Grace of Monaco

Also by Steven Englund

MAN SLAUGHTER

With Edward Ford:
FOR THE LOVE OF CHILDREN
PERMANENT LOVE

With Larry Ceplair:
THE INQUISITION IN HOLLYWOOD,
Politics in the Film Community, 1930–60

GRACE OF MONACO

AN INTERPRETIVE BIOGRAPHY

STEVEN ENGLUND

DOUBLEDAY & COMPANY, INC.
GARDEN CITY, NEW YORK
1984

Designed by Laurence Alexander

Library of Congress Cataloging in Publication Data

Englund, Steven.
Grace of Monaco.

Includes index.
1. Grace, Princess of Monaco, 1929– 2. Monaco
—Princess and princesses—Biography. 3. Moving-picture
actors and actresses—United States—Biography. I. Title.
DC943.G7E54 1984   944'.949'00994 [B]

ISBN: *0-385-18812-9*
Library of Congress Catalog Card Number 83–20742
Copyright © 1984 by Steven Englund

This book is lovingly dedicated to my aunt,
Virginia Simpson.

CONTENTS

PREFACE

In September of 1981, I wrote to Grace of Monaco to say what interested me in the story of her life. The organizing principle, it seemed to
me, was this: "You've lived according to the values you profess. Many
affirm traditional values, but rather fewer determine their lives by
them, particularly when difficult choices must be made and large temptations or successes bypassed for a greater good." I added that I felt this
hewing to purpose made her life "exemplary in ways that I, as a person, understand and find sympathetic, and which I, as a writer, believe
I could communicate to the public."

Before saying what happened next, I should perhaps tell the reader a
word or two of what motivated me to write this letter. Grace Kelly, the
movie star, had quite captivated me when I was a young boy. My ten-
year-old's infatuation with her was a joke in our house because it was
so out of character for me to care about *any* movie star, or anything to
do with the movies. Being raised in the loving but unstable home of a
fine, once successful, but declining screenwriter, I wanted only to flee
"show biz." The charm that "the movies" exercised over so many in
my generation never claimed me. For me, Hollywood was a depressing
reality which I escaped in aspirations and enchantments of my own—
notably, Roman Catholicism, academic and scholarly achievement,
East Coast style and values. Looking back, I am sure that what drew
me to Grace, aside from her beauty which utterly dazzled me, was her
much-reported disdain for Hollywood and our shared commitment to
"other" values, beliefs, and institutions.

Well, she went her way and I went mine. I remember being pleased
she married a staunch Catholic and (what I took to be) a Frenchman,
though I knew I would miss reading about her in the lines that my dad
thoughtfully underscored for me in *Variety* and *The Hollywood Reporter*.
I kept a very casual eye on her development.

When I finally started to think about a biography of her (early 1981),
time had changed many things. Politically, Grace couldn't have stood
much further away from me than she now did. I had been a strong left-
winger in the fifties, too, but then she hadn't been making public remarks that made her sound like a reactionary. Princess Grace was also
deeply involved in issues and activities—from breast feeding to poetry

reading by way of pressed flower collages—that interested me not at all. Finally, she was part of a society that aroused in me more sarcasm than fascination.

Nevertheless, the effect of these "downsides" was to magnify what I took to be the main issue: faith, and one's living of it. Grace and I shared ultimate beliefs, and nothing else; moreover, she had shown an apparent systematic and disciplined commitment to "our" beliefs and values that was far greater and costlier than my own commitment. The effort to investigate her life and report her success, if success it was, would edify—myself first, and then (I hoped) the reader. So I wrote to Grace.

It turned out she was interested. We met on Friday, the thirteenth of November, 1981, the day after her fifty-second birthday. I had suggested a lunch at the Algonquin, which I knew to be a spot she loved, but it suited her packed schedule better for us to meet late in the afternoon at the apartment of her friend Vera Maxwell, the clothes designer. Grace was tired and a bit frazzled, which showed in the dark circles around her eyes. I wrote in my journal afterwards, "She looked her age, but softly, lovely, matronly."

We had a good conversation. Among other things, she told me a detail of her actress's career that I had never known, though she expected I had. In her last live TV role (in 1952), she played a young American girl who meets an American boy in Monaco, and they fall in love. The part of the boy was played by George Englund, my stepbrother, then an actor. It happened that Grace knew my then sister-in-law, Cloris Leachman, from her Broadway and television days—which was also news to me.

Pleasantries and coincidences aside, we found we agreed on my approach to her life, which is to say we shared a sense of what was essential and inessential in writing about her. This said, however, two things prevented her from working directly with me: she had a very full plate of work (I had no idea till later how full "full" meant); and she wished to write her own life story one day. She may also have wished to consult other writers, but was too polite to say so. Grace asked me to stay in touch, to give her some of my books and articles to read. Later, she wrote me that if I wished to go ahead with my own biography of her, she would grant me more interviews and help me to see her friends. She even named one (Vera Maxwell) whom I later interviewed.

Before I had time really to begin my work, Grace tragically died. I nevertheless decided to go forward with the book. The result is this biography, which is an attempt at a serious appraisal of a life lived around a commitment to a specific understanding of the Christian faith and the values extrapolated from it. Although the book goes to considerable length to try to set Grace in her unusual historical circumstances, it is finally an interior view of a familiar set of struggles. As Grace understood *far* better than most, her story is a more common than exotic one, focusing on one woman's efforts, successes, and failures to be the best daughter, wife, mother, actress, and princess she could be according to the lights she chose to live by.

This is an "interpretive" biography because Grace's death prevented her from giving me the interviews that I needed to keep the historian in me from feeling tentative, i.e., interpretive. My subject lived such a fiercely private and inner life that I seriously doubt it would be possible for anyone, save perhaps her husband, to write other than an "interpretive" biography of her.

But lest the reader imagine I personally feel doubtful of my assessment, I should say that I was sorely tempted to use the following quotation from *Craig's Wife* by George Kelly (Grace's beloved uncle and favorite writer) as my epigraph: "It isn't an opinion I have of you at all, Harriet; it's *you* that I have."

In a book about a subject as "famous" as Grace, acknowledgments risk becoming window dressing. I shall limit myself here only to saying that I have interviewed a great many of Grace's friends, relatives (though not her children), and important associates in her multifaceted work. I am very grateful to them for seeing me and, in many instances, giving me (usually very gradually) their confidence. Their names are cited in the footnotes, together with the date(s) I saw them. As a general rule, once someone is footnoted, all his or her subsequent quotes may be considered (unless otherwise indicated) as coming from that interview. As to bibliographical references, the reader will quickly see that I have kept them to a bare minimum. I did so to facilitate reading and because the periodical literature on Grace is as well known as it is extensive. I have thus limited myself to footnoting quotations only where it seemed important for understanding or fairness to do so. Quotations from books, on the other hand, are all noted.

The suggestion that spurred me seriously to consider this undertaking came during an evening walk with my dear friend John Niespolo. In the course of gathering research, I benefited from two assistants of high caliber: Jane and Patty Polisar. My friend Jim Sutty made a splendid contribution to Chapters 2, 3, and 4 on Grace's film career, while Rachel Gorlin, a most talented writer-reporter, left her singular mark on Chapter 1. I am grateful to the fine writer and biographer, Donald Spoto, for his advice on the relationship between Grace and Hitchcock, and to Charles Stacy, M.D., for his advice in Chapter 11. Thanks to Daniel Harrison, Billy Heekin, Thomas Wile, Nadia Lacoste, John Carroll, Rupert Allan, Frank Cresci, Peter Skolnick, and Sally Parrish Richardson for their special help. At Doubleday, Katherine Precht and Anne Hukill were not only constantly helpful, but constantly patient and cool under pressure (which I often was not), while Dorothy Gannon was the best copy editor I've had in six books. If there are errors in these pages they are due to my stubbornness, not to Ms. Gannon's lack of vigilance. The loyalty and generosity of Vincent Curcio in scrutinizing every last syllable of a manuscript he disagreed with figure among the wonders of friendship.

As in my last book, so again, it finally comes down to two friends: Tom O'Brien, a fellow writer, and Lisa Drew, my incomparable editor. They both disapprove of my tendency to use the superlative so they leave me no way of thanking them properly. That this book *is*, and that it may contain something of value, is to a great extent their doing.

I have dedicated this work to Virginia Simpson because she stepped into a breach in a way that even the most responsible, generous aunt couldn't be expected to do.

Steven Englund
New York City
December 22, 1983

Monaco io sono
Un scoglio
Del mio non ho
Quello d'altrui non toglio
Pur viver voglio

(I am Monaco
A rock
I have nothing
And take nothing from anyone
Nevertheless I wish to live)

Grace of Monaco

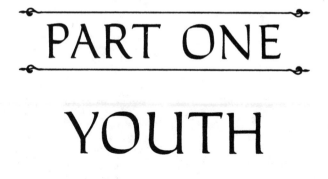

PART ONE

YOUTH

CHAPTER 1

THE KELLYS OF EAST FALLS

If you take the Chestnut Hill commuter train from Thirtieth Street Station, Philadelphia, eventually you cross the Schuylkill River on your way north. Before you get there, however, there is a railroad bridge high overground. It's a strange sort of place: there are tracks, trestles, steel girders, and little else, making one of those grotesquely beautiful rusty industrial islands common on the Northeast Corridor. The bridge is a sandy color, but on its sides you can see a montage of drawings. As you approach, you get a clearer view: tombstones, graffitied in punk style on the beige background. Each mock grave is outlined in black with a whitewash center and each has a name in the middle—James Dean, John Belushi, Jimi Hendrix, the alienated heroes of several generations of American youth. Incongruously at the far left end, there is another name: Princess Grace.

Many Americans harbor a special affection for Grace's memory, but few would place her in such company. Whoever did probably had an even more special regard, grouping her name with those of prematurely dead superstar antiheroes for very local and specific reasons. Only in Philadelphia could Grace Kelly be seen as an *outré* figure. Yet only there, in America at least, would she be called Princess Grace.

The reason for both facts is simple: Grace Kelly is part of Philadelphia's acquired royalty. Her father started by laying bricks, but ran for mayor of the city and even contemplated becoming senator of the state. He worked at a carpet mill at age nine, but his monument stands near the Schuylkill River, seated in a beloved scull, set to row his way to Olympian glory, an Irish Catholic Adonis. Grace's brother, a later champion, lives in the Palace, a penthouse atop a hotel in the center city. A local architect today seeks to raise money for a monument in Grace's memory.

All the grandeur started with bricks and mortar and retains some of its grass roots. Social mobility is extremely limited in Philadelphia—the Kellys could not have joined the same country club as the Biddles and the Cadwaladers, even if they had cared to. But their Irish Catholic working-class origins have made their successes representative; Princess Grace and her family have come to symbolize upward mobility for ordinary Philadelphians, who, like the Kellys, could not have grown up in the exclusive precincts of the Main Line or Society Hill. The Kellys are outsiders who made it and made it big—if not as big as their Boston "cousins," the Kennedys, then big enough to retain their local rambunctious glamour.

Grace Kelly—Princess Grace—had a character and career whose design was shaped by her Philadelphia roots as much as by Hollywood and Monaco. According to Rita Gam, a close friend, Grace had "the strongest sense of family of anyone I knew."* What did it mean?

When Grace's father, John Brendan Kelly, was born in Philadelphia's East Falls section in 1890, no one would have confused that principally Irish working-class neighborhood with such rich districts as nearby Germantown, let alone with Wynnewood or Bryn Mawr. East Falls—only about two miles from the center of the city—was in those days virtually a company town for Dobson's carpet mills, which employed all ten of John Henry and Mary Costello Kelly's children as soon as they were old enough to quit school. The employers tended to live in the *other* neighborhoods, though a few had mansions in the upper Falls.

Philadelphia is built of a series of such neighborhoods, each with separate and distinct characters. In the 1850s, when East Falls was first seriously developed around the expansion of Dobson's mills, it had the air of a town unto itself, growing off the then-remote banks of the Schuylkill River. Even in its early development, class distinctions appeared in East Falls; there were the solid working-class row houses of the "lower" Falls and the more genteel "upper" Falls, with its detached homes, tree-shaded streets, and minimal commercial activity. To the young Kelly sons and daughters at the turn of the century, the upper Falls must have represented heaven. It was a modest dream, a respectable place to live, lacking ostentation and pretension, but its lace-curtain dignity left it on the fringes of Philadelphia's social hierarchy, even its Irish gentility—that is until the Kelly family's achievements put it on the map.

The Kellys were a representative Irish-American family of their time. With ten children, John Henry Kelly was able to earn only enough to provide the bare essentials for his offspring, a fact his wife would not let him forget. Time for anything but work was hard to come by, which led some of the Kelly children to pursue escape assiduously. John B. sought it through his rowing; George, Walter, and their sister Grace (who died at age twenty) sought some refuge in the world of fantasy through the stage.

* Interview with author, October 28, 1983.

There were six Kelly brothers—P.H. born in 1872, Walter born in 1873, Charles born in 1880, George born in 1887, John B. born in 1890, and a sixth son, John, who died in childhood. They all eventually made their marks in life, but there is no question that they all started out at the bottom. Like his siblings, Grace's father, John B., went to work at Dobson's mills at age nine, but by the time he turned twelve, his oldest brother Patrick ("P.H.") had taken him on as a laborer in his own burgeoning construction firm, the first of many Kelly financial successes. The other sons did well also, but excepting Walter and George, they never strayed far from East Falls, preferring to be large fish in a small pond. However high they reached, their tastes remained parochial.

The Kelly household was matriarchal. John Henry Kelly and Mary Costello had an unfortunate marriage but she at least managed to instill esprit de corps, a strong sense of family in her children, particularly her sons. A fiercely intelligent woman whose drudgery-filled life must have been a bitter disappointment, "Grandma Kelly" transmitted to her children a thirst for experience and for the immigrant dream of an American "better life." She was strict but driven and drove her sons upward.

The spread in the siblings' ages meant that the boys weren't particularly close. Nevertheless, even as adults they looked after one another, imbibing their mother's clannish, almost tribal, passion. Walter lent John B. the money with which he started his business. George helped P.H. when his business fell on hard times. John B. helped George get an honorable discharge from the army service he so loathed, volunteering for a regimental boxing match to get liberty for the one brother who so scorned his sporting activities.

But, then, allowances were usually made for George Kelly, an exception to most rules about the Kelly brothers. Somewhat intellectually inclined, homosexual, disdainful of physical undertakings from sports to manual labor, George sought to conceal his lowly origins and reinvent himself as a patrician. He became a Pulitzer prize-winning playwright, but George Kelly's most successful character may have been himself. As Grace's foremost childhood link to the world of imagination and theater, Uncle George was an important reminder that one could make a career, not from bricks and mortar, but from make-believe. George also allowed her to understand, from an early age, that her father's way of seeing things was not invariably correct. "He was one of the few people who ever contradicted my father," she said with envy later. "He is the most wonderful and intelligent man I have ever known. Whatever he talks about, he makes you understand all its beauty and hidden meaning."

Little is known about George's early years, between the time he left

Dobson's carpet mills and turned up in 1910 as a twenty-three-year-old vaudeville actor on the boards of western Pennsylvania. For more than ten years George was on the road, performing in and eventually writing vaudeville sketches and one-act plays. Then, in 1922 his first full-length play, *The Torch-Bearers,* was produced on Broadway to considerable critical and popular acclaim. With the production of *Craig's Wife* and *The Show-Off* in the next several theater seasons, George's reputation as a "bankable" playwright became secure. His vaudevillian years had given him a keen sense of what would work onstage. In tune with the twenties, George's plays were witty and sophisticated while striking a high moral tone, but at their best, his characters attain a universality that only the finest artists can achieve.

The heyday of his career lasted at most fifteen years, for there was an Achilles' heel in George's talent, a certain brittle lack of compassion. As Joseph Wood Krutch wrote in the September 20, 1929, *Nation,* "Hate seems to be the real source of his inspiration, and one is almost inclined to suspect that behind the harshness of his attitude lies some personal experience which would have to be known before one could entirely understand the vehemence of certain emphases which destroy the proportions of the work for the ordinary spectator . . . He has idiosyncratic standards of judgment and he distributes rewards and punishments according to some personal canon of poetic justice which leaves the spectator less satisfied than resentful . . ."

A clue to George's bitter side emerges in his attitude toward women, an extreme example of a problem all his brothers seem somehow to have shared. In his plays, women are often hated, feared, and most of all misunderstood, as if a distant part of another world. When questioned about this obvious misogyny, George equivocated, damning and excusing at once: "Women almost invariably rely on intuitive reasoning or some other illogical basis. However, most of the traits in women to which men object are the result of women's treatment at the hands of men." No doubt George was thinking of the relationship between his mother and father. With his mother's dreams of education thwarted with no respite from childbearing, she turned her hostility toward her quiet husband, even her children. They received a minimum of affection from her, becoming primarily her weapons against the world. George was one of her greatest successes and failures.

Though the Kelly boys had managed to grow into self-confident men, each emerged from his mother's home scarred in his own way. Brother Charles's son, Charles Kelly, Jr., once observed, with less overstatement than one might hope, "There has never been a good Kelly marriage." It was a pattern that would continue.

Unlike his other brothers (George excepted), Walter, a famous vaudevillian who was well established by the time George entered the field, never married at all. Known as the "Virginia Judge" throughout his long career, Walter Kelly satirized rural blacks and the "southern justice" they received, though not with much compassion or social conscience. Curiously, Walter, not George, is remembered as the nonconformist and rebel by the family, although he must have fit in better at family gatherings than his effete sibling. Both of the itinerant thespian Kellys paid pleasant visits to East Falls, George less frequently than Walter. Walter doted on their mother and enjoyed his nieces and nephews. George, more often, wanted to play the piano alone. Walter died in 1938, when Grace and her brother and sisters were still quite young. However nonconformist and rebellious, he left to George the job of encouraging that streak in their brother's child.

Walter was close to John B. and in 1919 lent him the seed money for his own construction firm—Kelly for Brickwork—which continues in the family to this day. The firm grew considerably after the one serious dispute among the Kelly frères: P.H., who also owned a business, quarreled with his brother Charles, who worked for him. The argument became bitter, and John earned P.H.'s wrath for siding against him. Charles left P.H.'s firm to help manage Kelly for Brickwork, where he became the unsung hero of the business, running the proverbial "tight ship" while Jack dabbled in politics, women, sports, horse racing, and whatever else struck his fancy. It was not the luck of the Irish, but the luck of a youngest son that John B. profited even from his brothers' breakup.

But maybe John B. made his luck. He had won two Olympic gold medals as a single sculler by the time he turned thirty. He was energetic, aggressive, a promising businessman, dashingly handsome, an Olympic athlete to boot.

He could also marry most any woman he chose. In 1924 he chose Margaret Majer, a twenty-four-year-old physical education instructor. Margaret, as they said in those days, was quite a "go-getter," a match for Jack's assertive, physical lifestyle. With her two-year certificate from Temple (unusual enough in those days among working-class women), she became the first woman to teach physical education at the University of Pennsylvania. She had been a cover girl for a national magazine. On the surface, she seemed strong and self-assured, ready to handle a family, a household, and whatever life might have in store.

Despite (or perhaps because of) certain similarities between Jack's mother and his wife, Grandma Kelly did not take well to her son's German Lutheran bride. Margaret converted to Catholicism, understanding this was expected of her, but it apparently did more harm than good to her standing with her mother-in-law, making her even more of a rival. The enmity did not have time to go too far, however;

Mary Costello Kelly was dead within two years of Jack and Margaret's wedding. But other thorns would soon appear in the marriage.

Margaret's Catholic home was disciplined in its religious observance, as it was about most everything, but never seems to have been devout. Attendance at Sunday church in those days was routine for Catholics, but John B. did his duty only when he felt like it and only to maintain appearances. Kell, his son, never attended Catholic school, and Peggy and Grace, the older daughters, transferred from the strict Ravenhill Academy convent school to the secular, less regimented Stevens School in their early teenage years. "Our having a Catholic education was never terribly important to my parents," said youngest daughter Lizanne.† Spirituality, in short, was in low supply at the Kelly household; much more critical was Catholic teaching on moral uprightness and social propriety, which fitted easily with Margaret's own upbringing.

Their Irish background, on the other hand, seems to have held significance for all the Kellys, and some danger. The Kelly children took pride in the fabled Irish gifts for conversation, blarney, and conviviality that their father, man-about-town, came to exemplify in his time. But there was also a strong emphasis of male and female separateness in Irish culture: women tend the home while men stay out drinking and socializing. Margaret, whose father had died when she was a little girl, rapidly became disturbed by her husband's needs to live in a world of which she could be only one part. It was not what she had expected, and it began to poison things early.

Nevertheless, though Margaret and Jack clearly had differing views of what a marriage should be, they saw eye to eye on the basics of how to raise a family. They had to, for it came quickly. Peggy ("Baba") was born in 1925, John B., Jr. ("Kell") in 1927, Grace in 1929, and Lizanne in 1933. All were raised with firm discipline, some humor and quite a bit of "togetherness." Whatever his escapades, husband and wife were both determined that the John B. Kellys would be the ideal all-American family. Appearances were everything; unbecoming emotions were to be banished or suppressed. The Kelly family homestead, still standing in the upper Falls at 3901 Henry Avenue, projects a conspicuously solid image, and was meant to. The two-story brick neo-Georgian house, built by Jack with Kelly Company bricks at the time of his marriage, has an eminently respectable-looking semicircular driveway in front and a large backyard for the children. Jack Kelly had a black limousine. Upkeep of the grounds and the inside of the house was done mostly by servants, some of them live-in. As the children grew through

† Interview with author, October 15, 1983 (and subsequent quotes from Lizanne).

the years of the Great Depression, the Kellys continued to live as a prosperous family should, without being showy or vulgar.

From an early age the Kelly children were in the public eye. In addition to minding Kelly for Brickwork, Jack took the advice of friends who said he would make a great candidate for something, entering politics seriously in the early 1930s. As a Democrat in thoroughly entrenched Republican Philadelphia (they had held the mayoralty for sixty years), Jack Kelly hitched his fortunes and those of the city party to Franklin Roosevelt. In 1935, he ran a dynamic campaign for mayor; with the enrollment ten to one Republican, he lost by only 40,000 votes out of more than 700,000 votes cast. Old political hands still contend that the corrupt Republican regime stole the election from Kelly. The campaign was especially vicious, with rumor and innuendo wreaking havoc with Margaret Kelly's attempts to preserve the normalcy of her handsome Henry Avenue household.

Charles Kelly, Jr., Jack's nephew, recalls the Republican anti-Kelly whispering campaign of 1935, "People would call on the telephone and say, 'Is it true that Cardinal Dougherty is going to have an office in City Hall if John B. Kelly is elected mayor?' They [would] tell one story to the Protestants and another to the Catholics," Charles recalled. Among the Catholics, he claimed, Republicans whispered, " 'Is it true that Mr. Kelly sends his children to Protestant schools to be educated?' "‡

John B. lost graciously, composing some verse for the night of his defeat: "Be proud of your blackened eye/It isn't the fact that you're licked that counts, but how you fight and why/. . . For the harder you're thrown/the higher you bounce." In a nutshell, it was the Kelly family philosophy, taken to heart uncritically by all four of his children (though most of them were too young to have grasped what was going on that evening). Jack Kelly put great emphasis on the ability to fight and endure. The choice of fights, or their wisdom, were not things about which Jack Kelly gave much thought. He considered himself a man of action, a doer not a thinker, as were his wife and *three* of their four fair children.

The experience of Jack's mayoral campaign left "Ma Kelly" (as Margaret was known) determined to bounce back from her "defeat" as a wife. She tried to act on her horror of her husband's continuing political involvement. Kell put it this way after his mother in effect destroyed his own chance at the 1975 mayoral nomination: "Mother always felt that politics was a threat to the stability of her marriage. That's why she hates it so." In 1936, she forbade her husband to even consider accepting the Democratic nomination for U.S. Senate; in

‡ Arthur H. Lewis, *Those Philadelphia Kellys* (New York: Morrow 1976), p. 11.

1940, he stepped down (one gathers reluctantly) as head of the Philadelphia Democratic Committee, though his influence continued informally.

Ma Kelly was not wrong about the threats to her marriage. Originally through his political activities, and later through social and business connections, Jack Kelly was meeting and seeing other women. One friend of the family, Dorothea Sitley, long-time public relations chief at Gimbels Department Store, told Arthur Lewis that Jack ordered twenty-seven compact handbags with makeup in them (at $150 apiece) as Christmas presents for his lady friends.

But the threat to the Kellys' union did not come from Jack's flirtations or flings. In the late thirties, he became deeply involved with Ellen Frazer, the sister-in-law of one of his political nemeses. An attractive, well-to-do but down-to-earth divorcée, Mrs. Frazer lived in Chestnut Hill around the corner from one of Grace's closest school friends. As a result, her father was not eager for Grace to visit her chum's house after school; his black limousine was frequently in Mrs. Frazer's driveway in the afternoon. Apparently, John B. would have married Mrs. Frazer, had Margaret been willing to give him his freedom. To Margaret Majer Kelly, however, such a thing was unthinkable: the family must stay together no matter what the cost. Although the costs to the adults involved were doubtless high, Baba, Kell, Gracie, and Liz probably owe a significant part of their happy family life to their mother's "till death do us part" conception of marriage.

Jack Kelly did not spend an enormous amount of time at home with the kids and was certainly not as great a day-to-day influence on the children's lives as their mother. Indeed, he was, possibly, less a presence than Geoffrey Ford, known as "Fordie," the trusted and revered black manservant who was truly "like a member of the family." Nevertheless, Jack Kelly infused 3901 Henry Avenue with high spirits and lively humor. He was a merciless teaser (the sensitive Grace was most susceptible) and practical jokester, as well as an excellent raconteur. The Lone Ranger was one of his special enthusiasms. The kids once delighted him by sending in a label from Silvercup Bread and thirty cents for a Lone Ranger premium, a gadget that glowed in the dark; he played with it, flashing it on and off in the closet under the stairway, to the children's delight. His business acquaintances and friends also brought a broad range of visitors into the Kelly home, including Henry Fonda and Douglas Fairbanks, Jr. In good part because of Jack Kelly's social nature, 3901 Henry Avenue was the scene of many gala parties remembered fondly by the children. Whatever his defects as a father, his vivacity was infectious.

It was also needed. Jack brought a lighter side into the house, softening his wife's somewhat rigid approach. Years later Kell remarked on his mother: "Oh, that Ma Kelly, she's a tough one, a tough German cookie . . . Now, I wouldn't say that Mother's a Nazi . . . but sometimes I do refer to her as, quote, 'That old Prussian mother of mine.' "*

Her Prussian manners were not just figurative but literal. Once Ma Kelly took the German grammar books out after dinner for a lesson in her native tongue. "We gave her such grief when she tried to teach us German; we'd hide the grammar books. This was around the time of World War II and we'd complain how unpatriotic it was," recalled Lizanne with a smile. "I think Mother was disappointed."

The children did not often prevail over the will of their "Prussian" mother. Margaret Kelly distributed the allowance money parsimoniously. Lizanne noted that if one of them "wanted to get something extra [we'd] have to go to Fordie and try to bum some money from him." Swearing was completely verboten. Again Lizanne: "If you said something like 'that's a lousy thing,' oh, she'd have a fit!" Against such competition, Jack Kelly invariably came across as a *likable* father; in a Prussian environment, he brought all the strength and weakness of a hurly-burly Irishman. Irresponsible, he was also fun.

Lizanne believed that her father "left us girls to Mother; I think girls frightened him a bit." It is true that Jack probably was not sure how to deal with the emotional demands of young girls, and their father's distance did not stand them in good stead in their later intimate dealings with men. At any but an unconscious level, all three girls were thoroughly charmed by and apparently adored their debonaire father. Whatever his accomplishments and obligations, he remained quite in touch with the boyish part of himself throughout his life. Lizanne, now in her fifties, still has a portrait of young Jack Kelly hanging over a mantel in her otherwise unadorned living room.

Did the children know what was going on between their parents? Kathy McKenna, an assistant to Kell during his years as a Philadelphia City Council member and an astute observer of the Kelly family, told Arthur Lewis, "I don't know whether Kell was aware, actually aware of his father's other interests or infidelities. I think he undoubtedly *felt* it." None of the children was more likely to have picked up on the tension between their parents than introspective, intuitive Grace, though it is unlikely that she ever consciously knew the sources of the friction. The split between conscious and unconscious attitudes toward their family life is a crucial theme in the emotional development of the Kelly children. While at one level Grace and her sisters and brother grew up in a "happy home," at other deeper levels, there was little honesty and communication between family members; reinterpreting their relationships to one another would have been impossible

---

* Interview with author, October 21, 1983 (and subsequent quotes).

given the parents' upbringings where denial was essentially an emotional necessity. According to their code, betrayals of weakness or unhappiness were to be swept away by wholesome activity.

"Sports were a must in our family," recalls Lizanne. The whole family often spent Sundays at the Penn Athletic Club downtown, going to the circus or the movies as a reward later for a hard workout. Summers the Kelly family retreated to their beachfront house in Ocean City, New Jersey, where everyone swam and played outdoors. Ocean City—actually Margate, the nicest section of the town—is a summer resort near Atlantic City that has long been popular with Philadelphians, but not for its elegance. Unlike Long Island's Hamptons or Delaware's Rehoboth Beach, Ocean City has thrived as a haven for families. And there the Kelly family trudged each summer to romp with joy.

But even the supposedly leisurely summer recreation had an edge to it in the Kelly family. Sports were serious business, and competition was to be taken seriously. Grace, Peggy, Lizanne, and, especially, Kell were expected to exercise rigorously, and with Kell, someone stood over him, urging him on. Peggy and Lizanne needed no spur. As the son of an Olympic champion, their brother did not get off as easily.

When Kell reached his early teens, his father took it on himself to train him as an oarsman, an undertaking with great emotional significance for John B. Kelly, Sr. In 1920, the senior Kelly's rowing club, the Vesper Boat Club, was rejected in its effort to compete in the most prestigious rowing competition, the Henley Diamond Sculls. At the time, and for years after, Jack Kelly was to claim that Henley had forbidden him to enter because the snobbish Brits would not permit the presumably more brawny working-class to compete against "gentlemen." In fact, according to Roger Angell in *The New Yorker*, Henley had lifted its ban on rowers who did manual labor by 1920. It was nothing directed personally at Jack Kelly. Rather the Vesper Boat Club team was not admitted because of a fifteen-year-old dispute over how to define the amateurism of its members.

Perhaps Jack Kelly took Henley's rejection of his team personally, or perhaps he knew the publicity value of the story of his exclusion based on his class origins. Whichever it actually was, the tale of champion Kelly's cruel and unjust exclusion has made it into American amateur sports mythology. After John B. Kelly's rebuff by the Henley committee, as he himself put it, "I vowed that if I ever had a son, he would come back to Henley . . . beat the English in their most cherished competition, and make them like it—or else." Accordingly, young Kell was put through grueling training to become his father's instrument of revenge in a sport he, initially at least, "didn't particularly like." In addition to his Olympic honors (he won more medals than his father),

Kell took Henley in 1947 and 1949, but the athletic exertions deprived him, by his own admission, of most of the fun and spontaneity of adolescence.

The girls were spared the intense pressure their father brought to bear on Kell, and their accomplishments were much less stunning. Nonetheless, the desire for a better physical education program was an important part of Peggy and Grace's desire to transfer from Ravenhill Academy in East Falls to Germantown's Stevens School. Clearly, their parents would have had a hard time disagreeing with their daughters' insistence on an improved sports curriculum.

Another reason the girls wanted to transfer, of course, was their eagerness not to have to be subjected to the strict regulations of Ravenhill's Catholic nuns: uniforms had to be worn, and reports were sent home weekly to a pupil's parents on her work and deportment. The girls were given permission to transfer without much ado. At Stevens, a small girls' private school that catered mainly to daughters of "better (usually Protestant) families" from Chestnut Hill and Germantown, Grace and Peggy felt more at ease. Grace played field hockey and tennis and participated in athletics gamely, but never managed to live up to the accomplishments of the rest of her family—including baby Lizanne who became a champion swimmer.

§   §   §

Young Grace, however, found herself adrift in her family's sea of competition and activity. As a young child, she preferred reading or making up games and stories with her dolls to athletic exertion and joking around. Only Uncle George, of whom Grace apparently became aware about the time she turned six or seven years old, offered family sanction for her pensive, reflective nature. She looked to her parents more often for approval and affection than did her siblings—who seemed to be offered it more freely for their outgoing natures.

Certainly, Grace got little enough affection from John B. As one writer has noted, "As she was growing up, Grace could never figure out her father. Every girl craves attention and love from her father, but Grace, being subtle and sensitive, needed a special kind of suave, delicate handling that her father, a gruff man, may have been incapable of expressing."[†] Similarly, Kell's eldest daughter Ann has this recollection of her grandfather Kelly: "He didn't like real small children who weren't big enough to talk back to him. He also liked very brash children, not shy kids. He liked kids of the Shirley Temple type." Peggy, who came much closer to her father's ideal type of girl, overshadowed

† Maurice Zolotow, "Grace Kelly: Her Biggest Gamble," *The American Weekly*, April 29, 1956.

her younger sister. Even after Grace had become a famous film actress, her father was regularly quoted as expressing a sort of dubious surprise at his middle daughter's success.

Grace also had trouble eliciting from her mother the approval she craved. Like her husband's mother, Margaret Kelly didn't readily display affection and warmth. Whether or not this undemonstrativeness on her part drove her husband into the arms of other women, John B. Kelly's breaches of his marriage vows certainly did not make his wife any warmer toward, or more approving of, him or the children. With Grace especially, Margaret Kelly had problems relating. " 'There was always something a bit different, a bit withdrawn about Grace,' Mrs. Kelly reports. 'She was a frail little girl and sickly a good deal of the time, very susceptible to colds. She was completely self-sufficient and could amuse herself for hours by making up little plays with her dolls.' "

Indeed, young Grace did amuse herself quietly for hours at a time with her dolls and Nancy Drew mystery books. Lizanne once locked her older sister in a closet, and not a word was heard from her until someone opened the door several hours later. There was Grace serenely playing with her dolls. Lizanne observed, "Peggy was vivacious, my father's favorite, more of an extrovert and capable of being a real clown. Grace was very shy, pretty, reserved and calm. I was the brat sister making lots of trouble."

Among these vivacious, or noisy, doers, Grace was an outsider. When they all hit teenage years and took up competitive sports, Grace used an outsider's method to compete. Her need to excel in another area entirely was, of course, one of the reasons she began taking acting seriously. Like all of her passions, her feeling for acting went deep and was not easily visible on the surface. Since the age of eleven or twelve, Grace (as well as Peggy) had been appearing with the East Falls Old Academy Players, in juvenile and later ingenue roles. Ma Kelly's brother, Midgey, and his wife had gotten the girls involved, and Grace's interest and talent brought her increasingly better parts. From her start in *Don't Feed the Animals,* Grace progressed to parts in plays like *Cry Havoc* and, much to her delight, her Uncle George's *The Torch-Bearers.*

Of her performance in the latter, one of Philadelphia's major critics wrote: "Grace Kelly, John B.'s pretty daughter, made her appearance last night in Uncle George Kelly's comedy hit *The Torch-Bearers.* For a young lady whose previous experience was slim, Miss Kelly came through this footlight baptism of fire splendidly. Although father and mother beamed at Grace from the front rows and other friends were scattered through the house, it was largely a theatrical crowd this girl faced on her break-in. From where I sat it appeared as if Grace Kelly should become the theatrical torch-bearer for her family." Uncle George would doubtless have found the Old Academy Players an insufferable example of amateurism and could only have smiled ironically at this "compliment" to his niece. Through the Players and in Stevens School productions, however, the magic of the stage began to work its spell on Grace Kelly.

She did not—in fact was not expected to—feel like herself when she acted, and young Grace found that a liberating, heady sensation. Through the theater, like Uncle George before her, Grace was reinventing herself. As a performer, Grace elicited from her audiences approval that had eluded her at home (though perhaps this approval was not as deeply satisfying as for something she had done as *herself*—rather than in the guise of a character onstage). Ironically, her pleasure in acting involved what her parents all through her childhood had been urging her to be: someone other than who she was. Grace's calling required her to disguise herself, but now on her own terms rather than theirs. Moreover, she could out-Kelly the Kellys in one other way: the performing arts alone seemed to have a glamour exceeding—or at least rivaling—that of competitive sports. Grace began to believe that she had found a vocation in acting that allowed her to receive the emotional gratification that she had always craved. As a teenager, she redirected this craving into a strong drive to excel in Uncle George's domain, the theater. "Acting for a person as introverted as Grace," wrote Zolotow, "is a medium by which one may live out one's fantasies, which Grace found more gratifying than reality."

At Stevens, too, she was able to include in her school curriculum an area that was to become a lifelong passion: dance. At age eleven, after attending a matinee of the Ballet Russe and being fascinated with Igor Youskevitch, Grace first envisioned herself as a stage performer. She took ballet lessons for the next two years, as well as instruction in piano, but was never encouraged to take her dancing too seriously. She probably came to regret this as she got older and came to fully appreciate the ballet. Stevens School alumna Marie Frisbee Rambo recalls her friend Grace's interest in a modern dance class, which was given on Saturday mornings. "I was not as keen on it as she was, and I remember getting calls from Grace already at class on Saturday morning: 'Marie, where are you? You promised you'd be here!' "‡

Enthusiasm was one thing, however, and commitment another, and Grace was maturing at a time when a woman's commitment to a career was unusual. "Career girls" were rare in the 1940s in the milieu in which Grace and her sisters grew up. Young women were expected to prepare themselves to be capable mothers and homemakers, particu-

‡ Interview with author, October 21, 1983.

larly in the post-World War II economy of abundance with a booming birthrate. It was "unfeminine" in some fundamental way. Oh, working was acceptable for a few years, perhaps, while searching for the right husband, but a career was not to be taken seriously. Artistic endeavors, considered more "feminine" than most vocational possibilities, were acceptable as hobbies. Grace was not taken seriously by those around her when she confided her intention to become an actress; it was generally assumed that she would confine her theatrical activities to amateur (torch-bearing) efforts, combined with marriage and family duties.

It would have been very easy for Grace Kelly to have got married very young—as sister Peggy did when she married at nineteen. But if Grace did not push herself toward marriage, neither did her mother push her. As Princess Grace put it in 1974, "My mother was something like Queen Victoria in that she didn't believe in marriage for her girls. When I first heard of mothers trying to push their daughters into marriage, I thought, this can't be true; do mothers really do this? My mother was always the opposite. And I'm a little bit the same way with my own children . . . I want my children to marry for love."

Margaret Kelly's unwillingness to push her daughters probably had more to do with her dissatisfaction with her own marriage than with any confidence about her daughters' capability to achieve. This is hard to explain—for Margaret Kelly was, as Lizanne puts it, "a women's libber in her day"—but easy to document. Ma Kelly's main interest outside her home and family for years was the Women's Medical College of Pennsylvania, where she served on the Auxiliary and, from the mid-1940s to the 1970s, on the Board of Directors. Located near the Kelly home in East Falls, Women's Medical was the only all-female medical college in the country until it became coeducational in the early seventies. Margaret Majer had briefly taught physical education there before her marriage; her attachment to the institution was great. It was an unusual "charity" for a woman of Margaret Kelly's time and place to devote herself to; its distinctly feminist character was out of place in 1940s and 1950s Philadelphia.

Undoubtedly, Women's Medical's proximity to the Kelly home was one reason Margaret stayed so involved, but there was another far more significant one. The institution was important to her as a representation of female independence, harking back to her days as a young instructor on the campus. In 1946 she was one of the key board members in the fight to preserve the medical school's single-sex status. Yet, perhaps like most "advanced" thinkers, she had less courage of conviction when it came to herself and her family. She never encouraged any of her daughters to pursue a career in medicine—or any other field, for that matter. "She felt a bit insignificant around all the terribly intelligent women at Women's Medical," explains Lizanne. "Frankly, I don't think she thought we had the ability to go into something like medicine." Margaret Kelly, in short, didn't push her daughters—at least the oldest and youngest—into anything.

Early marriage was for Peggy Kelly an effective way to get away from home without having to continue schooling, though she wouldn't have put it to herself that bluntly. Lizanne hoped to marry after two years at the University of Pennsylvania, but was stopped by Ma Kelly who wanted at least one of her daughters to get a college degree. Bennington College's entrance requirements had ensured that that daughter was not going to be Grace. She had hoped to combine dramatic training with liberal arts at Bennington, but was crushed by her rejection for lack of sufficient high school math credits. (Princess Grace to this day is probably the school's most eminent alumna-manquée.)

But she was relieved on one level: never the most enthusiastic student, Bennington's rejection at least spelled the end of her academic career. But she felt at a loss as to how to pursue her consuming interest in acting without a college setting. Uncle George solved her dilemma with his advice: apply to the American Academy of Dramatic Arts in New York. Her parents made more than token efforts to talk her out of this plan; they did not see acting as a "serious profession," and, above all, they worried about what might become of Grace around people who lived life more "loosely." But once her mind was made up, Grace was impossible to dissuade. George Kelly's encouragement of his young niece added to her determination and helped seal the close bond between them that was a source of strength to her all her life, lasting long after she had given up acting.

What did George Kelly, not routinely fond of women, warm to in his brother Jack's middle daughter? Grace shared with her uncle a fiercely private side—a contempt for easy confidences and cheap display of emotion. Then, too, because of her hypersensitivity, she had, almost defensively, developed a rational approach to making decisions and dealing with people (the calm, professional manner she exhibited in Hollywood is a perfect example of this). And George must have been struck by her seriousness and strong will to do something so much unlike the rest of her siblings—as he had some forty years before when he left East Falls for the vaudeville circuit. Finally, he may have sensed in her his own tacit outsider's rejection of the "brash and sassy" personalities in the Kelly family, and a desire to "rise above" them, beginning (but not ending) with a created patrician demeanor. Perhaps George saw in Grace, or Grace in George, a mirror image.

Most significantly, the uncle who left so strong an imprint on his niece was himself a somewhat embittered, chastised man. His final plays on Broadway from his "first" period, ending with *Philip Goes Forth* in 1931, won nothing like the acclaim or commercial success of the earlier triumphs. So, with many a second thought, Kelly had followed the path of many of the fine writers of his era: he "went to Hollywood"—specifically, to M.G.M., where a two-thousand-dollar-a-week salary, a large private office, and a personal secretary awaited him. That, and little else, certainly few work assignments. As with so many of the other renowned "eastern" literary names who trekked west, Kelly was bought mainly to glorify M.G.M.'s masthead.

Eventually the studio got round to giving him some rewrite work, but things did not go well. A man of Kelly's singular, penetrating vision was equal to herculean literary tasks, but not inane ones. Helen Hayes remembered him when he was assigned to a film she was working on, *The White Sister*. Kelly was the second or third screenwriter to "take a shot at" a particular scene, but the dialogue he produced was "old-fashioned, a little stiff." "It was an impossible scene anyway," Hayes remembered, "Even Don[ald Ogden Stewart—a leading screenwriter] had failed with it. But they made such fun of George behind his back. I was appalled at the way they treated a man of his intelligence and distinction. I don't believe George was ever happy in Hollywood."*

In fact, George's feelings were more ambivalent than unalloyedly unhappy, for he liked the weather in Los Angeles and maintained a home there long after he quit at Metro-Goldwyn-Mayer. Then, too, as he would occasionally remind anyone who inquired, it wasn't as if Broadway had been so good to him after the first decade. Nevertheless Kelly's love of his art did not abate, and he continued to turn out plays in the midthirties and forties. *Reflected Glory, The Deep Mrs. Sykes,* and *The Fatal Weakness* were beautifully crafted, but flawed, creations; neither they nor his other plays in this era came close to achieving the success of *Craig's Wife* or his other twenties' plays.

Young Grace followed her uncle's declining career closely. He made many trips home, often staying in the large brick house on Henry Avenue. Loyally, she attended his performances, though on at least one occasion, a play closed before George could send her tickets. As she grew older and her own fascination with acting developed, George—or his image in her mind—was undoubtedly responsible for channeling her interest toward the theater, and away from Hollywood, which she, too, thought vulgar and commercial, unappreciative of true artists. George's glory was won on Broadway, so then would Grace's be. Fiercely protective of her uncle and his reputation, Grace would carry George's torch, some of his manner, and one or two of the chips on his shoulder (especially about Hollywood) throughout her life. In the most candid interview Princess Grace ever gave—to a trusted friend, the

* Interview with author, November 7, 1983.

screenwriter, Budd Schulberg—she spoke so passionately of Uncle George and of maintaining his reputation that Schulberg wrote, "I hadn't realized till now what a driving force it has been in her life."†

At George's suggestion, Grace applied to the American Academy of Dramatic Arts in New York City. For her audition she did a scene from his *Torch-Bearers* and a speech of Portia's from Shakespeare's *The Merchant of Venice*. Her auditioner remarked in his written report that her voice needed work, but that her dramatic instinct was "expressive" and that she seemed "promising." Accordingly, in 1947 the eighteen-year-old Miss Grace Patricia Kelly of Philadelphia enrolled in the Academy and took up residence at the Barbizon Hotel for Women. "We hoped she'd give it up," said Ma Kelly, while her husband noted, "Those movie people lead pretty shallow lives."

Her father, who knew only too well how "wicked" the world could be, insisted on the Barbizon, a hotel for single "career girls" run in the best college-dorm fashion of the times. Located in the stylish East Sixties, the Barbizon was a haven for girls from "good" families who had come to New York to make their fortunes. Men were absolutely forbidden to set foot above the first floor. An open, friendly atmosphere prevailed: clothes, party invitations, makeup tips, and the like were swapped regularly.

For Grace, the Barbizon was a congenial halfway point between her family's home on Henry Avenue and the "outside world." She was not interested in the glitzy clothes and the promise of a glamorous social life that had brought many of her fellow Barbizon denizens to New York. Even while maintaining a certain characteristic reserve—and taking her studies very seriously—Grace made several friends at the Barbizon.

The Academy was a rigorous introduction to the many aspects of an actor's craft. Grace studied everything possible, from voice (working at getting rid of her whiney, nasal twang) to fencing (later useful for her film *The Swan*). Improvisation was new to the somewhat inhibited eighteen year old. Princess Grace recalled, "We would be assigned to go to the Bowery and observe a drunk and then come back and act out a drunk. One of the oddest assignments we had was to go to the zoo and watch a llama. I never figured out why because few of us have been called on to play the part of a llama."

She frequently went home to East Falls for weekends, but the distance between her family's sensibilities and her own was widening. Kell remembers, "She started coming back in those days and saying things like 'I never admire anything physical in a man anymore. I only admire men's minds.' She came down to Philadelphia with this guy—a

† "The Other Princess Grace," *Ladies' Home Journal*, May 1977.

teacher at her school, I forget his name—and my parents were not too happy with him. My mother thought that if I were to bring around a couple of my big, fine-looking athletic friends, then Grace would see them in direct comparison with this guy and see what a creep he really was. So I brought these guys in—one of them was an Olympic butter-fly champion, one was a weightlifter, and the other guy was another good athlete, good-looking fellows. I gave them a clue that Grace's friend was a bit of a creep or something, so they walked in, met this guy, and gave him the grip. They practically put him on the floor." Kell paused for a broad grin. "My sister Grace was fit to be tied that I brought in these animals to assault her friend! I got the silent treat-ment for that one, all right. *But she did give up seeing that guy*" (Emphasis added).

§   §   §

Kell's story well conveys Grace's ambivalence about her family. The psychological pattern deducible from the anecdote would recur all her life: Grace's (apparent) flouting of Kelly family values followed by their disapproving reaction leading to strong guilt feelings in Grace and her eventual capitulation. She later described her striking out for the Academy and an acting career as a "rebellion," saying, "I did it. I rebelled against my family and went to New York to find out who I was, or who I wasn't." Yet in truth the kind of individualist thrust that made Grace's career was altogether too standard in the Kelly tradition to be called "rebellion"—*except* as a way of describing the guilt and enormity of feeling that doing anything against Kelly wishes raised in the heart of a girl as conscientiously devoted to her family as Grace was.

There was little of the stuff of a true rebel in Grace. Later, with her own children, she would say she understood "rebellion" and expected them to go through that "stage," yet when one of her daughters did, she did not really understand, for she couldn't fathom her motive. Hadn't she given her the one thing—the only thing—that she herself had lacked as a child: response and approval? What, then, the motive of a rebellion?

Individual identity, family membership are the two great threads—almost the dialectic—of Grace's life. As either grew, it threatened the other; yet in tense union, they created a changing whole greater than either part. From the fair Kellys, Grace received a physical beauty so extraordinary that, despite the derogations constantly repeated by one eager to be taken "seriously," it was always one of the pedestals on which her success reposed. From their full-throttled immigrant ambi-tion, she drew an energy and drive that, in three and a half years, put her eleven movies and one Oscar to the good and had made her one of the greatest stars Hollywood ever knew. From tough old Jack, the one serious Democratic contender in a Republican city, Grace drew the independence of mind and strength of will to do things her way, in Monaco as in Hollywood, even at the price of breaking with the studio that gave her her break. The list could be extended—religion, values, a "way" with people, loyalty, esprit de corps, a deep concern with charity and the public weal. *All* these things bore, in Grace, the Kelly stamp.

Yet from them, too, she received a burden of frustration and pain that, as Schulberg correctly sensed, she bore all her life. "My father was the central force in our family," Grace said, not once, but many times over many years. "We were all loud and sassy, but we always stopped what we were doing to listen to him." That beloved, charming, handsome father, for all his attractions, was also a monster—a man of such gigantic selfishness that he molded his own son into the instrument of his vengeance on Henley (for a slight, imaginary to begin with); an expert player of the double game, who cheated flagrantly on his wife; and finally a capricious father who played favorites with his adoring daughters, withholding and bestowing affection and approval according to an inscrutable whim.

In all his bluff give-and-take, Grace always came up shortest, as she herself later admitted in her more candid moments. "My sister was my father's favorite," Grace told a *McCall's* writer in 1974, "and there was the boy, the only son. Then I came, and then I had a baby sister, and I was terribly jealous of her. I loved the idea of a baby but was never allowed to hold it. So I was always on my mother's knee, the clinging type. But I was pushed away, and I resented my sister for years."

In the movie *High Society*, Frank Sinatra says to Grace, whom he half loves and whom he, as a reporter, has been watching carefully for some time, "I know that when your father hurt your mother, he hurt you." Grace's sisters claimed that, as children, they knew or sensed nothing of Jack's outside affairs. Grace herself, though she never spoke to even her closest friends of such things, made it clear in conversations with Rainier, that she had intuited the tension between her parents and, as she grew older, understood why.‡ Given her own frustrations with her father and her "clinging" to Ma for some of the response and affection he didn't give, it is equally likely that Grace identified with Margaret and took her pain personally. Grace would always say she admired her mother most for having preserved the family unity, with the clear implication that she understood that Ma did so despite (and to offset) the corrosive effect of her husband's infidelities.

The key lesson Grace took from watching her mother and her father

‡ Interview with Prince Rainier, September 12, 1983.

was to deny pain and, if that weren't possible, to suppress it—but, above all, not to show it. One of her favorite plays of her Uncle George's was *The Fatal Weakness* whose central character is Edith Espinshade, wonderful, hopelessly sentimental late middle-aged romantic, who has been two-timed by her husband. Toward the end of the play, after she has lost him to the other woman, Edith tells her best friend "I want to prove to myself that I am completely untouched by this entire thing." Her wish is, of course, futile, but the effort she puts into maintaining the facade is the point (or one of them) of Mrs. Espinshade's character.

Thus, Grace. As a young girl she wrote a poem about a "little flower" who is "lucky" because she soaks up sun and stands calm and pretty "while others have to fight and strain." But in the next stanza, she writes "But you must, too, have wars to fight/The cold bleak darkness of every night," and ends, "And yet you never let it show/On your pretty face." In short, "I'm all right, Jack" was something else Grace owed her father—her ego defense *par excellence*, not only vis-à-vis him, but to the world for the rest of her life. She rejected self-pity more sternly than any temptation she ever faced. The result was not altogether infelicitous. Grace's interiority and self-discipline contributed greatly to deepening the "character" that she hoped she had inherited from Jack. But the tension and hurt were often there, and the dissembling that Grace went through to hide them sometimes frustrated people close to her who wished to help and might have. It also contributed to her being misunderstood by the press and the outside world.

As the roll of Grace's achievements grew long and her fame became international, a new trait emerged in Kelly père—pique. His friend Paul Douglas, the actor, said that he found it "strange" to hear that a "champion" as well known as Jack Kelly was now being identified as "Grace Kelly's father." Doubtless, the experience of feeling the spotlight suddenly shift to his child was disconcerting for a proud and vain man like Kelly, but if he had possessed much of the "character" he was forever recommending to his children, he would not have told the press on the night Grace got the Oscar, "Peggy's the family extrovert. Just between us, I've always thought her the daughter with the most on the ball."

Not the least effect of statements such as these (and there were many) was to encourage the rest of the family to express their own natural resentment of Grace's fame, which they did. When *Time* did a cover story on his sister, Kell could find little more to say than to second his father's opinion that "There's been too much publicity about Grace" or to make fun of her taste in men. When Grace got back from making a movie in Africa and London, her sisters mocked what they called her "English accent," while their father "confided" to reporters, "I don't think she'll get swellheaded as long as her sisters have their breath." Finally, Ma Kelly authored a ten-part series for the Hearst publications recounting all manner of truths, half-truths, and falsehoods about her famous daughter's "romances."

A bit of hard teasing now and again was one thing, perhaps wholesome, certainly to be expected in a large Irish family. But the sort of punishment that perversely withheld esteem and organized derision inflicted on Grace was quite another. She was the Cinderella—sandwiched in between Kell the alter ego, Baba (Peggy) the favorite, and Lizanne the cosseted baby—and though she met her prince, she also carried aching scars from the ungallant, unbecoming remarks of her father and (through him) her family.

Unlike her Uncle George, Grace never adjusted to her outsider's status within the Kelly midst. She never gladly stood apart from them in the "superior" realm that her beauty, attainments, sensibility, intelligence, refinement, and celebrity or princely status could have provided. The ache of unmet childhood need throbbed in Grace's heart all of her life. The unfulfillable desire to please her father outlived Jack (who died in 1960) and endured in Grace in her attitudes and actions toward her siblings and mother. Her involvement with them was unquestioned—their weddings, babies, problems, divorces, and their needs were as much a part of her life as she could possibly make them from a distance of five thousand miles and vastly separate worlds. When she was with the Kellys, Grace's fame and accomplishments embarrassed and troubled her, for she sensed that they removed her ever further from the love and approval she craved but couldn't get from her family. So when in Philadelphia, the City of Brotherly Love, Grace rehearsed her old Cinderella part, reinserting herself back into the role of self-effacing, self-sacrificing "Gracie," available (now as star, now as Princess) to do everything they asked of her—a never-ending list of items. It struck her close friends and Monégasque family as strange, incongruous, and sometimes it upset them. But it was part of her burden, and she carried it as cheerfully as she could.

Grace herself only once adverted to the pain of her youth. In 1977, she told Budd Schulberg, a screenwriter and friend, who was interviewing her for the *Ladies' Home Journal:* ("It must have been a heavy load," I said to Princess Grace, "to keep up with the Kellys, to keep up with yourself—to be the best.") "Yes, it was—it is—a heavy load," Princess Grace replied. The silence that followed seemed to hold its own inaudible sentences. Loads are to be carried. Burdens are to be borne.

It remains true and noteworthy, nevertheless, that when all is said about the Kelly traits and the Kelly hold on Grace, the other branch of her life dialectic—her independence—was finally the stronger. *She left home*, the only one of her siblings (and only the third Kelly in several generations) to do so. She left home and made an extraordinary life for herself away from East Falls and utterly *different* from that which she had known there.

This, certainly, her family understood—they, best of all. Asked in a recent interview why Grace "turned out differently" from the rest of them, Kell replied without hesitation, "She got away from home early, before she got married." A touch ruefully he added, "None of the rest of us managed to do that."

PART TWO

PROFESSION

CHAPTER II

THE LOVE OF THE THEATER, THE LURE OF HOLLYWOOD

I think that the question of whether to be or not to be an actress is one that every woman must, at some time or other in her life, decide for herself.

—*George Kelly*, The Torch-Bearers

I hope to be so accomplished a dramatic actress that some day my Uncle George will write a play for me and direct it.

—*Grace Kelly, aged eighteen, in her application for admission to the American Academy of Dramatic Arts*

There she stood, alone, exposed, afraid. She was a grown woman but still a young girl, ingenuous but sophisticated, quiet but forceful. She was an Easterner seeking her destiny in the West and finding confirmation of her unspoken fears: the strangeness of western ways, the clash between her values and her new home.

It wasn't Grace Kelly, and it was: it was Amy Kane, wife of Marshal Will Kane in *High Noon*, the role that first gave Grace prominence in movies. It was far from her best performance, but it suited her, for Grace in Hollywood paralleled Amy in Hadleyville, though repelled not by violence but vulgarity. With their patrician, seemingly austere eastern sensibility, both actress and heroine had to struggle to find a place in, and make a commitment to, what they regarded as a crude, but exciting environment. The main difference is that Grace didn't find her Gary Cooper *there*. Hollywood fed her but starved her, too. So she left, and when she did, appropriately, she went back even farther east than she had come from.

Grace wanted to be a stage actress, but had to settle for being a movie star instead. Before that came some modeling, stints on early live television drama, and all too few shots at her beloved stage. Her career was a success story, and each phase of it brought her some genuine satisfactions. Yet the odd thing was, she never fit in. Independent-minded, cultured but not corrupt, reserved but more honest than the hype swirling around her, she struggled to preserve herself in the boisterous brave new worlds beyond East Falls. But since the self she would preserve was itself conflicted, she found little peace or lasting satisfaction.

§   §   §

Modeling was hardly something the eighteen-year-old niece of George Kelly dreamed about. On the contrary, she pooh-poohed the idea when it was first put to her by her good friend at the Barbizon, Carolyn Scott. But Grace trusted Carolyn, and Carolyn, in turn, trusted her own strong intuition that Grace definitely had the lines and the beauty of a model. In fact Carolyn was maybe surer that her overly shy Philadelphia pal had a future in modeling than in acting. So she hammered away at Grace to have professional photos taken and to submit them at the major modeling agencies. Carolyn learned to choose her arguments, and she early recognized that the "glamour" of modeling meant nothing to the theater-obsessed Grace. Nor, surprisingly, did the reminder that Grace's mother, as a sassy young beauty, had made the pages (and one cover) of several women's magazines cut much ice with her daughter.

But money talked. The prospect that Grace might pull down enough income to reduce significantly the amount she got from home—and maybe even to become independent of her parents—*here* was persuasive reason to follow Carolyn's advice. Under the banner of self-reliance, Grace presently got the pictures taken and sent them around. Almost immediately she got calls to come in, followed by a number of offers. She signed with a small but good agency and started out at the excellent wage of $7.50 per hour.

Carolyn's intuition was qualifiedly right—at least as far as the modeling went. Grace became a modest success very quickly. Her beauty could be made to come alive by a camera. The face which seemed so prosaic when unmade-up and buried in a book became glowing and inviting when a good photographer brought out its warm qualities. Grace became one of the better models in the business. Posing for Ipana, Old Gold, several brands of beer, clothes and fashions galore, she eventually started to earn the top fee of $25 per hour, or approximately $400 per week—a truly munificent sum in 1949, and more than enough to pay her way through her entire second year at the Academy. By then she had done more magazine covers than her mother and was being featured in advertising layouts and catalogues. Toward the end of her modeling career, she was starting to do fashion shorts for newsreels, two of which took her on trips to Paris and Bermuda. In sum, an overnight success in a tough business.

Nevertheless Grace never figured among the top flight of New York models. Photographers later tried to explain it with reference to her "natural limitations" in the breast department. Others, like Ruzzie Green, speaking to *Time* magazine described Grace as constrained within the style of being "what we call 'nice clean stuff' in our business. She's the girl next door. No glamour, no oomph, no cheesecake." But Grace's limitations as a model did not mainly result from natural or stylistic limitations. Grace might have been a leading model had she but cared to be. Future cameras and artists of the image would quarry out of Grace Kelly a great deal more than "girl next door" beauty. The speed, pressure, and purely commercial purposefulness of advertising photography undoubtedly precluded much experimentation with models, most of whom got slotted within a "type" in their first week at work, and Grace probably did not object. Her boundaries as a model were self-imposed, not physical limitations or the narrow impositions of current public taste. Grace disdained modeling for what she saw, rightly or wrongly, as its degradation or trivialization of the person of the model. She would say later that she felt "humiliated" at having to approach "strangers" with requests for jobs. Yet it was highly improbable that Grace the model ever had to approach anyone—her agency did that for her. In reality, Grace was articulating her acute inner discomfort at being taken for face value alone. Again and again this reflex led her to demur strongly where others might smile tolerantly.

As assignments in television and the theater increased, Grace happily quit modeling. Popular accounts of her early professional life would later record that at a certain point Grace's agents dramatically posed the choice for her: "Acting and modeling, you can't do both, which will it be?" In truth, such a question could never have occurred to anyone who knew the young Grace Kelly. She was ready to give up modeling almost before she could afford to. Her first professional theater role lay at hand—at roughly a fourth of the money she was making as a model.

§   §   §

Grace arrived at Bucks County Playhouse in the summer of 1949, excited and awed at the prospect of acting professionally. Showcase performances before overly sympathetic audiences of parents and fellow students had not evoked her best efforts. Bucks County, however, provided a different opportunity. One of the top stock companies on the eastern seaboard, it regularly employed some of the leading names and finest talents of the American stage—like Lillian Gish, Helen Hayes, and Ruth Chatterton, none of whom made more than five hun-

dred dollars a week. Any actor who was asked played Bucks County; it
was a signal honor to be invited and the selection of plays made the
experience challenging and wonderful. Grace made her debut the same
week as Jennifer Howard (daughter of the screenwriter and playwright Sidney Howard); their names would be recorded on a 1949
seasonal list that included Walter Slezak, John Carradine, Sylvia Field,
Florence Reed, Leo G. Carroll, and Eva Le Gallienne.

The owner-impresario of Bucks was Theron Bamberger, as unsenti-
mental and demanding a producer as Grace was likely to meet. Grace
passed the tryouts splendidly, but Bamberger's decision to give Grace
such a careful look in the first place—for there were many Academy
graduates more apparently able—probably had to do with his affection
for her family whom Bamberger knew well. His program note on
Grace said more about her relationship to three Kellys (Jack Sr.,
George, and Kell) than it did about the young actress or her professional background.

The play itself was even a Kelly production: *The Torch-Bearers*, her
Uncle George's great satirical comedy. His niece played the part of
Florence McCrickett, a young amateur actress. She did well, but not
memorably—as indeed very few neophytes ever did. If she left any
lasting impression on the small staff at Bucks, it was for her hard work
and seriousness of purpose. "She was all business; the theater mattered
to her terribly," recalled Elizabeth Mears, Bamberger's assistant. The
leading lady in the play, Haila Stoddard, had stronger accolades for
Grace: "Experience would later give Grace a host of things to draw on
when she was onstage, but even at this early time in her acting career,
she had an almost innate sense of what not to do. She effortlessly
avoided the common affectations or mannerisms of young actors." In
fact Grace must have done better than average, for she was invited
back a month later to play the rather larger role of the dizzy ingenue in
The Heiress—a part in which she was said to "glow."

The "glow" drew a reaction from an unexpected source. One day,
soon after returning to New York from Bucks County, Grace got a
breathless call from the East Coast offices of Twentieth Century-Fox.
The "celebrated director," Gregory Ratoff, was making a movie called
Taxi; he wanted to meet this young blond actress—and right away; this
afternoon in fact. Chary of movies and the "Hollywood" style from
listening to Uncle George talk about his M.G.M. experience, Grace
found the hype and urgency of the request false, distasteful. If she
couldn't manage to decline to meet Ratoff, she certainly refused to
endow the event with any mystical importance nor it to change her
habits. Dressed in her comfortable "New York costume"—old tweed
skirt, adored familiar shirt, hair uncurled, and without makeup—
Grace simply stopped by the Fox office en route to her acting class.

The scene that greeted her in Ratoff's outer office would have rattled a young woman of less pride or self-assurance than the nineteen-year-old Grace Kelly. Here sat close to a dozen competitors—beautiful girls, all coiffed and dressed and made up to the nines. The rest of the story is, of course, pure "Hollywood," though nonetheless true for that. At first sight Ratoff pronounced her "Perfect!" for the part of a young Irish immigrant girl, declaring "She is *not* pretty" (true enough; Grace's beauty, especially given her banal New York lifestyle, was hardly obvious). Ratoff ran a screen test of her for *Taxi* and said he must have her. The producer viewed the test, however, and contradicted his "celebrated director." Ratoff didn't get his "not pretty" Grace; he got the British actress Constance Smith, star of *Brighton Rock* and *The Thirteenth Letter*.

The rejection barely fazed Grace. A few weeks after the screen test (but before the producer's veto), Grace had what was to her a far more desirable and worthy assignment. In the fall of 1949, Grace Kelly got her first Broadway part—as the bewildered and anguished daughter to Raymond Massey's cavalry captain in August Strindberg's tragedy *The Father*. Massey himself cast her, though not till well into the run did he learn she was the daughter of his old sculling friend, Jack Kelly. (Left to her own devices, Grace never but never depended on her family.) In addition to Massey, another actor of high distinction appeared in the play—Mady Christians, with whom Grace struck up an affectionate, if respectful, friendship. Grace later told a reporter that she learned as much about acting sitting in her dressing room, "listening to Miss Christians talk" as she had in several years of private lessons and Academy instruction. The play was no hit however, largely because, in Brooks Atkinson's opinion, Massey's "ferocity of soul" was not up to his part. Though the New York *Times* drama critic found that Grace Kelly gave "a charming, pliable performance," she was soon out of work. *The Father* closed its doors after sixty-nine performances.

Grace was unhappy at the calm which now beset her career in drama after its strong beginning, but she didn't let it discourage her. Assiduously, she spent the 1950–51 season reading for dozens of parts —and got nowhere. One remembered disappointment was losing the ingenue role in a Clifford Odets play called *The Country Girl* (a part subsequently deleted from the film version). The rejection that hurt most, however, came at the hands of Helen Hayes. Grace very much wanted a role in *The Wisteria Trees*—a Joshua Logan adaptation of Chekhov's *The Cherry Orchard*, that was to star "the first lady" of the American theater. Grace felt she might have a good shot at the role, for she knew Hayes through her daughter Mary, a classmate of Grace's at the American Academy of Dramatic Arts. Personal considerations indeed played a role—but against Grace, not for her. Mary MacArthur had died tragically young, and her mother felt honor bound to select Mary's best friend, Bethel Leslie, to fill a role that would have been Mary's debut on the Broadway stage. Unfortunately, Miss Hayes told Grace none of this, but let her read for the part as if she had a chance, then rejected her. Leland Hayward, the producer, tried to argue Hayes out of her "sentiment" saying that Grace "is going to be someone really big," but the actress would not be moved. She defended her decision on artistic grounds as well, saying that Grace had too weak a voice for the theater. Years later, Hayes told Grace, "I did Hollywood a big favor [in rejecting you],"* but Grace certainly hadn't seen it that way at the time (or later). She wasn't simply disappointed but also hurt by Hayes's rejection—perhaps because she intuited (or learned of) the futility of her reading. Not a person to harbor grudges, Grace made an exception in this case. Several years later, she was still "smarting" over that rejection, said her then roommate Rita Gam.

Adducing "what went wrong" at auditions was a futile pastime, but Grace, like any actress, did it constantly. Sometimes she figured the problem was her height: at five six and a half, she stood a bit tall for ingenue parts. On occasion, at their request or her own suggestion, Grace read lines in her stocking feet. She later told a reporter, only half in jest, that she felt she landed the role in *The Father* simply because "Mr. Massey and Miss Christians happened to be tall, too." Other times, she thought maybe casting directors found her too leggy or too chinny or too inexperienced. Undoubtedly, Grace was occasionally thought too beautiful, and (in at least one instance) too plain. The one category Grace believed she fit perfectly was "the too category." One serious problem that afflicted her at this stage was her voice: it was still too reedy, high, and thin. Grace could shout but she couldn't always project.

Nevertheless she made progress. Many times in her life, Grace would befriend people who played critical roles in her career or her work. A talent more than a calculation, this tendency nonetheless served her extremely well—and never more decisively so than with Edith (Edie) Van Cleve, her first agent. One of the better-known and most trusted agents at the most powerful agency in the country, the Music Corporation of America (M.C.A.), Van Cleve was not likely to confuse sentiment and work. She preferred to cultivate painstakingly a small "stable" of carefully chosen candidates rather than play the odds by formally representing dozens.

Edie was deeply preoccupied with developing a preoccupying young actor named Brando when a colleague called to say he knew of an Academy graduate with "strong possibilities" for motion pictures. Van

* Interview with the author, November 7, 1983.

Cleve went to a showcase production of *The Philadelphia Story* and there saw Grace Kelly in her first role. The young actress had breathtaking beauty, she felt, and an impressive, if understated, and very eastern style. She also had acting talent, though Van Cleve saw that both it and her beauty needed careful development if they were to shine. Enamored of the theater, Grace thought only of getting back on the stage (it didn't have to be Broadway). Enamored of success, Van Cleve was already wondering if Grace's future might not lie on the screen where her beauty—"incandescent, beguiling"—could be magnified and exploited. They had several talks; the actress said she wished to avoid "Hollywood," stating the usual satchel of understandable, if predictable, utterly East Coast prejudices. For the moment there was no conflict, however. Edie strongly felt Grace must hone her acting ability and that could not be done in front of a movie camera. Personal affection for Grace led Edie not only to push a little harder for her client-friend's career but also to play a more direct role in her professional formation. At her instigation, Grace began intensive private acting lessons with one of the most fashionable coaches in New York, Sanford Meisner, of the Neighborhood Playhouse. She also jumped back into summer stock work. Finally, Edie introduced Grace into the newly developing medium of television.

§ § §

Television then had nothing like the negative aura it later acquired. On the contrary, between 1948 and 1957, television was one of the liveliest, most creative and exciting arts in America. Networks were not yet bloated bureaucracies, mostly devoid of ideas and courage, vying with one another to underestimate the taste and educability of the public. Rather, they were laboratories in which a vital new medium was being developed, and they attracted many of the very finest young, creative, and performing artists in the nation. Disdained by the theater and menaced by the studios which defensively forbade their contract artists from working in television, the early networks had no choice but to call on fresh talent—who, in turn, were only too delighted to respond.

The world Grace found in the New York TV studios had a palpable excitement and esprit de corps that she and her colleagues would never forget, even though nearly all eventually migrated away from television. Not only was the quality of live drama on the "Philco/Goodyear Playhouse," "Studio One," and "Playhouse 90" extremely high, but the adventure and pleasure—the sheer comradely fun—of working on them proved a unique experience for many artists.

Such shows were also a perfect forge for shaping and annealing young actors, though perhaps "crucible" would be a better word for the fearful heat and pressure of early television. Contrary to casual expectation, live television was far more akin to a traveling stage troupe than to moviemaking. If something went wrong once the show began airing—from muffed lines to absent props to faulty sets—there was no stopping for retakes; nothing but nothing could be done. The actors stood out there alone; they had to be able to improvise, knowing full well that the high price of a flub was its visibility, not just to an audience of a few hundred (as in a theater) but several million viewers. Television was for the swift-witted, the surefooted, and (because the quantity of shows was high and the range of acting parts extensive) the versatile. Beauty, moreover, wasn't enough. Television technology and camera artistry didn't yet approach the levels of movie cinematography and cinematographers. A beautiful face couldn't get magnified, searched out, and enhanced in its every facet because the equipment wasn't adequate. In other words, you had to be able to think quickly, to move fast, to expect the unexpected, and to act.

Which is what Grace did. As Edie Van Cleve pulled down assignments virtually weekly, TV shortly replaced modeling as Grace's bread and butter income in the year or so (1950–51) before she went to Hollywood. Early on, Van Cleve introduced her client to the most gifted of a large group of gifted teleplay producers, Fred Coe. Like Grace, Coe's first love was the legitimate stage, where later on he would produce *Two for the Seesaw*, *The Miracle Worker*, and *A Thousand Clowns*, among other Broadway successes. When she worked with him, however, Coe had turned his attention to television where he was producing the "Philco/Goodyear Playhouse," a weekly series that presented hour-long original dramas or adaptations of plays, novels, and short stories created by gifted young writers from Paddy Chayefsky and J. P. Miller to Sumner Locke Elliott and Tad Mosel. Working out of an old, cramped radio studio in Rockefeller Center, directing unknown actors with the names of Eva Marie Saint, Paul Newman, Rod Steiger, and Walter Matthau, Coe and his team turned out dozens and dozens of productions (including *Marty*, *The Catered Affair*, and *Dinner at Eight*) that not only pulled down thirty Emmy nominations (Coe won three Emmys in 1955 alone) but shaped the genre of dramatic plays on television for years to come.

A shy, lonely man of great personal reserve, Coe nevertheless specialized in intense professional relations. If he liked an actor or writer, a kind of "love affair" bloomed between them, as Coe systematically worked to evoke the most from him or her. The producer was immediately captivated by Grace Kelly's combination of beauty and manner. "She had talent and attractiveness," he said later, "but so do a lot of other young people in the theater who never become stars. The thing that made her stand out was something we call 'style.' " That "style," however, wasn't easy to explain. Sometimes Coe called Grace "the essence of freshness," but other times she was "queenly"; and, still other times, she was "the kind of girl every man dreams of marrying."

But if Coe had a hard time capturing Grace in words, he did well by her on the television screen. Snapping her up, he cast her first as the lead in a production of Sinclair Lewis's *Bethel Merriday.* Then he gave her the lead role in *Ann Rutledge,* a drama about the woman who captured the young Abraham Lincoln's heart. From there, he gave her other assignments, most notably the lead in an adaptation of F. Scott Fitzgerald's *The Rich Boy* that won Grace considerable acclaim. By no means all of Grace's work for Coe was in leading parts, but few of the roles he gave her were uninteresting or unchallenging (though after a period of time, Grace worried that she might be getting typecast playing rich men's daughters). No producer-director with whom Grace ever worked had a higher opinion of her nor pushed her harder than Coe. But then no other producer-director expressed the concern, as Coe did, that Grace had a slight tendency to depend on her unique "look," which was always in demand, and therefore not to push herself as hard as she should have. He went so far as to say that Grace was "lazy" about extending herself to the limits of a natural talent that he regarded as of the highest order.

Grace worked for many other TV producers besides Coe, including the one man who could be named in the same breath with Coe as *the* pioneer of live television drama: Worthington Miner. The other programs she regularly appeared on were generally the best and the most popular in the business—e.g., "Kraft Television Theatre," which specialized in costly, elaborate productions and hired actors like Lee Remick, Anthony Perkins, Joanne Woodward, and Cloris Leachman; the "Nash Airflyte Theater"; "Prudential Family Playhouse"; and "Treasury Men in Action" (a high-grade crime series with Lee Marvin, James Dean, Jason Robards). Grace also did a one-shot appearance on "The Web" in 1950, and she starred in *50 Beautiful Girls,* a rather atypical episode of the show "Suspense."

Grace appeared several times in a very popular series that specialized in psychological dramas and mystery, "Danger." Grace did two episodes for the director, Ted Post, who called her "a very cool, lucid actress with a regal bearing." The adjectives, Post agreed, suited the first role Grace played for him—a countess in a French revolutionary thriller—but they also suited Grace, in his opinion. "She was no [Eleonora] Duse, but she gave a very believable performance," he said.† Was Post surprised that Grace went on to be so successful? "Yes and no," he replied, adding a postscript that countered the Coe viewpoint. "Her

† Interview, October 26, 1983.

beauty alone was spellbinding and would have won her great attention. But Grace was also *very* determined and worked hard. She listened to you and applied what you said. She learned."

It wasn't all sweat and grit, however—far from it. Grace and her young co-workers delighted in the comradeship and intimacy, sometimes even the silliness, of their little world. To break the tension and exhaustion of hours of work, the actors would often play a game called "giggle belly." They would lie on the floor with their heads on each other's stomachs, then somebody would tell a funny story, and start to laugh, at which point his belly would make his neighbor's head bounce, whose subsequent laughter would then make *his* belly bounce, etc., until in short order the floor was covered with insanely laughing actors. The greatest sources of mirth (then, and for the rest of their lives) were bloopers and mishaps occurring before the camera. Talking twenty-five years later with an old colleague from live TV, Princess Grace could barely manage to get a typical story out without collapsing in laughter: "[In this episode], it was Christmas time, and a wonderful English character [actor] and I were coming to bring an orphanage a hot pie for Christmas. But the pie was too hot, so I set it down and the old actor stepped in it. He came limping into the orphanage with half the pie spread over his shoe. 'Look what we brought you—this nice, hot pie—Merry Christmas!' "

Any account of Grace Kelly's training as an actress that failed to emphasize the critical role of live TV would be negligent, for not only did she learn a great deal in working on teleplays, but she also became a bigger success—both artistically and financially—here than in the theater. In all, the young actress appeared in sixty teleplays in only thirty months—a remarkable record that didn't even take into account her appearance on something called "Hollywood Screen Test"—a high-level talent show for young actors of some experience who were looking for "the big break." (Besides Grace, Mercedes McCambridge and Edward Everett Horton got their "breaks" on this show.) A biographer was on the mark to conclude "When the definitive story of New York television is made, the name of Grace Kelly will be synonymous with the early fifties period along with Maria Riva, Mary Sinclair, and Felicia Montealegre. They were the stars."‡

§   §   §

Yet for Grace, as for most of her colleagues in television, there was never any question of lingering in the world of the twelve-inch screen. More stubborn and determined than most, Grace kept her hopes pinned permanently on the stage. ("I remember she was always a little

‡ Gwen Robyns, *Princess Grace* (London: W. H. Allen 1976), p. 61.

removed," Coe reminisced in 1956. "[She was] not a snob, but she had her eyes set on a very high goal early in her career.") Van Cleve, on the other hand—though doing her best to secure Grace what theatrical opportunities she thought useful for her—kept looking for film opportunities. Before long, therefore, Edie landed Grace her first movie assignment.

Among the spectators during the eight-week run of *The Father* was one of the most powerful and perceptive producers in Hollywood, Sol Siegel, who was then preparing to make a melodrama called *Fourteen Hours*. Taken with Grace's looks, he told his director, Henry Hathaway, to see the play. After, they decided to approach Kelly through Van Cleve and offer her a small but important role in their film. Grace would play the part of a woman preparing to divorce her husband, who changes her mind after seeing a pathetic unhappy man standing on a skyscraper ledge, thinking to jump. The movie, though it boasted a cast that included Paul Douglas, Barbara Bel Geddes, and Agnes Moorehead, was no great success, but it served to get Grace known "in the business."

And "the business" was where M.C.A. was subtly nudging Grace, whether she knew or liked it or not. M.C.A. had a very powerful West Coast office where, ignored by his client, an agent and future friend was working hard to get Grace in pictures. Jay Kanter was as competent as Van Cleve, but had nothing of Edie's hard-driving personality. In the laid-back world of Hollywood, however, the extremely personable, soft-voiced Kanter was perhaps more suited to his territory. The goal on which the twenty-five-year-old agent had his hopes set for client Kelly in the spring of 1951 was a western melodrama of virtually classical unity and spareness. It was called *High Noon*, and it was to be produced by Stanley Kramer from a script by Carl Foreman, directed by Fred Zinnemann. These were men already well along their paths to becoming the major producer, writer, and director that posterity knows. Kramer was already one of Hollywood's most successful young independent moviemakers, with *Cyrano de Bergerac*, *The Men*, and *Home of the Brave* to his credit. Foreman had written screenplays for *Home of the Brave* (1949) and *The Men* (1950); and Zinnemann had directed *The Seventh Cross* (1944) and *The Men*.

Foreman had actually heard of Grace first, even before Jay Kanter made her existence known to Kramer. A close friend of screenwriter John Paxton, Foreman had seen his buddy's film, *Fourteen Hours*, and had remarked on the "extraordinary attractiveness" of the young blonde in that minor part. At the very next story conference he told his colleagues about her. They saw the film, then summoned photographs of Kelly from Kanter, and then summoned the actress herself. Grace made a famous appearance in Zinnemann's and Kramer's offices wearing white gloves. "It wasn't so much the gloves themselves as that she had the personality and manner to go with them," said Zinnemann. "Actresses are usually [pause] more uninhibited." But neither the gloves nor the "eastern seaboard style" clinched it; Grace Kelly was hired, in Zinnemann's words, "because she was a *very* pretty girl."

Grace herself was hardly blasé at the success of her fast trip to Los Angeles. She was fully aware of the quality and success of Kramer's output and she respected his writer and director greatly. Still, being Grace, she had her concerns, which she aired with Van Cleve and (by phone) with Kanter. The chief one was simple: fear of any entangling contract that would tie her to a Hollywood studio. On graduation from the Academy, she had rejected out-of-hand a standard seven-year contract that major studios commonly offered beautiful young actresses on the gamble that one in a hundred of them could become a star. To Grace such an arrangement resembled indenture and implied self-betrayal. As she had no wish for a Hollywood career in any case, she told her agents, she wouldn't consider a term contract. When she got the *High Noon* offer, moreover, Grace hoped to spend the summer of 1951 doing plays. She had received a third invitation to the Bucks County Playhouse, and afterwards, an invitation to perhaps the most prestigious stock repertory company in America, Elitch Gardens, in Denver, Colorado.

Van Cleve reassured her client about the question of a contract. As an independent filmmaker, Kramer was not in the business of retaining artists beyond the picture at hand. Grace could make *High Noon* with every expectation of returning to New York immediately after production. As for Bucks County and Elitch Gardens, Edie agreed that it would be priceless experience for a serious actress and was therefore prepared to gamble. Officially, *High Noon* was to start shooting in the spring of 1951, before Elitch even opened its doors. But Van Cleve, knowing that Hollywood shooting schedules rarely unfolded as set, figured Grace might sneak in a season on the legitimate stage before she had to report to the sound stage. She guessed correctly.

In August, Grace opened at Bucks County Playhouse in *Accent on Youth*, a play by Samuel Raphaelson, in which she played the female lead—an adoring secretary to an aging playwright. It was not a brilliant production but the experience was memorable for Grace because of the testing she received at the hands of her male counterpart. Jerome Cowan had been in his day a rather well-known Hollywood star of B pictures, but for several years Cowan had been undergoing the galling experience of watching his career as a romantic lead fade. Unfortunately he had not the mettle to fade gracefully. Young Grace Kelly met the full force of his frustration and unhappiness. In Cowan's opinion, the woman cast as his co-lead was a raw tyro whose beauty and relationship to George Kelly were her only assets and whose skills certainly did not merit a major role opposite a "major actor" like himself. He aired these feelings liberally—"throwing his swash and buckle all over the place," recalled colleague Natalie Core. The result was an extremely intimidated Grace. "She had no trouble understanding what was the real source of Cowan's tetchiness, and she felt sympathy for the man, but he made life very hard for her," continued Core. At first, Grace nearly buckled under the pressure. She could barely remember her lines for her fright, and she depended on Core to cue her through rehearsals of *Accent on Youth*. Gradually both pride of craft and her ability to act on Core's advice put Grace beyond the range of poor Cowan's rantings. When *Accent* opened, she gave some of her best performances.

After a week at Bucks County, Grace flew to Colorado. Elitch gave her one of the best summers of her life. She arrived at this overbuilt, Tivoli-like "garden" with enthusiasm and determination, but also with a trace of anxiety. The actors who had played on the Elitch stage included most of the greatest names of the American theater and screen: Bernhardt, Fairbanks Sr. & Jr., Mary Pickford, George Arliss, Tyrone Power, Sr., and Edward G. Robinson. In Grace's time, they included many who had gone on to movie stardom—José Ferrer, Tyrone Power, Jr., Walter Pidgeon, Pat O'Brien. Grace felt profound respect for such tradition, and, as at Bucks County Playhouse, she very much hoped she would make more of an impression than as a beautiful ingenue. Her first play was F. Hugh Herbert's *For Love or Money*, in which she had some success with a fairly difficult part—a role that had, in fact, launched a stage career for June Lockhart. She followed this with an even better portrayal in *Legend of Sarah*. Then came *The Detective Story*, *The Man Who Came to Dinner*, *The Cocktail Party*, and *Ring Around the Moon* in which she won some of the best accolades accorded the Elitch actors that season.

The weeks at Elitch sped by idyllically. Grace's reputation as a stage actress was beginning to establish itself for more reasons than her beauty or her name; she had won the affection and respect of all her colleagues; and a romance with fellow actor Gene Lyons was rapidly developing into the deepest relationship she'd ever had with a man. Nothing, she told her friend and co-actor, Whitfield Connor, would have pleased her more than "to stay here forever."

One day in the middle of summer, as she was preparing enthusiastically to open in *The Glass Menagerie*, Hollywood laid its claim. Grace called Whit aside and said that she had a problem. She showed him a telegram she'd just received from a producer whom she called "Mr. Stanley Kramer." In it, Kramer formally reiterated his offer of a role in *High Noon* and requested her immediate arrival in Los Angeles to begin filming. Grace confided her mixed feelings to Whit. She was greatly tempted to take the movie part, she admitted, but on the other hand, she hated to leave Elitch where she was now beginning to come into her own as a stage actress. Secondly, she wondered if, in any case, she wouldn't have to turn "Mr. Kramer" down because of her contract with Elitch. Could she in good conscience break it? Touched by a decency, naiveté, and artistic commitment that he did not customarily associate with Hollywood-bound actresses, Connor reassured Grace. Not only could she legally and ethically leave Colorado before the end of the season (actors did it all the time, he said), she would be crazy not to, he told her.

§   §   §

Thanks to three fourths of a season at Elitch, Grace arrived in California far surer of herself than when she had done *Fourteen Hours*. Nevertheless, she came with the understandable trepidation that any stage actor must feel at the thought of appearing before the searching eye of a camera, close up. Poise, memory, character, intelligence, one's "whole" appearance—the usual qualities that produce a fine dramatic actor—do not count, or count very differently, on a motion picture screen. Grace's single film experience (in *Fourteen Hours)* had left her— and the writer-producer of the film, John Paxton—ambivalent. There was little doubt that her beauty could be translated onto the screen and even be magnified by the camera. But the editing process had so whittled down and (in Paxton's eyes) deformed Grace's main scene in the film that it was impossible to judge what could be expected of her as a screen actress in a major role.

In addition, the men who hired Grace for *High Noon* were no longer sure that they'd done the right thing. Their doubt had nothing to do with Grace's abilities, however. At the time she was hired, Kramer, Zinnemann, and Foreman had yet to cast an actor in the all-important male lead of *High Noon*, Marshal Will Kane. The budget for the picture was very low, as independently (nonstudio) financed films tended to be. The last of a five-picture commitment that Kramer Productions had made with United Artists, *High Noon* would be no Technicolor blockbuster with big names. If the movie made money, as its makers hoped, it would be on account of low budget and high art. The man who played the role of Kane would be no box office giant.

Then, hardly a fortnight after Kramer had given M.C.A. the "yes" on Kelly, he found to his astonishment that no one less than Gary Cooper wanted the lead in *High Noon*—and for far less money than he usually received. In retrospect, it was understandable: Coop hadn't had a hit in a long while. But at the time, his acceptance brought, first delight and amazement, then distress in the offices of Stanley Kramer Productions.

For it suddenly struck everyone they now had one potentially large problem at hand: Coop was fifty; the Kelly girl who would play his bride, twenty-two. "You can bridge some gaps with makeup and camera angles, but almost thirty years?! Wouldn't the whole film fall out of kilter?" Foreman worried. "Wouldn't we now be obliged to explain why Marshal Kane—hardly what you'd call a conformist—was marrying a child?" Foreman's worry was Zinnemann's, was especially Kramer's. The producer felt outright that Kelly was now miscast. Yet there wasn't time to start the search for another, older actress, nor could Kramer bring himself to call M.C.A. and buy out their client's one-picture contract (though financially it would have been easy to do so—Grace was only making five hundred dollars a week). "She was just too special, her face too attractive and photographically interesting," Zinnemann explained. "We stuck with her." So off went the telegram to Elitch: Grace should report for early September shooting.

Starting actors and actresses nearly always strive to be liked, are rarely objectionable; rudeness, irresponsibility, and personal idiosyncrasies come with the territory of fame and wealth. Nevertheless, Grace's modesty, friendliness, sympathy—"The total absence of anything suggesting egocentricity or greed" (Foreman)—immediately impressed her co-workers and distinguished her from most other apprentice actors. She seemed to be immune even from the common contagion of competitiveness. But she—or her beauty—could arouse strong jealousy in others. The fine actress Katy Jurado (a star in her Mexican homeland) was convinced that Zinnemann was "half in love" with Grace and was giving her far more camera play than her role called for—and at Jurado's expense. Kramer, too, studied the early footage (the "dailies") and wondered if Kelly wasn't being "overemphasized." He had figured Jurado, not Grace, was the female lead—"the spur of the film," as he put it. Fortunately he said nothing to the volatile Mexican star, while Foreman reassured Jurado that "Fred's close-ups simply give Grace a chance to come on as strongly as you do." (To which Jurado replied, "You bet I'm strong. I don't care how many goddamn close-ups he gives her, people are going to remember *me.*") Yet even at the height of Katy's bursts of Latin sarcasm, she never alleged that Grace herself had anything to do with Zinnemann's cinematic overindulgence.

Such disharmonies were minor and infrequent, however. The pleasure of making the picture matched the artistic quality attained in the product. The film was soon regarded as a masterpiece. Looking back, it is very possibly the finest film in which Grace Kelly ever played, even though she herself would perform far better in future parts. In the event, the worrisome "age problem" never materialized. No one noticed or commented on the generation and a half separating the conscientious sheriff from his equally principled bride (nor does Katy Jurado come off as less than a sultry beauty giving a first-rate performance).

The critics were very kind to Grace, though none of them expended much space on her performance. The actress herself, however, often criticized her work in this, her first important motion picture role. "Everything is so clear working with Gary Cooper. When I look into his face, I can see everything he is thinking. But when I look into my own face, I see absolutely nothing. *I* know what I am thinking, but it just doesn't show. I wonder if I am ever going to be any good." Grace's words, frequently quoted or paraphrased in a number of publications (notably a *Time* magazine cover story), were by far the harshest—and in fact the only serious—criticism she received for *High Noon*. Later retrospective analyses of Grace's work tended to ignore or minimize her judgments in view of *High Noon*'s achievement and her own future success.

Yet there is some truth in Grace's subjective appraisal. On camera, her eyes, for example, reflect far more thought and intelligence than feeling. Even at peak moments—as when the ex-convict Frank Miller (Ian MacDonald) grabs her as a hostage—the terror in Amy's face looks manufactured. And there is only slight preparation for the grand emotional burst where she confronts Cooper and almost deserts him.

Grace's performance is obviously as well thought out as a young stage actress could make it—and get away with, since a theater audience could not see directly into her face. On camera, however, the character of Amy is distant, removed—a state of affairs aggravated by Grace's voice, with its careful stage enunciation and sharply noticeable East Coast (even semi-English) accent. At the critical extreme, Stanley Kramer never did alter his opinion that Grace was "miscast," that she and Cooper "weren't convincing as a couple," though he did not communicate this to Grace nor mention it publicly in her lifetime. Foreman spoke of a "tinny quality" in Grace's portrayal—again a deficit intensified by her high-pitched voice. Zinnemann, though convinced from the outset that Grace would one day be a major star, believed that the actress "may have appeared rather bloodless and flat" as Amy Kane. The director said he hadn't had time to work "really closely" with Grace during the filming. But on reflection, he wasn't "at all sure I could have significantly improved her performance, and I might well have inhibited her [with too much direction and criticism]. She was a very young actress."

Indeed, Grace was *a very young actress*, but here it worked in her favor. Her youth combined with those same "unemotional" traits which she herself criticized created a performance that was objectively far more praiseworthy than subjectively fulfilling. As a budding actress, Grace had reason to worry about her corseted emotion, or her aloofness, or the occasionally soprano staccato of her voice, but *as Amy Kane*, she was almost typecast. Despite all the worries about age, appearance, makeup, and voice, Grace came off well precisely because the part called for someone very much like the young Grace Kelly. In a later cover story on Grace, *Time* called her "awkward" among the locals of Sheriff Kane's bailiwick, but that is exactly what Zinnemann was striving for. Her stiffness and remoteness coincided with what Amy ought to have been feeling as a displaced, slightly repressed and inhibited eastern Quaker girl caught up in a bloody vendetta on the morning of her wedding. The plot of the movie meant everyone must desert Cooper; the core of Grace's role was that no one understood *her* and her repulsion for the exaggerated emotions of frontier life. Amy's near exit on the noon train was thus symbolic of Grace's own one-foot-in, one-foot-out relation to Hollywood. Playing herself to a degree, Grace proved an excellent foil for the drama that Zinnemann and Foreman created, a striking contrast to Jurado and a complement for Cooper. An experienced, older professional actress would have had to possess very considerable acting talent indeed to do what Grace did (and somewhat rued) naturally.

§ § §

You have a form of respectability that requires a certain anchorage in the conventions.
—*Florence McCrickett, in* The Torch-Bearers, *by George Kelly*

With considerable relief Grace returned to her apartment on East Sixty-sixth Street in the late fall of 1951. She had enjoyed the actual shooting of *High Noon*, but she hadn't much liked living out of a suitcase at the Chateau Marmont. This rather ostentatious neobaroque instance of Hollywood hostelry, towering over Sunset Strip, meant little to Grace, despite the news that Bette Davis and Joan Crawford often resided there. At this early point in her career, although she knew practically nothing about life in the show business capital, Grace felt certain it wasn't for her. And in case Grace flagged for a moment in cherishing this prejudice, her family stood by with reinforcements, literally. At John and Margaret Kelly's "suggestion," Lizanne and Peggy accompanied their sister on the month-long safari into darkest movieland.

The Manhattan life to which Grace returned with such relish was a rich mix of a few fine friends with a myriad of activities. The friends with whom Grace spent most of her social time were largely newfound and young—aspirants, as she, for careers in show business. Edie Van Cleve was the exception; she was thirty years Grace's senior and a highly accomplished professional. All her life, Grace displayed a special regard for older people, often (but not always) women. Usually persons of considerable quality and attainment, they aroused strong feelings of respect, almost deference, in Grace, whose identity as daughter and niece was never far from her heart. Older people also brought out in her physical affection, warmth, and spontaneity which many of them—though parents in their own right—had never received to such a degree before and which they cherished in "Gracie."

Grace's closest friends among her contemporaries at this time included her other agent, Jay Kanter (who then moved to Los Angeles), as well as a colleague of his, John Foreman. Young bachelors for the nonce, Jay and John shared an apartment in Grace's building (Manhattan House) and baby-sat Henry, her parrot, when she was away on a play or movie. Grace also remained close with two friends from her Barbizon days, Prudence ("Prudy") Wise, her ex-roommate, and loyal Carolyn Scott, who dubiously trooped off to Grace's every showcase and performance, wondering if the girl had it in her to be the actress of her dreams. Another lifelong intimate friend was Sally Parrish Richardson whom Grace met in her last year at the Academy, and who roomed with her for a period at Manhattan House. Finally, there was Natalie Core, whom Grace met at Bucks County and who got her through the jarring episode with dyspeptic Jerome Cowan. To her great pleasure and relief, she saw a lot of Natty in live television.

Grace's collection of New York intimates really was a circle. To a remarkable degree, they came to care for each other as well as "Gracie." As a group, they possessed certain qualities that Grace both shared and prized—warmth, spontaneity, sincerity, artistry, a dash of craziness. Decades later, they didn't recall so much what they did together as the candor, excitement, and enjoyment of their interaction. "We gabbed and giggled a lot," said Judy Balaban, who married Jay Kanter, just before Grace left New York. Judy excepted, the gang tended to come from a social-economic class one or two removes below the Kellys, yet not so distant as to create problems on that score. They all had strong personalities and identities, moreover, and intense drives to succeed. They weren't *just* nice folks; they were, without exception, nice folks with considerable talent, ambition, and the capacity for hard, directed work. Finally, too, the capacity for loyalty. Thirty years later, they were still Grace's friends.

Her friends, in short, were vital to Grace, but they never occupied as much of her time as her work did. An actress, like any artist, may draw on all experience in the practice of her art. The more extensive her "kit" of resources, therefore, the better her chances of understanding and rendering a part. Grace could no more separate leisure from professional activity than any of her colleagues. When she wasn't rehearsing or performing, she was studying voice, music, dance, photography or reading books and plays and thinking about their characters. The four years in New York before Grace became a star were the only taste she ever had as an adult of privacy, simplicity, and personal freedom. Far, far sooner than she expected or than part of her wished, her life would alter drastically, and not entirely for the good. But the base she built for herself in these years always held. As did the friends.

Grace had one serious romance in these years and several casual relationships. One of the latter was with the rising young actor, Oliver Thorndike, whom Grace met during her second appearance at Bucks County. An extremely handsome man and very promising dramatic actor, Thorndike played the young villain to Grace's ingenue in *The Heiress*. By several reports, he fell quite hard for Grace, who did not fully return the affection, but went out with him for a while until she met the man who held her heart in these early years. Even then, she deftly managed to transmute the tie with Thorndike into a platonic friendship, which lasted until his tragic early death a few years later.

When Gene Lyons arrived at Elitch Gardens in the summer of 1951, he was regarded within the New York acting profession as one of the most promising actors of his generation. Born and raised in Pittsburgh, of Irish descent, Lyons spoke with a slightly British intonation. He was husky, square-shouldered, and good-looking but not in the "standard leading man" way. Rather, he had reddish-blond hair, a slightly turned-up nose, and a permanent flush on his cheeks. Some said he resembled a young Charles Bickford; others said Arthur Kennedy; and at least one close friend of Lyons's called him "a male Irish Katharine Hepburn." Gene could be quiet and withdrawn; those who didn't know him well sometimes mistook Lyons for a "square." The set designer Bob Markell, who worked with him on several "Danger" episodes, called the actor "a bore with a strong chin and weak opinions. He could have been a Canadian Mountie, or, better yet, a Dudley Do-Right [a cartoon figure of the era]."*

Others felt differently. Director Ted Post, who worked frequently with Lyons in live TV and became something of a friend, considered him possessed of an insightfulness he had seen in no actor except Marlon Brando. Lyons pulled down brilliant reviews in a television adaptation of Jean Cocteau's *The Eagle Has Two Heads* that Post directed. Other emergent directors—Sidney Lumet, Franklin Schaffner, and Martin Manulis—agreed that Lyons had intelligence and great

* Interview, October 23, 1983.

talent, but that he required getting to know. "If you made the effort," Post said, "you found in Gene a highly sensitive, giving man. In fact he was so sensitive and introverted [that] I sometimes wondered if he wasn't self-destructive."†

Lyons's love before he met Grace was another aspiring young actress, Lee Grant. She had met Gene in a Broadway show in 1949 and was so impressed with his ability that she urged him to try out for the Actors Studio—the era's elite training ground for actors. (Teachers like Elia Kazan, Harold Clurman, and Lee Strasberg taught students like Brando, Newman, Julie Harris, Eileen Heckart.) "Gene was the sort of fellow who wouldn't have tried out on his own," Grant said. "He had an elegant, reclusive facet to him that just wouldn't have impelled him to do something *for* himself. Gene had a horror of aggressive or competitive behavior."‡ He and Grant tried out together and were accepted. They also fell in love and had an affair for the next two years, during which time Lyons's TV and stage career boomed.

Asked what attracted her to Gene, Lee replied, "So many men are boys; Gene wasn't. He was self-contained, responsible, mature. He had a personal code of ethics that he never betrayed—not to hurt people, not to lie or cheat to get ahead." If a little bit the "straight-arrow," Lyons nevertheless had a "devastating wit, with the accuracy of a Benchley or some other member of the Algonquin Round Table set." What finally held her to him, however, were Lyons's interior qualities. "Gene had an inner fragility and loveliness that were very special and very endearing."

After a two-year affair, Grant and Lyons parted ways, but remained friendly. The actress, feeling constrained at living entirely in the entertainment milieu where Lyons was content to stay, was moving toward political consciousness and making new friends. "I was full of questions. Gene admitted he didn't have the answers, but said he wished he did." A while later, they met and Gene "told me he was deeply in love with Grace Kelly. 'This is it, Lee,' he told me. 'I'm going to marry her.' "

Grace confided to no one at Elitch what drew her to Lyons that summer, but within a fortnight it was apparent to everyone at the Gardens that the two were "a thing." Whitfield Connor, who was as close as anybody to the pair, said he believed Grace was attracted to Lyons's remarkable self-possession, which bordered on the dour or phlegmatic. "Looking back I can see how Gene had some of the traits of the counterhero of the next generation," said Connor. It seemed to the other actors that possibly Grace fell first for Lyons, but that he

† Interview, October 26, 1983.
‡ Interview, November 3, 1983.

then reciprocated in force. When Grace left to do *High Noon*, the normally nonchalant Lyons was visibly agitated and upset. He went so far as to telephone Whit Connor, who happened to be in Los Angeles at the same time as Grace, and entreated him to use his influence with Grace to remind her of her commitment to the theater and of her distaste for Hollywood. (Connor gently declined the charge.)

Grace of course needed no admonition where such things were concerned. She rejoined Lyons in New York in the fall and their romance continued—but not unobstructedly. Elitch had been an idyll, New York was life, and Philadelphia was alarmed. For starters, Gene was a decade older than Grace and he was separated from his wife. Although he eventually won an annulment of the marriage, the Kellys reflexively disapproved of Lyons and didn't change their minds. Lyons was an actor, and Ma and Pa Kelly resolutely refused to admit that Grace could be happily married to anyone in her own profession, even if he were becoming a star (as Lyons seemed to be doing). Jack and Margaret might have intervened less forcefully but they knew that Grace's feelings for Gene ran deep. The message from home was unambiguous: date him if you must, but don't get any notions of marriage into your head.

Grace did have such notions. She was by now deeply in love with Lyons, very possibly for the same combination of strengths and "fragility" that had drawn Lee Grant to the actor. Then, too, like Lee, Grace shared with Gene the daily intensity and intoxicating excitement and comradeship of successful young actors in live television. But undoubtedly the strongest, and headiest, bond between the two was their mutual love of the theater and their hopes to succeed as dramatic actors. In this regard Gene was the leader and enchanter, for his career was far ahead of Grace's. (He would shortly make a major hit on Broadway staring in *Witness for the Prosecution.*) Lyons hoped that he and Grace might evoke theatrical stardom out of one another. Possibly, too, he thought it might be possible to get Grace into the Actors Studio, though that would have been unlikely at her modest level of accomplishment. In any case, before these things could happen, a severe obstacle arose within the relationship: Lyons's drinking. In 1949, Lee Grant had noticed that "Gene loved his Bushmills [Irish whiskey]," as she put it. Others among Lyons's colleagues were less euphemistic. They said the actor had a serious drinking problem that worsened every year. "I don't know what drove him to drink," Ted Post said. "We'd meet at Walgreen's and talk sometimes, and I could see that things were eating him. He was self-destructive, but he wasn't the type to talk a lot about himself, especially if it was to complain."

Though an alcoholic, Lyons nevertheless functioned. His drinking problem was something only he and his intimates knew about. As an actor he was famous for dependability and professionalism. He and Grace continued to date. They frequently went to the theater together, often ending the evening with supper at the Algonquin, whose oaken paneling and literary ambience Gene adored and taught Grace to do. But though they saw a good deal of each other, Grace steadfastly hung back from becoming Gene's fiancée. His drinking problem predated her appearance in his life, and she probably sensed she would not be able to eradicate it. It poisoned their relationship, and it left Grace increasingly vulnerable to pressure from home and the demands of work. Those demands, meanwhile, were irresistibly pushing Grace (against her own and Gene's wishes) into movies, not the theater.

They continued to see each other in the few months before Grace left for East Africa to do *Mogambo* in 1952. M.G.M. internal memoranda, in fact, referred to Lyons as Grace's fiancé. But by the time she got back to the United States (and moved to Los Angeles), the two drifted apart. Lyons took their breakup very hard indeed. By the midfifties, his career finally began to register the effects of his alcoholism. Within a few years, he was reduced to the tragic state of asking old friends for money. Later, Gene pulled himself together and enjoyed a brief revival in a character role on the television show "Ironside." He died in the early seventies.

§   §   §

Curiously, for all that *High Noon* would one day figure proudly in Grace Kelly's "filmography," it contributed little to launching her as a movie actress or a Hollywood phenomenon. Kramer was correct in believing, "You certainly could not have foreseen from *High Noon* how far, and how fast, she'd go." Grace hadn't been back in New York a month (and was earnestly going from Broadway tryout to Broadway tryout) when news came from the coast that the director John Ford wanted Grace for the second female lead in a movie to be called *Mogambo*. His choice had had nothing to do with *High Noon*, nor even *Fourteen Hours* (neither of which he had liked her in); rather he took Grace on the basis of what she had thought was her ill-fated screen test for *Taxi*.

The brainchild of truly unexpected parentage—Stewart Granger and Marlene Dietrich—*Mogambo* (the word means "big gorilla" in Swahili) was to be an unabashed remake of a 1932 romantic hit, *Red Dust*, starring Clark Gable, Jean Harlow, and Mary Astor. According to the scenario of its recasters, the new film would be set in Africa (instead of Southeast Asia) on the estate of a big game hunter (instead of a rubber planter). But the heart of the story was the same—a love triangle among three Hollywood stereotypes: a great white hunter, a sultry chorus girl of easy virtue, and the reserved wife of an English engineer. Although Dietrich never saw herself in the film, Granger, anxious to keep the hold on big adventure films that he had recently won with *King Solomon's Mines,* naturally cast himself as the lead. Dore Schary, head of production at M.G.M., at first bought Granger's casting, then abruptly changed his mind when Clark Gable asked to play his old part ("We've got to keep the King happy, no?").

The *Mogambo* offer disturbed Grace. Accepting it would mean abandoning her hardworking, restrained New York life, with its rarefied theatrical ambitions, the predictable schedule of classes, the tryouts, music and voice lessons, its built-in hours for reading, its small dinner parties with close friends, and its frequent visits home. *Fourteen Hours,* the *Taxi* screen test, and even *High Noon* hadn't seriously interrupted this intense and fulfilling pace, let alone subjected it to serious threat in the form of real temptation. *Mogambo,* however, would be a big budget blockbuster from the home of the blockbusters, Metro-Goldwyn-Mayer—the epitome of "Hollywood" and the studio system. The names assigned to the picture were "stoppers" in every suit—from Gable and Ava Gardner and Ford to producer Sam Zimbalist and screenwriter John Lee Mahin (who had written the wonderful screenplay of *Red Dust).* Grace was being made an awesome offer. It was not so much the money (Grace could make slightly more modeling full time) but the opportunity to establish herself as an actress before the entire country, even the world.

On the other hand, there would be no possibility that she could accept Ford's choice without signing a good fraction of her future over to M.G.M. in a standard exclusive term contract. Moreover, as she must have known, there was no likelihood of further avoiding close contact with a world that, until now, Grace had regarded with quiet disdain and disapproval. Grace was a careful planner and reflective analyst and must have worried over the options. She also realized the moment she read the script that her part—the prim, almost haughty bride of a bland and silly English cuckold—was hardly appealing, either from an actor's or a spectator's standpoint. One consideration weighed against all the drawbacks, however. If the part of Linda Nordley could not call upon or display great dramatic prowess, the movie camera might "discover" a brilliant new star in the Hollywood pantheon. This was a temptation that even Grace could not overlook. The dimensions of the success and fame within her grasp extended far beyond anything the stage could provide.

Edie Van Cleve and Jay Kanter were keenly aware of these attractions, but they knew enough not to press such arguments on Grace overtly. Instead they, along with Lew Wasserman (of the M.C.A. Los Angeles office), concentrated their energies on the tactics of bet-hedging in the negotiations underway with Metro. At her instructions, they insisted that Grace must not be treated like a "starlet" and would not take up permanent residence in Hollywood. She would not do more than three films a year, for which she was due, in addition to her salary, a twenty-thousand-dollar-a-year bonus. And, most important of all, she would get one year off in three to return to the New York theater.

From his experience as an agent, Kanter frankly doubted that mighty M.G.M. would ever bow to such terms, coming, as they were, from a comparative unknown. If he and Van Cleve and Wasserman pressed their demands with dead-earnest conviction, it was because they had their backs to the wall. To Grace, this was less a commercial negotiation than an inner trial about her own faithfulness and integrity. Her points (particularly the last) weren't negotiable; they were the minimum concessions necessary to neutralize her conscience and overcome her ambivalence. They were the only way she would go to Hollywood (via Kenya). Anything less, and she'd happily use Metro's noncompliance as a reason to "return to the theater." Kanter pondered ruefully the fate which had brought him two such gifted but stubborn friend-clients as Marlon Brando and Grace Kelly. "Every other actor in the world, even stars, pressed you [the agent] for work. But with Marlon and Grace, it seemed like the thing they dreaded most was me calling to say I had a movie deal for them. Not doing *Mogambo* would not have fazed Grace for one second. On the contrary, I actually think she'd be relieved of the burden of a very painful decision."

Metro-Goldwyn-Mayer happily left Grace on the horns of her dilemma. After a good bit of raised eyebrows and harrumphing about precedents, studio executives Mannix, Thau, and Hendrickson acquiesced to the terms. Hidden within the legalese and technicalities of the interoffice memoranda that passed among their offices over the Kelly contract, there was a distinct impatience and disbelief that any unknown actress could make such a fuss over "stage play engagements" when she could be doing "photoplays." But John Ford and Sam Zimbalist were certain they needed Grace, so the front office complied. M.C.A. got what its client wanted and Grace, after some final anguishing, signed on the dotted line.

Or tried to. Ironically, British Actors' Equity very nearly saved Grace for the theater, at least temporarily. The news of Grace's casting as Linda Nordley was still fresh—she hadn't yet actually signed her contracts—when the British actors' union filed a formal protest with Her Majesty's Government. How, the union demanded to know, could M.G.M. get away with using an American actress to play the part of a British wife in a movie that would nearly entirely be shot within the British Empire? A million had already been spent erecting *Mogambo*'s elaborate fortresslike location in Kenya, while M.G.M.'s large studio at

Boreham Wood outside London was the designated site for shooting all of the movie's interior sequences. Unless the studio could bring enough counterpressure to bear on Her Majesty's Government, Grace would have to be sacrificed to British trade union policy.

It came right down to the wire. Grace got her passport, her shots, and her plane ticket; she took her wardrobe fittings and studied her lines. Meanwhile M.G.M. was negotiating to engage an English actress (Virginia McKenna) for the part of Linda Nordley—just in case. Simultaneously the studio informed M.C.A. that Miss Kelly could sign her contracts, but only with the strict proviso that they would be nullified if the studio lost its appeal with London.

In the end, permission was granted and Grace climbed aboard a TWA superconstellation bound for Nairobi. She joined the rest of the cast—Gable, Gardner, and the well-known English actor, Donald Sinden, who played Linda Nordley's husband, Donald—at the *Mogambo* settlement, described by one writer as "a luxury hotel under canvas."* As on *High Noon*, Grace got the highest possible marks for professionalism and collegiality, but, surer of herself this time, she was far less shy and remote in Africa than she'd been in Los Angeles. The result was that Grace impressed people with the multifacetedness and quality of her personality. Merely the introductory smile she flashed Donald Sinden merited a lengthy paragraph of eloquent description in memoirs he wrote three decades later. Sinden, of course, like screenwriter Mahin and director Ford, also commented on Grace's "amazing prettiness," while Clark Gable spoke of her beauty to everyone he met. On the other hand, Grace also made a lifelong attachment with Ava Gardner, on whom her beauty made less of an impact than her sincerity, loyalty, and humor.

Especially the humor—rich, homey, uninhibited, constant—so unanticipated a resource in this patrician blonde from Philadelphia. Again and again colleagues commented on Grace's spontaneous wit—including impersonations and accents—or her painstaking pranks. She had intended to give Clark Gable a pair of knitted socks for Christmas (shooting ran on into the winter of 1952–53) and knitted away in a frenzy during her spare moments all fall. But presently it became clear the socks wouldn't be ready, so Grace devised an alternative gift. Every few days, she stole a small domestic article, including a large wool hunting sock, from Gable's tent. When Christmas Eve rolled around, she hung up his sock, filled with his own possessions. Later, she self-defensively labeled her caprice "a silly gesture," but the truth was that it quite touched everyone who knew of it, most of all the friend on whom it was pulled.

* Roland Flamini, *Ava* (New York: Coward, McCann, & Geoghegan, 1982), p. 181.

What impressed Gable and the others even more was Grace's tire-
lessness in getting the most out of her presence in Africa. She was the
only member of the cast, for example, who bothered to learn Swahili
well enough to order a meal. She was equally fearless as well as energetic in her intention to see as much of Africa as she could "so I can tell
my grandchildren about it someday." On days off, while the rest of the
cast slept in, Grace piled out at dawn and went hunting with Gable
even though it meant jostling around in the back of a jeep across miles
of dusty flatland. She was a fine shot, and she was even game to step
into a picture with several natives and display her section of a twelve-
foot python that Clark killed.

Sometimes lonesomeness struck the twenty-four-year-old. Gable
once found Grace on an isolated stretch of beach on the Indian Ocean.
He watched her for a while, sitting with a book on her lap, gazing out
to sea. A lion walking far down the shore eventually decided Gable to
join Grace. He found her with tear-filled eyes. "Oh, Clark," she said, "I
was reading *The Snows of Kilimanjaro* and got to the part where the
leopard gets frozen in the snow, and I looked up and there was that
lion walking along the shore. He's out of his element, too." Other
times, Grace's homesickness waxed less poetic. Donald Sinden recounted that one night Ava Gardner came to his tent and asked if he'd
seen Grace, who, she said, had run off in a stream of tears in the midst
of a talk they were having. Sinden and Gardner went in search of their
friend and found Grace sobbing uncontrollably. There was little they
could do to mollify her, but the next morning she was up early and off
on a safari with Gable and "Bunny" Allen, the English hunter who
had been hired to advise on the picture.

§   §   §

As a remake, *Mogambo* failed to attain the freshness, vigor, and pace
of its predecessor—a doubly curious drawback considering that both
motion pictures had the same scenarist (Mahin) and male lead. At the
risk of over-simplifying, *Red Dust* was very much a thirties' product,
replete with smart, rapid-fire dialogue, lively tempo, and youthful
stars, who turned in more convincing portrayals than their successors
(Ava Gardner excepted). *Mogambo* was fifties all the way: sprawling,
implausible, slow; heavily reliant on thin-plotted high adventure and
brilliant camera work. The Technicolor rendering of the falls at Rift
Valley in the moonlight constitute some of the finer cinematography of
an era enchanted with it. But that wasn't enough to save what John
Ford himself referred to as "a popcorn eater's movie." Ford was unquestionably a great director, but here in East Africa he encountered
overwhelming problems. From the first day, *Mogambo* brought him
nothing but headaches—personality conflicts between him and Gable;

endless technical and logistical difficulties; enervating arguments with Culver City. Complicating matters, Ford's health was very poor. He not only spent a good deal of the time bent double with stomach cramps from dysentery, but, much worse, began experiencing the serious problems with his vision that would eventually lead to cataract operations (only partially successful) and thoughts of premature retirement. Frankly, the director had one goal in Kenya: to get out as fast as he could before the awful burden of this huge film crushed him completely. In the words of his biographer, "If John's life were to be plotted on a graph, *Mogambo* would represent an important downward turn."†

Under the circumstances, Ford had no time for young Grace Kelly, who turned in a good performance, but no more, as she herself recognized. Many figured no more was possible; John Lee Mahin himself called the role of the prim and naive Mrs. Linda Nordley "a thankless task." Grace's every line abounds with insipidness—"This [the compound] is charming. Everything so neat and clean. I'll be unbearably frank and say I didn't expect it." Ava Gardner, however, has some superb quips ("These animal-catching characters don't have very many nerves, just one big one"). In their scenes together, the Nordley character comes off the complete fall girl:

MRS. NORDLEY Who's the Mr. Thompson famous enough to have the gazelle named after him?

ELOISE KELLY He's a third baseman, hit a home run for the Giants once. Won the pennant.

None of this is Grace's fault, of course, and the question is, not whether her character is interesting or sympathetic or easy to play, but how well she plays it. In this respect, *Mogambo* runs curiously parallel to *High Noon*. Again, she's well cast as the stiff and uncompromising "lady" to her rival's sentient *femme fatale;* again it works precisely because Grace can not only get away with emotional and physical inhibition but can use it as a positive asset in the part. Her slightly anglicized pronunciation—which, cleverly, Grace did not accentuate for the part —fit Linda Nordley perfectly. Her trammeled emotions—heightened by a continuing rigidity in her arms and torso—endow her with an appealing vulnerability that eluded Mary Astor in *Red Dust*, even if her performance outshone Grace's in passion, terror, and anger. Grace's best scenes come, not surprisingly, in the too few instances when she manages to tap her own well of feeling. Being held by Gable in the moonlight by the falls (Grace later called it "Clark's *Gone with the Wind*

† Dan Ford, *Pappy: The Life of John Ford* (Englewood Cliffs: Prentice-Hall, 1979), p. 257.

embrace"), she suddenly uncovers in her eyes a surge of childlike eros, which, coupled with her beauty, is momentarily breathtaking.

As in *High Noon*, so in *Mogambo*, the critics proved friendly, if cursory and undemanding about her performance. Grace was nevertheless not pleased with it, and, given her standards, was right not to be. By her own lights, Grace was absolutely correct to expect more of herself once it became clear that John Ford was too preoccupied to be even a Fred Zinnemann in his handling of her. Given her fine training, her considerable stage experience, and her high dramatic standards, Grace might have gone further in directing herself. But she permitted herself to play a kind of caricature of "the proper English wife"—stressing all the obviously British adjectives and adverbs, saying her bland lines with one-dimensional sincerity rather than infusing them with irony, and in general taking uncostly advantage of her own personal inhibitedness. As a result, Linda Nordley lacks the depth to make credible the profound emotional transition to falling in love with the hunter, Victor Marswell (Gable). This was the great difference between Mary Astor and Grace Kelly; the former hadn't a fraction of Grace's beauty, or even promise, but from the start she portrayed a character who suggests some mystery and hidden capacity for love. Grace produced a Linda Nordley that satisfied John Ford, the Metro front office, the Academy of Motion Picture Arts and Sciences, and even the critics. But not Grace Kelly.

Nevertheless, there is more to be said about *Mogambo*. The question arises why didn't Grace show more initiative? Part of the answer, no doubt, is that she was young and shy and far from home, and heaven knows, one did not truck with John Ford with impunity. Yet Grace had already displayed great stubbornness and mettle, when issues greatly mattered to her, e.g., standing up to Jerome Cowan, or driving a tough bargain with M.G.M. In the case of *Mogambo*, perhaps, the issue simply wasn't *that* momentous to her. In her public and private statements, she often tended to trivialize the movie and her reasons for doing it. ("I wanted to go to Africa and get to do a picture with John Ford and Clark Gable.") *Mogambo*, one suspects, never had great merit in her mind—less due to the role she played than for the significance of the movie in her life. *Mogambo* was Grace Kelly's entry, via the term contract with M.G.M., into that world that she had heard Uncle George deride many times; it was also, though she doubted it at first, her exit from the theater which George had once conquered and where Grace so ached to establish her own identity. Hence, the reflex—odd in her—to poor-mouth *Mogambo* and to seem to regret going with Metro. "I could kick myself [for signing]," she told a reporter for the Los Angeles *Times* several years later.

At the time she admitted that, her anger was presumed to stem from financial resentment. Metro got off cheaply as the Grace Phenomenon built, though not unfairly: no studio or executive producer could have predicted the rocketing trajectory of Grace's success in motion pictures or negotiated contracts to keep pace with it. But salary and perks were a red herring. Grace's resentment originally had been self-directed, gradually got projected onto the studio and particularly the film which started it all. Schary and the Metro executives could never understand Grace's disdain for her first M.G.M. film. Defensively, they began to say out loud what every producer in Hollywood already knew —that *Mogambo* had made Grace Kelly a star. What they didn't know was *that* was the problem.

CHAPTER III

THE RELUCTANT
MOVIE STAR, I

I've been at the studio for years and years. In all that time there's been nothing like it. What gets me is that when all of the hullabaloo started, she'd only really been seen in one picture. We can't keep up with the demand for interviews with her. We even had somebody here from The Saturday Review of Literature. The Saturday Review of Literature! *I've never dealt with* The Saturday Review of Literature *before.*

—*Studio Publicity Man*

It surprised me so, the way everybody enthused; because I didn't think I'd done anything so extraordinary.

—*George Kelly,* The Torch-Bearers

The Hollywood which Grace Kelly unintentionally took by storm was an industry in crisis. The habit of moviegoing was steadily declining in America since the War, largely (but not only) thanks to television. By the late sixties, the number of admissions to movie houses sold each week fell by two thirds. Smaller audiences spelled diminishing profits for the studios, which, in turn, began to cut back on the number of films they made. The crisis wasn't the "decline and fall of Hollywood," a frequently heard refrain, but it caused the movie business's hardest times since the Depression.

When Grace signed with Metro, the general industrywide decline was producing a particular problem: a dearth of fresh stars. Despite the apparently impressive roster of front-line stars at the major studios, age and changing fashion had overtaken the time-honored Old Guard, and too few new troops were being recruited to replace them. The same frightened, conservative reflex that led front office executives to reduce output also imposed restraint on their old practice of "nailing down" dozens of players in term contracts. As a result, the gambles that had created several of the major careers of the thirties and forties were made far less often in the fifties. So who were cast in the leading roles of all these remakes and play adaptations and musicals? The great names of the era—Crawford, Cooper, Gable, Tracy, Bogart, K. Hepburn, Davis, Cagney—were all deep into middle age. The rapport could not be great between stars in their late forties and fifties and a ticket-buying audience that ranged in age from fifteen to twenty-five. Fresh faces to suit changing tastes were badly wanting.

But what faces, what tastes? It was certainly clear that "traditional" looks could not be altogether bypassed. Among men, the dawning popularity of Charlton Heston, Rock Hudson, and Richard Burton testified to the continuing hold of the heroic style among moviegoers. Yet more excitement was generated by a very different sort, the antiheroes: Montgomery Clift, Marlon Brando, and James Dean.

Among leading women, the situation was similar. The only new superstar of the time was Marilyn Monroe. She was an absolute phenomenon, to be sure, but also a tribute to the residual strength of an era that was passing. There would be other "bombshell" beauties in the fifties, of course—Elizabeth Taylor, for example, had just evolved from child to adult lead in *Father of the Bride*—yet among female stars, as among males, the shift away from tradition was definitely discernible. Forties' sex symbols—Betty Grable, Hedy Lamarr, Jane Russell, Lana Turner, Rita Hayworth, Ava Gardner, Gloria Grahame—gave way to the "ladies," women who combined beauty with breeding and elegance, and perhaps a touch of hauteur.

Not that the "lady" look was new. The thirties and forties boasted Norma Shearer, Ingrid Bergman, Deborah Kerr, Olivia De Havilland, Joan Fontaine, and Greer Garson. But these stars portrayed more or less refined ladies in distress; the "ladies" of the fifties were supposed to be active and have minds of their own. One interesting and lovely such actress was a French girl recently arrived in Hollywood, Leslie Caron, who had won acclaim for *An American in Paris*. And, in the same year as Grace moved to Los Angeles, another actress named Hepburn —this one with a rare combination of refinement and pixy charm— gained attention with *Roman Holiday*. Two more aspiring brunettes who well captured the look of the demure, unsexy beauty were Jean Simmons and Donna Reed. In sum, Grace Kelly arrived in Hollywood at a time when the prevailing fashion very much suited what was seen as her "look."

Grace never liked the idea of a "look," and in this regard she also represented a change in Hollywood. Confining a movie star to a precise, predictable image was already becoming a dated, much-criticized policy by the fifties. As a strategy, it had been the by-product of the studio system in its prime, when well-manned publicity offices sought ways to make distinctions among the scores of contract players working at a studio and to promote the careers of certain, carefully chosen individuals. But the prevailing mood of the fifties was more individual-ist, less corporatist. If studios now hesitated to sign up new players, the more conscious and talented of the new players paused long and hard before "signing away their lives" to one studio. Some began to believe that successful careers were best made out of the roles and films and particular director-producers an actor chose, rather than by mindless submission to a studio's identity and policy.

Grace belonged to the new breed of actor and shaped some of its destiny. Signing an exclusive contract with M.G.M. to do an African adventure movie with Clark Gable was itself almost an outdated satire of a Hollywood plot; Grace began regretting her action virtually be-fore she took it. She would come deeply to resent being tied down in this old fashion—especially to the M.G.M. dinosaur who grandly re-fused to recognize the times. After decades of profit and undisputed rule, Metro was beginning to feel the reins slipping from its grasp by the midfifties. At a time when rival studios like Columbia and Twenti-eth Century-Fox were coming on strong with imaginative, compara-tively low-budget masterpieces like *Picnic, From Here to Eternity, All About Eve*, and *On the Waterfront*, Metro's aging executives could do no better than *Quo Vadis, King Solomon's Mines*, and *Mogambo*. They were all money-makers to be sure, but not the sort of thing to long appeal to an East Coast actress with serious dramatic background and aspirations. Again and again, Grace would reject their tired old formulas and steady diet of pop musicals and pulp big-budget adventure movies in favor of more interesting projects at other studios.

Such projects were not slow in appearing.

§ § §

Location shooting on *Mogambo* finished in the early spring of 1953. The cast and crew reassembled in London to complete the picture with interior shots at M.G.M.'s Boreham Wood studio. Grace was eager for shooting to end so she could return to the United States to do a play, *The Moon Is Blue*, at Playhouse Park in Philadelphia, a theater which she respected and knew well, for her family had contributed to it over the years. The prospect of performing in her hometown both attracted and frightened her. She hadn't been home long when Jay Kanter called to say that Alfred Hitchcock wanted Grace for the female lead in his new picture.

It pleased Grace that the movie in question was to be a screen adap-tation of a play. *Dial M for Murder* was a mystery-melodrama by the English playwright Frederick Knott; it had enjoyed great success in London and on Broadway in the 1952 season. The script followed the play faithfully, to the point—this also pleased Grace—that the movie would take place all on one set. *Dial M for Murder* was more than an adaptation, Grace felt; it was a filmed play.

Hitchcock hired Grace for what he believed *he* could do with her. *High Noon* and a preview of *Mogambo* had left him unimpressed. He felt that Zinnemann and Ford had been ineffective in exploiting the young actress's beauty and special appeal. The Fox screen tests for *Taxi*, however, reinforced Hitchcock in his intuition about Grace. It wasn't her skill at portraying the immigrant Irish girl but her appearance on-screen that caught, and held, his eye and confirmed in him the feeling Grace had "quality." "You could see her potential for restraint," he said later. Certainly the reality of restraint was present in their first interview, for Grace choked—worse than she had with Zinnemann. Never good at small talk, still less so when the matter was employment and her interlocutor a famous, revered older professional, Grace sat stone-still and said almost nothing. "In a horrible way it seemed funny to have my brain turn to stone," she said later. The director's brisk reaction to the encounter—he had already decided to hire her—was to say to an associate that he would "definitely have do something about [lowering the pitch of] her voice."

"The best directors are those who become emotionally involved with what they're doing," Grace said when asked about Hitchcock. Certainly after Zinnemann's comparative detachment and Ford's outright indifference, Hitchcock's lively interest in her came as a great gratification and relief. Yet, in retrospect, "emotional involvement" was almost a euphemism for the obsessive concern that the director of *Dial M for Murder* displayed for every detail of his new leading lady's work. Fortunately, for Grace's sake, Hitchcock was still at a point in life where his *idées fixes* about beautiful actresses were not altogether inflexible. For example, he and she collided on the small but critical matter of Grace's costume in the scene where she confronts her would-be killer. Hitchcock's prior idea, strongly held, was that she should wear a rich, profuse red velvet robe that would accentuate her blond hair and, via lighting and shadow, infuse the scene with a certain "effect." Grace understood his point, but felt very strongly that such a costume wasn't right for the part. She stood her ground and told him, "I don't think that this woman is going to put on this great fancy robe if she is getting up in the middle of the night to answer a ringing phone and there's nobody in the apartment." Hitchcock asked her what she would wear then, and Grace replied, "I'd just get up and go to the phone in my nightgown." He admitted this was a better idea.

What would later be seen as Hitchcock's vision for Grace Kelly— subtle, cool, elegant facade covering wells of passion, sweetness, and humor—emerged only gradually. In *Dial M*, this vision is hardly realized. The movie is in no sense Grace's. Her role as the beautiful wife of a sociopathic sophisticate planning to kill her for her money is a richer part than anything she'd had previously, but is still squarely overshadowed by the male leads—all three of them. The part made no demands on Grace; all she had to do was look beautiful in full-face shots with rear lighting and speak the patrician English that suited her almost too perfectly.

Only once did something new emerge: Grace's eroticism. Hitchcock would make it standard in his next two Grace Kelly movies. In *Dial M*, it climaxes the early scene where Margot Wendice (Grace) is talking with her American friend (Robert Cummings) and suddenly embraces him and gives him a very full kiss. The naive, childlike vulnerability of Linda Nordley in *Mogambo*—sweetly appealing, but not especially apt or interesting—is here replaced by the purposiveness, craft, and passion of a woman conducting an affair behind her husband's back. Unfortunately this one scene was the start and finish of Margot Wendice's character evolution; thereafter, she returns to being what movie mogul Harry Cohn used to call "a reactionary—[s]he reacts to what everyone else is doing."

To his credit, Hitchcock also succeeded in lowering Grace's voice, and—after many retakes—in evoking genuine terror from her, something Ford had not done. Grace conveyed other emotions more convincingly as well—shock, grief, listlessness. Yet *Dial M for Murder* is mainly foretaste and promise, not realized potential, where Grace was concerned. The film mostly looks backward, not forward. Not only does Grace still betray elementary problems (e.g., what to do with her hands and arms), but she still gives a frustratingly overcontrolled and self-conscious "performance." Hitchcock had not yet taught her how to draw on her inner qualities or how to give rein to her emotions.

§　　§　　§

One wonders when Grace Kelly became aware that Hitchcock was infatuated with her. Probably not during *Dial M*. While mindful of the galvanizing effect she often had on men, Grace had too reverential a regard for "Mr. Hitchcock" to permit herself to analyze him as she might have a younger, more obviously available and interested man. She would have had to be propositioned by Hitchcock before she would have considered formulating a reproach against him. The director hadn't yet given way to the painfully apparent and destructive passions he harbored for leading ladies (notably Tippi Hedren), but there was little doubt in the minds of his close associates that by the completion of *Dial M*, Hitch's interest in Grace was compulsive and amorous. "He would have used Grace in the next ten pictures he made," said screenwriter John Michael Hayes, who worked closely with Hitchcock in this period. "I would say that all the actresses he

cast subsequently were attempts to retrieve the image and feeling that
Hitch carried around so reverentially about Grace."

Hayes knew that Hitchcock wanted Grace for his next film, *Rear
Window*, before Grace herself knew it. As *Dial M* drew to a close, the
director grew agitated; the only time he became calm and could confront the completion of the current picture was when he was actively
planning the new one—for Grace Kelly. Indeed, *Dial M* was still in
production when Hitchcock called in Hayes, whom he had assigned to
write the script for *Rear Window*, and instructed him to get to know
Grace. "See what you can do with her dramatically," he said. Hayes
spent the better part of four or five days with Grace. "I was entranced
by her," Hayes said. "I hadn't expected to be, but I was. I couldn't get
over the difference between her personal animation and, if I may say
so, her sexuality, and the subdued role she was playing in *Dial M*, not
to mention her other pictures. There was an alive, vital girl underneath that demure, quiet facade; she had an inner life aching to be
expressed, but she wasn't drawing on it." Hayes then met with Hitchcock and made the strongest possible case for a script that would draw
on "both parts of her nature." Hitchcock enthusiastically agreed; in
fact, typically, he appropriated Hayes's ideas for his own. (Also
Hayes's vocabulary. Hitchcock was especially taken with Hayes's use
of the word "patrician" to describe the more apparent of Grace's two
"natures." He walked around the set saying "patrician" whenever her
name came up.)

The end of shooting came in late September and Grace returned to
New York. Though Hitchcock had spoken to her about *Rear Window*, a
firm deal hadn't been made mainly because Grace had other plans, or
rather hopes. Indeed, she had hoped she wouldn't be available for TV
or movies at all in 1952. After nearly a three-year absence from the
Great White Way, Grace had finally landed a part in a comedy by
William Marchant, *To Be Continued*, directed by Guthrie McClintic. It
opened at the Booth Theater in April with a remarkable collection of
distinguished Broadway veterans—Neil Hamilton, Dorothy Stickney,
Luella Gear, and John Drew Devereaux. Unfortunately, they closed
two weeks later (Grace's notices were mixed and mild). Now in late
summer, she had received a call from Jean Dalrymple, the manager of
the City Center Theater in New York. Dalrymple said she had seen
Grace in *The Father* and admired her for her seriousness and charm.
She informed Grace that they were reviving the play *Cyrano de Bergerac*
for a limited run at the City Center in November. The star would be
José Ferrer, but the female lead was open. Was Grace interested?

Was Grace interested? Perhaps the most romantic part in an extrava-
gantly romantic play, Roxane appealed to Grace more than almost any
other part in the classical repertoire. Cyrano's love is a kind of lyrical,

feminine ideal: exceedingly beautiful but also tenderhearted and ardent, a person whom everyone loves on sight. To her close friends, and in her own heart, Grace *knew* she had a Roxane in her. She identified with the part and strongly believed that with the right director (in this case, Ferrer himself), she could make her inner Roxane public. Grace especially wanted to land the part to remind herself, and others, that her chosen world was the stage. One lived *by* certain things (e.g., movies) but one lived *for* others. Roxane was altogether in the latter category.

So Grace gave an emphatic "yes" to Dalrymple and begged her to entreat Ferrer to hold off choosing an actress until she could read for the part. At Dalrymple's suggestion and through her arrangement, Grace even contrived to rehearse herself in the role with the man who had directed the original 1946 Broadway production of *Cyrano*, Mel Ferrer (no relation to José). The moment *Dial M* was finished, Grace raced home and settled down to work with Ferrer.

In late October, she read for the part of Roxane. Unfortunately, fate as well as artistic judgment conspired against Grace. When she mounted the stage at City Center, she had a bad cold. Mel Ferrer and Jean Dalrymple tried to intercede on her behalf and get José to put off the reading, but time pressures weighed heavily on the director. Even had he been well disposed toward Grace, Ferrer could not have let her off the hook. He did permit her to come back and read a second time, however. Even then, the actress could barely get her voice beyond the first few rows. "Joe kept telling her to project," Dalrymple remembered. "He finally said to Mel in an exasperated voice, 'Tell the girl to talk louder!' " Grace did her best, but it wasn't nearly good enough. When she left the stage, Ferrer looked around at everyone and said bluntly, "There, I told you. She hasn't got the experience; she's not a pro. It wouldn't have mattered even if she didn't have a cold. She's not right."

Grace was "a good scout" about losing the part, but she confided to Jean that it was a "great disappointment" to her. "I sensed that somehow or other the role symbolized something for Grace," Dalrymple said. The part went to someone else. Ironically, and to Grace's double disappointment, it went, not to a renowned lady of the stage, but a glamorous movie star, Arlene Dahl. (Dalrymple explained the choice thus: "Arlene was the closest thing I could find in a hurry to the genteel, soft-voiced, beautiful Grace.")

More ironically, while all of this was taking place, Hitchcock and screenwriter Hayes were tailoring a new part for Grace which had some of the very same qualities of Roxane. Ferrer may have worried that Grace couldn't project the lushness of romantic feeling needed in

Roxane, but it was precisely that gamble—that Grace had it in her—which Hitchcock took, and won big, in *Rear Window*.

The part of Lisa Fremont is the personification of the beautiful and successful career woman; Edith Head summed up her costume designs for the role as clothes that display "money, taste, and discrimination [and try] at all times . . . to suit the occasion." So far, no Roxane. But the inner Lisa, which so enthralled Hitchcock and which he so masterfully evoked on camera, had a quality of winsome amorousness that recalled the great heroine. The Lisa whom Lisa delights in showing to her lover, Jeff (James Stewart), is a melange of the playful and the sensual, at once both innocent and highly seductive. Hitchcock termed Lisa's appeal "sexual elegance," but the phrase is overblown, like his fondness for Hayes's word "patrician." Lisa Fremont is certainly sexual *and*—thanks to Edith Head's stunning wardrobe, elegant—but basically she is a sentimental girl in love with her guy.

Grace, though still smarting from the *Cyrano* miss, saw this instantly; she didn't have to be told what a fine part Lisa Fremont was for her. She told her sister Lizanne that Lisa reminded her of Nancy Drew in the beloved stories of her youth. At the moment when Hitchcock's call arrived, she had another offer—the female lead in *On the Waterfront* (subsequently played by Eva Marie Saint). This project had the built-in attraction of being filmed in New York, but it didn't strike Grace as anything like the opportunity, the occasion, that playing Lisa Fremont would be. With only one afternoon of reflection, she chose to return to Hitchcock.

"Hitch really threw himself into *Rear Window*," said Hayes. "He was determined to ferret out Grace's romantic potential." The ferreting proved even more painstaking than *Dial M for Murder*, if only because —to accept the compelling case of biographer Donald Spoto—Hitchcock was by now deeply, if unconsciously, in love with Grace. In the previous movie, he had spent nearly a week shooting the brilliant murder scene, with its overtly sexual overtones. In *Rear Window*, the director demanded twenty-seven takes of one simple scene where Lisa plants a kiss on Jeff's forehead. On opening day of shooting, he and the entire crew labored for thirty minutes to capture just the right close-up insert shot of Lisa's shoes—a shot later discarded. (He said to an inquiring assistant at lunch, "Haven't you ever heard of the shoe fetish?") Through it all, Grace was her director's faithful, protean instrument.

With one notable exception—in the scene where Lisa produces a sheer negligé (from her overnight case, as witty and pithy a piece of character development as there is in the whole film) Hitchcock took one look at Grace in the nightgown and summoned Edith Head. "The bosom is not right," he euphemized, "we're going to have to put something in there." Shooting came to an abrupt halt while Head took

Grace to her dressing room and gently explained "Mr. Hitchcock's worry." But the normally docile actress put her foot down. First, she said, falsies would show through the negligé; secondly, she didn't and wouldn't wear them, period. So the two women spent a few minutes fussing—making apparent "adjustments"—and when Grace returned to the set, she "stood as straight as possible." The ruse worked; Hitchcock pronounced himself satisfied. "See what a difference they make?" he said grandly.*

With such esprit de corps, *Rear Window* was a dream of a picture to shoot, despite the director's finicalness. Now a veteran, Grace felt more at home on the Hitchcock set. Playing the part of Lisa had the effect of bringing her out more than had been the case on *Dial M*. She mischievously flirted with the men on the set, openly adored and flaunted her costumes, and, in Hayes's words, "enjoyed, and made all of us enjoy, her chance to be utterly feminine."

§   §   §

A favorite topic of discussion in New York and Hollywood, in 1954 or 1984, is the question of what makes a movie star. Outsiders usually resort to "the mysterious chemistry" between the performer and the moviegoer and leave it at that. But film executives can rarely resist the temptation of trying to prime the Bunsen burner or stir the test tube. Sometimes, with vast expense and effort, it works.

Usually it doesn't. Marion Davies might actually have had a more successful career if William Randolph Hearst's "interest" hadn't "destroyed the gay spontaneity that made her so charming in real life."† Similarly, not all the horses and men of studio king Samuel Goldwyn could make a star of the foreign-born beauty Anna Sten. Nor could Fox foist off the French actress Simone Simon on American audiences. In Grace's era, the authoritarian director Otto Preminger thought to make a star of the young girl who won his much-ballyhooed national "search" for a newcomer to play his *Saint Joan*. Again the public had the last word; though a druggist's daughter from Marshalltown, Iowa, Jean Seberg did not "play in Peoria." On the other hand, when the "mysterious chemistry" works, it may set off a reaction of heat and light far beyond the capabilities of studio alchemists to foresee or comprehend, let alone control. Such was the case at hand.

The Grace Kelly Phenomenon broke upon the world before it broke upon the city. The last to grasp what was happening was Grace's own publicity department at M.G.M., though in fairness to Howard Strickling and Morgan Hudgins, who were undoubtedly among the best in a

* Donald Spoto, *The Dark Side of Genius: The Life of Alfred Hitchcock* (Boston: Little Brown, 1983), pp. 348–49.
† W. A. Swanberg, *Citizen Hearst* (New York: Scribner's, 1961), p. 411.

sordid business, they barely knew Grace in early 1954. She had done only one picture for Metro, *Mogambo* (not released until late 1953), and that had been filmed entirely on location. Following this, she had been "loaned out" twice, to Warner Brothers and Paramount, for the Hitchcock pictures. In between, Grace stayed at home in New York.

Moreover, *Mogambo* was a hit that established Grace Kelly as a fixture in the Hollywood firmament, but it did not make her a star, let alone a phenomenon. Metro had many far bigger names (Gardner, Taylor, Turner, etc.) and far more demanding egos to take care of; Grace, frankly, got lost in the rush. In February, she was nominated for an Oscar for Best Supporting Actress for her role as Linda Nordley. The nomination apparently surprised M.G.M. as much as it also pleased them. (The Award went to Donna Reed for *From Here to Eternity*. Grace hadn't the least expectation of winning; she was merely gratified, if incredulous, at being nominated.) But in March, the studio's publicity department wrote to inform higher-ups that while "we would like to have the services of Miss Kelly for a magazine and newspaper campaign and a TV commercial with Lustre Creme Shampoo," the Lustre Creme people "at this writing are not in favor of using Miss Kelly" because she "is not a big enough name." Vera-Ellen was deemed preferable.

But something was happening. If publicists didn't know, a few editors did. Hardly more than a fortnight after the Lustre Creme letter, the editors of *Life* took something of a calculated risk and ran Grace Kelly on their cover. The accompanying text tried to justify the choice with an awesome leap of faith: 1954, the editors declared, would turn out to be "A Year of Grace." That could be, but it certainly was not so in early spring when *Life* made its decision. At that time Grace was still being carried along more on potential than delivery. She had just finished shooting three films *(Dial M, Rear Window,* and *The Bridges at Toko-Ri)* and was starting *The Country Girl*, but none had yet been released.

For a month, the responsible editors must have rued their prediction. *Dial M for Murder* had its moment in midspring, and Grace, for the fourth time in a row, got passed off with sunny incuriosity ("she does a nice job," wrote Bosley Crowther). Then, *Rear Window* was released. That did it. In what motion picture executives are always referring to as "Peoria"—i.e., the vast U.S. hinterland between the two coasts—many movie houses began quietly adding the name "Grace Kelly" to equal billing with "Hitchcock" and "Stewart" on the marquees and in their advertising. At about the same time, the publisher of the extremely powerful *Hollywood Reporter*, W. R. Wilkerson, wrote a special signed column about Grace, which he ended with the prediction, "It won't be long before this attractive kid will be the Number One feminine box-office attraction of the world."

It was the best bet *Life* ever made.

§ § §

Masks are arrested expressions and admirable echoes of feeling, at once faithful, discreet, and superlative. Living things in contact with the air must acquire a cuticle, and it is not urged against cuticles that they are not hearts; yet some philosophers seem to be angry with images for not being things, and with words for not being feelings.

—*George Santayana*

At its simplest level, the "Grace Kelly phenomenon" was the huge geyser of public renown and acclaim that shot up around Grace after mid-1954. Seemingly from nowhere, she hit number one in the box-office derby within six months of Wilkerson's prediction, and never fell below number three in her years in Hollywood. Following the break of the *Life* cover, Grace was besieged with requests for interviews by nearly every major and minor general-reading publication in America. In just the twelve months following *Rear Window*, she was the subject of cover stories in *Look, Time, The Saturday Evening Post, McCall's, Ladies' Home Journal, Redbook, Collier's,* and *Cosmopolitan*. The list of major features alone, not counting the hundreds of newspaper stories on her film career, runs to well over three dozen entries—more than many stars accumulate in a lifetime of moviemaking. From comparative obscurity, Grace Kelly became the most popular and talked-about actress in the country in the space of the last six months of 1954. Whether for her acting talent, her social background (often imagined), her mystery, her ladylike qualities, her "sexual elegance," or simply, for the way her blond beauty was stunningly revealed on the movie screen, Grace attracted hundreds of thousands of devoted fans. They proved faithful. Not only through 1956 was Metro deluged with more fan mail for Grace Kelly than for any other star under contract, but letters continued to pour in for years following her retirement. Many fans indeed continued to follow her life with sympathetic interest to the very end. In short, not only was 1954 "A Year of Grace," so were 1955 and 1956.

(Grace's first fan letter was from a teenage girl from Oregon, who wrote after seeing *Fourteen Hours*. Thereafter the actress's most enthusiastic and loyal fans remained women. The reason for this might have been that Grace, while beautiful, struck male moviegoers as unattainable. A sociologist, Thomas Harris, wrote a master's thesis at the University of Chicago comparing Grace Kelly's appeal with Marilyn Monroe's. He quoted director Billy Wilder on Monroe: "Perhaps her

secret is that when the common man looks at Monroe he thinks he'd
have a chance." But when the common man looked at Grace Kelly,
wrote Harris, he knew he couldn't get to first base.‡)

"Who *is* Grace Kelly?" If any question lay at the center of the uproar
now heard on all sides about the young actress, it was this one. At first
it seemed merely a question of correcting the misimpressions that the
role of Linda Nordley had created. Studio spokesmen aided by Grace's
friends, relatives, and colleagues took pains to dispel the myth that
Grace was the daughter of "a gigantic millionaire," that she occupied a
"glamorous Manhattan penthouse," or that she had gone to an English
finishing school. *Time* magazine summed it up neatly when it noted
that people tended to assume Grace Kelly was a Main Line debutante.
She wasn't, *Time* wrote, "though she is the next thing to both of them."

Many of Grace's costars broke their usual practice of avoiding the
press except when absolutely necessary and went out of their way to
shed light on a woman whom they obviously esteemed and regarded as
unique. Cary Grant, who gave some serious reflection to the matter,
put it thus: "She owns a controlling interest in her own mind." William Holden, on the other hand, overspoke from the heart, "She has
become a symbol of dignity and all the good things that are in us all."
Even the laconic, ironic Hitchcock became nearly cloying on the subject of Grace: "She is a very handsome woman, extremely intelligent,
extremely sensitive with a tremendous sense of humor . . . she has
character without faults." Edith Head patiently explained that Grace
wasn't always "cool and collected" ("Annoy her and she boils . . .
There's a lot of solid jaw under that quiet face of hers."); Van Johnson
called her "the thoroughbred type"; and one former Paramount executive wrote an article trying to "explain" Grace to the public. Nor, of
course, was the press at a loss in finding words for the new actress: she
was the "mistress of underplay"; she had "ladylike virtue"; "underlying sex appeal"; "maturity," "grace," "refinement," etc.

But the best general answer to the who-is-Grace-Kelly question came
from Grace's costar in *Rear Window*. "This girl has crossed up everybody by turning the Cinderella story upside down," said Jimmy Stewart. "She came out here to Hollywood from a happy home, where she'd
been loved, kindly treated and well educated . . . [She went] to a good
dramatic school. She took her work there seriously, and afterward
worked in television, in summer stock and had a small part on the New
York stage. By the time she reached here she was a skilled and competent actress. She wasn't found behind a counter in a drugstore or
luncheonette or at a drive-in. She didn't have to be nice to this guy or

‡ Gordon Gould, "Hollywood's Secret: Sex Symbolism". Chicago *Sunday Tribune Magazine*, January 15, 1958.

that guy to get ahead. And no producer would have thought to tell her 'I'll make you a star, but I'll have to pull your teeth out and put caps on them, and dye your hair, and give you a new name, and tell you where to stand and talk and how to spend your free time.' Nor did Grace, once a star, cover up for lack of self-confidence and ignorance by playing the part of hail-fellow-well-met and slapping electricians on the back. She's a lady and she expects to be treated like a lady. She's on time to work, she does what she's told to do, and because she does it without a sweater-girl buildup—which is the traditional way to do it— there are folks who think she's either high-hat or some kind of enigma. I've got news for you," Stewart said, in classic Stewart style, "maybe she's just shy."

If the people who pressed the who-*is*-Grace-Kelly question had simply wanted a good answer, they could well have settled for Stewart's generous but accurate estimate. In retrospect, however, it seems fairly clear that some of the impulse to throw up one's hands in apparent despair or exasperation about ever "knowing Grace Kelly" stemmed from something other than confusion. In the early fifties, it was still standard policy for the front office to dominate the professional *and* the personal lives of their players, particularly the stars. While the front office determined stars' "images" and selected their films accordingly, the publicity offices superintended their personal lives—passing on their dates and mates, organizing their weddings, expediting their divorces, covering up their scandals, etc. Nine tenths of Grace's fellow stars sighed and carped at this state of affairs, and a few periodically threw celebrated tantrums, but they all submitted because, finally, they depended on studio paternalism to run their lives. They had never known life any other way, and they didn't feel as though they had an alternative.

This was not the case with Grace Kelly. From the start, she showed herself at once too shy and too stubborn to play by all of the studio rules. In the professional arena, she took more initiative in choosing films outside the Metro pale than was considered accepted protocol for a young female star in that era. But at least in the activity of filmmaking, she acknowledged M.G.M. had a call on her. In her personal life, by contrast, it was hard for Grace even to conceive the notion that the studio would orchestrate it, let alone permit it to do so. When Metro's publicity department asked her for the "standard data" about her physique—i.e., the measurements of her bust, waist, and hips—she refused to provide it. (So one prurient columnist asked Grace directly for her "vital statistics." She replied, "It's nobody's business. A person has to keep something to herself, or her life is just a layout in a magazine." In a much-quoted retort, she told another reporter, "It's nobody's business what I wear to bed.") Moreover, Grace scrutinized studio publicity about her and her movies to make sure it was, if not tasteful, then honest. She obliged M.G.M. to recall, at some expense, ads that promoted one of her pictures by depicting a Grace Kelly-type figure clad in a Jungle Jane skintight suit and flaunting larger breasts than Grace possessed.

On the other hand, after some initial confusion and hesitation, Grace did her best to understand and accommodate the demands of the publicity machine. This was a painful but urgent learning process. The more Grace tasted the consequences of indulging her shyness, the more she recognized she had to open herself up. The workaday press not only stormed her gates and made life difficult, they tended to misread her silence as disdain. Worse, so did many of her colleagues in the picture business. By the middle of 1954, therefore, Grace was starting to make strenuous efforts to adapt to the needs of her new career. Throughout the rest of her life in pictures, she acceded gracefully to most of the publicity demands of great celebrity—the endless requests for interviews and photographs, the ubiquitous autograph seekers, the concern for one's appearance and one's "image," and for being seen in the right places with the right people, and, finally, the strict containment, if not denial, of the private (on behalf of the public) self. In order to do this, Grace had to create a "mask"—the necessary "cuticle" of which George Santayana spoke in the quotation earlier. For a sensibility as fine and a privacy as guarded as Grace's, the alternative to a mask, in the annihilating atmosphere of Hollywood, was the risk of self-destruction. The displays of cheap candor and self-revelation that many stars engaged in would not merely have revolted Grace's sense of discretion but rapidly have undermined her peace of mind and her identity.

So Grace pulled behind a facade, a persona—an act of self-protection of which many Hollywood personalities availed themselves. But there were differences. Grace's persona was mainly self-created, not studio constructed and supervised. Moreover, in Santayana's terms, it was "faithful, discreet, and superlative": faithful because it reflected her real personality; discreet because it also protected it; and superlative because so original and flexible. Grace did not tell the whole truth about herself, but she didn't lie. The dissemination of confected, flattering stories and hyperbole to newsmen who knew perfectly well this was *ersatz* material struck Grace as unbecoming not only to the disseminators but to their listeners (and to their readers).

If the press could trust Grace, she felt she must try to trust them, thus violating studio publicity departments' adversary view of the world. She often received journalists by herself, without the hovering presence of a studio flack. She refused to be "coached" on how to give "quotable" answers; rather, she gave answers with factual, unemotional, concise straightforwardness. She had, for example, very few anecdotes to recount because she was far too new at moviemaking to have accumulated amusing vignettes. And she said so. She also declined outright to answer impudent questions. On the other hand, knowing that her public image was neither "quotable" nor immediately warm and accessible, Grace made sure she was not always hiding behind her wall. If she trusted her interviewer, she made efforts to offer him or her glimpses of the personality and sensibility underneath the "cuticle." On at least one occasion, she invited a writer (Maurice Zolotow) to dine with her in her apartment in Los Angeles, cooked him dinner, answered his questions, and generally treated him nearly as she might have a New York friend.

The results of this policy might have proven disastrous. Given her youth and inexperience with the press, Grace might have been wrong to trust the decent instincts of men and women generally credited with instincts only for the jugular. But the thick dossiers of Grace Kelly clippings from this era amply show that she was justified in her guess that popular writers were not only decent but intelligent. The result of taking writers seriously was that Grace avoided being taken one-dimensionally for her mask alone. Writers like Zolotow, Pete Martin, Isabelle Taves, and numerous others vied with one another to plumb the actress's "unseen side" as well as paint the beautiful surface. Nobody neglected to report that underneath the "patrician reserve" lay interesting complexities, qualities, vulnerabilities. Indeed, if there was any cliché in writing about Grace Kelly the actress, it was this more-to-her-than-meets-the-eye psychologizing. Ironically, often there wasn't. Grace's mask worked well because she wasn't always wearing it.

The studios and their publicity departments didn't like it. Grace might have enjoyed sophisticated professional help in presenting herself, but instead, all too often, she was undermined. Anita Colby, the consultant to David Selznick on whom the character of Lisa Fremont was modeled in *Rear Window*, wrote an entire piece about Grace Kelly around the thesis that "in Hollywood this woman is misunderstood." Less misunderstood than resented. By the end of 1954, it was apparent that a certain important faction of "opinion setters" in the business was choosing to hold onto their early misimpressions and misinformation about the new star. One producer (who, typically, refused to let his name be used) said Grace had "stainless steel insides"—a quote that made its way into several articles and angered and hurt Grace ("That was gratuitously cruel," she told friends). Another producer (equally nameless) referred to Grace with a derogatory remark of Oscar Wilde's: she was "the sphinx without the mystery."

But it was the studio publicists, with their false candor and mock despair, who were Grace's true antagonists. A woman in the Paramount publicity office told several reporters that Grace's composure was "simply the most inspired technique I have ever seen for getting ahead in [the] industry." Another official source at the same studio volunteered that "the New York taxi drivers can't believe that Miss Kelly is a movie star because she doesn't look like one." Speaking "confidentially" and, of course, not for attribution, publicists enumerated "reasons" why Grace was a "puzzle": she lived like a young actress instead of a "movie star"; she drove a small rented car; she made her own clothes because store clothes were too expensive.

These facts were not untrue. Grace first lived in Hollywood in a simple one-bedroom apartment which she shared with actress Rita Gam. She got around town in a rented Chevrolet, though she hated driving and once told a reporter that her first "luxury" would be a chauffeur, not a maid. In the rare moments of free time, she occasionally made some of her own clothes, e.g., an organdy stole, and undoubtedly she believed prices at the Beverly Hills shops were high.

But none of this need have been regarded as exceptional, let alone exceptionable. Intentionally or unintentionally, however, those guardians of the Hollywood fantasies, the studio publicists, inflected their references to Grace with dubiety and incredulity that then sabotaged her own sincerity and straightforwardness. Certainly, they in no sense accepted Grace's own persona or helped to present it with admiration and pride, as publicity offices should have done. Instead, official studio "explanations" and "confidences" about Grace were far too often filled with disbelief and facetiousness, and even the best writers would quote them, coming as they did from an "inside source." A Metro flack "despaired" of providing anecdotes about the actress to an inquiring journalist: "I don't think Grace would let an anecdote happen to her." But the prize for wide-eyed disingenuousness went to the M.G.M. publicity man who greeted writer Pete Martin with this irresistible piece of candor: "I'm hoping you'll tell me what the excitement about this girl is all about."* Being straightforward, Grace made a major mistake with Hollywood mythmakers: she made a myth beyond their imagining.

§   §   §

In the M.G.M. roost of squawking hens, a chicken like Grace Kelly hadn't much priority. Metro had Ava Gardner, Elizabeth Taylor, Eleanor Parker, Lana Turner, Debbie Reynolds, Esther Williams, Jane Powell, Cyd Charisse, Deborah Kerr, June Allyson, and Greer Garson. There were too many stars, too few roles. Accordingly, M.G.M. was pleased to consent to Hitchcock's request to borrow Grace for *Dial M for Murder*—charging him what was considered to be the very reason-

---

* *The Saturday Evening Post* (October 30, 1954)

able fee of $20,000. According to the prevailing system, only M.G.M. could pay Grace's salary since she was under contract to that studio, though loaned out to another. Grace's salary for six weeks of filming came to $7,500. M.G.M. thus netted $12,500 on the deal. The studio would do approximately as well on *Rear Window* and a bit better on *The Bridges at Toko-Ri*. By comparison other major stars were regularly loaned out for six-figure sums. Metro was happy with its profits, but annoyed at Grace who had taken it upon herself to enter directly into contractual arrangement with Warner Brothers. Such a display inclined one to wonder if this modest and retiring beauty wasn't a tad headstrong.

The impression was reinforced when, even before the completion of shooting of *Dial M for Murder*, Grace's agent was requesting another loan-out for a second Hitchcock picture. Again, interoffice memoranda make it clear that M.G.M. executives believed that Grace and Hitchcock had arranged the deal between themselves and simply "informed" the "home" studio; but again M.G.M. consented and set a $25,000 fee for Grace's loan-out. Then, for the third time in the same season (fall 1953), a request for a Grace Kelly loan-out arrived on Benny Thau's desk and was granted. It was from Paramount again, this time not on behalf of Hitchcock, but the production team of William Perlberg and George Seaton. They wanted Grace for a film set during the recently ended Korean War, *The Bridges at Toko-Ri*.

The producers were fortunate, indeed, that their inquiry to M.C.A. (Grace's agent) arrived at a time when she had no theatrical offers, hence no reason to keep her in New York. Nevertheless, her interest in the movie was understandably low, for the part was minor: Grace would play the wife of a reactivated lieutenant (William Holden) in the Navy Air Force. The point of the film was to show real war conditions in Korea, leaving very little "love interest." Grace's part barely occupied 20 percent of the script; three male actors, excluding Holden, had larger parts than she. Yet Perlberg and Seaton stubbornly wanted the "right actress"—one with "a combination of cool beauty and inner warmth," who wouldn't be too demanding or expensive. Not surprisingly, they interviewed dozens of candidates before they found her. "Grace didn't put on an act," Perlberg said, adding that other girls arrived looking like Sadie Thompson. "Grace was dressed as if she were window-shopping—glasses and flat-heeled walking shoes."

Perlberg and Seaton did better by their "unknown talent" than she by them. *Bridges* was completed in the fall of 1954, but not released until early in 1955, by which time Grace had not only won the New York Film Critics Award and the Oscar for best film actress of 1954 for her work in *The Country Girl*, but had become one of the media events of the decade. When *The Bridges at Toko-Ri* opened at Radio City Music

Hall, it was advertised as a Grace Kelly movie, while the credits featured Grace's name below Holden's but above those of Mickey Rooney and Frederic March. Despite the hype, however, the role of Nancy Brubaker, as *Time* put it, "does little more for Grace than establish that she has a better figure than normally meets the eye" (January 31, 1955). The New York *Times* called her "briefly bewitching." The New York *Herald Tribune*'s reaction—"Everyone knows how nice it is to have her around"—was more typical. For most critics, Grace's personal standing and her acting promise meant far more than her work in the Holden movie.

To M.G.M., however, Grace was now pure gold. With the completion of *Bridges*, Grace had now made three pictures away from "home" and become one of the hottest properties in Hollywood. The studio's old indifference to their world-famous "contract player" gave way to public statements of exaggerated pride and endless internal deliberations about "how best to utilize Grace Kelly's services." But Schary, Thau, and Mannix found themselves in the frustrating position of holding the ace of spades and not being able to play it. Grace's contract called for her to make only three "photoplays" a year, which she would have done by July 1954.

However, since a contract was no impediment as long as Grace *wanted* to make a film, the larger problem was that she seemed to be looking for properties outside of Metro. She had adopted M.G.M.'s habit of benign neglect and had her head turned by more farsighted producers. Hitchcock discerned her ambition when he said, "So far she had only played leading women. She has yet to play the character about whom a film is built. That will be her big test." She found it.

§   §   §

In January of 1954, Jennifer Jones—Mrs. David O. Selznick on Christmas cards—got pregnant. A man of Prussian determination where his wife's career was concerned, Selznick telephoned William Perlberg to say that if he and Seaton would only move quickly into production on their next project, Jennifer could play the lead, as planned, before her condition showed. The producer team reflected for an afternoon and realized the risk was too great. Jones would have to be replaced.

The project in question was a screen adaptation of Clifford Odets's play *The Country Girl* (for whose Broadway production Grace had tried for a part and been turned down). In a town where *The Creature from the Black Lagoon* and *The Crimson Pirate* were the actor's standard fare, and *The Robe* was *haute cuisine*, a title part such as that of *The Country Girl*'s Georgie Elgin was instantly the most talked-about and sought-after role in Hollywood. With Jones's departure from the lists, a free-for-all now opened among several of the ranking female stars. The ingenuity and rivalry aroused were marvelous to behold. The careful timing of agents' calls, the calculated hints dropped to friendly columnists, the minuet of dinner parties, the pressure put on "darling Phyllis" Seaton by "dear friends" made the Oklahoma Land Rush seem edifying by contrast.

But Perlberg and Seaton both knew whom they wanted: Grace Kelly. Her work in *Bridges* brought them to the same conclusion that Hitchcock had reached: the actress was ready for a major role that would display not only her beauty but her acting promise as well. The problem was, they didn't figure they could get her. Metro was in no mood to farm out their prize calf another time. "We have big plans for Grace," Schary told the producer team when they made the first inquiry. He added, "We'll let you know," but Perlberg and Seaton knew the answer was no. Which didn't mean they took no for an answer. Perlberg and Seaton knew Grace better than Schary did; the Metro chief would first have to persuade Grace with his "big plans." Breaking strict protocol, the two producers sent to Grace personally a copy of the script for *The Country Girl.* ("Just say that I suspect Seaton and he suspects me," Perlberg coyly explained it to the press after the movie was released.) Then they waited, letting beautiful stars compete for the role they wanted Grace to have.

M.G.M. certainly did have plans for Grace Kelly. Its story department was now a whirring hive of activity on her behalf. In late winter, a release from Howard Strickling's publicity office informed the press of plans to put into immediate production a picture entitled *The Cobweb* —a love triangle in which "Miss Grace Kelly" would costar with Robert Taylor and Lana Turner. The newspapers and columnists were no sooner starting to mull this over when, a few weeks later, another Strickling release rescinded the previous decree and offered new news. Now "Miss Grace Kelly" would be playing in *The Long Day*—a romance set in the early West during the Indian War of 1870. In this movie "Miss Kelly" would have no major female star to contend with. It was, said Strickling, "a starring vehicle" for her alone.

The problem was, nobody checked this out with "Miss Grace Kelly" and her agents before releasing it. The actress wanted nothing to do with either film, the more so as she had read George Seaton's script and loved it—and wanted to do it almost as badly as a Broadway play. Grace called Kanter in New York and her M.C.A. agent in Los Angeles, Lew Wasserman. She told them her wishes and asked for advice. They were not optimistic; M.G.M., they said, was trying very hard to make up for its earlier neglect. Shouldn't she now try to accommodate them? Client was adamant. M.G.M., she said, hadn't come up with a single worthy role for her since *Mogambo*—a dubious part in any case.

She insisted M.C.A. submit her name for *The Country Girl*. If Metro stood firm, she would quit show business and "return to the legitimate stage."

For all that Grace would have had a hard time supporting herself on "the legitimate stage," Kanter and Wasserman didn't figure she was bluffing. On the contrary, they glumly believed she was deadly serious and would renounce her stardom even before it blossomed. They agreed to do as Grace wanted, but they advised her to keep a low public profile. M.G.M. had already expressed quiet displeasure because Grace acted too independently in making outside deals. Above all, Schary and Mannix must not have their pride put on the line by Grace's obvious participation in the now-raging *Country Girl* sweepstakes. Grace agreed. Not only did she not publicly press to play Georgie Elgin, she let it "slip" that "I'm not big enough yet to ask favors or tell [producers] I want certain roles. I'll just have to wait and hope."

Meanwhile, Wasserman negotiated, as Van Cleve and Kanter had often done—with back to the wall. If he lost this deal, he lost a major client, and show business lost an important talent. In fairness to them, the Metro executives with whom Wasserman talked were also aware both of Grace's worth to the studio and of their own personal esteem and affection for her. Too, they knew what a fine role was being offered their star. Accordingly, although Schary drove a hard bargain, it was clear from the outset that he would give way. For a fifty-thousand-dollar fee, Paramount could once again have Grace Kelly for a Perlberg-Seaton film. The moment the scheduled six weeks of shooting *The Country Girl* was completed, however, Grace was to commence a Metro film—*Green Fire*, with Stewart Granger. For every day that she was late, her "borrowers" would have to pay five thousand dollars in penalties. Wasserman, Paramount, Perlberg, Seaton, and Grace Kelly all accepted.

Leaving only Bing, the other star of *The Country Girl*, unsatisfied. Sight unseen, Crosby hadn't cottoned to Kelly. Sounding like Jerome Cowan at the Bucks County Playhouse, the crooner harrumphed and objected when his producers had whispered to him that they were in secret negotiations with the M.G.M. star. Grace, he complained, was altogether too glamorous to play the part of a downtrodden, homely, loyal but worn-out and frustrated housewife with intellectual overtones and a country background. She would have to be far more experienced than Crosby thought she was to bring off a part so distant from herself. Perlberg and Seaton allayed Crosby's fears as best they could; the singer reluctantly agreed to see how things worked out.

The Country Girl is not the finest film Grace ever played in. It is not nearly her most finished role, nor her most entertaining. But it is, perhaps, the best job of *acting* she ever accomplished. Her timing, delivery, voice, and accent are all vastly improved over her earlier films; she has overcome the occasional awkwardness with her arms and hands. In her best scenes (nearly always with Holden), Grace understates as well as ever, while attaining certain emotions better than ever before: sarcasm, anger, listlessness, bleakness. In large part her success may have been due to how much Georgie Elgin she (and director Seaton) were able to ferret out of Grace. Crosby had it wrong when he supposed the actress and the part lived light-years apart. For from it. Anyone who dropped by Grace's New York flat risked catching her as William Holden does in her first scene in the movie: unmade-up, wearing glasses, pumps, and an old cardigan, and with her nose in a book. Moreover, Georgie's loyalty, persistence, and self-sacrifice as well as her obvious intelligence and her conventional morality (she sticks with her marriage despite sore temptation) all suited Grace to a T.

What was new was for Grace to go public with elements of her inner self. Certainly she had no professional experience with a role such as Georgie. Rarely had she ever played a part that entirely broke through the Grace Kelly mask and certainly never on the screen. In that sense *Country Girl* was a first and a last. In order to do it, Grace had to call on all the technique which school and the theater had given her. If it is apparent that she is "acting," it is equally certain she is acting well. Her characterization is thus more impressive than poignant. By comparison, Bing Crosby's performance (in a far less sympathetic and attractive role) is more natural and convincing.

The severe blemishes in *The Country Girl*—among them the fact that its central figure, in either her moments of defeat or victory, is no more a "country girl" than Marie Antoinette in shepherdess garb—are not the fault of the actors but the writer and director. Grace's colleagues and co-workers on the set were deeply moved by her work. At the completion of shooting, they all got together—including the gaffers, electricians, and grips as well as the various screen artists—and presented her with a plaque: "To Grace Kelly. This will hold you until you get next year's Academy Award." And as for Bing, after one week of shooting, he told George Seaton, "I'll never open my big mouth to you about a casting problem. I'm sorry I had any reservations about this girl." His feelings by then went beyond the movie, as we shall see.

CHAPTER IV

THE RELUCTANT
MOVIE STAR, II

I'm going back to New York, to the peace and comfort of a quiet room.
—*Georgie Elgin, in* The Country Girl
(screenplay by George Seaton)

Dore Schary once said of Grace that she "has a motor racing inside of her, although it turns over quietly." The young actress's motor never purred more efficiently than in 1954 when the sheer volume and velocity of her work were prodigious. *The Bridges at Toko-Ri* finished production in early March, yet before April Fool's Day, Grace was back on a Paramount set to begin *The Country Girl*. This film ended shooting in late April. Without a breather, Grace stepped on a plane for Barranquilla, Colombia where, with many, many a regret, she kept her promise to Metro-Goldwyn-Mayer to do *Green Fire*. Shortly after, it was off to Europe for *To Catch a Thief*. Pace *Life*, it was "A Year of Grace"—and an intense struggle with her studio.

If any artistic career must have its nadir, *Green Fire* was Grace's. M.G.M.'s "big plans" for a star known for her conscientious pursuit of acting challenges turned out to be a costly adventure-morality tale about emeralds, bandidos, and true love on the upper Magdalena River —in CinemaScope, costarring Stewart Granger. "I don't want to dress up a picture with just my face," Grace had once said. "If anybody starts using me as scenery, I'll return to New York." That much-quoted Kelly refrain, which had got its speaker out of a number of similar projects, was never more apt than now. The men making the movie were more interested in Grace's looks and style than her ability. In his memoirs, Stewart frankly admired his costar's "fabulous behind." He wrote, "Grace had one phobia, her behind. For me it was the most delicious behind imaginable, but it did stick out a bit and she was very self-conscious about it. Our last scene was played in a torrential downpour and when the final kiss came we were both soaking wet, which accentuated that fabulous behind. To save her embarrassment I covered it with both hands. She was so delighted at finishing the film that she didn't even object, but if you look closely at that kiss you'll see Grace give a start as those two eager hands take hold."*

Andrew Marton, the Hungarian director of the movie, was no less taken with the actress. He later "explained" his choice of Grace for *Green Fire* by commenting succinctly, "She walks like a sexy duck." Marton even defended Grace against her own mother. Ma Kelly was in the wardrobe room one day, long after, when the company was back from location, filming interiors in Los Angeles. She cast a critical eye on Grace, who was being dressed, and said, in front of several of her colleagues, "You know, Gracie, you really don't have a lot up here [indicating the chest], do you?" Everyone was embarrassed. Marton later remarked chivalrously that he preferred Grace's "quality to quantity" in the breast department.

In *Green Fire*, Grace does little more than look and sound like Deborah Kerr, while changing from one florid skirt to the next. No one resented this more than she—particularly since, as the filming dragged on, it seemed somewhat likely that Grace wouldn't be able to return in time to keep an appointment with Hitchcock for his next picture. Rain, 120-degree heat, flies, faulty equipment, and local political problems conspired to choke progress. But those loyal inamoratos of Grace's behind—Marton and Granger—exerted themselves and the crew to see that shooting finished in time for the anxiety-ridden star to catch a flight for France where she was to begin *To Catch a Thief* on the Riviera.

Grace flew to Paris amid general incredulity in Hollywood that M.G.M. had really given way on this, her fifth loan-out in eight months. When Hitchcock had first suggested *To Catch a Thief*, it seemed certain that Grace would not be allowed to accept his offer. Both Louella Parsons and Hedda Hopper announced in print that the deal hadn't a chance. Don Hartman, Paramount's chief of production, was said to be "extremely reluctant" to pick up the phone and ask his old friend Dore Schary to defer to him for the fourth time that year. Only Grace—and through her, Hitchcock, and then Cary Grant—stubbornly believed she would get to play the part of bored, spoiled Frances Stevens, the artful and witty daughter of an American oil heiress. In very Frances Stevens fashion, Grace reassured Edith Head a dozen times: "No matter what anyone says, dear, keep right on making my clothes. I'm doing the picture." Grace knew she had two aces up the long sleeve of her white glove: her ever-ready (if never-tried) willingness to close up shop and return to New York à la Georgie Elgin, and her awareness that M.G.M. in fact wanted something only Paramount

* *Sparks Fly Upward* (New York: Putnam, 1981), p. 306.

The John B. Kellys, circa 1936. The "baby," Lizanne,
is in front. From left to right behind her:
Grace, Peggy, Margaret (Ma), John (Pa), John Jr. (Kell).
Credit: United Press International Photo.

Grace in her modeling days, 1951.
Credit: Skyline Features.

Grace playing in the TV role of a provocative chorus girl, 1952.
Credit: Skyline Features.

Grace in bobby sox. Credit: Skyline Features.

Grace and the "King" (Clark Gable) in Mogambo, *1953.*
Credit: The Penguin Collection.

Grace and Jimmy Stewart in Rear Window, *1954.*
Credit: Patron, Inc.

Grace and Oleg Cassini, 1954.
Credit: The Museum of Modern Art/Film Stills Archives.

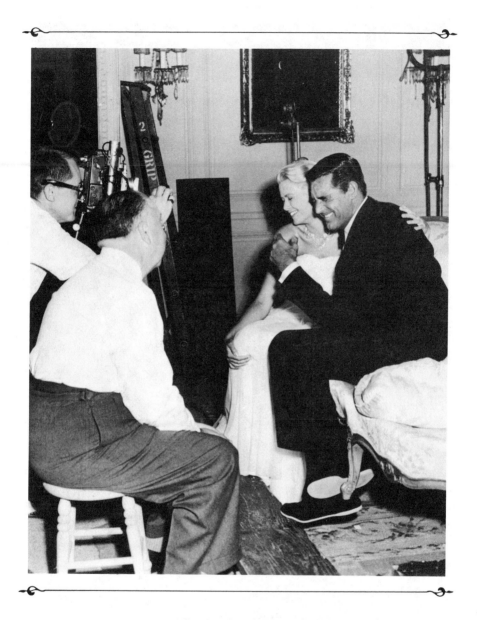

Grace and Cary Grant "blowing" a scene in To Catch a Thief
(1955) while director Hitchcock (center) looks on.
Credit: The Penguin Collection.

*Grace receiving the Oscar for Best Actress
of 1954 for her performance in* The Country Girl.
Credit: United Press International Photo.

could give—William Holden, to play a part in a forthcoming Metro picture.

M.G.M. got Holden, and fifty thousand dollars; and Grace got to go to the French Riviera to do her third Hitchcock picture, but she arrived in a state bordering on clinical exhaustion. The demands of the previous months had taken their toll. The actress was pale; shadows surrounded her eyes; she complained of insomnia and, extremely uncharacteristically, irascibility. She had begged to be allowed to stay over in a Paris hotel for a few days "to sleep," but the cost of adjourning production was prohibitive, and Grace was ordered to report. It was a credit to the friendly atmosphere of the set that Grace recovered as fast as she did.

Friendly, but hardworking, Hitchcock never demanded more of his actresses than in scenes of passion or violence. Thanks to biographer Donald Spoto, we now know that much of this "perfectionism" was attributable to his unacknowledged infatuation with Grace and the sexual frustration he felt at its unrequitedness. Sadistically, he put his leading lady through considerable torment. Cary Grant recalled the scene in the film where he jerks Grace's arm and slams her against a wall. The director rehearsed it nearly a dozen times even before filming, though it was not a particularly complicated or telling scene and was physically hard on the actress. During intermissions, Grace would quietly massage her wrists while wincing in pain, but in a moment would take her place back under the lights for more shoving. On the other hand, Hitchcock's obsession with Grace had its more agreeable moments. The whole point of the masked ball at the end of the picture was to show off Grace Kelly in a shimmering gold silk ball gown. Indeed, throughout the shooting, Hitch's interest in Grace's clothes was never less than avid. (He hired Edith Head to create a wardrobe that turned out to be "a costume designer's dream . . . the most expensive setup I've ever done," Head wrote years later. "Hitchcock told me he wanted her to look like a princess. She did.")† Though Head was the best in the business, Hitch left no detail to her judgment but made every decision himself. Similarly, though his makeup man, Harry Ray, was also one of the finest in Hollywood, the director intervened constantly. (Ray never thought Grace needed much makeup, however. "Her skin was just gorgeous," he told a journalist. "All I had to do was add a little cheek rouge, a soft pink lipstick and a little mascara. It took me seven minutes flat. She was the first woman I ever worked with that I didn't have to put foundation on. I have never met anyone with skin as lovely as Grace's.")

† Edith Head and Patty Calistro, *Edith Head's Hollywood* (New York: E. P. Dutton, 1983), p. 110.

The entire cast and crew were of course delighted to be spending a spring on the Côte d'Azur, but no one more so than Grace. It was apparent to everyone on the set that she thought the Riviera the most beautiful place in Europe. Only the rare occurrences of late-shooting or complete fatigue could daunt Grace in her enthusiasm to see the sights—whether in the sun-bleached towns and cities dotting the coast, or on drives into the surrounding Maritime Alps to discover this or that restaurant or hideaway. She went so often and was so gregarious, that everyone from Harry Ray to John Michael Hayes to Doc Erickson and Herbert Coleman (the associate producers) got a chance to go with her. Several have memories of accompanying Grace to Monaco. Casino gambling seems to have ignited her initial interest. Grace kept talking about roulette until finally John Michael Hayes said they had to visit the world-famous casino at Monte Carlo. He, Grace, and Betsy Drake (Cary Grant's wife) drove there the next weekend. During the trip, Hayes patiently explained his system of betting and of conserving money. Grace grew as excited as a child listening to this; she raced for the gaming tables as soon as they arrived and didn't return for an hour. When Drake and Hayes saw her again, she was triumphantly waving a fistful of francs at them. ("It probably wasn't more than thirty-six dollars in U.S. money, but it was a million bucks to Grace," Hayes said.) Then the three took a drive around the Principality, marveling at the beauty and variety of sights offered. Grace was especially entranced with what she had heard about the gardens on the high plateau called the Rock.

"Whose gardens are those?" she inquired.

"Prince Grimaldi's," replied Hayes, adding, "I hear he's a stuffy fellow."

"Oh, I'd like to see his flowers," Grace said wistfully.

To Catch a Thief fully justified whatever small suffering its director exacted from its leading lady. Grace as actress attains the particular fire-and-ice vision of herself that Hitchcock had been developing and striving toward in three films. Where Lisa Fremont *(Rear Window)* was seductive, Frances Stevens is a seductress. She has all of Lisa Fremont's sophistication (and more), but with an additional, splendid gift for high banter and amorous innuendo. In exchanges such as the following with John Robie (Cary Grant), Grace's timing is dead-on, while her inflection of innocence is laced with just the right whiff of irony:

STEVENS *[at a picnic lunch]:* I've never caught a jewel thief before. It's so stimulating! *[Offering him cold chicken]* Do you want a leg or a breast?

ROBIE You make the choice.

STEVENS Tell me, how long has it been?

ROBIE Since what?

STEVENS Since you were in America last.

Perhaps the highpoint of Grace's performance comes in the scene where Stevens invites Robie to dine alone with her in her suite at the Carlton. The following dialogue takes place against a background of Bastille Day fireworks:

STEVENS If you really want to see fireworks, it's better with the lights off. I have a feeling that tonight you're going to see one of the Riviera's most fascinating sights. *[Dressed in a strapless, low-cut evening gown, she moves closer.]* I'm talking about the fireworks, of course.

ROBIE I never doubted it.

STEVENS The way you looked at my necklace, I didn't know. You've been dying to say something about it all evening.

ROBIE What, about me staring at it?

STEVENS No, you've been trying to avoid it.

ROBIE May I have a brandy?

STEVENS Please.

ROBIE Would you care for one?

STEVENS No, thank you. Some nights a person doesn't need to drink. Doesn't it make you nervous to be in the same room with thousands of dollars worth of diamonds, and unable to touch them? Like an alcoholic outside of a bar on Election Day.

ROBIE Wouldn't know the feeling.

STEVENS All right, you've studied the layout, drawn your plans, worked out your timetable, put on your dark clothes with your crepe-soled shoes, and your rope, maybe your face blackened. And you're over the roofs in the darkness, down the side wall, to the right apartment, and the window's locked. All the elation turned into frustration. What would you do?

ROBIE I'd go home and get a good night's sleep.

[Stevens asks Robie if he intends to rob the villa they have been in earlier.]

ROBIE Tell me, have you ever been on a psychiatrist's couch?

STEVENS Don't change the subject. I know the perfect time to do it. Next week the Sanfords are holding their annual gala. Everyone who counts will be there. I'll get you an invitation. An eighteenth-century costume affair. Thousands upon thousands of dollars of the world's most elegant jewelry. Some of the guests will be staying the weekend. I'll get all the information and we'll do it together. What do you say?

ROBIE My only comment would be highly censorable.

STEVENS *[reclining on the sofa, her diamond necklace glittering around her neck]:* Give up, John—admit who you are. Even in this light I can tell where your eyes are looking. *[Close-up on the necklace]* Look, John—hold them—diamonds! The only thing in the world you can't resist. Then tell me you don't know what I'm talking about. *[The fireworks burst in the background. She kisses his fingers one by one, then puts his hand underneath the necklace. Cut to close-up of the fireworks.]* Have you ever had a better offer in your whole life? One with everything!

ROBIE I've never had a crazier one. *[Cut to fireworks.]*

STEVENS Just as long as you're satisfied! *[Fireworks.]*

ROBIE You know as well as I do this necklace is imitation.

STEVENS Well *I'm* not! *[They kiss: cut to fireworks, then back to the long kiss, then back to a climax of fireworks. Fade-out.]*

Hitchcock had a simple comment on Grace's performance: "She can play comedy not only sexily but elegantly. It's a quality most [actresses] do not have." The relaxed playfulness, self-assurance, and youthful beauty displayed here still do not make one think of *Cyrano's* Roxane, once Grace's favorite heroine; there is too much mischief for real nobility. But the sophistication and wit of Grace's Frances Stevens might have won for their interpreter serious attention for a role in a Molière comedy.

Grace's accomplishment in *To Catch a Thief* is the finer, moreover, because the film itself is, by Hitchcock standards, unclever and rambling. The movie was a commercial success, but enjoyed mixed critical acclaim. Some reviewers considered Cary Grant passionless and unconvincing, at best a Henry Higgins sort of lover. Certainly he gave Grace nothing like the strength she needed from male co-leads (Holden, Stewart) to shine. Bosley Crowther, for one, wrote that only the dazzling Riviera setting endowed the romance between John Robie and Frances Stevens with a taint of credibility. Many critics scored Hitchcock and Hayes for the excursiveness and implausibility of the plot, while praising them for the brilliance of the dialogue. But Grace received plaudits universally. This time, the "cool" beauty was the fire to Grant's ice.

§   §   §

"No, personally, I think she's speaking more in anger than in sorrow."

—The Torch-Bearers, *by George Kelly*

The armistice with Metro-Goldwyn-Mayer broke in late 1954. Only considerable goodwill, great patience, and the blunt, ongoing fact of

Grace's absence kept the peace as long as it held. Following the shoot-ing of *To Catch a Thief,* Grace finally took a desperately needed rest. She and her sister Peggy made a wonderful two-week trip to Jamaica where they sunned, wined, dined, and Grace read Jacques Cousteau. Following this vacation, Grace returned to her beloved apartment on East Sixty-sixth Street.

At no time, however, was she out of touch with her employer. In-deed, at the request of M.G.M.'s publicity department, Grace tolerated a photo-feature piece to be done on her for *Collier's* while she was in the Caribbean. But she was, frankly chary of the studio, and had been for several months now. Only cramped shooting schedules had prevented her from personally registering her displeasure over *Green Fire*—a dis-pleasure redoubled by M.G.M.'s provocative and deceptive advertising posters for the newly released film (featuring an exaggeratedly volup-tuous Grace Kelly imitation in a Jungle Jane suit utterly unrelated to her character or costuming in the movie itself). Grace told her agents that, as kind as Dore Schary and his colleagues in the Thalberg Build-ing were to her personally, they simply had no understanding of her particular interests, aspirations, or talents as an actress.

Metro, also, felt its patience running low. As hard as it was to admit, Grace had become a problem child, though of a new kind. Here was no chronic tardiness or absence from the set, no difficult temperament to work with, no scandalous personal life, no demands for more money. But Grace troubled them more: a deeply ethical and fine person, she seemed to Metro to be acting in bad faith. Specifically, she would not do M.G.M. movies. *The Cobweb* and *The Long Day* were, in Metro's eyes, top-drawer projects, with big stars and big budgets, yet Grace seemed to have declined them both out of hand. In fact, she had given the matter some thought, but in the end, had no interest in doing a picture in which she costarred with another female (Lana Turner in *The Cob-web*), nor, still less, another *Mogambo* or *Green Fire* sort of adventure. Metro's executives either didn't grasp these reasons or discounted them. It was virtually impossible for any studio to alter its basic image and filmmaking policy.

So M.G.M. kept trying, but in their way, not Grace's. While she was in Cannes, the story department came up with yet another expensive historical extravaganza—a film adaptation of Sir Walter Scott's novel *Quentin Durward* to star Robert Taylor "or the equivalent." A script was duly dispatched to M.C.A. and duly returned by Miss Kelly. Grace had taken one look at the scenario and realized it offered her nothing by way of challenge or possibility for growth. "All the men can duel and fight," she told a reporter, "but all I'd do would be to wear thirty-five different costumes, look pretty and frightened. There are eight people chasing me, from an old man to the head gypsy. The stage directions on every page of script read, 'She clutches her jewel box and flees.' I just thought I'd be so bored." To Hedda Hopper, Grace described *Quentin Durward* as "a cowboy story with armor." Nevertheless, M.G.M. publicity insisted she was doing the movie and later had to issue retractions when she would not.

Grace's battle with the studio wore on. The fall of 1954 found the actress in New York, searching for interesting theatrical projects. As of the seventeenth of September, she had entered the third year of her contract with M.G.M. She could, if she chose, now take time out to do a long-running play, but fine parts on the stage were hard to come by. In Broadway casting offices, Grace's screen fame held less purchase than it did in Hollywood. Her dramatic talent was untested compared to the theatrical lights who competed with her for major stage parts. In Hollywood, however, speculation raged about Grace's theatrical prospects. The incorrigible trade papers, the *Hollywood Reporter* and *Variety*, had it that while vacationing in Jamaica, Grace had either attended or thrown a party for the celebrated English playwright Noel Coward, with the purpose of discussing either his writing a new play for her or her doing an American revival of one of his classics. Grace laughed off these rumors. Playwrights like Coward, she informed columnist Radie Harris, did not clutch breathlessly at every new motion picture star who appeared on the horizon. She would have been "flattered beyond words" just to meet Coward, let alone to act in one of his plays, but she hardly expected that Coward knew, or cared, much about Grace Kelly.

No sooner deprived of one fantasy, the "trades" leaped to another. Now, they "reported," Grace would do a new play written for her by her uncle, George Kelly. Again, however, movie columnists were hopelessly out of touch with the Great White Way. Though one of the grand names of the American stage, the author of *The Torch-Bearers* and *Craig's Wife* had not had a new production mounted in New York since 1946 when *The Fatal Weakness*, one of his finest plays, closed after a disappointing run. Kelly soon quit Manhattan for Laguna, California, where he wrote only three more plays (all completed well before 1954) and then retired. In any case, Grace's fame was not yet alone sufficient to stage a new George Kelly production on Broadway. By the time it was, she was no longer acting.

Even while trying, without success, to land a major role on the New York stage, Grace's attention could not long turn from Hollywood. Whether she liked it or not, it was where her life and self-interest lay. And M.G.M. was not flagging in its efforts to interest her in a picture. In place of *Quentin Durward*, the studio now offered two properties—*Something of Value*, an adaptation of a soon-to-be published novel about the Mau Mau uprising in Kenya; and *Jeremy Rodock*, a western costarring Spencer Tracy. This last feature was a major plum from M.G.M.'s table, as *Variety* and *Reporter* vied with each other to point out. If Grace accepted the part, it would mean that in just two years in pictures, she would have costarred with most of the major actors in Hollywood. In a business where names counted for almost everything, what could she complain about?

Determined to try her hardest to be fair, Grace flew to Los Angeles at the end of January 1955, to confer with Dore Schary and the Metro brass. They gave her the latest version of the *Rodock* script and a copy of galley proofs of *Something of Value*. Internal M.G.M. office memoranda also indicate that the executives were prepared to discuss salary with Grace, should the issue arise.

The issue did not. Though Grace would soon be making $1,250 a week, which by 1957, would have risen incrementally to $2,500, this was a derisory sum to pay a box-office star of Grace's magnitude. She was making half of the salary Metro paid its top screenwriters, who were the lowest faces on the studio totem pole of artists. By way of comparison with her fellow actors, Metro paid Ava Gardner a per picture sum that worked out to three times what Grace got; Gable got five times as much. To try to compensate Grace, M.G.M. paid her a bonus for 1954 of $20,000, but the studio still came off the winner. It not only paid Grace a fraction of the bonus it paid other stars, but took in $140,000 in loan-out fees for her, while her accumulated salary and bonus came to $120,000. In effect, M.G.M. had had Grace's services for free in two pictures and was still $20,000 to the good.

None of which disturbed Grace enough to raise it as a bargaining issue. She, as everyone, was certainly aware of the disparity between her worth and her remuneration, but to her, unlike most, salary was not an issue. This was a hard point for Hollywood to grasp. Louella Parsons, who liked Grace and championed her, nevertheless radically misread the actress's demotion of the salary issue as disdain: "Salary doesn't worry Grace because her father has plenty of money." But Grace would have stood on a breadline before she took money from home. From Grace's perspective, the point at hand was 100 percent *artistic:* would Metro understand this actress's aspirations and interests and respond to them or would it continue to try to force her into that studio's star mold? To offer her a handsome raise in weekly salary, at this point—as M.G.M. was undoubtedly prepared to do, if pressed— would have confused the issue.

There was another problem. In the very moment Grace was agreeing to give serious attention to Metro's latest submissions, she already had a project that deeply interested her: *Giant*. Like *The Country Girl*, only more so, the role of Leslie Lynnton Benedict in George Stevens's upcoming production of the Edna Ferber novel was an incessantly discussed, widely coveted role in Hollywood. Grace had only one thing going for her—her friend William Holden, the only star yet cast in the huge-budget picture,‡ who was strongly plumping for Grace with Stevens. The latter, together with the Warner Brothers brass, frankly preferred Elizabeth Taylor, but in late winter of 1955 it seemed dubious she would recover in time from her recent cesarean section to begin shooting in April. So Warner's lodged a pro forma bid for Grace with M.G.M.; but they held out slight hope that Metro would release her.

And indeed M.G.M. did not. The studio reacted with uncharacteristic speed and directness. Schary himself took a call from columnist Louella Parsons to say that there was no question of Grace's doing *Giant:* "We are not going to loan out Miss Kelly for *Giant* or any other picture. She is coming back to M.G.M. very shortly. We've already agreed to loan out Elizabeth Taylor [for *Giant*], and that's that." Then he added, "We feel Miss Kelly has certain obligations to us. After all we were the first to give her a chance. All of her offers came after *Mogambo*. She has a contract [with us] and she has only made two movies for us. Maybe she has a few complaints, but we are all perfectly willing to discuss whatever is wrong. We want to keep her. We think she is a great artist and we are going to see that she gets the right vehicle."

Grace did not buckle. In a move that surprised everyone—Metro, her agents, her friends—Grace calmly announced she had carefully read *Jeremy Rodock* and *Something of Value*, and although both properties contained things of value, they were not "right for me personally." Her reaction foreclosed even a friendly discussion of the scripts. In the context of Schary's published remarks, it was a recklessly provocative position for a twenty-five-year-old, freshly minted movie star to take with the head of production of the mightiest studio in Hollywood. The press further "amplified" Grace's meaning to include the implication that she had little wish even to try to find "the right vehicle"—which was not true (for all that Grace perhaps had private doubts that such an effort would prove fruitful). Columnist Mike Connolly expressed this position in memorable "trade-paperese" when he wrote, "Looks like Grace Kelly is really persona non grata out Ars Gratia Artis way—and out to break her M.G.M. pact."

Metro had a final weapon in its arsenal. Placing an actor on "suspension" was strong medicine, though in fact it was used from time to time (e.g., on Grace's friend Ava Gardner). A suspended actor could no longer receive his salary nor make a motion picture anywhere in the world (at the risk of legal proceedings). Suspension was first mentioned the previous spring when Grace declined *The Cobweb* and *The Long Day* out of hand, but rejected for two reasons. First, Grace remained per-

‡ Holden eventually declined the role.

sonally very popular with everyone in the company, from hod carriers to vice presidents; it would not be good for morale to "put her in the deep freeze," as the saying went. Secondly, there was no promise that Metro could win the ensuing battle of appearances. Grace was not only very popular, she was every day reaping more honors and accolades. She also had the advantage of fighting for artistic principle rather than for higher pay or to try to defend some indefensible personal misconduct. Even Grace's slightly negative reputation as "Miss Goody Two-shoes" would set her in good stead in this war of moral appearances. Metro guarded slim hope that suspension would work on someone who so brazenly threw her salary, her celebrity, and her future in pictures at risk.

Nevertheless, Grace left Schary no out. With columnists "betting" openly that Grace would "win," too much face was now at stake. With genuine regret, he set the gears into action. On February 26, Loews Inc. notified Grace by telegram that she was "instructed" to report to the office of Sam Zimbalist (the producer of *Jeremy Rodock*) at M.G.M. headquarters in Culver City. Several days passed; Grace did not report. A telegram from Marvin H. Schenck, vice president of Loews, then formally suspended her "until the completion of [the role assigned her in *Jeremy Rodock*] by another person." Since the script revisions weren't even finished, let alone a shooting schedule set, that might be some time.

Grace counterattacked subtly. In her first public reaction, the actress immovably occupied the moral high ground of surprised ingenue. She was, she said, "bewildered and disappointed," and she hoped that Metro's executives "are not too mad at me." They had "a good talking point," she granted, in wanting her to do another M.G.M. film after the loan-outs, but she had turned down the roles they'd offered "because they're parts I couldn't see myself as playing." Grace continued, "It's my first experience with a thing like this, and I guess that there is nothing that I can do but sit here and wait till they want me back. I feel very strange not getting a salary anymore." She added a coda that some columnists believed was facetious and some took literally, "It's difficult. I'm afraid I'll have to stop decorating my new apartment for the present."

At once conciliatory, candid, and disingenuous, Grace's statement made it all but impossible for the studio to paint her as a headstrong wrecker, which, in any case, it did not try to do. Indeed Metro did very little but wait while its brass conferred and conferred. Occasionally the press resurrected some of the old clichés of 1952–53. Kendis Rochlen, a columnist in the Los Angeles *Mirror-News*, quoted a passel of "unnamed sources" in "the business" (quite possibly one or two of whom were associated with the M.G.M. publicity department) who invoked against Grace the hoary bromides, "She won't live here and when she is here, she doesn't join in any of the movie colony's activities"; "for my dough she's a cold dame who can't forget she's going to inherit a few million bucks"; and "Grace Kelly doesn't mind being a big star, but at the same time she thinks she's too good for Hollywood." As a rule, however, the press, even the movie press, proved itself more Grace's friend than adversary. A gossip columnist of the Los Angeles *Examiner* let drop the opinion that "I wouldn't be one bit surprised if Grace Kelly gets her way and is given permission to play in *Giant* after all."

In suspending Grace, Metro hoped that the shock of such a measure might bring even Grace to her "senses." When it early became clear that no "enlightenment" was taking place, Metro didn't know what to do. The Motion Picture Academy of Arts and Sciences solved M.G.M.'s problem.

§   §   §

Grace probably would have won her battle with Metro, but winning the Oscar for *The Country Girl* clinched it early. The award was the climax of a long period of harried expectation and excitement. The tension and anticipation engendered by Academy Awards night are great any year in Hollywood, but rarely more so than in 1955, and rarely more focused on one race: that for the Oscar for Best Actress. For here Hollywood had one of its most implausible but delicious scenarios: the best actress might very well be one of its own outlaws.

The outpouring of critical and popular acclaim that Grace received for *The Country Girl* was extraordinary. "Intense, perceptive . . . the lovely Miss Kelly will get her share of praise . . ." Bosley Crowther had written and was fully borne out as the accolades poured down on Grace after the film's release in December 1954. The praise ranged from the fulsome to the thoughtful, but it never meant more to Grace, as she told her friends, than when it spoke of her achievement in theatrical terms. *Cue* magazine, for example, called the acting "as close to theatrical perfection as we are likely to see on-screen in our time." With dithyrambs such as this floating around about Grace Kelly, it was a foregone conclusion she would receive her second Academy Award nomination in as many years. Her receipt, in January, of the New York Film Critics Award, only confirmed Grace as a top contender for the Oscar.

It was far less certain that she would win it, however. Two of the other nominees had truly distinguished themselves, Audrey Hepburn for *Sabrina* and Judy Garland for *A Star Is Born.** But it was generally assumed that Hepburn, though her acting set a standard for a certain kind of charm and loveliness, would not win for the second year in a row against such formidable opposition. (She had won in 1953 for *Roman Holiday.*) Garland, on the other hand, was a sentimental favorite among many voters for the successful Operation Bootstrap that *A Star Is Born* represented in her own life. Grace, typically, felt she would not win. She went with the Hollywood conjecture that gave the Oscar to Judy Garland.

But she wanted the Award. In part it would vindicate her to her parents in her choice to come to Hollywood in the first place—a decision about which Grace was wracked with mixed emotions, now more than ever. Moreover, it would work greatly to her advantage in this seemly but no-quarter contest with M.G.M.

The studio, for its part, was rapidly having enough of playing the part of heavy in this one-sided scrap. As the Awards ceremony neared, and speculation mounted that Grace could well win, M.G.M. had to face the prospect that it might be trapped in an appalling public posture of having suspended the Best Actress of 1954. It is clear from internal documents that Schary, Thau, and Hendrickson were searching for pretexts to lift the suspension almost as soon as word of its application had got out (at the end of the first week of March). At a conference on March 18, Benny Thau proposed that the studio lift suspension in return for Grace's agreeing to act in the film adaptation of Elizabeth Barrett Browning's autobiographical *The Barretts of Wimpole Street.* Metro had informally sounded out the actress about the project, and although she hadn't been positive, she at least hadn't given a definitive no, Thau reported hopefully. He added, "If she turns down *Barretts* we can suspend her again." Thau's colleagues agreed that this plan would "place us in a sounder position than we now are [in]." Even if they had to suspend Grace soon again, she could at least go to the Pantages Theater in good standing, and twenty million TV viewers couldn't be told by commentators that M.G.M. was an ogre.

When she drove to the theater, Grace was on the surface a picture of composure. She was accompanied by the French actress Zizi Jeanmaire, Don Hartman, head of production at Paramount Studio (which had released *The Country Girl*), and her dear friend Edith Head, who had designed Grace's dress for the evening. The dress was an aquamarine sheath gown with spaghetti shoulder straps and a matching evening cloak. (Head to the press: "Some people need sequins; others don't.") Grace wore a pair of elbow-length white gloves and carried a

---

* The other nominees were Jane Wyman *(The Magnificent Obsession)* and Dorothy Dandridge *(Carmen Jones).*

handmade petit point evening bag. Her hair was styled in a chignon, and as they entered the huge, neomedieval lobby of the Pantages, she picked up a small yellow rose and pinned it to her bun.

William Holden made the Award to Grace, a touch that added to the emotion of the occasion, for by then the two were good friends. Grace accepted it in a hushed voice made tremulous with emotion.† She had prepared no remarks, nor, before such an assemblage, would the thought have even crossed her mind to improvise a speech. She said only one short sentence, "The thrill of this moment keeps me from saying what I really feel." Later, though, her pluck returned. When photographers asked her to pose for them, kissing the winner of the Award for Best Actor, Marlon Brando, Grace replied with a smile, "Well, I think he should kiss me." Brando didn't need a second bidding.

One reporter, a man with a good memory, asked Grace, "Now that you're back on salary, you can finish decorating your [New York] apartment, can't you?" The young actress smiled impishly and granted, "It looks like I might, doesn't it?" Afterwards, she, together with most of the winners, went to a party at Romanoff's. Then Grace went home—and cried.

In the Kelly manse on Henry Avenue, the family was watching the Awards. When Grace won, John B. told friends (and later the press): "I can't believe it. I simply can't believe Grace won. Of the four children, she's the last one I'd expected to support me in my old age."

§   §   §

"Think what it means to be a swan . . ."

The picture industry press had no doubt who was left standing in the Metro-Kelly square-off. "Grace Kelly Wins Point, Also M-G Reinstatement" read the *Variety* headline of the twenty-fifth. Pieces in the *Hollywood Reporter* and the *Los Angeles Times* and *Examiner* said essentially the same thing. Within a fortnight, moreover, the newspapers were reporting the demise of Grace's association with *The Barretts of Wimpole Street.* Nobody at Metro had thought to consider the fact that Miss Barrett was forty-three in the play, while Grace was twenty-five. For this, and for other reasons, the actress declined the role that Schary and the studio publicity department had announced she'd be playing. Yet nobody at M.G.M., Benny Thau included, suggested she be suspended a second time.

Instead Metro continued to ply Grace with suggested projects. Even

† Interestingly, Grace might have had two nominations and even won two awards if she had accepted the role in *On the Waterfront,* for Eva Marie Saint won the Award for Best Supporting Actress.

now the studio seemed not to comprehend both what was right for the actress and what she herself wanted. Admittedly it is always a difficult task to separate an artist's subjective perceptions of self from an objective assessment of her abilities and suitabilities. Metro was in a business where to fail at this too often was to fail period. The studio, moreover, had certainly had plenty of painful experience from which to learn about the complex person whom their standard contract denominated "Artist, Grace Kelly." Their choice of projects in the post-suspension period was not always poor, but they were inappropriate for her as an actress. The most exotic idea M.G.M. tossed at Grace was the lead in Tennessee Williams's masterpiece, *Cat on a Hot Tin Roof*, with screen treatment by Dore Schary himself.‡ The role of Maggie, with her raw mouth and earthy style, and her brimming, frustrated sexuality, is the epitome of inelegance, the opposite of glamorousness. The offer flattered Grace (and stunned her agents), but it would have challenged her talent to its outermost measure, and, frankly, beyond. One fully understands why she thought about it hard—and declined.*

Myth would later have it that the idea for making a movie of Ferenc Molnar's play, *The Swan*, occurred to M.G.M. as an afterthought to Grace's and Rainier's wedding announcement (January 1956): art imitating life, as it were. In fact, the idea of Grace's playing Princess Alexandra in *The Swan* had been suggested to her the previous April, before she'd even met Prince Rainier. Metro's story department had thought it a perfect part for her. Grace, with her special interest in theatrical roles, especially classics (major or minor), eagerly read it. The drawback was that this was another ornate period piece à la *Quentin Durward*, with everyone decked out in elaborate costumes, bowing to one another, and speaking stuffily; and Alexandra herself was (at first glance) a rather treacly and passive character, acted upon by strong-willed others. Nevertheless, the central motif of *The Swan*—the subordination of love to duty—was a strong and universal theme that personally interested Grace deeply. Uncertain, she hesitated a time and scanned the alternatives: *The Opposite Sex* (a rather frivolous musical comedy) and *Designing Woman* (a romance, to costar Stewart Granger). From such an array of scripts, *The Swan* was by far the least objectionable. Grace would have much preferred *Giant*, but that was not an option. The alternative was to exhaust Metro's goodwill with further rejections, or to leave pictures entirely. For now she chose *The Swan*.

‡ George Cukor was supposed to direct. No one in Hollywood knew much about the new Williams's play at this time. The Los Angeles *Times* referred to it as an "untitled comedy of manners" (October 23, 1954). They cannot be blamed, however. Williams did not even finish the third act of *Cat* until virtually the night it opened at the Morosco Theater, March 24, 1955. (My thanks to Donald Spoto for this information.)
* The part eventually went to Elizabeth Taylor, a hot Hollywood sex goddess. On the stage the part was brilliantly nailed down by Barbara Bel Geddes.

She was rewarded (among other ways) by getting to learn to ride sidesaddle without even having to leave New York. Grace took equestrian lessons in Central Park where she attracted small knots of helpful fans, cheering her on and giving advice about how not to fall off the horse. The shooting turned out to be even more fun. In September, the cast assembled at M.G.M.'s Culver City lot to do the interior shots, then very soon after left for location shooting at Biltmore House, an awesome model of a French Renaissance chateau built by George Vanderbilt in Asheville, North Carolina. Working many weeks together in comparative isolation, the cast drew close to one another. Even as M.G.M.'s publicity department industriously churned out pieces for the New York *Times* describing Grace as "friendly but reserved,"† the actress herself was winning a reputation among her colleagues for her warmth and spontaneity. Alec Guinness was so touched by Grace's qualities of "thoughtfulness and pure fun" that he began a friendship with her that endured a lifetime. Although she had not been introduced to Guinness, she drove to the Asheville airport to meet him (he called it "a charming gesture"). Within a day or two, "reserved" Grace drew the English actor into the jokes and games that dominated leisure time on the set. They played word games, invented cryptograms, and sometimes acted just plain silly (Guinness: "The other day I told her a joke and Grace actually fell off the couch laughing.") Sometimes it was less innocent. Together with her accomplice Jessie Royce Landis, with whom Grace had worked and become friends on *To Catch a Thief*, Grace made life at Biltmore House "wonderfully miserable" for the hapless Guinness. On learning that Guinness had received a fan letter from an adoring local woman named Alice, "Roycie" and "Gracie" arranged to have him paged every few hours at the hotel by "Alice." Guinness's life was plagued by the unseen "Alice" for days. It took him weeks to figure out the truth.

The Swan was the only picture where Grace received lead billing and in an impressive lineup: Guinness, Jourdan, Landis, Winwood, Moorehead. This said, it is not one of her best films. In fine, vintage M.G.M. fashion, the production is a costume maker, cinematographer, and set designer's delight—as pleasurable, and as filling, as a tray of canapés or wedding confections. The Hungarian-born director, Charles Vidor, had worked his way up from B pictures in the thirties; he was now turning out standard studio fare on the order of *Hans Christian Andersen* or *A Song to Remember*. He was rather better at capturing eras, moods, vistas, or objects on camera than at directing actors in

† While every other major actor in the picture, from Jessie Royce Landis to Louis Jourdan by way of Estelle Winwood, Agnes Moorehead, and Brian Aherne was described with unalloyed praise. ("Appalachian Molnar" by Howard Thompson, the New York *Times*, October 9, 1955.)

a story. The vexing problem with *The Swan* was that he could not sound a consistent tone or set a single tempo. At times the film seems a comedy, other moments, a melodrama. In the absence of a fine, strong director, or a dominant male costar (such as Holden had been for her in *The Country Girl*), Grace was not able to hold herself from drifting back to bad habits. She began "to act" again. The result is an Alexandra who is something of a caricature of the Grace Kelly mask. John McCarten of *The New Yorker* noted that "She tends to enunciate with the nicety of a small girl reciting an elocution lesson . . . Her emotions seem clogged; where they are intended to flare, they simply become somewhat strained and reedy. The eyes squint and the lips pucker, but the effect is one of shallowness—a shallowness all the more regrettable because the depths are there, but not fully tapped."

Still, Grace never disgraces herself or even performs badly in *The Swan*. She had learned a good deal about comic acting from Hitchcock, and she produced a couple of splendid moments in *The Swan*. Guinness himself remarked on Grace's skill in the scene where Alexandra makes a gauche curtsy and bumps her head on Crown Prince Albert's chin. She managed the extremely intricate timing with perfection in *one take*. (Guinness: "It takes good acting to make gaucheness graceful.") The film's visual strengths play to several of the actress's major trumps. Vidor achieves a linear, statuesque view of Grace's beauty that in some scenes (e.g., the ball, the final balcony scene with Prince Albert) is quite memorable. But even here, one wishes for the multifaceted shades and movement that encased and enhanced Grace's beauty in Hitchcock's adoring hands.

With the completion of *The Swan*, Grace's home studio had yet to demonstrate that it knew how to exploit the resources of its most talked-about acting talent. Time was running out; Metro had one last chance.

§　　§　　§

Tracy's just exceptionally strong-minded, and very, very *wonderful, always.*

—*from the screenplay of* High Society, *by John Patrick*

It was classic Metro-think. *The Philadelphia Story*, a film adaptation of the eponymous Philip Barry play, had been a profitable and celebrated triumph in 1940. It had virtually assured the careers of Katharine Hepburn, Cary Grant, and James Stewart. A decade and a half constituted enough (barely) of an intermission to justify a remake, at a time when good ideas were few and far between in Hollywood, and surefire screen *originals* almost unheard of. As a tribute to the induplicability of the original movie, the new version would carry a different name, have different stars in a different setting, and follow a slightly different line. It would be a *musical* adaptation, filled with wonderful songs sung by the two ranking crooners of the era, accompanied by the ranking jazz instrumentalist.

And, since the studio was Metro-Goldwyn-Mayer, home of the grand and grandiose, *High Society* would be set in Newport, Rhode Island, with songs by Cole Porter, sung by Bing Crosby and Frank Sinatra, accompanied by the trumpet and band of Louis Armstrong, and starring . . . Grace Kelly.

Grace Kelly? This might have been reckless casting indeed—perhaps the sort of frantic wish to please the star that had led Metro six months before to offer her the wildly inappropriate role of Maggie in *Cat on a Hot Tin Roof.* Whatever plaudits Grace had accumulated as an actress, no one *ever* dubbed her the successor to Katharine Hepburn, nor thought her a logical choice for the lead in a *musical.*

But this time the gamble paid off, richly.

The Philadelphia Story is urban, urbane, and brittle; it requires principals who are both sophisticated and deadly serious. *High Society*, by contrast, unfolds in the more casual milieu of aristocratic Newport at Jazz Festival time. The accent is on the lush, the glamorous, the agreeable. The happy ending, which emerges as a surprise in the 1940 film, is easily foreseen from the outset in the new version. Hepburn's Tracy is older and smarter; she is headstrong, bullying, and a tad malicious. Her rancor toward Dex (Cary Grant) is genuine; her barbs sharper. The one crucial trait which Hepburn certainly has in abundance, and which *any* Tracy must possess, is command—she must call the shots.

In *High Society*, Grace does just that. Though her billing receded to second (after Crosby, ahead of Sinatra), her performance is superb. For the only time in her life Grace Kelly dominates a motion picture. In *The Swan*, she had been the focus of attention, but as a piece on a chessboard moved by other characters—notably her mother (Jessie Royce Landis). Even Hitchcock hadn't let Grace be both the main focus of interest *and* chief cause of action in a film. Metro, whether by design, default, or desperation, finally did.

Grace gives us a strong but not venomous Tracy Lord—a characterization harmoniously in tune with the altered setting of the story. Her Tracy is a spoiled, petulant, naive child, often unhappy, sometimes charming, but—and this is decisive—no less in control of events and people than her predecessor's. After a hesitant beginning, that fact is established when Tracy meets and disarms the two interloping reporters from *Spy* Magazine. The parody of petty bourgeois perceptions of high wealth that Tracy is supposed to provide must leave the sardonic journalists in confusion about what, exactly, they are seeing. The temptation to ham it up would undoubtedly be great for a young actress, especially given that she must speak lines in precious French while fluttering about in a balletic mime. To give in to that temptation would mean losing her mastery over the two reporters, a mastery the plot requires. Grace resists the temptation. When she departs the "south parlor," she is and stays mistress of the action—through rumbas and drunk scenes, behind the wheel of a Mercedes, or in a score of scenes with strong costars. She does it, not by her beauty or her glamour, nor with the force of mind and will that Hepburn effused naturally, but with a canny skill at timing, manipulation, and comedy.

This is not to say that Grace Kelly is *better* than her predecessor, who won the New York Film Critics Award and an Academy Award nomination for her rendering of the role, and who possesses one of the great talents in American drama. Hepburn also had eight years of seniority on Grace at the time she played Tracy Lord, not to mention the invaluable experience of having played the part onstage. Knowing all this full well, Grace, at twenty-six, nevertheless, set the knowledge aside and sculpted out her own very different and appealing version of a role that was in the public mind all but inseparably associated with another actress. It is a comment not only on her skill, but also on her individuality, and even sangfroid.

§ § §

The most remarkable features of Grace Kelly's career as a film actress are her youth, her range, and her development across so brief and intense a span. She was twenty-three when she started. In four and a half years and eleven pictures, working with Hollywood's best and best-known screen artists, Grace took on lead roles in two melodramas, three mysteries, one western, two adventure movies, a war story, a period piece, and a musical comedy of manners. She never did badly; and only in her M.G.M. pictures *(High Society* excepted) was she merely adequate. For the rest, she displayed either high competence or real excellence.

More impressive than Grace's range, however, was the trajectory of progress in her art. *High Noon* was important, not for her performance but as a wonderful introduction to the business. It exposed Grace to the highest quality of artistic associates that Hollywood had to furnish, and it reinforced her innate taste and standards of excellence. *Mogambo*'s significance in Grace's career was elsewhere: it squarely confronted Grace with both her principal temptation and her major problem as a screen actress. The problem was her inhibition of emotion. The temptation: to run for cover within the stereotype M.G.M. and Hollywood in general offered her. To Grace's credit, she stubbornly refused to let the praise for *Mogambo*—praise she rightly attributed to her novelty and beauty, not to her acting (despite the Academy Award nomination)—trap her in Linda Nordley-type roles or distract her attention from improving her work. The juxtaposition of *High Noon* and *Mogambo*—of Zinnemann and Ford—demonstrated to Grace, moreover, how vital to her improvement was a strong, attentive director who understood her deficiencies and was interested in her as a screen actress.

Enter Hitchcock. His immense contribution to Grace's development lay in his intuitive understanding of Grace's psychology. Whether consciously or unconsciously, the English director was aware of Grace's subliminal fear of self-revelation and self-betrayal, fear that led to her constricting her emotions before the unblinking gaze of the motion picture camera. Grace's contemporary, Audrey Hepburn, was fortunate in that she naturally, instinctively, cottoned to the camera. In Grace, however, something deep inside her was terrified by the intimacy and penetration of the camera. She had a performer's desire, to be sure, but her instinct was theatrical—to entertain across a space through the mediation of intelligence and interpretation, with the techniques of voice, inflection, movement, general appearance, etc., and all the other devices of stage acting.

Infatuated with Grace's reserve and beauty, Hitchcock recognized that the key to unlocking her cinematic potential was to get Grace to stop leaning on "acting" techniques alone, and to draw instead upon her emotions in rendering a part. He easily won her trust with his seriousness, intelligence, and a strong paternal presence. His own physical modesty and apparent emotional containment also undoubtedly commended him as a person Grace could rely on not to "expose" her meretriciously. Over the course of three films, Hitchcock succeeded in drawing forth Grace's gift for romancing the camera with her beauty—few angles or shades of which the director neglected in his careful exploring of her physical presence. Equally importantly, he helped her discover her wit and seductiveness.

There was, nevertheless, a limit to what Hitchcock had to give Grace (or any actor). Actors mattered less to him than realizing his own vision, pursuing his own compulsive project. In his slick, manufactured movies, one can easily, as one reviewer noted, ". . . look beyond the actors and enjoy the view without missing anything important."‡ In *To Catch a Thief*, Grace sparkled with real luster, but she could go no further with Hitchcock. The two best roles he gave her were, in the final analysis, unsympathetic, two-dimensional manipulators of men.

Her next challenge was films where quality acting was the heart of the matter. In *The Country Girl*, Grace performed less than brilliantly.

‡ Quoted in Spoto, *The Dark Side of Genius*, p. 367.

One can sympathize with Garland's fans; she deserved the Oscar more than Grace. But then Judy Garland, a veteran actress at thirty-two (who had been in show business since she was four), was playing a part virtually cut to every wrinkle of her identity while Grace, at twenty-five, barely an apprentice, had taken on a complex character lead far, far afield from the Grace Kelly *persona* or her prior film repertoire.

The ultimate challenge for any actor would include either the lead in a story that revolves entirely around one person or with the lead entirely unrelated, even diametrically opposed, to the character and character type of the actor herself. *The Country Girl* satisfied only the second of these criteria. The play and movie are misnomers in this regard (as well as others): they are not mainly about the "country girl," but her husband. Important as Georgie Elgin is, the story and the movie are finally Frank's, and Bing Crosby was the true (if unsung) hero of the film. Grace could therefore rely on others—usually Crosby, sometimes Holden—to carry most of the weight. Ideally, Grace's next step might have been a role that met both criteria of excellence.

In the event, *High Society* satisfied only the first. Nevertheless, the burden on Grace was great even if the role was tailor-made to the popular notion of Grace Kelly. In the great Hepburn's shadow, Grace's strength of professional identity was tested. But according to Celeste Holm, Grace knew how to handle the problem: "She was less dependent on other people's response than any actress I'd met in Hollywood. She had an extremely strong will, but also great politesse. She was keenly aware of whose footsteps she was following in, but finally she was even more aware of who *she* was," Holm said, then added, "She was George Kelly's niece, that's who. And she knew it. It gave her a kind of stern pride."

What was perhaps meant only kindly and rhetorically turns out to carry analytic weight. The resource which Grace may indeed have called upon to render her portrayal of Tracy Lord was—one may speculate—her Uncle George. Certainly the fine comic portrait she provided is not only worthy but reminiscent of a George Kelly character —e.g., Mrs. Espinshade's daughter, Penny, in *The Fatal Weakness,* a play Grace knew well and loved. Hitchcock was never more on the mark when he said that the vehicle most likely to take Grace "to the top" was sexy, elegant comedy. By the end of her career, the actress revealed genuine artistry for comedy. If M.G.M. had decided to do a film adaptation of *The Misanthrope,* they would have been within their rights to cast Grace as Célimène.

Viewing the pageant of Grace's career, some, at the time, were led to wild hyperbole. Jimmy Stewart said of his friend that "She had it in her to become another Garbo. Garbo played everything: tragedies like

Camille, comedies like Ninotchka, romance like Queen Christina. Grace could have played all these roles." Others put it more justly and judiciously when they emphasized Grace's rapid improvement and her continuing promise. But even with the more critical, Grace's remarkable ascendancy made one pause. Stanley Kramer put it thus: "I *never* thought of her as a great actress, just a good to very good actress. But then you never could be sure because she never got tested greatly. She might have risen to greatness." Foreman, Grace's first screenwriter, said, "The thing about Grace was, toward the end of her career she improved so quickly you thought she might even surmount her beauty." Zinnemann, who wasn't especially enamored either of Grace's Hitchcock films or *High Society* summed it up best: "She would unquestionably have become a very important star—first, because of her beauty, but very soon after, for her personality, the way her mind worked. She would have been more than a movie star."

And yet posterity has not been kind to Grace Kelly the actress.* In its ardent affair with her beauty, her glamour, and, mostly, with the unprecedented social phenomenon that her short career and its conclusion generated, collective memory (aided by the press) has tended to neglect Grace's cinematic achievement and forget her promise. In this gradual depreciation and forgetting, Grace herself participated. Her pride, her modesty, and her ever-ready willingness to trivialize "show biz" led her both to underplay her film accomplishments and—very occasionally, very slightly—to magnify what was truly a minor career in the theater.†

Yet it remains true to say that after *High Society*, Grace Kelly was arguably one of the most promising actresses in America. In forty months and eleven movies, Grace had learned, developed, and, indeed, produced enough for the most serious screen artists to believe she might have it in her to cross the wide gap between high movie star competence and truly fine acting. When the "Bryn Mawr voice and mannerisms" and the breathtaking photogenicity are laid aside, there is still something left over. As crucial as cinematographers of the qual-

---

* A change may be taking place since Grace's death. At *Rear Window*'s revival in 1983, David Denby asked in *New York* magazine, "Can Grace Kelly really have been called 'icy'? She's straightforwardly sexual here—nothing 'indirect' (Hitchcock's word) or reserved about her." (October 17) Vincent Canby was more encompassing in his review of *Rear Window*. He said Grace's eleven films "firmly established a witty, sexy screen personality that no one since has ever matched." (New York *Times*, October 9) Denby and Canby's views come at the end of a quarter century of silence or undervaluation. It remains to be seen if Grace's death will spark a renewed interest in her as an actress and a serious critical re-evaluation of her work in movies.

† In 1980, Princess Grace wrote a spare and eloquent Introduction to the polished brochure of the Académie de Danse Classique Princesse Grace. Referring to her great love of ballet, she wrote, that it was "with a pang of regret" that she gave up dance "for the theatre." Not movies, the "theatre," (spelled in the English style).

ity of a Robert Burks and Robert Surtees were to creating Grace Kelly's transcendent screen beauty, or as major as Edith Head's contributions were in costuming the actress, there was still a crucial, growing "further element." According to Donald Spoto, Hitchcock's biographer, Grace "charmingly captured the spirit of her era in movies—the search for illusion." But at certain moments in certain films—e.g., the scene in *The Country Girl* that takes place in the alley behind the theater where Georgie Elgin and Bernie Dodd (William Holden) have their first confrontation—Grace stepped beyond being "a charming example of the search for illusion" and gave one reason to believe she might have carried her torch into the subjective realism of sixties films.

But she did not. Instead, she left the business just when she had reached the end of her beginning. She was twenty-six years old.

Whence came the coherent direction and dynamism of Grace's performance in *High Society?* Chuck Walters was an effervescent, gracious director, with a gift for setting musical numbers, but he was far from a Zinnemann, Ford, or Hitchcock. Nor did Grace develop the kind of synergy with Crosby and Sinatra that sustained her so well with Holden, Stewart, and Gable. Perhaps *the* most remarkable thing about her last, most promising picture was that Grace created and evoked her own performance. Her self-confidence and maturity were never greater than in the months just before, and during, *High Society*'s making. The most extraordinary irony of Grace Kelly's career as an actress was that those very developments in her heart and personal life which marked her coming of age as an actress also resulted in that career's sudden cessation. Why?

CHAPTER V

HOMELESS IN A HOMELESS PLACE

We all loved her. You can't work with Grace Kelly without falling a little in love with her.

—Fred Coe, producer

Work dominated Grace's time in these years, but work brought little lasting satisfaction, only celebrity. Actual picture-making—the memorizing and delivering of lines, the takes and countless retakes, the A.M. calls and commissary food, the lights, cameras, and hours of *inaction*— had its novelties and thrills, and brought great satisfaction to the young actress, but they could not finally fill the hollowness at the center. Indeed, the constant tension and stimulation they generated posed a problem in their own right. Unwinding at the end of a long day was necessary, but not easy.

Harder by far was shucking off the effects of the false excitement— the chimeras and illusions, the daily bombardment with attention and stimuli—that came with the territory of "Big Hollywood Star." Many of Grace's fellow stars took refuge in coping mechanisms. Drugs, alcohol, conspicuous consumption, eccentric social behavior gave the acting profession an almost infamous renown. Grace had no interest in these. The sole antidote for her was a stable, succoring private and inner life, but they, in turn, required a family of one's own and regularity of daily rhythm. Only the smallest handful of actors succeeded at having stable families. The requirements of job and the ethos of Hollywood sapped the base on which family life must stand. The spirit of self-sacrifice, moderation of expectation, general peace of mind were not qualities that celebrity and glamour cultivated; shooting on location destroyed any possibility of regularity of family life, while shooting at the studio more often than not devoured an actor's energy.

Hollywood, wrote Grace's friend David Niven, "was a hotbed of false values . . . but it was fascinating, and *if you were lucky*, it was fun." Grace was not lucky. Years after, looking back on Hollywood from the richness of family life in Monaco, Grace loyally defended "show biz," spoke pleasurably of the absorption and challenge of screen-acting. But at the time, she lacked Niven's crusty self-possession. For the few, like Grace, who keenly felt the ache and understood its cause, Hollywood could never be home. She told a journalist, "At times I actually hate Hollywood. I have many acquaintances here, but few friends." The friends came—the men in droves, but the end of the story was the same as the beginning. She remained a stranger. "Always seated askew, as if on the arm of a chair; ready to get up, to leave." Gide's words apply to more than restless French writers in the thirties.

Grace nevertheless resourcefully attempted to build some kind of "life apart" in Hollywood. With stubborn devotion and ingenuity, aided by her family and one close East Coast pal who came west, Grace carved out little niches and havens that provided sustenance and some alternative to the jealous demands of "the business."

The necessity of setting up temporary residence in Los Angeles became unavoidable with the completion of *Mogambo* in the late spring of 1953. Having signed a contract with one studio, with a new film about to begin shooting at another, and with the dead certainty of other films after that, Grace had no prospect of being able to live in New York for an appreciable period of time until the fall of 1954, when her contract with M.G.M. stipulated she had a year off for "stage plays." Grace might have chosen to live out of a suitcase in the Beverly Hills Hotel, but she knew that would only exacerbate her homesickness. So, instead, she set briskly about building a home away from home. She took a small two-bedroom apartment on Sweetzer Avenue, the actual center of the old Hollywood. Once the hub of show biz fashionability, downtown Hollywood had lost most of its cachet when Grace moved in. Most of the studios were there, but no longer most of their well-paid artists, who had migrated west closer to the ocean. Sweetzer Avenue was déclassé, and the industry press would soon poke some fun at Grace for living where call girls beckoned to passersby. But at least Grace's neighborhood was a lively community. She could not have afforded a sprawling residence in Bel-Air or Beverly Hills, but she would also have died of loneliness out in one of their splendid, isolated canyons. Grace was a young actress and a would-be New Yorker, preferring spunk, not space.

With Grace, Prudence Wise moved into the stucco "modern"-style, two-story apartment building with the kidney-shaped pool. Prudence was a close friend from the Barbizon days, who had agreed to work for Grace as her private secretary. But she was no factotum. On the contrary, beloved "Prudy" was the first of many friend-protectors whom Grace kept by her side over the years. All politesse, efficiency, and no-nonsense to the world, at home, Prudy was Grace's confidante, playmate, and shrewd counselor. She fully grasped the threats to Grace in the new environment and dedicated herself to fortifying Grace's life apart.

The two girls were soon joined by a third, Rita Gam, who had known Grace faintly from live television and modeling in New York, and, like her, had gone on to a career in pictures. To judge Rita by her appearance and casting was to entertain every fantasy and scenario but the truth. A sable-haired, lustrous beauty, she was the harmony to Grace's melody. Directors always selected her for the demicharacter roles. From the nervy and sassy or brazen and bawdy to the sultry and shady, Rita was always the "best friend," the rival, the "other girl," the faintly nefarious foil. She had, for example, been chosen by John Ford to replace Ava Gardner in *Mogambo* if that apostle of temperament and tumult had one more time "seceded," as the *Hollywood Reporter* put it, from the picture.

So much for the Gam *persona*. The real Rita was about as soft-spoken, as unworldly, as insecure and scared as any seventeen year old who ever ran away from home with just her pair of skis. This she had done, seven years before, in the company of a youthful Broadway waif named Sidney Lumet. The two had married but not settled down, and the miracle was they lasted the five or six years they did. Now, in this summer of 1953, with her marriage on the rocks, soft-spoken, sweet-tempered, shy Rita Gam found herself living out of a suitcase in the Beverly Hills Hotel, waiting for shooting to commence on a thing entitled *Attila the Hun*, in which she would play the sensitive role of concubine to the scourge of Asia. Despondent, feeling out of the swim of things at the Beverly Hills poolside ("this vulgar display of Hollywood's finest female flesh, oiling, turning and seducing for a crack at the big time"),* she thought seriously about going back to New York.

Then the phone rang: "It's Grace Kelly here. Why don't you come around for coffee this afternoon?" The apartment Rita found was filled with the "inspired clutter" that was always the hallmark of "Gracie's place." It was a "very personal, feminine and sentimental" sort of place, "filled with snapshots, sketches and souvenirs from [Grace's] first films. Everywhere there were pictures of her family." The girls talked about their careers. Grace burbled out stories of Africa and of Gable; she proudly displayed her collection of amethyst-veined rocks that she had insisted on shipping back all the way from Kenya, but which seemed to Rita as "strangely out of place in Hollywood's cardboard apartments."†

* The Rita Gam quotations on this and the next page are taken from her article, "That Special Grace" (*McCall's*, January 1983).
† The overweight of Grace's baggage was so expensive that the studio complained to her agent.

But no more out of place, perhaps, than the two girls themselves. Rita and Grace admitted to one another their mutual hesitations and anxiety at this outpost duty they were doing in a "foreign" land. And they talked at length about "the conflict between the drive for perfection in our work and the kind of life we both ultimately wanted to live." Then, as naturally as if she were inquiring if Rita wished more coffee, Grace asked her if she'd like to move in with her and Prudy. Rita had no second thoughts. The home that the girls had created away from home was irresistibly beckoning. She joined her square friend in the refuge behind Prudy's protective ramparts.

The world they created was nourishing and sweet and altogether homespun—in humorous contrast to the lives they led at the studio. "While [Grace] was exhausted from a day of serious acting [on *Rear Window*], I was sore from having ridden horses through fire [in *Attila the Hun*]." They flung themselves into exercising ("the battle of the bulge was never far from our minds") till Rita found Grace asleep one evening when she should have been doing toe-touchers. But it really didn't matter; the arduous life of acting took a grateful toll in calories. If they were awake enough to cook and eat, the girls could stuff themselves with Grace's "classic tomato spaghetti" or Rita's "homespun beef stroganoff," and drink as much champagne as they liked. ("Grace loved it, so we always kept some on ice.") Then, with a last mite of energy, they would go for long jaunts through old Hollywood, waving greetings at the affable ladies of the night who walked sentry duty on Sweetzer. "Looking back," Rita Gam wrote lovingly, thirty years later, "we were terribly naive, considering that the world saw us as glamorous movie stars. We . . . played like Nancy Drew and her pals, in a more innocent time, even in the loopy, hyped-up enclave that was Hollywood."

Occasional weekends, Grace would drive down to Sun City to see Uncle George who lived there in retirement with his lover and secretary, William Weagly. Sometimes George drove up to L.A. Few in the Hollywood Grace knew remembered George Kelly from his Metro days, but for the actress, George was a stronger presence than most of the people she saw each day. He no longer openly poor-mouthed the picture business, yet his manner, erudition, and reputation were a constant reminder to Grace of her unfulfilled theatrical aspirations and of the dangers of a studio contract and the life it brought with it.

§   §   §

Splendid affection between Gable and Kelly in love scene at falls.
                              —*Cablegram from John Ford, director of*
                              Mogambo *to producer Sam Zimbalist*

The shooting of *Mogambo* required, all told, just under five months—most of them spent in isolation in the luxury dome that M.G.M. thoughtfully constructed for its artists in the middle of a subtropical jungle. The familiarity of convenience and moviemaking, however, by no means dispelled everyone's feeling of total isolation. The actors and crew were now residents of a remote and perilous land where lions roamed freely at the periphery of bivouacs and strange birds called to each other through the nights in haunting, disconcerting refrains—a land and a time in suspension, where standards, conventions, responsibilities were harrowed and weeded for the planting of new erotic, ephemeral blooms.

The Gable of 1954 was a sagging shadow of the youthful *bell'uomo* who so understandably captivated Mary Astor in *Red Dust*, but he had the appeal of a man in pain. Since Carole Lombard's death, "Clark was lonely and restless, always searching for someone to replace Carole but never finding her."‡ In recent years even his career had hit a slump. The King, as he was called, had had a short-lived marriage with the English aristocrat, Lady Sylvia Ashley, which had ended in a divorce a few years earlier. Now Gable was back on the hustings. For John Lee Mahin, screenwriter for *Red Dust* and *Mogambo*, and close friend of many years to Gable, it was never a question of whether the great star would "make a move," only how Grace would receive it.

At twenty-three, Grace Kelly had not been away from familiar faces and places for longer than a fortnight. Now she was eight thousand miles from Manhattan House, obligated to spend eighteen weeks working at a new and frighteningly demanding job, with associates of legendary names, in an encampment bounded on two sides by rivers with alligators in them. She was determined, she was game, she was oh-so-scared, and she took support gratefully from wherever it came.

Life in the encampment quickly fashioned its own relationships—largely, if not entirely, a reflection of the hierarchy of work. The leading actors and other screen artists created their own little society apart from the crew, the extras, the workers. In this little aristocracy, there was, from the outset, no mistaking that Grace was, as cameraman Bob Surtees put it, "that pretty girl at Clark's side." It would be hard to overstate the reputation that the King still enjoyed with women of Grace's generation (or the preceding; Ma Kelly grew "weak in the knees" at the mention of Gable). The first words out of Grace's mouth when she called Philadelphia in a purr of excitement to tell her mother about *Mogambo* were these: "I'm going to Africa [slight pause]—with Clark Gable!"* There was, in short, a special romantic aura about the

‡ The words are John Lee Mahin's, from an interview with the author (April 8, 1983).
* Mrs. John B. Kelly, "My Daughter, Grace Kelly: Her Life and Romances," as told to Richard Gehman (*Los Angeles Examiner*, January 15–24, 1956). Installment VI.

King that no young girl, certainly no actress, could have possibly over-looked, or wished to.

He displayed a special regard for her from the day she arrived, when he met her at the airport and drove her to the Kenya National Park for his personal tour and commentary. Thereafter Gable's invitations to do things and go places with him were constant. They were easy for Grace to accept. The two of them shared a robust enthusiasm for "wholesome" activities like sightseeing, big-game hunting, and early rising that, to say the least, bored many of their colleagues (notably Ava). Grace readily understood Clark and enjoyed being with him. The virile, handsome outdoorsman whose fearlessness and bravura won the respect of natives and white hunters alike, recalled to her many of the more agreeable traits of her father and brother. And although she was not often attracted to men of that mold, in this instance, the circumstances, and the man, were unique.

Finally, perhaps most significantly, the two needed each other. As Grace distracted Clark from the malaise that suffused his life in these years, she leaned on him for guidance—sometimes even direct advice—in her first major movie role. She called him "Ba," which was Swahili for "father," and, as one writer noted, not too far off from Lombard's "Pa."†

Does all this permit one to state categorically that Grace had a full-dress love affair with Gable? No. A future lover of Grace's—Oleg Cassini—stated that when he casually put this question to Grace one day, she replied that she had not.‡ In her series of articles, Margaret Kelly also denied it, but with sufficient hedging as to beg questions: "Why shouldn't she have cried over [Gable]? . . . After all, she'd just spent five months working and practically living with an attractive, kindly and sympathetic man. Gable was all of those things." Mrs. Kelly assayed Grace's feelings for Clark as "a schoolgirl crush," but what she did not take into account in print was the all-important circumstances of a complaisant, exceptional fate that brought two attractive actors together as screen lovers in an African adventure-romance. Few of Grace's friends, including Cassini, and still fewer of those who saw her and Clark together in Africa disputed that she harbored strong feelings for him during the shooting. What precisely happened between them can never be known. That Grace was a little in love should probably not be doubted.

Had Kenya been closer to the quivering noses of the hound dogs of movie gossip, or had Grace Kelly been the household name she was soon to become, the relationship with Gable would have hit the pages

---

† Roland Flamini, *Ava* (New York: Coward, McCann & Geoghegan, 1983), p. 184.
‡ Interview with the author. New York, April 28, 1983.

of the scandal sheets far sooner. In the event, it was not until the eve of the completion of location filming that rumors of this "May-December" association began to crop up. Shortly before leaving for London to shoot the interiors of *Mogambo*, Gable received a cable from the English equivalent of Louella Parsons. He read it to Grace: "Rumors sweeping England about your romance with Grace Kelly. Please cable confirmation or denial." They decided the best way to handle such speculation was casual facetiousness. At the airport, the King read the cable aloud and announced grandly: "This is the greatest compliment I've ever had. I'm old enough to be her father."

Quite true. "Ba" had twenty-eight years and a set of false teeth on Grace, and if those differences had perhaps counted for little in the never-never land of southeast Africa, they rapidly took on considerable heft in London. During the weeks of shooting at Boreham Wood, the two continued to go out *very* discreetly, but it soon became clear to Grace, if not to Clark, that the relationship could only go forward as a friendship. If Grace needed any reminding, her mother flew to London within a day or two of her daughter's arrival. Mrs. Kelly was only *too* delighted to dine with Clark and go to the theater on his arm, but the question could not even arise as to how she would view him as a serious suitor for her daughter. The same adamantine objections would have held for him as had for Lyons: he was an actor and he was a divorcé. (Lyons eventually managed to get an annulment of his marriage, but that does not seem to have altered Ma Kelly's feelings about him any.) Gable's greater fame and wealth would not even address, let alone overcome, the religious and social objections of the wife of a conservative, self-made, Irish Philadelphia bricklayer.

But this time no argument arose to trouble the relationship between mother and daughter. At its height, Grace's affection for Clark never approached the love she had felt for Gene Lyons. Grace departed London in tears, but she departed as Clark's friend, no more nor less. For his part, Gable bowed to force majeure gallantly and philosophically. When, a few months later, a newspaper columnist reported that Clark had given her a diamond bracelet, Grace called him up and demanded, "Well, where is it? I'm waiting." Gable chivalrously stuck by his policy of waving off questions about his relationship with Grace with exclamations like "I'm old enough to be her father," while Grace simply refused to say anything but this: "I am very fond of Clark." They remained good friends until his death in 1960. Thereafter Grace remained very friendly with Clark's last wife, Kay, who, with her and Clark's young son, John, visited Monaco. Her husband, Mrs. Gable said, had always spoken of Grace "in a very special way."*

* Interview, April 11, 1983.

§   §   §

The Hollywood press didn't really know to run with the Gable-Kelly liaison until it was over. Perhaps irritated at having been caught napping, the columnists soon had their ears and mouths full when Grace returned stateside and began shooting *Dial M for Murder* on the Warner Brothers lot in Hollywood. Ray Milland, Grace's costar in *Dial M*, was forty-five in 1953, six years younger than Gable. He had been married to his English wife, Muriel, for twenty-one years, but that fact did not forestall his developing an infatuation for the blond actress playing his wife in the film. Telling Grace that he and his wife were separated, he asked her out several times. In a friendly way, Grace accepted; Milland was an actor she not only respected but was grateful to for the advice and support he gave her on the set. It is highly doubtful she felt anything more.

She hardly had time to. Almost instantly the press got wind and misread Grace's, if not Milland's, interest. Columnists hostile to "cool Miss Kelly" condemned her as a husband-stealer. As Kendis Rochlen wrote in the *Mirror-News*, "She's supposed to be so terribly proper, but then look at all those whispers about her and Ray Milland." But the very Catholic Louella Parsons, rushed to her coreligionist's defense, writing that "I happen to know that Grace is a strict Catholic girl brought up by a strict Catholic mother"—as if *ipso facto* these circumstances precluded any dalliance. In fact, it was true, however, that Grace had been surprised to learn that her occasional dinner partner was not, in fact, separated from his wife. She was undoubtedly sorry to learn that Ray had misled her. But frankly, she didn't understand what the fuss was about. Knowing her own feelings for the actor had never gone beyond friendliness, Grace saw nothing wrong in dining with him, regardless of the status of his marriage. (Muriel Milland lived in England—with her husband when he wasn't on location.) It happened that Milland—desiring to establish his availability in Grace's eyes—had misrepresented himself, but that was his problem, not Grace's. (Another of his problems was domestic. A schism erupted in the Milland ménage due to Milland's infatuation. Muriel, however, did not divorce him, and eventually they were reconciled. Years after, columnist Sheilah Graham, who appears to have received confidences from Milland and his wife, summed up Milland's *folie* thus: "It came over him in a rush: that the whole thing whatever it was, had been make-believe, and that he had been in love all the time with his very understanding wife, Mal [Muriel's nickname].")†

For a few of the more confirmed Grace-haters, the actress was per-

† New York *Mirror*, April 12, 1962.

manently encumbered now with the reputation of husband-stealer, although she had quit seeing Milland after the completion of their picture together. Hostile or sympathetic, several columnists misread Mrs. Kelly's and sister Peggy's trip to Los Angeles as family concern over the Milland affair. But there was no Kelly "concern" because there was no Kelly romance.

After *Dial M*, the press's interest in Grace's personal life relaxed temporarily. The most speculative curiosity could turn up nothing to drool over in Grace's fond friendship for Jimmy Stewart, with whom she was making *Rear Window*. In the months she lived with Rita and Prudy, Grace had no steady boyfriend. The girls occasionally showed up at Hollywood soirés ("We were invited to many of the 'Group A' parties," Rita remembered), but after a few negative experiences with the local garden-variety clutchers and grabbers, they learned to keep more to themselves. Rita recounted one memorable evening in her *McCall's* memoir on Grace. Charlie Feldman was an agent in the halcyon days when producers still ran studios and agents were generally regarded as the lowest form of Hollywood life. One night he lured Rita and Grace to his home on the pretext that he was having a "dinner party." "We drove up Benedict Canyon in Grace's mustard Chevy and arrived at Charlie's to find that there were no other cars in the driveway. We looked at each other as a discreet butler led us past two dim chandeliers in the hallway and then into the living room. Then we met 'the party'—Francisco (Baby) Pignatari, the South American playboy, and our host, Charlie Feldman. The gentlemen stood there in all their sunburned glory, smelling of expensive cologne and dressed in slick, expensive casual clothes and cashmere sweaters. They looked rather like plastic dummies from Bloomingdale's menswear department . . . The evening proceeded to go downhill from there. Grace sat straighter and straighter behind her glasses and poker face. As the dinner progressed, we noticed that the lights were getting dimmer and dimmer, and by the time we had finished the *coq au vin* Pignatari's hands were groping my knees.

" 'Let's go,' I whispered to Grace in a panic.

" 'Let's wait for dessert—it might be good,' she whispered back."‡

With the opening of production on *The Country Girl* in the spring of 1954, a costar's amorous interest provided the press with the makings of another Grace Kelly affaire manquée.

Bing Crosby's opposition to Grace's hiring for the key role of his wife was well known. Equally publicized was the crooner's sensational

‡ "That Special Grace," *McCall's*, January 1983, p. 32.

change of heart at the end of the first week of production, by which point he had already fallen violently enamored of his blond costar and asked to take her out. He even spoke privately with fellow actor William Holden to inquire of his feelings for Grace and ask him "to stand aside."* Holden graciously did so, but he harbored doubts about Bing's chances. He was right to doubt. Crosby was a practicing Catholic and a widower, which might have figured to his credit in Mother Kelly's eyes except that his cause with her daughter was lost from the outset. Grace never felt more than platonic affection for Bing.

For a time Bing courted Grace ardently, showering her with dinner invitations, which she sometimes accepted to be affable. The papers applied a bellows to what they called a "spark," but were reduced to subterfuge in order to convey to readers the impression of a flame. A picture in the *Herald-Examiner*, captioned "Hollywood romance," shows Grace and Bing alone in a restaurant. A closer look shows Grace smiling attentively away from Bing (on her right). It turned out that sister Peggy was seated at the table as well, only the editors thoughtfully cropped her out (undoubtedly on the theory that "two's company . . .").

Rebuffed, the singer tried to make it appear as if he'd never pleaded his case. "If I were fifteen or sixteen years younger, I'd fall willingly into the long line of limp males who are currently competing madly for her favors," he told Pete Martin of *The Saturday Evening Post*.

One male, however, was not limp and did not compete, because he didn't need to. Bill Holden was by universal agreement one of *the* most well-liked screen artists in the business. Relaxed, polite, charming, he was as agreeable as he was handsome; he displayed none of the egomania that characterized so many leading actors. He simply had no enemies. Like Gable, Holden was one of whom it could be said that he was both a man's man *and* a lady's man, but while he took his male pals for granted, he actively sought out the company of women. Holden liked women in general; at a time and in a business where there were few mixed gender friendships, Bill had female *friends*. But there was no question that he was also one of the great "lovers" of his era.

He and Grace met on the set of *The Bridges at Toko-Ri*. Bill had told several friends how eager he was to work with the new, highly touted star—to see if she was the cool cucumber that some made out. Like most who met Grace on the set, Holden instantly found her to be warm and admirably hardworking. She found him, frankly, one of the most attractive men she had ever met. But he was married to, and

* *Golden Boy, the Untold Story of William Holden*, by Bob Thomas (New York: St. Martin's Press, 1983, pp. 97–98). The other Holden quotes are from *ibid*.

living with, a most charming lady. There could thus be no question for Grace of dating Bill Holden.

Except that he would not take no for an answer. He was incredibly persistent—but in a delightful, jocular, sophisticated way, with none of that edge of frantic infatuation that had marred Milland's and Crosby's self-presentations (and proven an easy tip-off to the press). He was also the absolute master of the *beau geste* because he had the bigness of heart to underwrite gestures. When Grace was signed for *The Country Girl*, Holden shocked the film world by voluntarily giving up second billing to her. It was an unheard-of offer, and his agent must have howled. (George Seaton said to Holden: "You're the first actor in Hollywood history to lower his own billing.")†

And, if such a demonstration of nobility were not enough, Holden even quietly stepped aside in his pursuit of Grace when Bing Crosby— not even a particularly close friend of his—asked him to be permitted to try his hand.

After Bing failed, Bill quietly stepped back into the pursuit. Aware of Grace's concern about Mrs. Holden, Bill brought her into friendship with Ardis. *Confidential* magazine ran a salacious account of what it called Holden-Kelly trysting, adducing for evidence the fact that the actor's white Cadillac convertible was seen occasionally parked outside Grace's Sweetzer Avenue apartment. *Confidential*, however, had not done its homework. The car was indeed owned by Holden, but belonged to—as everyone knew—Ardis. Several times, four at least, Bill had picked up Grace and brought her home for dinner with him and Ardis. (*Confidential* editors might also have considered that Grace would hardly conduct an affair from an apartment she shared with two roommates, especially the redoubtable Prudence Wise.) Holden demanded—and got—a retraction from *Confidential*. He even called Hedda Hopper in order to get the correct version of the story out. But he added a disingenuous coda, "I don't understand all this publicity about Grace. I like her, but I don't think she's the *femme fatale* she's built up to be. She's pretty *femme*. But she's not *fatale*."‡

The remarks may have been intentionally deceptive, for it is possible that by then Holden and Kelly were involved—not "fatally", to be sure, but intimately. According to Holden's biographer, Bob Thomas, twenty-four-year-old Grace was charmed, nudged, and finally swept away by the irresistible, if irresponsible, star. Unfortunately there is no evidence to prove that, nor, still less, to specify what "swept away" did, and did not, entail. Holden took Grace for a weekend to his Palm Springs home, but was disappointed when she brought Prudy along

† Thomas, *op. cit.*, p. 97.
‡ Quoted in Thomas, *op. cit.*, p. 98.

for the ride. Thomas writes, "Bill solved the problem by taking Grace on moonlight horseback rides into the desert," but his implied conclusion—that Holden seduced Grace—is more persuasive to a biographer of Holden than of Kelly. It is unlikely that Grace would have let herself become emotionally involved with a married man, particularly when she was friends with (and periodically seeing) his wife. Grace may well have harbored special feelings for Holden and even continued discreetly to see him for a time after *The Country Girl* was completed, but there probably would not have been more to it than that.

§ § §

I felt like a streetwalker. Fear covers everything out here like smog. There is no respect for privacy.

—*Grace Kelly*

By the spring of 1954, Grace's personal life was swiftly becoming one of the hottest items of discussion in the Hollywood press. Reading the gossip columns, one would have got the impression Grace Kelly had come to town to be a courtesan, not an actress. The publisher of the *Hollywood Reporter*—a publication that had certainly contributed its share to the rumor mill—took pen in hand to remind readers, in a front page editorial, that scandals were beside the point. "This gal's sailing in the romantic department—which is good box office," wrote W. R. Wilkerson, "but Grace Kelly is going to be one of the great stars of the picture business not because of romantic items—Kelly's lovers—but because she's a top actress."

Grace herself writhed under the microscopic scrutiny; she let her bitterness show in occasional interviews where she contrasted the Hollywood lifestyle to New York's, to the former's disadvantage. Sometimes her perceptions of the differences were peculiarly her own. For example, she told a journalist that "asking a friend to dinner here is such a thing. It involves a complicated phone call or even a more complicated telegraphic invitation. In New York you see your friends easily and with no folderol." Later in the same interview, she complained that merely walking down the street in Los Angeles was "dangerous" because a girl might falsely be taken for a prostitute. But it is no farfetched deciphering to suggest that Grace was flailing out at more than differences in social protocol between one region and another. (If anything, the worlds Grace knew best—Philadelphia and New York—were socially more formal than the notoriously casual southern California movie community.) What bothered Grace was not formality but the jackbooted invasion of her privacy, by the remorseless, relentless scrutiny of public view. It is unlikely that anyone could have mistaken Prudy, Rita, and Grace for streetwalkers, and if he had, Grace would normally have been the first to laugh—that is, unless her Ma and Pa Kelly-trained conscience was bothering her.

The effective disguise that Grace put on in the year or so before she met Oleg Cassini—her first publicly acknowledged *beau*—was the appearance of running an innocent, homey social life that was in no way romantic, let alone promiscuous. She also maintained an absolutely unbending policy of politely ignoring *all* questions about her personal life. Her friends and her mother and sisters, who came to town frequently, supported the policy with a different strategy. They, unlike Grace, could sometimes seem to be "coaxed" into "letting you in on a little secret." Louella Parsons delighted in recounting the cutesy story, told her by a Grace intimate, of the young movie star's "great love"— the actor Douglas Fairbanks, Jr. "He kissed her goodnight," Parsons wrote, "and she knew she would never wash off that spot on her face again." Grace's sister Peggy gave out a much-quoted statement, that went far toward establishing Grace's preference for family fun in the press's eyes: "Her phone rings constantly. I know because I had to answer it [when I spent time with her] in Hollywood. But she almost never went out. Even when she had a night off she would rather go out for a big dinner with me and have a lot of laughs. Family laughs." Rita Gam, described as "an actress who double-dated with [Grace]," was quoted as saying, "She's darling and lots of fun, but let a man get ideas and she'd reach in her bag and pull out her horn-rimmed glasses and put on the clipped English accent. I've never seen such an efficient technique for freezing a wolf."

Certain writers thought they smelled a wolf in sheep's clothing, but even they complimented Grace on what Madeleine Ryttenberg called her "new system for dealing with whispers, innuendo, and raised eyebrows." Scoop Conlon, a well-known PR man in Hollywood who was also a good friend of the Kelly family, told one writer, "It's my hunch Grace does [these things] deliberately. She is very cagey about doing anything the gossip columns can hop on. Put yourself in her shoes. If you felt you'd been put upon by the tiger cat gossip columnists and rumormongers, you'd watch your conduct in public extra carefully."

Neither the Louella Parsons nor the Scoop Conlons were entirely right. If Grace's "policy" proved effective, it was because it lay so near the truth. And the truth was that Grace was always a family girl, and a woman's woman, before she was a man's. Between the time she moved to Los Angeles and the time she began seeing Cassini, Grace—despite all the gossip—had no serious romances. Her private life was the society of friends, usually female. Here Grace was relaxed and happy as a giggler, a prankster, a gifted mimic, and a softhearted confidante. She adored Prudy and Rita and a small handful of other West Coast friends (Edith Head, Harry Ray, a makeup artist at Paramount, occasionally

Alfred and Alma Hitchcock), and she enjoyed frequent visits from her family, especially Uncle George. But the company of available and overtly interested men made her nervous. Her dating, often than not, had the reality as well as the appearance of a junior high school romance with Prudy Wise, Rita Gam, or one or more of Grace's sisters (not to mention Ardis Holden) playing chaperone.

If anything, Grace needed a romantic life. She was lonelier for a man than she perhaps realized herself. Though she said little about him to her friends, it was clear to them that she missed Gene Lyons, even though she was aware the relationship could not have gone on. As for Gable and Holden, those quasiromantic friendships must have reminded her of what she wanted and didn't have (and couldn't, with them). For all the pleasures of life at Sweetzer Avenue, it was a holding action—until the need to go on location for the next picture, until she could move back permanently to New York, until she met a man with whom she dared conduct an open relationship.

§ § §

I am an aesthetic man. I like things of beauty.

—*Oleg Cassini*

Describing Grace's first romance since Lyons demands the superlative.

Epicurus has no more ardent, adept knight-errant in our times. He was born in Paris in 1913, the son of Countess Marguerite Cassini, daughter of Tsar Nicholas II's ambassador to the United States, and Alexander Loiewski, a ranking diplomat in the Imperial Russian foreign service. He was raised in Florence where his mother ran a successful salon of high fashion, and when the time came, he followed in her path. In another era, he would have chosen a more romantic career, but a canny and determined realist, Oleg first found ways to pay the bills and only then indulged the tastes of a courtier. An enduring anachronism, few have bested him at combining the flare of a *mousquetaire du roi* with the unbending self-discipline of a shopkeeper.

By the early 1950s, Cassini had become an American citizen. He made his home in New York, but his presence in international high society, both as couturier and cosmopolite, was secure. Leading hostesses not only wore his fashions, but invited him to their soirées. Together with his older brother Igor—better known by the byline of his gossip column, Cholly Knickerbocker—Oleg set a standard of charm, wit, and Old World manners. An acknowledged connoisseur of women, he had been married and divorced twice, though he was still in his thirties. His first wife was the cough-syrup heiress, Merry "Madcap" Fahrney. The union was brief. (Miss Fahrney had four more husbands to go before she was through; Oleg was her fourth.) A greater love match by far was Oleg's second marriage, to Gene Tierney, the actress, with whom he had two daughters. But that relationship also bowed to the conflicting demands of dual careers and sensitive egos, and 1953 saw Oleg free again.

In the summer of that year, he and a close friend went to see *Mogambo*. Leaving the theater, Oleg said to his friend, "You know this girl, Grace Kelly, she's going to be my girl." The friend laughed this off as unlikely: "Who says you can just walk in and pick her up?" Cassini replied, "I do." A few minutes later, they entered a small French restaurant on the East Side of Manhattan. As he prepared to sit down, Oleg glanced to his right and there, at the adjoining table, sat Grace. She was having dinner with a close actor friend from television days, Jean-Pierre Aumont.

As luck and the familiarity of European society would have it, Oleg and Jean-Pierre knew one another, though they were far from intimates. Oozing geniality, Oleg nevertheless greeted Jean-Pierre, conferring a grand smile on his "old friend." No fool, Aumont saw who, and what, was coming, but he had no chance to take evasive action. Common courtesy obliged him to introduce Oleg to Grace. Then Aumont sat there, roiling with irritation, while Cassini gushed well-turned compliments to his dinner guest.

"Having started out this strongly," Cassini said thirty years later, "I was in my own mind committed. I had no choice but to deliver. I went on a campaign, absolutely the greatest, most exhilarating campaign of my life, using every bit of fantasy and energy I had. The goal to get this incredibly beautiful, superficially cool woman interested in me."* A realist, the designer knew perfectly well he had neither the looks nor the fame of a Holden, a Gable, or an Aumont—nor, for that matter, their wealth. He played to the strength that had already got him what he had. One of his heroes, Frederick the Great of Prussia, had said, "L'audace, l'audace, toujours l'audace," and Cassini imitated the audacity by plying Grace with *style*.

Within twenty-four hours, several dozen roses of varying shades arrived at Grace's New York apartment; they carried no card. The next day another shipment, then another, followed, on the third day, by a telephone call: "This is your friendly local florist." With a trace of asperity, Grace demanded to know who was on the line. Oleg replied that she would find out in the fullness of time, but for the moment, would she—on just the slender assurance that she had indeed met her

* This, and subsequent, direct quotes are from an interview with Cassini in New York, April 20, 1983.

caller—have dinner. Grace hesitated, then suggested that "the voice" join her and Peggy for lunch that day. "Fine," said the voice.

Grace certainly remembered Oleg when she saw him the following afternoon, but after a pleasant lunch, she did not encourage his ardor. She told him that she was moving to the coast shortly. The news did not daunt Cassini. He went frequently to Los Angeles, he replied. Would she mind if he contacted her there? She would not. Oleg took that as carte blanche to launch an amorous operation as intricate and carefully wrought as a counterespionage infiltration. Flowers, small presents, billets-doux, telephone calls fell on Grace, unexpectedly but dependably. Weeks became months. Gradually, very gradually she began to get caught up in the intrigue of the game. Her responsiveness, muted at first, became progressively warmer. At just that moment, Oleg stopped all communication. He learned from L.A. friends that Grace was going to a party at the well-known show biz watering hole, the Mocambo. With the help of a good friend (the agent Ray Stark), he got himself an invitation to the party and a beautiful date. Came the evening, there was Oleg—fox-trotting, rumbaing, tangoing, mamboing across the floor with a skill calculated to show up 99 percent of "those beefily handsome blond American boys so reminiscent of Grace's brother." Instantly Grace was at his side, and with a look too keen and a voice a tad tremulous, said, "Why Oleg, why didn't you *tell me* you were going to be in town? *Please*, come sit with us."

Thus opened, in the middle of 1954, a romance more suggestive of a chess game than of a love affair. Indeed love is an ill-chosen word to render the tension, the mutual fascination, the subtle manipulations that characterized this remarkable and curious alliance. Grace had never met a man remotely like Cassini. Taken on the superlative terms he set, he simply towered over the sweet, tame American men-boys whom Grace had heretofore dated. He punned in three languages and his reading ran from Proust and Colette to Manzoni, Tolstoy, and James. He could discriminate among cognac snifters, knew the preferability of Roederer Cristal to Dom Perignon, was familiar with when to use a *révérence* and when a full bow and generally displayed a foresightful thoughtfulness that left *nothing* to be desired. Grace was due in New York for an evening en route to Cannes? Then Oleg got a friend at the Carlton to get them adjoining rooms. She didn't feel like driving to Philadelphia (she never liked driving)? Why, Oleg was there with the limo.

One evening, early in the relationship, Grace called Oleg at his mother's home on Long Island where he happened to be spending a weekend. She was depressed, she said, and wondered if Oleg would come and cheer her up. *Would he?!* Cassini was so taken away at the thought of being needed by her that he raced out behind the house and took a dive into the pool, fully clothed. It was empty. The next day he showed up at Grace's place in L.A. with a huge bulbous, broken nose. She took one look at him and slammed the door. "She was not without humor, dear Grace."

Cassini succeeded to some degree because he possessed an intuitive grasp of a certain side of Grace that matched Hitchcock's. Not for nothing did their romance attain its highest luster while Grace was shooting *To Catch a Thief*. Oleg brilliantly mined the Frances Stevens vein in Grace—the rich, beautiful intriguer, as much a rival as a lover to John Robie (Cary Grant), whom she finally ensnares with his own game. And indeed Grace displayed the same adeptness at this game of romance. Early in their relationship, she sent him a postcard with the message: "Those who love me, follow me. G." And Oleg did; he followed her wherever she went—including Europe. She proved a better player than her teacher, for Oleg made the fatal mistake of falling deeply in love with his quarry. Grace never really did with hers.

Their romance reached its height on the Riviera, where Oleg outdid himself *à outrance*. There were long drives through villages in the Maritime Alps, dinners of *cuisses de grenouille provençales* and Montrachet '49, discourses on culture, gastronomy, literature, and couture, bringing the two an intimacy that moviedom would soon deny them. The two could luxuriate in evening tête-à-têtes in place of two- and three-hour long-distance phone calls between Los Angeles and New York. Their affair flourished on the Riviera because again, as on location with *Mogambo*, Grace lived in a fantasy world where conventions were suspended, privacy permitted, captivation encouraged, and a master enchanter was at work.

But the tenure in fairyland was this time far briefer. Within six weeks, Grace and Oleg were back in the United States to greet a gale-force explosion of media interest in their relationship. Cassini, after all, was the first man to be publicly acknowledged as Grace Kelly's boyfriend. He therefore came in for a critical review from the studio (M.G.M.), the family, the friends, and, not least, the press that few human beings would tolerate let alone pass unscathed. The less so Cassini, who, as the ex-husband of Gene Tierney was a well-known and much-criticized figure in Hollywood. Every columnist in the business ran nearly daily updaters on the Cassini-Kelly pair. Many were hostile to the designer, deeming him too devilish, as Hedda Hopper said, for the "ethereal Miss Kelly." (In another column, she wondered aloud in her column why, with all the good-looking men in town, Grace had to pick Oleg Cassini. She concluded, "It must be his mustache." Oleg was one of the few to take Hedda on full face. In a square-off that became famous, he replied to this column with a telegram:

"Dear Hedda, I see what you mean. I'll shave mine off if you shave yours."

The Kellys were worse than the columnists and their rudeness almost pushed Grace into marriage. Their blind and downright opposition caused Grace to start to see Oleg, not as a partner in a game of love, but as an ally and symbol of the very freedom and independence that had led her to opt for a career in acting in the first place.

"The mere thought of Grace's considering a divorced man was distasteful to us."† Mrs. Kelly arrived for lunch with Grace and Oleg within a week of their return from France. (They had embarked separately, hoping to defuse some of the anticipated maternal explosion. Grace took the boat with Hitchcock and the cast; Oleg took a plane.) Not one given to euphemism or excessive decorum, Ma Kelly weighed right in. "Oleg," she said, "you're terribly charming and continental, and I can certainly understand Grace's wanting to date you, but as a marriage risk you're very poor."

Unexpectedly, Cassini defended himself. How could she expect that a man nearing forty wouldn't have been married before? He still enjoyed the friendship of his recent ex-wife, Gene Tierney, and he was the soul of responsibility and affection with his children. He could hardly be accused of fortune-hunting ("I'm a good earner, just as your daughter will be"). And, finally, "I utterly reject the charge of running around with women. I date, certainly—that's to be expected from a normal man—but once I am involved with a woman, as I now am, I do *not* date others." Then, with a certain temerity, Cassini turned to the offensive. How, he asked Mrs. Kelly, could she attack his supposed promiscuity, on the one hand, yet condone the homosexuality of a close family friend (he cited a name), on the other. "It behooves you to try to be consistent in your Catholicism, does it not, Mrs. Kelly?" Finally, in a veiled allusion to her husband's philandering that no one missed, he said, "You know, I've always said that before one accuses another person, it is a good idea to be sure of one's own ground."

The onslaught took Ma Kelly by surprise. Grace's silence seemed to betoken some compliance with her lover's words. Addressing now "Mr. Cassini," rather than "Oleg," Margaret Kelly agreed to acquiesce in their dating if he and Grace would forestall any announcement, or even talk of engagement for six months. Grace needed "at least" that much time to see things clearly, for "you are, Mr. Cassini, as you well know, *a very charming date.*" She added that she hoped he would be able to join the family for a weekend in Ocean City where they were living for the summer. It was a command performance. Grace was pleased by it; she felt sure that Oleg would charm the Kellys en masse as much as

† Mrs. John B. Kelly, Sr., *op. cit.,* January 21, 1956.

he had fascinated her. Cassini knew better; he made the trip south with, as he liked to put it in French, *"mort dans l'âme* [death in my soul]."

George Kelly might have done justice to the evening meal that Oleg shared with his brother's family at their beach house on the Jersey shore one Saturday night in the late summer of 1954. The "treatment" meted out to the interloper by his girlfriend's relatives was classic Kelly. Before Oleg even arrived, her brother Kell had been threatening to "kill him if he walks through the door." (He had called him an "oddball" in the newspapers.) It was an execution all right. Oleg was met with utter silence from John B. Sr. and John B. Jr. At the dinner table they hardly even looked at him. Mrs. Kelly was polite but distant. Grace's sisters were manifestly cowed by their parents' hostility and said little. The one friendly face Oleg encountered at this interminable meal was that of young Donald LeVine—Lizanne Kelly's handsome aspirant fiancé. Said Cassini, "Donald was Jewish, so he, too, was in bad odor with the family, though not so bad as I. He was the only person who talked to me. We were the pariahs."

Grace herself was simply numb—no doubt, with mortification and disappointment. She had endlessly reiterated to Oleg, "Once they see how fine you are and how important to me, they will come round." The realization was that Mr. and Mrs. Kelly were manifestly not to be budged by their daughter's feelings came as a stunning shock. Cassini interpreted it as Grace's "momentarily glimpsing that her family regarded her as a prize possession, a property, like a racehorse, that must be handled, above all invested, wisely—not wasted." Others maintained that Grace's parents simply did not believe Oleg would make Grace happy, even though Grace did.

The Philadelphia episode so appalled Grace that it kept her with Oleg several months after doubts had undermined her faith in their relationship. In early 1955, it was clear that in their game of love, Grace was now the dominant player; by the force of both circumstance and will, Oleg was *her* escort, she no longer his pupil. This fact was clear to all who spent time with them together. It occurred to more than one of Grace's close female friends that compassion, more than passion, held the actress in a romance she was sure would go nowhere.

Grace herself was growing steadily more confused. On the one hand, she did not wish to hurt Oleg nor appear to dismiss a relationship that everyone—not least her own family—considered to be serious. On the other hand, she was fast coming to understand that a game of love is not love, and that style and panache are not essence—indeed, may, in certain instances, amount to a betrayal of essence. If many people she loved and respected did not take Oleg seriously, it was perhaps because he, by his own admission, was playing out a transparent fantasy. Oleg may have helped her to see that her family regarded her to some degree as a "prize possession," but how did he regard her? "I was as much in love as I could be," he would say many years later, adding, "It's very difficult to discern here what was a game, and the desire to win. The more it went on, the more it became imperative for me to win her. Maybe if she hadn't been Grace Kelly, I would have said to her mother right off, 'Okay, you win.'" For whatever reason, by the spring of 1955, the ties between Grace and the man regularly referred to as her escort and even fiancé-to-be were growing tenuous.

Oleg worsened matters now by betraying his darker side. As he saw Grace's feelings changing, he gave way to jealousy and anger that swiftly doomed the relationship. Grace herself had been looking for some "sign," as she put it, that things were quits between them. That sign arrived when Oleg threw a fit of pique over Frank Sinatra. One day, Grace telephoned Oleg in New York to ask him if he would mind her going out for an evening with the well-known singer. Frank had expressed a strong interest in meeting her, she said, and while she wasn't interested in Sinatra romantically, she certainly would like to have dinner with him. And one other thing: the time of the proposed date would be an evening of the coming weekend—when Oleg himself was due to be in Los Angeles.

Bruised over the ongoing pummeling he was taking in the columns about not being "good enough" for Grace, Oleg instantly bristled: "Yes, I *would mind*. How in hell do you think it'll look in the papers if you're photographed on Sinatra's arm going into Chasen's while I'm sitting in my room at the Beverly Hills Hotel? That's all Hedda [Hopper] will need to write tomorrow morning, 'Great! Cassini is out of the picture.' So, no, you do *not* have my permission."

Grace nevertheless went out with Sinatra. It did not end the Cassini relationship then and there, but it sounded the death knell. Grace still saw in Oleg a symbol of her independence from her family, and for that reason alone—and inertia—she continued to date him into the spring of 1955. Then something old surfaced in a new way.

§   §   §

Grace did not wish to go to Cannes to represent the American film community at the International Film Festival of 1955. She was busy changing apartments in New York, moving to a lovely two-bedroom flat on Fifth Avenue overlooking the Metropolitan Museum. She had hired the noted society decorator George Stacey whose work she admired in the pages of *Vogue* to help her, but she made it clear from the outset he was an *adviser*. The two threw themselves into the search for the "right" pieces (mostly for eighteenth-century French, as it turned out), and Grace did not feel like stopping this altogether agreeable work to go to Europe.

The man who persuaded Grace to go was Rupert Allan. Grace had met Allan in the spring of 1953 in London when he was an editor-writer for *Look* magazine, doing a cover story on the "event of the century," the coronation of Elizabeth II. They met, rather briefly, while the elevator in the Savoy Hotel climbed five floors, and they came to know each other better the following week at a party at Ava Gardner's flat. A soft-spoken, gentle man, Allan radiated an inner kindness and trustworthiness that set him apart from the journalists Grace was used to. Allan, in turn (after initially wondering "what all the shouting was about—I mean, there she sat, rather unprepossessing in a sweater, tweed skirt, and loafers"), soon saw qualities in this woman that interested him. He wrote a story on her in *Look* which charmed Grace. A few weeks later, she invited Allan to her apartment for dinner in New York. There began a friendship that endured to the end.

Now, in the spring of 1955, Rupert thought it ridiculous that Grace did not take a vacation in Cannes. He assured her what a good time she would have at the Film Festival. Handling the press took a bit of savvy, of course, and heaven knew Grace would want to avoid the embarrassment that struck Robert Mitchum the year before,‡ but Rupert said he'd be there to deal with the journalists, so Grace could relax and have a good time. He pressed hard and Grace finally agreed.

And was glad she had, for in addition to the sand, sun, and stars, she received a call, the day after her arrival, from one of her favorite old beaux-friends, Jean-Pierre Aumont, the very man who had so regretfully introduced her to Cassini. Though admittedly their friendship had somewhat receded in the glare of the ensuing Cassini-Kelly match, Grace had never lost her very tender feelings for the handsome actor she had first met in New York, in live television. It was in early 1952 that Grace and Jean-Pierre had enacted the parts of Mr. and Mrs. John Audubon in a historical teleplay called "The Way of an Eagle." Like other would-be Grace-suitors, Aumont had had his work cut out for him. The young Grace paid him no particular heed whatever and politely declined "Monsieur Aumont's" lunch invitations. Finally, "I became furious. We had been rehearsing in a dance hall, and there were slogans written on the walls. On about the third day, I took her by the arm rather firmly and, pointing at one, said, 'Look at that, please.' The

‡ Mitchum fell for an old paparazzo trick while he and his wife were representing the United States at Cannes in 1954. A rather buxom floozy suddenly accosted him and, with *poitrine* suddenly bared, turned herself and the star to the cameras. A gentleman to the last, Mitchum covered her endowment with his hands. The shutters snapped and the next day the pictures went round the world.

slogan read, 'Ladies, be kind to your cavaliers. After all, men are human beings, too.' "* Grace smiled and went to lunch. Soon they became friends. A running gag between them for years after was to repeat to one another the lines that had been given the bird-crazed Audubon in the teleplay. "Look, dear, a wren (or a sparrow or bobolink or whatever)!"†

Now, in the wake of the Cassini affair—and once again away from hated Hollywood—Grace was delighted to hear from him—perhaps in part, frankly, because he was so different from Oleg. Without Cassini's intellect or complexity, Aumont also lacked his obsessiveness; nor did he make a cult of "style." He didn't have to. He was just himself—casual, wantonly affectionate Jean-Pierre, one of the handsomest actors in France, a hero of the Resistance, a major figure on the European (and soon the American) stage and screen, and the widower of Maria Montez. For Grace, this was quite enough. Aumont was twenty years her senior but that made no difference. She spent every moment she could spare from official duties to be with the man she called, simply, "Pierre."

The trouble was the press was everywhere due to the Festival. Grace and Aumont used every bit of ingenuity they (or Rupert Allan) could come up with to elude reporters and photographers, but finally, the paparazzi were victorious. At the end of the Festival, *Life* magazine published a sensational sequence of photographs, taken with zoom lens, showing the "lovebirds" at lunch on the balcony of a small French restaurant. In the several cuts, Jean-Pierre is seen holding Grace's hand; the two snuggle and caress; they kiss. In short, a rather endearing and lovely, innocent set of amorous gestures, badly misconstrued by publication as photographs in the largest picture magazine in the world. (Some journalists speculated that Aumont, desirous of exploiting Grace's unique publicity value, had let the photographers know where they would be lunching. Aumont denied it, and no one has ever stepped forward with proof.)

The *Life* photos abruptly ended the Kelly-Cassini affair in the press's eyes. Now the frenzied word flew about that Grace and Jean-Pierre were "altar-bound," as the trade papers put it. Aumont, amused at all the hoopla, answered a reporter's question—"Would you like to marry Grace Kelly?"—with what he intended as a facetious reply, "Who wouldn't?" Considering the press's misconstrual of these words, it was fortunate indeed Aumont hadn't replied "I do," or the couple would have been pronounced man and wife.

It has generally been assumed that this first successful penetration of

* Jean-Pierre Aumont, *Sun and Shadow* (New York: W. W. Norton, 1977), p. 150.
† Interview with the author, Paris, May 24, 1983.

her privacy that the *Life* photos represented utterly scandalized and shook Grace.‡ Indeed, some said she was reduced to lying to the press, e.g., as when she announced in the immediate aftermath of the *Life* brouhaha that "Jean-Pierre and I are just good friends." Such an interpretation overlooks Grace's aplomb and, above all, her sense of humor. Grace was angry, unquestionably, but she was not shaken, and she certainly didn't lose her wit. On the contrary, in Tracy Lord fashion Grace sweetly finessed the boys on the bus, few of whom suspected, let alone shared, her sense of high jinks. Only gossip writers would fail— in the wake of a published photo sequence manifestly depicting two *inamorata*—to report a line like "just good friends" without seeing the tongue in Grace's cheek.

And she kept it there, too. She told one reporter that although there was no truth to *current* rumors of a romance with Aumont, "There would have been two years ago." That instantly set the press to clucking over the "two-year secret affair" between Grace and the French actor. But anyone who knew Grace well knew that during her time in television she had been deeply in love with Gene Lyons. And of course it was common knowledge whom the next major relationship brought to Grace's side (Cassini). In between, she had been seen at dinner or out on the town with many men—among them Aumont—but at no time had anyone close to Grace, or from afar, pegged her as in love with Aumont. (Aumont, too, placed the really intense period of their relationship at Cannes, not earlier.)

From flippant, Grace turned to flagrant when she and Jean-Pierre hit Paris immediately after the Cannes Festival. They took adjoining suites at the swank Raphael Hotel, well-known oasis of Ingrid Bergman and Greta Garbo among many other glamorous names. They then proceeded to enjoy one another's company in cavalier disregard of the now-hysterical press—sallying forth to the theater and ballet, dining with Jean-Louis Barrault and Madeleine Renaud, attending Patachou's premiere, visiting Saint-Germain-des-Prés and Montmartre, and generally doing what comes naturally in Paris in the spring. And for Grace, that spring, this meant continuing to stick it to the press. She "announced" to a group of reporters that she saw "no obstacles to marrying a Frenchman," adding with furrowed-brow sententiousness, that "Love is not a question of nationality . . . I love France and the way Frenchmen's minds work." This all got reported with poker faces, so that soon newspapers from Liverpool to Kankakee had Kelly and

‡ Mrs. Kelly wrote to that effect in her famous series (see Installment VII, January 21, 1956 in the Los Angeles *Herald-Examiner*). So did biographer Gwen Robyns in her book (*op. cit.*, pp. 106–07).

Aumont, variously, eloping, intending to engage, intending to marry, or simply falling madly in love.

The truth lay nowhere in between. After the painful, drawn-out termination of the fantasy-bound, talky affair with Cassini, Grace at twenty-five simply had a wonderful, passionate fling with an old beau.* Within a fortnight, however, she returned to Hollywood and to her career. After all this crescendo of speculation about a great love, she saw Aumont precisely once in the next year—when he flew to North Carolina for a brief visit while Grace was making *The Swan*. When her mother casually inquired if Monsieur Aumont should be "invited to Philadelphia," Grace—perhaps thinking of the generous reception accorded Cassini—replied, "Mother, dear, that's entirely up to you." (By then, Ma Kelly had been let in on the truth behind all the reportage. Grace had wired her mother from the Raphael a lapidary message: I HAVE LOST NEITHER MY HEART NOR MY HEAD.)

§   §   §

In fairness to Hollywood, it is hard to imagine *any* career that would have bestowed great peace of mind on Grace Kelly in these years. For her, a certain amount of constant discontent was a psychological necessity—a concomitant of the conflict going on in her heart. Grace was impaled on two very fundamental, but contradictory, needs: to defy and to satisfy her parents. The former had led her to the remarkable acts of independence that built a major film career in three years. But the latter endowed her with values, prejudices, sensibilities, and aspirations that stood at cross-purposes with the world in which she created her career. Saddled as she was with unfulfilled theatrical aspirations and a George Kelly down-the-nose-squint at "movieland" on the one hand, and the uninspected belief that family and children were life's *summum bonum* for any serious woman on the other, how was she to find peace of heart as Hollywood's newest celebrity?

What is remarkable is that to some degree, Grace succeeded in evading the traps of "stardom." She managed to create a life apart from movies: in Los Angeles with Rita and Prudy; in New York in her new apartment (her permanent residence in early 1955); and on both coasts, for a brief time, with Oleg. She not only held on to her older friendships during the Hollywood years, she made several important, lasting new ones: Rita Gam, Edith Head, Judy (Mrs. Jay) Kanter, Rupert Allan, Alfred Hitchcock, and Cary Grant, among others.

Grace, finally, was no naïf and no prude, but she *was* an innocent— an innocent armed, but an innocent nevertheless, who met life's chal-

---

* Aumont, for his part, may have come to take things a little seriously toward the end, but it is unlikely. When I asked him if Grace had been "one of the several great loves of your life," he replied, smiling, "No. But it was a very tender friendship."

lenges with an innocent's strengths: hard, self-critical work; self-control and discipline; religious faith; and close friendships. Only in her lethal sense of humor did she perhaps display a measure of worldly sophistication, but even her play tended to lie closer to "fun and games" than to high wit. But underneath the humor and the cool and the daily pleasures she made for herself, the pressure mounted in Grace. The problem was not mainly the life in the goldfish bowl that stars perforce led; Grace wore her public mask as creatively and honestly as it could have been worn by one so young and so mistrustful of the screen actor's career. The problem was that an innocent's strengths, even arduously applied, could not finally render up a believer's fulfillment in an agnostic's land—could not, to paraphrase C. S. Lewis, provide heavenly comforts on earth. Grace drew increasingly profound meaning and fulfillment from her work—indeed, she would not realize just how much until she left it—but that was not enough to satisfy the voices in her conscience and heart. Those voices told her that a life of screen-acting exacted too many sacrifices. They reminded her of the frustration of deeper needs—for a family and for spiritual growth and expression—that was constantly pulling her gaze away from the work at hand, keeping her restless.

Then, too, there was loneliness and the frustration of emotional-sexual need. The failure of the Cassini relationship and the public scandal of her "tender friendship" with Aumont dramatized for Grace the seeming impossibility of carrying off *any* amorous relationship while she was a screen star. This not only threatened to preclude the possibility of a family, but also worried her for what she feared were its ethical consequences. The Cassini relationship and the flings (whatever they amounted to) with Gable, Holden, and Aumont were *not* associations of which she was especially proud. Rita Gam "suspected that Grace was used by some of these men. For them, it was not serious, for her it was. They could not have suffered as desperately, or as silently, as she did."† Gam underestimated how much suffering Grace's men went through on her account (Oleg Cassini, for example, would, in some regards, never get over losing Grace), but Gam is correct that Grace herself suffered deeply from guilt in these years, though she spoke about it to her friends only obliquely.

Grace typified her era and breeding with her romantic idealism. (Cassini called it "phony idealism," yet he developed a case of it vis-à-vis Grace before he was through.) She had a tendency to fall in love with—even momentarily consider marrying—nearly every man she seriously dated. Not to do so would have risked being profligate in her own eyes—a conclusion all the easier to arrive at for a girl raised in a

† Interview with author, July 19, 1983.

world that looked on actresses as, in the final analysis, akin to whores. But the readiness to fall in love led to exaggerated expectations and misplaced emotions, followed by disappointment—and, of course, more guilt.

In addition to idealist, Grace was also a serious, as yet uncritical, Roman Catholic. Cassini contrasted her religiosity with the laissez-faire Catholicism he saw among Europeans. "I know for sure that she went to confession regularly—I sometimes accompanied her to the church—and I believe she was often troubled in her conscience." She couldn't *not* have been. Judy Kanter, perhaps the most reflective of Grace's intimates in that era, expressed it thus, "If one has carefully defined values, as Grace did from the time she was very young, then breaking the rules brings very little pleasure and much remorse and guilt."‡ That Grace "broke the rules" in mind, not act, would have carried little weight in her scrupulous conscience.

In short, by the late fall of 1955, Grace was wrestling with guilt and a good deal more. She was back in her studio's favor, but M.G.M. was not in hers. Its executives continued to try to mold Grace into their kind of star, and she continued to hold on to different aspirations both as an actress and as a person. She hated the Hollywood lifestyle, she was exhausted from shuttling back and forth between there and New York, and she was witnessing what she took to be the collapse of her emotional life. Under the circumstances, it is a wonder she stayed so long in movies.

The failed relationships with Lyons, Cassini, and the others had at least taught Grace some important lessons about what she did want and need in a man. Unknown to her, the right man had already turned up.

‡ Interview with the author, April 14, 1983, Los Angeles.

CHAPTER VI

LETTING GO GRACEFULLY

The art of living is the art of letting go gracefully.
—*George Kelly*, The Fatal Weakness

They met in his gardens, on her second day in Cannes. It was not love at first sight, but, at most, an extremely pleasant publicity encounter. On the train from Paris, Grace had run into Pierre Galante, a journalist with *Paris Match* and husband of Olivia De Havilland, and had promised him to do a photo spread with the Prince of Monaco. Grace didn't feel she could say no; besides, she was eager to see the gardens after her previous visit when shooting *To Catch a Thief.*

It had been a hectic morning before the photo session. She and Galante left Cannes late and then had been delayed en route. They arrived at the Palace a few minutes after the arranged hour, but the Prince was late, too, it turned out. He would be arriving presently, an aide-de-camp said; his personal banner fluttered over the Palace in anticipation. More minutes passed. Grace surreptitiously consulted her watch; she *had* to be back in Cannes by five to preside at a meeting of the American delegation to the Film Festival.

Rainier arrived with a boyish smile and demeanor, terribly sorry to have kept everyone waiting, and artlessly putting them at ease. He spoke to all, seemingly not willing to address Grace directly or even look at her carefully. Would she like to see the Palace, he inquired. She had already been guided through it by his aides, she replied. So the Prince showed them to the gardens. With pride, Rainier led them first to his small zoo—two lions, a few monkeys, and a beautiful Asian tiger given him by the Emperor Bao Dai of Vietnam. As he talked of his beasts, the Prince lost all trace of his earlier shyness or embarrassment; his animation grew. Among the group, only Grace responded wholeheartedly to the Prince's enthusiasm. Within a few moments, it struck Galante that the two of them were lost unto themselves. "We felt like indiscreet onlookers," wrote the journalist years later.* Rainier put his

* *Grace de Monaco* (Paris: Hachette, p. 12).

arm into the tiger's cage and petted the animal, who bared its teeth by
way of gratitude. Grace was deeply impressed at the Prince's ease and
courage with animals. They chatted quietly to themselves as the photographers hurriedly went about their job. In fewer than forty-five
minutes, the session was over; the party took its leave.

On the return trip, Grace was subdued, saying only to Galante, "He
is charming." She added a "very, very" to the "charming" when she
saw Olivia De Havilland at the meeting of the American delegation
(for which Grace was an hour late), and she said the same thing to
Rupert Allan later that evening. Indeed she repeated the same phrase,
with or without the "very's," in a postcard to her mother and to anyone who inquired—including Jean-Pierre Aumont.

And that was all.

§   §   §

*You see, my greatest difficulty is knowing a girl long enough and
intimately enough to find out if we are really soul mates as well as
lovers.*

—Rainier III, Prince of Monaco

Two months later, two of the Kelly family's closest friends, Edith
and Russell Austin—"Aunt Edie" and "Uncle Russ" to the Kelly children—came to the Riviera on vacation. Looking for things to do, they
read in the paper that the Sports Club of Monte Carlo would be holding its first gala of the season on the coming weekend. The Austins
very much wished to attend, but all the tables had been booked for
weeks. Edie idly suggested to her husband that he contact the Prince
and say he was a friend of Grace Kelly's. "Maybe he can help us get a
table." Austin figured he had nothing to lose, so he called the Palace
and left a message to that effect with one of H.S.H.'s secretaries.
Within a few hours, the Russells got a call from a certain Father Francis Tucker, an Oblate priest assigned by the Vatican to be Prince
Rainier's chaplain. He was also his close friend. His Serene Highness
was pleased indeed to welcome friends of Miss Kelly's, the priest told
the Austins. Tickets to a front table at the gala would be brought by
messenger to their hotel that very afternoon. Moreover, if the Austins
found it convenient to do so, H.S.H. would enjoy having them to tea at
the Palace the next day. The Austins replied that it would be *very*
convenient.

The tea itself was a somewhat staged affair, with the Russells talking
nervously about America in general and the Kelly family in particular,
and His Highness listening politely. As they took their leave, Russ
Austin actually urged the Prince of Monaco to "drop round for a visit"

at the Austins in Margate, New Jersey, next time he "happened to be in the U.S."

History, and Russell himself, have credited Austin with a certain audacity in the service of Cupid, but the likelihood is strong that he would not have spoken so forwardly to Rainier if Francis Tucker had not earlier given him the high sign, or indeed encouraged him to invite the Prince to Margate. If there were any ghost in the machine at this time, it was the wily courtier-priest, more Jesuit than Oblate. Tucker, formerly of a Philadelphia parish, had had his Irish eye set on the Catholic Grace for a long time now, deeming her an eminently suitable candidate for his wife-hunting master—"My Lord Prince," as Tucker enjoyed calling Rainier in the old manner. After the garden photo session, where the priest had not been able to be present, he had written to Grace a rather strange note: "I want to thank you for showing the Prince what an American Catholic girl can be and for the very deep impression this has left on him." Whether or not that statement rang entirely true at this time for Rainier, the notedly religious Grace certainly made a "very deep impression" on his chaplain.

Rainier had disclaimed any immediate plans to visit the United States, but four months later, he showed up in New York accompanied by Tucker and his private physician. An official release explained that the Prince of Monaco was in the United States for a routine medical examination at the Johns Hopkins Hospital. Father Tucker, however, had sent word of H.S.H.'s arrival to the Austins. They contacted the Kellys and—in a kind of "Lucy and Ethel" fashion—laid their plans. Rather than the Austins inviting the Prince and Fr. Tucker to dinner, they decided to hold the event chez Kelly in East Falls and on Christmas Eve.

That the Kellys wished for their daughter to be settled down, preferably out of the picture business, with a husband and children was very old news by late 1955. The alarm built into Margaret Kelly's gyroscope sounded nearly every time Grace was reported dating a new man. Her husband had dropped so many quotes along the lines of—"I'd like to see Grace married; these people in Hollywood think marriage is like a game of musical chairs"†—that only tyro reporters printed them anymore. Lizanne Kelly had finally got permission to marry the nice Jewish boy, which she did in June, leaving only Grace unwed among the girls. All teary-eyed at her sister's wedding, Grace had asked her mother when she thought she would meet the right fellow, to which Mrs. Kelly replied, "Honey, your prince charming will come along."

† Even "Kell bel" got in his two cents in *Time*'s cover story on his sister: "I generally don't approve of these oddballs she goes out with. I wish she would go out with the more athletic type. But she doesn't listen to me anymore" (January 31, 1955).

Now that there loomed the slightest chance that a real prince was in the offing, the Kellys were leaving nothing to chance.

Grace, for her part, knew nothing of the plots going on behind her back. Throughout the fall she was absent from Hollywood and New York, on location in North Carolina, shooting *The Swan*. Rupert Allan contacted her there in December to say that *Look* wanted to take some photographs of her and Rainier as part of a feature the magazine was doing on "the bachelor Prince." *(Look* had already won Rainier's assistance in the profile. When contacted by the editors, the Prince said he would be visiting the United States in the fall and added that he would like to visit Miss Kelly on the set of her next picture. He alluded to the *Paris Match* piece and suggested *Look* might like to take its own pictures of him and Grace.) Grace said she wouldn't mind in the least, but added when she saw Rupert smile, "If you think there's some romance going on, you're wrong. I haven't heard one word from him."

In any case, the Prince did not get to North Carolina before the M.G.M. expeditionary force left. Grace completed *The Swan* in Los Angeles. Shooting ran over schedule, and Grace was so frenzied to make it home for Christmas that faithful Rupert came over to help her pack. "We drank champagne splits," Allan remembered, "and chased Oliver [Grace's dog] who had her gloves in his mouth, and she left the next day. Not a word was said about Rainier because there was simply no reason to. She hadn't a thought about him." Grace left next morning for New York. She spent one day seeing her old pals, Judy and Jay Kanter, and Natty (Natalie) Core, then she left for Philadelphia. She arrived, innocently, at 3901 Henry Avenue on the day before Christmas Eve.

Three days later, Judy Kanter received a call from Grace. "Judybird, could you come round tomorrow at noon for lunch? I'm having breakfast with John (Foreman), but I want to see you separately. I have something to tell you both." Judy couldn't bear the wait and "shrieked" at Grace, "You've just *got* to give me a clue." So Grace did. And Judy Kanter was "shocked." Her husband, when he found out, was "absolutely astounded."

Approximately the same day, Natty Core got a call at her New York apartment. Grace asked her to drop by; she had "something to tell you." An hour later, Natty Core was "startled."

Three days later, Rupert Allan, who had been on a rather remote assignment for *Look* in Colorado, was driving back to L.A. and he happened to hear on the radio the news about Grace. He was "flabbergasted."

Grace Kelly was engaged to His Serene Highness, Prince Rainier III of Monaco.

What had happened?

§   §   §

*For my money, he's a real man. Not one of those milksops you gener-
ally take up with.*

> —*Mrs. Stevens to her daughter,
> Frances, in* To Catch a
> Thief

Yes, I knew Mother liked him, for she said so.
> —*George Kelly,* Craig's Wife

The Prince, Fr. Tucker, and Rainier's private physician, Dr. Donat, arrived as planned for Christmas Eve dinner. Grace had had one day's warning. She was nervous but far from unhappy at the prospect of seeing Rainier again. While the guests talked convivially and laughed at Fr. Tucker's wit, Grace and Rainier gradually drifted off by themselves in conversation, much as they had done in the Palace gardens in Monaco. After dinner, sister Peggy suggested that the "young people" come over to her house to continue the party. At the same time, Fr. Tucker asked to be taken to the rectory of a local parish where he was spending the night with a priest friend. Rainier was clearly reluctant to leave, so John Kelly, Sr., eagerly offered to drive Fr. Tucker. Grace and Rainier went to Peggy's.

When John Kelly returned, he told his wife with considerable pleasure that Fr. Tucker had said that the Prince wished to marry Grace. So that was it. The best-laid plans of Russells, Tucker, and Kellys had succeeded as far as they could. Now it all hung on what was going on between the principals.

At Peggy's, the actress and the Prince stayed apart from the others as best they could without being rude. (Grace joined her sister in a mock fashion show of old hats.) At 3 A.M., they returned to the Kellys. It seemed clear to Mrs. Kelly that the Prince wished to stay over, so she invited him and Dr. Donat to take the guest rooms. Rainier instantly accepted. Grace later drifted into her mother's room, looking radiant. Margaret, who just *had* to know what was going on, asked Grace what she thought of the Prince. "She hesitated, as though she did not want to reveal the full extent of what was going on inside her. 'Well, I think he's most attractive in every way.' Then she added, 'Yes, I think he's very nice.' "‡

All the next day, the Prince and Grace, though never alone, stayed largely to themselves. They were obliged to part for the evening, as Grace had a dinner date (with Philadelphia friends) that she'd made

‡ "My Daughter, Grace Kelly—Her Life and Romances," Installment VIII.

before she knew of Rainier's visit. The Prince returned to nearby Wilmington, Delaware, where he stayed with Donat and Tucker. But the third day, he returned to Philadelphia and spent the entire day with Grace. By dinner time, nothing was announced, yet everything seemed to have been decided. When the Prince went back to Wilmington for the night, Grace sat down with her parents, holding her mother's hand, and talked about Rainier. From her daughter's rush of emotion, Margaret Kelly "knew that she was going to accept him if he asked her."

Grace and her Prince spent the next several days together in Philadelphia, then New York, going to parties, seeing her friends, and mostly talking. On the twenty-ninth, five days after she had met him for the second time, she called her mother to say she was "very much in love." With that, the Kellys called Fr. Tucker to tell him the news. He smilingly told them that Rainier had already called to say the same thing. The priest and the parents met for dinner on the thirtieth at the Austins in Margate. There, Tucker formally notified them that his "Lord Prince" wished to marry their daughter. Margaret Kelly could hardly contain her excitement. The three discussed a great many related topics—Rainier's parents' reaction; Grace's future as consort of a sovereign; and so on. Then Jack Kelly gave his "consent," contingent of course, he noted, on his daughter's.

It soon became consecrated "truth" that, in John Kelly's portentous words to Fr. Tucker, "a title does not impress us. The only thing my wife and I are interested in is the happiness of our daughter." However "sincere" the Irish democrat in John Kelly may have thought he was being when he said that, his wife hit the reality of things a lot closer whack when she bubbled to journalists, "Imagine, the daughter of a bricklayer is going to marry a *prince!*" Ma Kelly had originally thought the sovereign in question was the Prince of Morocco, and had had to be told where and what Monaco was, but thereafter, her joy knew few bounds. A close family friend of the Kellys told a journalist a few months after, "During those hectic days in December and January, when the Kellys were entertaining Rainier, I sometimes got the feeling that Mrs. Kelly was more excited about the Prince than Grace was." The truth was that John, and especially Margaret, Kelly were immensely impressed with Rainier's innumerable titles, his glorified social status, and (far from least) his wealth. "The happiness of our daughter" mattered deeply to Jack and Margaret Kelly—but largely as *they*, not Grace, defined it.

The official version carried in the press (and in the Prince's authorized biography) maintained that the Prince asked the actress to be his wife on New Year's Eve at a private party. But from Grace's talks with her closest friends, it seems certain that he had posed, and she answered, his Question closer to the twenty-eighth, if not even earlier. Rumors, of course, had been wafting through the media since Grace and Rainier appeared together in New York (on the twenty-seventh). On the fourth of January, they went out on the town *en couple* with Malcolm and Carolyn (Scott) Reybold and John and Sally (Parrish) Richardson, ending up at the Stork Club. Their appearance instantly raised press speculation from a breeze to a cyclone. (The Broadway reporter of the New York *Journal-American,* Jack O'Brian, was present at the Stork Club and sent Grace a note, reading: "Dear Grace, I understand you will announce your engagement on Thursday or Friday." Below this he had drawn two boxes, labeled "yes" and "no," together with the instructions, "Answer one, please." Grace showed the note to her friends, including Rainier, then walked over to O'Brian and said hello. He asked if congratulations were in order. She replied that she couldn't answer his note "tonight." He begged to know if she could answer it Friday. Smiling, she whimsically chose to be frank: "Yes, Friday." The media took this as advance confirmation.)

On the fifth, the official announcement was made simultaneously in Philadelphia, at a country club luncheon for major Pennsylvania political dignitaries (but no movie people), and in Monaco, where excitement ran even higher than in New York or Hollywood society. At the Philadelphia Country Club, Grace and Rainier cooperated good-naturedly while batteries of photographers took their pictures. The Prince seemed far shyer than his fiancée, who sat beaming, wearing a twelve-carat solitaire diamond ring that the Prince had given her for the engagement. Later, scores of journalists followed the Kellys et al. home to Henry Avenue where Margaret made the mistake of admitting them in the front door. They climbed over the furniture, spilled over into bedrooms, descended on the neighbors, and generally provided a discomfiting foretaste of what the family would be in for in the next few months.

One reporter asked Grace an extremely forthright, if utterly apt, question: was this, he wanted to know, an arranged marriage, or, to employ the French term, an *alliance de convenance?*

The question merits serious attention. Did Grace Kelly marry for love?

§   §   §

By the end of 1955, the pressure on Grace as an unwed female, and a movie star to boot, was staggering. Being a bachelor posed far less of a problem in Hollywood than being a single woman. In a community oriented to couples, with so many eligible women, single men were in great demand. The position of the unmarried female, however, was, in a word "desperate.""* This held true, if differently, for a movie star like Grace. She had suitors aplenty, but with them came the stifling pressure of speculation and gossip.

The alternative for nearly all stars was to throw themselves into their work while maintaining an active "dating" life, maybe even marrying every so often (à la Taylor and Monroe), and damn the critics. For Grace, this was unthinkable; the only thing thinkable was settling down. Judy Kanter, who saw a lot of Grace at this time, summed it up thus: "As totally dedicated as she was to her work, and increasingly proud of her achievement in it, and as busy and full as her life seemed to be, and as many friends as she had, and options she could have chosen, I don't think any of us doubted for a moment that what she *really wanted* to do was marry, have a family, and settle down. And it was also absolutely clear, especially as time wore on, that she wasn't going to sail along for fifteen or so years before she did it."† Such words well capture Grace's mind-set at the conclusion of the Cassini affair. Grace herself told a *Collier's* interviewer, who was searching for the "key to Kelly," "I'd love to get married and have children." She then declined further comment, explaining, "If you want a thing badly, you mustn't talk about it. It's the sure way to lose."‡

Grace's greatest problem by far was not gossip or workload but finding an eligible man. The history of her romances and "tender friendships" before Rainier is the history of failed attempts, often a prelude to a successful marriage. A young girl, momentarily awash in emotion, Grace may have fantasized or even talked marriage with a number of men, from Lyons to Aumont. But only Grace would have known how *truly* intent she was on actually marrying anyone before Rainier. We have only external evidence with which to glimpse (poorly) a profoundly inner, mysterious process.

A careful weighing of the record of Grace's actions and her close friends' later judgments show that only Gene Lyons and Oleg Cassini ever got serious mention as marriage candidates. Yet even here the disclaimers and likelihoods (retrospectively constructed, to be sure) are too many to conclude that, parental disapproval waived, she would probably have married either man. On the contrary, she would probably have not.

The early months with Lyons were clearly a passionate affair for

* See Cynthia Hobart Lindsay's fine socio-psychological discussion of "The Social Behavior of the Human Male and Female—in Hollywood" (*Holiday*, May 1954). She writes, "The dearth of men in a community of beautiful women is its major social tragedy. Mike Romanoff once looked around his famous restaurant and said, 'The Cinema Colony is filled with single women who have reached that desperate age when their voices are changing from no to yes.' " (p. 48.)
† Interview with author, April 14, 1983.
‡ Evelyn Harvey, "The Key to Kelly" (June 24, 1955).

Grace. But the actress was all of twenty-two and twenty-three at the time, and soon into their relationship, Lyons began to slip back into serious alcoholism. However hard Grace strove to help him and to succor the relationship, and however worried the overanxious Margaret Kelly became on this account, it is inconceivable Grace would have married such a shadow as Lyons soon became. Reminiscent in many ways of the character Frank Elgin from *The Country Girl*, Lyons never shared with Grace the strong, happy years that Georgie Elgin enjoyed with her husband and which gave her reason for hope, hence the will to stick it out.

As for Cassini, it is hard not to conclude that this relationship was inherently doomed by its very terms of definition. A profound, but brief encounter (on location in the Riviera), based on Oleg's mad pursuit and his entrancing "game," the relationship was a study in fantasy, style, and surface. On retrospect, it seems to have consisted of Oleg's holding up a mirror to Grace and, for a time at least, entrapping her with her own vanity. Cassini's perception of the exterior and style of Grace, the dazzling young movie queen, is coruscating and accurate, but amounts to a photographer's depiction rather than a portraitist's. It ignores the actress's interior, which Oleg never seems to have been concerned with, let alone explored or cultivated.

If their relationship endured beyond that phase, it did so mainly because for Grace, Oleg took on symbolic value in her quiet struggle against her parents' attempts to control her life. But the living heart of the relationship appears to have expired far earlier than the corpse stopped twitching. Not one of Grace's closest friends in this era believed she would actually wed Cassini, though the newspapers (and Margaret Kelly) said otherwise. But Rita, Natty, Judy, and others saw how comparatively little respect or concern Grace seemed to bestow on Oleg after the initial part of the affair was over. Thereafter, he seemed to Grace's friends to be her adoring puppy who followed her from place to place in obedience to her postcard message ("Those who love me, follow me"). This "command" notwithstanding, the surest way to lose Grace's respect was literally to heed that narcissistic message. Given Oleg's wild chase after his aesthetic dream, he could not have done other.

Grace emerged from these (and the smaller) relationships sad, lonely, and guilty. But she seems to have pondered her failures and learned from them—not only about love, but about what she required in a marriage partner. The greatest lesson she learned was the common but vital one that loving a man was only one element of a successful relationship—necessary, but far, far from sufficient. Grace loved readily, as is often the case with people who have been loved abundantly. She respected rather more stringently. The man whom Grace would marry must be more things than "lovable." He must, first and foremost, be a man of sufficient inner strength to withstand the pressure of being married to a movie star, even an ex-movie star, and not be dwarfed, awed, emasculated or diversely overwhelmed by this fact. He would be a man of substantial personal authority and will, though neither authoritarian nor willful. Given the circles in which Grace traveled, he would probably, therefore, be a man of significant accomplishment and/or position, and very likely of wealth. He must also be a man of religious beliefs, ideally a Roman Catholic who practiced the faith. Relatedly, he must be someone committed to having a family, who accorded childraising an extremely high priority in his life.

Such a checklist, of course, provides only the roughest approximation of qualities, rapports, and circumstances that could "work out" or not, depending on a virtually infinite number of contingencies. The one thing Grace would *have* to find in a husband was a man anchored in her own tradition of faith and morals and committed to Christian ideals—beginning with the family, of course, but not ending there.

In the latter part of 1955, Grace was far riper for the picking than she or her close friends recognized, mainly because she was so absorbed by her work. But work, as we have seen, meant less to her than other priorities. As the year waned, she yearned not so much for rescue as for fulfillment.

The Grimaldi prince, for his part, may have yearned for rescue— from matchmakers. Rainier was *not* frantic to find a bride—as the press universally reported or posterity has imagined him. Indeed, he thought himself, at thirty-two, young enough to enjoy the bachelor life and trust to providence to find him a bride. Nevertheless, few around him, even among his acquaintances, could resist the temptation to play go-between. "Everybody was trying to marry me off . . . It was hard for me to go anywhere in company, even to invite anyone to my home." Matchmakers sprang up at every turn to introduce him to "this young lady I just know you're going to adore as much as we do."

In fact, the Prince was not keen to fall in love too soon again, having just recovered from the painful end of the long-term affair with a French actress. He had loved Gisèle Pascal deeply—perhaps even contemplated abdication for her—but had ultimately chosen duty and had broken off a relationship with a woman who could not bear children. In the years since their separation, Rainier found it difficult to get used to living as the object of constant gossip, speculation, and other people's marital schemes for him. (The most incredible of which surely must have been *Look* publisher Gardner Cowles's plot to land Marilyn

Monroe as Rainier's bride. The sordid "plan," of course, accomplished nothing except to disgust the Prince.)*

Romantic myth, prompted by "the Cupid priest" (Francis Tucker), has it that Rainier was smitten with Grace the first time he met her. It would be far closer to the truth to say he was impressed with her—her calm, her articulateness, her sweetness of disposition, all of which diverged from the image he had of her from the press and the movies. On later hearing about Grace, Fr. Tucker (who knew Philadelphia and knew of the Kellys) was quite taken with what he presumed to be Grace's suitability for his "most Catholic Lord Prince," but the Oblate was still fairly new to Monaco, and though he and Rainier would develop a good friendship, the priest had no license whatever to make marital inquiries on the Prince's behalf. In sum, when Grace and her small retinue took their hurried leave of Rainier and his Sumatra tiger, she left a man slightly more charmed than she herself had been— enough that he would encourage the *Look* European editor to arrange another photo session that would bring him together with Grace, but not enough to do anything about it when schedules changed and the session had to be canceled. Had the Austins not contacted the Palace in September, and had Tucker not been on hand when they did to rekindle Rainier's flame, there would have been no issue to the original meeting.

It would be interesting to know what transpired between Grace and Rainier when they met for the second time on Christmas Eve of 1955. In his authorized biography, the Prince—far from self-revealing at best —elides the whole topic of what took place between him and Grace as they got to know each other at the Christmas Eve dinner and after: "Naturally I enjoyed talking to Grace Kelly—we had a laugh remembering our earlier acquaintance—and this, I think, was where some understanding developed between us . . . From this situation, I suppose events moved quickly—only it didn't seem like it at the time . . . [Proposing] wasn't a sudden thought—I think we were both ready for marriage." These words (published in 1966) led people to assume that Rainier, at least, entered the match as an act of reason.

The fallacy of concluding that his proposal was purely, or mainly, calculated came from inducing inner feelings from public presentation. In addition to being an intensely, almost fanatically, private man, Rainier III was the titular and functioning chief of state of a very old European principality where (as Grace would soon discover to her dismay) the most finical formalities of address and style were observed. More than any movie star was he obliged to wear a public mask of

* Interview with Prince Rainier, September 12, 1983. Subsequent quotes are from this interview unless otherwise indicated. For details on the Monroe scheme see Robyns, *op. cit.*, pp. 134–36.

sobriety and judiciousness. Then, too, Rainier at that time was not the sort of man to admit to himself, let alone reporters, a "weakness" like love. In my interview with him in 1983, Rainier was more revealing. "It's very hard to explain," he said, "but it was something we both felt intensely. We knew we could make our lives together, and that now was the time to do it. We weren't children. We had both been through hard experiences and had learned from them what we were really looking for in marriage. That's what decided us to go ahead. It wasn't irrational, it was very thought out, but it was also very romantic. I realize it shocked people. That's probably why there was so much speculation it wouldn't last. Well, it did."

Those who saw Rainier during those extraordinary days after Christmas—including Donat and Tucker in his own suite and many of Grace's friends—attested at the time to the applicability of the word "romantic." They remarked on the look in his eye, and the quiet rapture of his smile for his bride-to-be. He loved. But he had come to the understanding, as Grace had, that love was not reason enough for marriage. Rainier personally wanted a woman who was beautiful, intelligent, of good humor, and with character, but if that were sufficient, he would have married Gisèle Pascal. The pain of ending that relationship annealed Rainier's identity as Prince. He intended to marry a woman he loved, but also one who also possessed the qualities to make an apt consort for a sovereign. She would have to be (or become) Catholic, be able to bear children, and generally possess, to some degree at least, the abilities to do the work of a Princess.

Thus, their agendas—reflecting their discrete experiences and needs—were only similar, not identical. Grace still hoped she might continue to work in her profession, although she wished to devote herself mainly to what they both hoped would be a sizable family. As will shortly become clear, Rainier knew from the outset that his wife could not remain an actress. He may have regretted this necessity (he certainly disliked appearing to be the "heavy" in the eyes of the American public and M.G.M.), but he accepted it. Grace would have a harder time doing so.

Even about a family, however, the couple was not at one in their intentions. In the most perceptive article done on Grace Kelly the actress, based on extensive talks with his subject, Maurice Zolotow wrote, "What is it that [she] . . . is seeking from marriage? I believe it is love, companionship and children. Up to now she has been deprived of emotional fulfillment. As an artist she has known tremendous success. As a woman, she has had moments of romance, has been courted and kissed—but she has not known complete happiness."† Grace was

† *American Weekly*, April 29, 1956.

investing her entire career in a new, and for many people, far less wonderful undertaking than making movies. She was going to devote herself completely to her husband and children. She innocently expected her husband to do the same. She would have many lessons to learn. As much as he loved his wife, Rainier "belonged" to himself or his wife and children less wholly than Grace belonged. He was, first and foremost, a ruler, and only next a private citizen. Grace at twenty-six simply had no way of understanding what that meant. She knew family duty, to be sure, from her youth on Henry Avenue, but duty in that context was a relatively simple and external constraint compared to the powerful concept that Rainier naturally understood and would eventually need his wife to understand, too.

§   §   §

I've been in love before—but never in love like this before.
—Grace Kelly

It would be hard to overstate the stupefaction with which the news of Grace's engagement was received by her friends, who had had even less warning than Grace herself of what lay in the offing. Although nobody, not even Hedda Hopper, failed to wish Grace and Rainier well, more than a few commentators opined that the alliance was a "marriage of state"—Most forcefully, Oleg Cassini.

"Grace Kelly," he said, "played the game absolutely by the book. Brought up very strictly in an atmosphere of brutal competition and an ethic of success, she learned from the start to live by the rules of appearance—socially, religiously, professionally. She was an establishment person through and through."‡ Cassini granted that Grace made "little thrusts of independence"—else he couldn't explain her stubborn devotion to their own relationship in the face of implacable parental disapproval—but finally these "thrusts" proved to be recessive, not dominant. "She came out of a milieu very similar to that of the Kennedys in Boston," he said. "Like them, the Kellys saw the world as the enemy." Imbued with an immigrant psychology, the whole focus of life for the Kellys was to impose the family socially, financially, professionally on an alien world. Every event in an individual's life was family-centered, said Cassini, *"only* the family was to be trusted—along with a few proven friends, retainers, and camp followers who were judged by their blind loyalty." The family was a thoroughgoing patriarchy; sons were preferred to daughters, but all children were regarded as potential sources of family advancement, in Cassini's view. It

‡ This and subsequent quotes are from an interview with Cassini in New York on April 28, 1983.

took Jack Kelly a comparatively long time to recognize Grace's worth to the family—the patriarch had a very East Coast definition of value that was fixated on education, athletic accomplishment, and elite business and society ties—but once he did so, Grace's life was even less her own than it might have been.

Marriage was regarded as a crucial means for family advancement via their daughters. Cassini believed that the senior Kellys saw marriage as social alliances that had to be very carefully assessed. "For Grace to have married a matinee idol or a clothes designer would have done no good at all," he said. On the battlefronts where the Kellys were engaged, Hollywood counted for little or nothing. Indeed, Grace's stardom was a dubious asset. Of itself, it did nothing to further the Kellys in their climb up the ladder toward parity with the Biddles or the Cadwaladers. But it might prove useful in landing her a good match.

At first, Rainier was mysterious to the Kellys, surmised Cassini, but once John Kelly had inquired of the man's fortune and standing, the Prince swiftly came to be seen as very definitely "a good match." "For all the obvious reasons," said Cassini, "Rainier brought the highest prestige that was religious as well as social and financial". Princes of Monaco are *Catholic* princes, closely associated with the Vatican. The Kellys stood to gain on all fronts. All that remained was to secure Grace's cooperation, and that was a foregone conclusion once she had separated from Oleg—an event, in Cassini's opinion, that amounted to *the* critical loss in her battle for independence. Thereafter, she returned to being a dutiful daughter, available for her parents' schemes and to fulfill their hopes.

If this view seems extreme, lacking in charity and reeking of sour grapes, one must consider that no one less than Peggy and Lizanne came to essentially the same conclusions as Cassini concerning the engagement (if not his characterizations of their family): "It was never a fairy-tale romance," said Peggy. "It was just a very nice agreement," said Lizanne.*

But as little as Hollywood understood Grace, still less did her family or her ex-lover, in this regard at least. Their conclusions about the engagement have all the merits of plausibility except truth. Cassini's analysis of Kelly family psychology is extreme but accurate. Nevertheless, it misses the point about Grace. Grace was no rebel, but still less did she intend to live out her life in the shade of the family tree, conforming to all of the family's values and expectations. "Little

---

* Quoted in Stephen Birmingham, *op. cit.* Based on interviews with the sisters, Birmingham concludes: "A 'nice agreement' may not sound much like love, but it was what Grace Kelly wanted . . . Love, in time, might come later." (Stephen Birmingham, "Princess Grace: The Facts Behind the Fairy Tale", *TV Guide*, February 5–11, 1983, p. 6.)

thrusts of independence" is an impotent euphemism to denote the personal qualities of endurance and self-reliance with which Grace moved out of the family at age eighteen and turned herself into a fine and immensely successful actress eight years later. "Little thrusts" would not have sufficed to escape the gravitational pull of East Falls.

To some extent, the Cassini and Peggy-Lizanne viewpoints said more about their espousers than about Grace. They made the mistake of confusing the admittedly absorbing, eye-catching circumstances and the externalities of the brief courtship for the substance of feeling between Grace and Rainier. Seeing in the principals *only* two exceedingly careful planners, and judging by projection of their own values, Peggy, Lizanne, and Oleg, among many others, missed other essential facets. The underlying truth was that beneath the social advantages of their match (of which Grace and Rainier were perfectly aware), theirs was an engagement of youthful passion and love, *as well as* of other elements. It was also the engagement of two shy adepts, both long accustomed to shielding their emotions behind masks. The inner Grace, who chose her closest friends mainly for their qualities of trust, warmth, playfulness, and goodheartedness, who had given her heart already to more than one man, and who hated Hollywood largely because it judged everything and everyone by surface facets, would not have entered into "a marriage of convenience" anymore than she would have married *simply*, on impulse. Grace was an exceptionally responsive person; it was by no means out of character for her to fall deeply in love, and very quickly. She was also exceptionally responsible and self-shielding. Once she had decided to wed, the engagement would be presented to the world in the world's terms.

That is not how she presented it to her intimates. She didn't tell them "I've decided to marry the Prince of Monaco"; she burbled: "I'm in love with a wonderful man." It wasn't a social climber, nor even a rebel in the Kelly midst, but a blissfully happy, radiant girl who reached "Judy-Bird" and Jay, and John (Foreman) and Natty and Rupert and Rita (among others) to give them "the wonderful news." Neither in implication or word did Grace ever describe her engagement as "a very nice agreement." The Kellys saw it thus; for them, Grace was rescued from an actor's fate by a "good marriage," and the family now claimed a Prince with two dozen titles. But Grace saw it differently and with good reason.

And you know, I think it might be a very smart move on your part—
if you were just to let the public remember you as a great actress. I
mean to vanish, as the poet says, right in the heyday of your glow.
　　　　　　　　　　　　—*George Kelly*, The Torch-Bearers

The shock waves generated by the announcement of the engagement hit Hollywood hardest. Grace of course had had no chance of keeping M.G.M. well briefed on her news. The studio's publicity department galvanized itself quickly, however, and though it wasn't able to halt the stampede on Henry Avenue, thereafter Morgan Hudgins and several associates stepped into the breach. Having been more ill-served than well by professional publicists, harassed Grace finally got some protection. Over the next several months, M.G.M. brought its entire weight and finesse to bear on seeing to it their best-known star got good press. Internal studio documents fascinatingly record the various ways its flacks could pressure or cajole journalists into serving M.G.M. ends. Interviews with Grace herself, or with other stars, were given only if writers promised to show copy in advance and permit corrections. Maurice Zolotow, for example, (who was cooked dinner by Grace at her home) appears to have agreed to delete Grace's measurements as well as references to her disagreements with her mother despite the fact that much of Zolotow's "thesis" focuses on Grace's divergence from her family. Even his throwaway thumbnail sketch of Nadia Woods, an acquaintance of Grace's, as "a dazzling little brunette number" had to go because the studio, at Grace's behest, found it offensive.

Mrs. Kelly Sr.'s articles on her daughter's "romances" were, of course, a nightmare for Grace and for M.G.M. They could do nothing about the American publication of the ten-part series, but they got the French press to rewrite objectionable portions as well as reduce the overall length of the pieces. At Grace's furious insistence, Ma Kelly started claiming that the long article was "rushed out of her" by the editors, adding she hadn't had time to check it carefully, hence that it contained innumerable errors. (The errors were indeed there, but not because the editors or co-writer misunderstood Mrs. Kelly, but because, as Grace knew all too well, her mother hadn't always known what was going on.)†

Good press, or not, it was just too much press, and often it pried too deeply. Innocent remarks, quoted in and out of context, but never spoken with publication in mind, haunted everybody close to the betrothed. The problem was, nobody but Grace, and not even she, had any experience with *this* intensity of news coverage. Kell, for example, sounded either fractious or noodle-brained when *Time* quoted him to the effect that "I don't think we can make a sculler out of [Rainier].

---

† Other times, whole features were conceived by Strickling or Hudgins who then "placed" them with favored magazines and writers, e.g., The *Ladies' Home Journal* piece which interviewed many of Grace's male co-leads was set up by Metro. Occasionally, a journalist was "disciplined." A certain Bill Tusher of the scandal sheet *Parade* was threatened with being barred from the Metro lot for a piece entitled "The Skeletons in Grace Kelly's Closet."

He's not tall enough. But I hear he's a terrific skin diver." His father, meanwhile, was assuring everyone who took notes how utterly unimpressed he and the family were by "royalty," whereas the Prince's wealth was a subject of great interest. ("I asked him for a rundown on his finances. When he got to one million dollars, I stopped him.") Kelly Sr. was even quoted giving some of the most obtuse paternal "advice" any future son-in-law ever had to publicly endure: "I told him that I certainly hoped he wouldn't run around the way some princes do, and I told him if he did, he'd lose a mighty fine girl." Margaret Kelly just told people she called him "Rai."‡

There were deeper problems than these that the overextensive coverage aggravated. For one thing, Rainier was not at all accustomed to the time and courtesy that American notables automatically granted to the press. In Morgan Hudgins's eyes, the Prince badly needed "a lesson in public relations," for he tended to grow impatient *way* too quickly. (At the press conference in the Kelly home, while all about him were still enjoying the melee, he grew restless and growled in a stage whisper to Tucker, "After all, *I* don't belong to M.G.M.") In subsequent weeks—from the Night in Monte Carlo Ball to numerous semipublic appearances at restaurants and coming and going to parties —Rainier's temper flared often, while even his princely manner seemed imperious to American reporters.

And not just to reporters, but to the Kelly family as well. For example, when the question of the site of the forthcoming wedding arose, the Kellys assumed they would organize it in Philadelphia. The Prince, however, early on implied it might have to take place in Monaco. At the time of Grace's return to Los Angeles to complete *High Society* (mid-January), the venue was still in doubt. The Kellys, longing to hold it at St. Bridget's Church where Grace had received first communion, simply went ahead and made the mistake of announcing these plans before they had checked it out with Grace and their future son-in-law. Unfortunately, the Kellys' all-American expectation failed to consider the exigencies of Monégasque pride and princely politics. Rainier had by now been in touch with his government and realized that the wedding must be held in the Principality. Within a day of Mr. and Mrs. Kelly's "happy announcement," Rainier's *chef de cabinet* and his Minister of State "informed" the press that the wedding would take place in the Principality's Cathedral of St. Nicholas (where previous Monégasque sovereigns had been married).

‡ Inanities were by no means the monopoly of the Kellys. Someone as presumably savvy with handouts as Jimmy Stewart was quoted all over for saying, "If she had married one of those phony Hollywood characters, I'd have formed a committee of vigilantes . . . I'd slit my throat if Grace ever did anything *not* like herself." (Parton, *Ladies' Home Journal*, March 1956.)

Margaret Kelly mounted a stiff rearguard action. "Nothing is de-cided," she told a reporter tartly. She and John offered a compromise: why not split up the event, holding the nuptial mass at St. Bridget's; the civil ceremony in Monaco? Rainier, now reminded of political *force majeure*, made it clear that this too, was unacceptable. Grace, caught in between, but sensing necessity's drift, said, "It doesn't make any differ-ence [where the wedding takes place]." Margaret and John graciously capitulated.

A far more major cleavage separated Rainier, Tucker, and Dr. Donat from 175 million Americans (minus the Kellys): the matter of Grace's future as an actress. But for the intensity of coverage, the issue might have got resolved gradually, naturally, by Grace and Rainier, as it should have been. Instead, the constant hammering of reporters' ques-tions presently elicited answers from several parties—answers that di-verged sharply. Here, M.G.M. publicity was of no help handling the press, for the studio itself was very much partisan.

In mid-January, Grace returned alone to Los Angeles to go back to work. She had other things to think about—notably, acting. She was facing the biggest part of her career—Tracy Lord in *High Society.**
Whether slyly or innocently, M.G.M. released statements noting that Grace Kelly had four years left in her contract; her next film, after her wedding, would be *Designing Woman*—a movie about the life of fashion designer Helen Rose, that would star, besides Grace, Jimmy Stewart and Cyd Charisse. At about the same time, Alfred Hitchcock was quoted by the *Journal-American* in some, for him, astonishingly doltish remarks. He was "very happy," he said, that Grace had "got such a good part [as Princess of Monaco], but all this talk about her retiring is a lot of nonsense." It was also reported that "Hollywoodites" were laying ten-to-one odds "that her future highness never will give up her exciting movie career to be a housewife." (The writer had obviously not seen the house.)

Grace's own words could be seen as vacillating. On the one hand, she told Los Angeles *Times* reporter Edwin Schallert on January 22, that she wished to take a long vacation from acting, adding that she was much less interested in her career now than prior to her engage-ment. On the other hand, she stated flatly that she would make at least one film after her wedding *(Designing Woman)*. Weighing the evidence,

---

* A wealthy socialite, Tracy was supposed to wear a fancy engagement ring. The first day on the set, Grace politely asked director Chuck Walters if she could wear her own engagement ring. Facetiously, Walters asked to inspect it first. In Celeste Holm's words, "Grace brought in the next day a diamond as big as a skating rink—deep, brilliant, colorful." Pleased, but a little embarrassed at the fuss it caused, Grace said, "It is sweet, isn't it?" That was her "downfall," said Holm. "There were shrieks of laughter on the set and, till the end of shooting, Grace was teased about her 'sweet' diamond ring." Inter-view, July 20, 1983, New York.

Schallert concluded it was fairly clear that Grace "will retire from filmmaking as soon as feasible." Other journalists concluded differently, however. Based on answers Grace gave at a Chicago press conference in mid-January, *Sun-Times* reporter-columnist Irv Kupcinet believed the actress would continue to act.

It is unlikely that remarks like those to Schallert or Kupcinet indicated any profound psychological ambivalence in Grace about quitting her profession. At the time she strongly believed she wished to throw herself into marriage and child-raising. But she was aware that formal retirement was a very great step to take and she wished to discuss it with Rainier in tranquility after their marriage. The Prince, however, had his mind made up now and wanted the word out—particularly as the American press badgered him on the subject. He was not sensitive to Grace's concerns not to stun her millions of fans nor to renege on contractual obligations she believed she might still have with Metro. Grace at this point thought she might be permitted to wind down her career gradually. Depending on mood or moment, she sometimes (as with Schallert) focused on the winding down, while at other times (as with Kupcinet) emphasized the gradualness of her retirement by discussing her "next film" or noting that "I am sure there are many affairs and obligations in Monaco that will fall to me." The press dependably wondered aloud if this "shilly-shallying" pointed to "predomestic discord among the lovers."

Even so, nothing might have badly disturbed the waters if Rainier hadn't acted like a prince. Statements referring to Grace's "role" as Princess of Monaco (or, worse, "Princess of Graustark") raised his hackles. He had only recently become aware of the reservoir of ignorance, and, worse, derision, that existed in the United States about Monaco. To the Prince's European way of thinking, if anything were liable to tongue-in-cheek facetiousness, it was movies, not Monaco. Americans credited the movie world altogether excessively, he felt. Unfortunately, he chose to say these things bluntly rather than lightly. Having joined his fiancée in Los Angeles on January 25 (he took a rented house in Bel Air; Grace lived in similar circumstances not far away), Rainier gave an impromptu press conference, without benefit of Morgan Hudgins or anyone else from the Metro publicity department. Marriage, he stated, would mean the end of Grace's career, full stop.

Far from bringing the debate to a full stop, however, as Rainier intended, his words only fueled more speculation about "predomestic discord." Irv Kupcinet, for one, whipped off a P&C (personal and confidential) telegram to Metro wondering, "Doesn't Prince Rainier's statement conflict with her own feelings and Metro's contract?" Most other journalists didn't bother to inquire, but leaped to write "yes" to Kup's query. Though privately Metro executives had begun counting

on Grace's permanent departure, publicly the studio stood stout in its
optimism that Miss Kelly's contract was "in force" and she would not
quit acting. Unintentionally, the Prince might have put Grace in a
somewhat embarrassing position except that Grace proved herself very
adept at issuing Delphic replies to inquiries about her future. As late as
her shipboard news conference, before embarking for Monaco, Grace
elided a definitive statement of retirement: "Right now I'm too interested in my marriage to think of the movies."

The Prince's flat statement on Grace's future certainly won him no
friends in the movie industry, a fact confirmed when His Serene Highness and his father, the Comte de Polignac, visited the Metro lot in
early February to watch a day's shooting of *High Society* and have lunch
with Dore Schary. A witness to this ill-fated meal was Celeste Holm,
who had been surprised to be included in a group of eight that included executives and aristocrats and no other actors (save Grace herself). Holm said, "I was nervous as a pregnant fox in a forest fire
because Chuck [Walters, the director of *High Society*] never finished a
sentence without a four-letter word in it. In those days we didn't use
words like 'shit' and 'goddamnit' all the time, as we do now. I could tell
that Grace was panicky. We sat there in the elaborate executive lunch-
room making polite conversation about how similar California climate
is to Monaco. Then, innocently, Dore inquired of Rainier how big
Monaco was. The Prince replied with the exact count in acres, at
which point Dore said, 'Jeez, that's not even as big as our back lot.' It
just fell out of him. It was utterly tactless. Maybe Dore felt Rainier had
it coming [for taking Grace away from Hollywood], though I honestly
don't think he meant any harm by it. The silence that followed was
deafening. I figured anything was kosher if it drew attention away
from that reply, so I immediately stuck my fork into my steak and
splattered juice and gravy all over the tablecloth, and exclaimed loudly,
'Dear me, you can't take me any place.' "†

Grace was not being coy to say she would do another film for
M.G.M. after *High Society*. For, seeing the end, and anxious to reap as
much as possible before Grace retired, Metro's executives came up
with a "compromise." They would concede (but only tacitly) that *Designing Woman* was out of the question *if* the Prince and his bride would
give M.G.M. exclusive rights to film the wedding. The studio quickly
learned what shrewd and hard bargainers the Monégasques could be.
According to the agreement painfully arrived at, a thirty-minute film
—with the pretentious title *The Wedding of the Century*—would be shot,
not by M.G.M. cinematographers, but a Monégasque company under-
written by the studio. Metro could not even claim that this was the

† Interview, July 12, 1983.

"official" filmic record of the nuptials,‡ though the Franco-Monégasque camera team would be granted certain unspecified "rights" of
access denied to others. The Monégasques would split any profts fifty-
fifty after Metro pocketed a 30 percent distribution fee. (Grace's and
Rainier's share was given to the Monégasque Red Cross.) M.G.M. only
managed the moot point that the film would not "count" against the
films "required" in Grace's contract.

This not-so-clever deal brought Metro considerably more expense
and headache than profts, but its larger interest was Grace's long-
range future. However certain *she* may be that her marriage was forever and her retirement (eventually) permanent, the studio had a
vested interest in planning for other possibilities. Many of Metro's
executives, beginning with Schary, had warm personal regard for
Grace, but they all had business reasons for keeping their claim to her.
For whatever mix of sentimental and material reasons, the studio provided Grace with a remarkable number of benefts. They paid her a
bonus (for 1956) of $65,166.66; they maintained her on salary (at $1,500
per week) for nearly four months after she left Los Angeles; they paid
the full cost of her wedding dress ($7,266.68 in materials and manufac-
ture, not to mention the salary of the dress's chief designer Helen
Rose); they sent Grace's studio hair stylist, Virginia Darcy, to Monaco
and kept her there on salary (at $300 per week plus expenses) for sev-
eral months; and finally they threw in, gratis, Morgan Hudgins to help
out with the public relations at the wedding.*

But even M.G.M.'s large and expert publicity department could
barely cope with the demands for information and interviews, let alone
carry out its usual practice of trying to control what was said. By the
spring of 1956, the press was caught in the paroxysm of the Grace
Phenomenon. The combination of movie fame coupled with Grace's
"royal connection" and the forthcoming nuptials generated an interest
in her so bottomless that no amount of media attention seemed to
slacken it. Some indication of the dimensions of the publicity phenom-

---

‡ *The Wedding of the Century*, filmed in CinemaScope, was nevertheless distributed by
Loews Inc. (M.G.M.) in a bath of publicity unmistakably implying that it was indeed
"official."
* M.G.M. kept its candle in the window for Grace until the expiration date on her
contract, plus a six-year "extension" of very dubious legality, which is to say until November 15, 1966. In her files in the Metro Archives, one can see that someone methodi-
cally drew arrows, week by week, through approximately 520 weeks on a "layoff sheet"
that is sometimes marked "Grace Kelly" and other times "Princess Rainier." Even after
1966, the studio, though long since under new management, continued to favor Grace
whenever it could, e.g., providing her free of charge prints of several of her films. Even
then, material aims got admixed with personal goodwill, as indicated in the memoranda
that flowed back and forth among executives, chewing over the question of whether $250
per print wasn't a rather expensive "present" to be offering the Grimaldis, but on the
other hand, it was only good business . . . etc. (M.G.M. Archives).

enon may be had by noting that only the coronation of Elizabeth II (in 1953) drew as much attention.

For all of Howard Strickling's and Morgan Hudgins's assistance, the main burden weighed on Grace, gradually undermining her health, goodwill, and happiness during what should have been one of the happiest times of her life. The one person who might have helped her was not able to stay with her. The Prince returned to his Principality in February where he had a wedding to plan and affairs of state to look after. Rainier, in any case, found the current din hellish and was constantly at a loss for how to deal with it. He attempted to slip out of the United States incognito, but "C. Monte" was hardly an indecipherable alias, and by the time H.S.H. got to Idlewild Airport, he could no longer duck reporters and photographers. Gamely, he fielded questions and "confided" to the press, "No more movies for Miss Kelly!" Asked if he were weary of publicity, Rainier made one of the greater understatements of the day: "A little bit. I expect that people will soon get sick of [all these stories]. I know I am."

Alone, Grace faced the fusillades: "How long will [your marriage] last?," "How many children are you going to have?," and "Do you call Rainier prince?" (Her answers to the above three: "A Roman Catholic marries for life," "That's out of my hands," "I call him Rainier.") She fielded these inanities so effectively that one reporter compared her to Joan of Arc before the court. Day after day on the set of *High Society*, Celeste Holm marveled as Grace courteously dealt with questions that "would have driven me right for the asker's jugular." Often Grace kept her composure, quoting Oscar Wilde, "There are no indiscreet questions, only indiscreet answers." What did nettle her, sometimes greatly, was embarrassment caused to others on Grace's account. At the 1955 Academy Awards presentation (where she gave the Oscar for Best Actor to Ernest Borgnine), she was furious when reporters and photographers paid more attention to her than to the winners. Similarly, Rita Gam's wedding in Manhattan was intended to be a private affair. Having won a divorce from director Sidney Lumet, Rita was marrying Tom Guinzberg, son of the founder of Viking Press. Grace was one of her bridesmaids, but her presence at the posh Sutton Square townhouse where the event took place ensured the presence of dozens of journalists who overran the facilities and showed no interest in the bride and groom nor any of the (mostly literary) celebrities on hand. Grace kept her pluck, however. When one photographer asked her if she wanted a wedding without publicity, she replied, "Yes, a nice secret one like this."

Keeping the press at bay was hardly the only thing Grace had to do in these frantic weeks before she left for Monaco. Top priority, of course, was *High Society*, whose shooting ran slightly over schedule, finishing in March.† Grace enjoyed making the film almost more than any other and drew closer to the cast and crew than on any previous movie. (She adored the going-away present the cast gave her: a "loaded" roulette wheel.) Near the completion of *High Society*, her parents and some close friends of theirs turned up in Los Angeles and had to be squired and feted for a week. Throughout this period there was an endless round of showers, celebrations, and farewells that Grace had to attend or hurt people's feelings. The Academy Awards were her last West Coast obligation. On the very first available flight next morning, she fled for home.

The pace and busyness of her Hollywood existence, though more frenzied than usual, were tolerable because Grace was used to it, *there*. In New York, on the other hand, she ached to be able to take her own quiet farewell of the city, her home, the few intimates, the pastimes she loved best. She did her best to say a good goodbye. She appeared unexpectedly at the Central Park riding stables to take a final, sidesaddle trot, but the paparazzi appeared soon after, in force, and the sentimental trot became a wild Grace chase through the tree-lined byways and alleys of the Park. (She later wrote a note to her pal Celeste Holm, then an officer of the Friends of Central Park, "Dear Celeste . . . Keep up the good work and be sure they keep the *bridal* path open.")

Her trousseau dominated Grace's last two weeks in New York. Even after she became a leading actress, Grace took no great interest in clothes. It came as a big surprise to Grace to learn that she had been voted one of the Ten Best-Dressed Women of 1955. Left to her own devices, she tended to wear sound, sober, sensible garments. Oleg Cassini called this penchant her "Bryn Mawr look," adding, "Grace wanted to be considered serious. A consuming interest in apparel was not, in her eyes, the hallmark of a serious person." Her good friend, Edith Head, wrote that "Offscreen she was not the best-dressed actress in Hollywood, but she was always fastidious about the way she looked."‡ (That judgment was pronounced in 1981, however. In 1955, Head's reaction to Grace's being named one of the best dressed was stronger: "All I can say is that miracles do happen in that field too," she told journalist Pete Martin.)

In films, of course, Grace (like any actor) had slight say in what she wore (though her friendliness with Edith Head permitted a certain collaboration in her costume designs for *Rear Window* and *To Catch a Thief*). Off the screen, the social demands of being a leading actress

† Ever the dependable trooper, Grace finally succumbed under the current strain. Her studio attendance record for the last month of filming show eleven "late" notices and two illness reports—extraordinary for her; but still far below average for most stars.
‡ Edith Head & Patty Calistro, *Edith Head's Hollywood* (New York: E. P. Dutton, 1983), p. 108. Subsequent Head quotes are from the same source.

obliged her to start giving more attention to wardrobe. Even then, her personal interest was in modest clothes, and her expenditures (except for gloves—a small mania for her*) remained discriminating and comparatively thrifty. She also tended to rely heavily on other people's advice—especially (while they were dating) Oleg Cassini's. Oleg regarded Grace as "a great diamond" and dressed her accordingly. ("You don't clutter up a diamond," he said, "with lots of arabesques and curlicues. Only homely women need busy dresses. Either you focus on the person or on the dress. With [Grace], there was never any question. Nature had already created it; at most I created just the envelope.") His designs for Grace were subdued, sophisticated, elegant dresses that set into relief her finest features: her hair, shoulders, arms, skin texture. "Grace felt she had a little bit of a derrière problem," added Cassini, "so I tried to deemphasize her behind in my creations for her." (Edith Head always said Grace's best feature was "her perfect carriage"; her only flaw, "a waist that was much too small.")

Grace did not depend for clothes just on Cassini, even when they were lovers; she used other designers, including one, Vera Maxwell, who became a lifelong friend. When the wedding was announced, a kind of competition broke out among designers to create her wedding gown. As Metro was Grace's studio, it was only natural that M.G.M.'s chief designer, Helen Rose, got the job—especially since Metro was covering all the expenses. (Acadamy Award-winning Rose was almost a legend in Hollywood. Grace was scheduled to play her in the film *Designing Woman*, a glossy version of Rose's life.) Unfortunately, that left show business's "other" costume design legend, Edith Head, miserable. Edith was not only a personal friend of Grace's but had wrought creations for her of such sexiness or magnificence (in *Rear Window* and *To Catch a Thief*) that the dresses themselves contributed singularly to Grace's movie fame. Edith did no less brilliantly in dressing Grace "down" for *The Country Girl* where the actress was obliged to look like a forlorn, dumpy housefrau. (That had required some getting used to for the neat and fussy Grace, but eventually she climbed into her part. Head said to her one day, "Grace, I didn't think we could do it, but you look truly depressed. I congratulate you.") But while Edith yearned to design the wedding dress, she took her lump gamely, and set immediately to work on creating the light gray silk ensemble with tiny white hat and long white gloves that would be Grace's going-away suit when she embarked on the S.S. *Constitution* for Monaco.

Grace's extraordinary popularity as an actress naturally influenced fashion. Something called the "Grace Kelly Look" emerged to become

---

* Edith Head recalled a visit to a glove store in Cannes where Grace bought so much that neither she nor Edith could pool the cash to pay for her purchases.

one of the most pervasive and perduring styles of the fifties. The "look" emphasized low-heeled shoes, tweeds, sweaters and gently flared skirts, simple patterns or solids in beige and pastel colors, soft- (not hard-) finished fabrics, uncomplicated hairstyles, discriminating use of makeup (no false lashes or exaggerated shaping of the mouth), and simple, elegant jewelry (or none at all). Grace herself had a hard time accepting the idea she had authored a fashion "look"; her tastes in clothes, she said, were far from novel. On the contrary, they ran to "classic" features that strove to outlast modes and fashions. She was nevertheless pleased to receive the Neiman-Marcus Award for consistently high standards of taste and fashion; she even flew to Dallas to receive it.†

When the time came for Grace to select her trousseau, she characteristically called in an outside expert, who was also a friend: Eleanor Lambert, a well-known fashion authority. Between them, they came up with a large selection of clothes from a wide gamut of designers— Ben Zuckerman, Fira Benenson, Galanos, and Branell (evening dress); Pauline Trigère, Harvey Berin, and James Galanos (cocktail wear); Adele Simpson, Christian Dior, Larry Aldrich, Traina Norell (day clothes); Claire McCardell, Brigance, B. H. Wragge, and Marquise (sportswear). Her hats came from New York's Mr. John; shoes—all of them with low heels so she wouldn't stand taller than the Prince (five foot seven to her five foot six)—came from Delman's of Fifth Avenue.

Remarkably, almost all of the designs were American. Grace's single favorite designer was Ben Zuckerman. The most expensive item in her trousseau was a full-length Canadian sable coat at $7,200; a mink jacket ran $4,800. Nevertheless, the cost of the new wardrobe—whose principal items included six cocktail dresses; four summer dresses; two evening gowns; two ball gowns, several coats, and a dozen hats—ran around $25,000.‡ This was a hefty figure in 1956, but hardly exceptional next to the sums that other international celebrities and socialites spent on clothes.

In the last analysis, however, Grace's real tastes prevailed. Loyal Rupert Allan, helping her pack her suitcases on the eve of her departure for Monaco, couldn't help noticing, and remarking on, the dozen or so pairs of old jeans and faded shirts and blouses that she had

† The high promotional value of a superstar may have played some role in Grace's selection, however. Stanley Marcus wrote a letter to his "dear friend," Dore Schary, beseeching him to let Grace be a day or two late for shooting *High Society* so she could make a second appearance at his famous Dallas department store. Her popularity with the clientele, wrote Marcus, was unique. Schary, who had his own store to run, politely refused. Marcus didn't come off badly, though. Among other things, Grace got her bridesmaids' dresses from his store.
‡ This did not include all the clothes she wore in *High Society*, which Metro gave her as one of its many wedding presents.

crammed in on top of far more costly apparel. "For heaven's sake, Grace," he said, "you're *not* taking those with you, are you? You'll never wear them." "Oh yes, I will," came the response, "most of the time."

> *There's always been something so terribly touching to me about two people standing up before all the world and promising to be faithful to each other while ever they live . . . It's so beautifully trusting. And I seemed to sense that this afternoon for some reason or other, more than I ever have in all the countless weddings I've been to . . . They looked so terribly young. And those words are so frighteningly solemn.*
> —Mrs. Espinshade in George Kelly's
> The Fatal Weakness

> *Walking up the aisle, I thought, "Here I am. This is a one-way street now. There's no way out of this."*
> —Princess Grace (1976)

Grace and Rainier might have been meant for each other, but Monaco and the media certainly were not. According to the previews, which endowed the wedding with the significance of the coronation of Elizabeth II, the two of them were supposed to have a fairy-tale wedding: "Hollywood Princess Weds Real Life Prince," ran the prewritten headlines. What it became instead was one of the first of many modern "media events," so saturated with coverage that the presence of the reporters threatened to become the story itself.

It is easy to become indignant and sarcastic about the press and the tasteless, mindless reporting that dominated its coverage of the wedding. The disaster that took place in April was not entirely its fault. It resulted rather from a disproportion between the size of the media blitz and the resources and expectations of a principality and a prince that didn't even have a press office.

The unfortunate result was that Grace's reign got off to a rocky start.

§   §   §

Grace's embarkation from New York on the rain-swept morning of April 4 should have been a warning. Within minutes of her arrival at the S.S. *Constitution* at Pier 84, the carefully planned press conference degenerated into a riot. Two hundred and fifty reporters and photographers, including many veterans of the business, pushed, shoved, and punched each other, shouted rudely at Grace and ignored all pleas to behave from the several press directors on hand (representing M.G.M. and the American Export Line). The actress did her best to answer their questions, but the mob overwhelmed her until she and a companion had to retreat into a corner of a cafe where they were extricated by security officers. The dean of New York shipping news reporters, Edmond Duffy, wrote that it was the largest, most boisterous press conference he had witnessed in three decades of waterfront reporting.*

Frazzled, Grace took refuge in her stateroom only to find, sitting incongruously amid gifts, flowers, luggage, telegrams, and the voluminous folds of specially hung silk wall cloth, a large, nervous weimaraner puppy, the ill-conceived present of Philadelphia friends of the Kellys. The commotion had liquidated what slight continence the high-strung animal had, and as Grace came into the room, the odor of excited puppy wafted from the bed.

The voyage out was one continuous party for Grace's friends and relatives, but a time of reflection for the bride. Also a time of comparative relaxation contrasted with the madhouse from which Grace had just escaped and the one toward which she was heading. To be sure, there were shipboard parties nightly, but they were far from the formal affairs with strangers or near strangers that Grace had had to attend in the preceding months, and besides she could leave when she wanted to walk on deck. She did that a lot. She later told a writer that staring into the fog of the first night, she felt "as if I were sailing off into the unknown. I couldn't help wondering: 'What is going to happen to me? What will this new life be like?' "

The wedding company divided naturally into two groups—the bride's friends and contemporaries and the Kellys and their set. Grace hung out with the former but was more than dutiful in her attention to her family and their Philadelphia crowd. She also gave press interviews and exclusive sessions to each of the photographers aboard, yet withal, had some opportunity to relax, to attend to correspondence, talk intimately with close friends, and, each evening before retiring, to walk alone along the boat deck and collect her thoughts. Toward the end of the voyage, the *Constitution*'s sister ship, the S.S. *Independence* steamed by close enough to flash the message "Good luck, Gracie!"

In the event, luck entirely evaded the betrothed in the next few days. The wedding was a circus, in terrible contrast to what bride and groom desired. Grace and Rainier approached the event with a mixture of awe and sentimentality reminiscent of the indestructibly romantic George Kelly heroine, Edith Espinshade, in *The Fatal Weakness*.

---

* A dozen or so representatives of the press were sold cabin-class tickets on the *Constitution*. Originally, Grace attempted to prevent any journalists from sailing on the ship with her. She asked American Export Line not to sell a ticket to any reporter, and the company agreed. Such a howl went up from the press that the actress relented. The line sold cabin-class tickets to reporters, who bunked four to a cabin. Grace even acquiesced in holding several shipboard news conferences. Nevertheless, the dissonant note that had been sounded at the pier conference did not completely abate.

For them the wedding was to be an intensely personal experience. Perhaps once, as Grace and Rainier looked at one another in the terrible solemnity of the Cathedral, and promised to forsake all others, the obnoxious world momentarily vanished. For the rest, however, their wedding belonged to the crowd—the crowd of dignitaries in the church, the journalists outside, and the thirty million in nine countries watching on television.

The public character of the wedding was made clear to Grace even as she descended the gangplank of the Prince's yacht, the *Deo Juvante II*, which took her from the *Constitution* to the shore. The yacht was now hers, a wedding present from her groom.† Rainier greeted her quite formally with a handclasp, no kiss or even embrace. The gesture was in part intentional, a sign to everyone that here, if not in the States, the most traditional standards of propriety were observed; it also fit the Prince's shy and undemonstrative public demeanor. Somewhat nervously, Rainier whispered to his future princess that the large saucer-shaped white hat she wore obscured her face and would not permit her future subjects to get a good look at her. But there was nothing Grace could do; her luggage was not at hand and the cavalcade had to begin. They drove in an open car along the streets of the Principality; Grace waved as best she could while clinging to a hat that filled like a sail in the gentlest breeze.

The timetable that the Prince and his staff had sweated over for weeks was remorseless in its unfolding of events—receptions, visitations, dinners, galas, and ceremonies—but this was not what nearly ruined the next seven days for the principals. Neither did the presence of vastly more tourists and spectators than anyone had planned for, for the crowds were good-natured and tolerant. "Impossible to imagine confusion here," Morgan Hudgins cabled his boss, Howard Strickling, at the end of the first day, but even confusion per se wasn't the culprit. Rather, what broke the spirit of the occasion was an unseemly, complex, gigantic tug-of-war, or series of tugs-of-wars, that gradually arose between journalists and the bridal pair, between the Monégasques and the Americans, and among the invited guests themselves.

Most of these struggles were identical to those that had been taking place in the United States, but here they were greatly magnified on so reduced a stage in so foreshortened a time frame. Well over fifteen hundred media representatives, from dozens of nations and hundreds of publications, descended onto one-half square mile of ground. They outnumbered the Monégasque army eight to one, the guests more than three to one; they outnumbered the police, including the reserves sent

† Its Latin words mean "With God's Help," the motto of the Principality of Monaco.

in by France; and at many events, they even outnumbered the crowds of spectators.

The Principality had made too few provisions for even a third this many journalists. A well-equipped and experienced press office would have barely coped with such demand, but in Monaco that spring, there weren't even daily communiqués, briefings, and picture sessions, let alone arranged exclusives and interviews. Rainier's ignorance of reporters' needs quickly generated their contempt, then fury, then aggressive and ingenious counterattacks, especially by photographers. At the start, Walter Carone of *Paris Match* brought off a daredevil stunt when he jumped out a small porthole in the S.S. *Constitution*'s stern into a speeding motorboat, from which he was able to get exclusive pictures of Grace as she boarded the Prince's yacht.

Carone set a standard for guts and nerve that galvanized his colleagues. Camera-laden, they now swung from rafters and crawled along eaves, hid in bushes, accosted guests, formed phalanxes or threw themselves in front of cars, argued and even fought with police and staff, climbed (indeed, according to one observer, seemed to live) in trees, and stood in the rain for hours—usually for far less than Carone got. Whether polite or pugnacious, the photographers were always pitiable, except perhaps to Rainier. He was particularly incensed when several photographers donned priests' cassocks to penetrate the Palace. (Ironically, Rainier's Genoese ancestors had taken Monaco with just such a ruse in 1297. Disguising himself and a few men as Franciscan monks, Francesco Grimaldi penetrated the fortress, then overwhelmed the guard and threw open the gates. To Prince Rainier, however, precedent did not excuse the photographers' sacrilege.)

Their reporter colleagues were generally older and proved less nimble. They fed on speculation (how long would the marriage last?), on rumor (in six years of ruling, Rainier never waved to his subjects until Grace taught him how), on cutesy trivia (was Rainier's nickname pronounced "Rah," "Ray," or "Shorty"?), or on themselves (reporters reporting the reportage). And they often made little effort to keep their resentment at the treatment they received out of their copy. Monaco came in for heavy doses of sarcasm from workaday journalists who reached for easy irony when a nuanced description of a complex and foreign reality eluded them. Monaco, which had been a "golden fairyland" or "kingdom of happy ever after," became, in the hands of peeved scriveners, "that pinpoint municipality," "the preshrunk principality," "this financially juicy plum of a principality," "this postage-stamp realm," and (after several bejeweled guests reported the burglary of their ornaments) "the light-fingered fairyland."

If this were not enough to ignite fury in the hearts of Prince and subjects, they had also been constantly reminded for nearly four months now that Grace Kelly "belonged" to the American people, that she would be bored and restless in a "seedy, rundown place full of empty mansions haunted by European families long since forced to take jobs guiding schoolteachers and driving Paris taxicabs," and that the marriage wouldn't last. Fred Sparks was a Scripps-Howard staff writer whose prewedding piece deserves to be quoted at length, for nothing less conveys the tone, and captures the outrage, that was a large section of American journalistic "wisdom" on the Grimaldi-Kelly match. Sparks wrote:

> *I will be willing to put a reasonable sum in a time capsule to be opened in five years and on my sum I will write: "Grace Kelly is no longer married to the prince—if she ever married him." If I am wrong this money goes to the home for aged feature writers . . . I hate to be offering Grace any advice but she is public property like the Mona Lisa and I urge her to stop, look and listen before she lets her head be turned by dreams of marbled halls. The marbled halls of Monte Carlo . . . lack central heating and the plumbing would worry a camel and the furniture belongs in a museum and collects pyramids of dust . . . We need [Grace] at home acting and laughing that laugh that makes young men fling kisses across the darkened theater. I want to see her radiant for thirty years more and raise a crop of American kids as pretty as herself or as rugged as her daddy and brother, who are natural athletes with the physique and coordination of an Irishman crossed with a Greek god.‡*

Similarly, the well-known reporter Dorothy Kilgallen alternated between giving breathless news bulletins, such as Rainier and Grace were dancing "cheek-to-cheek" at a prenuptial gala in the Monte Carlo Casino, and issuing absurd forebodings on the order of "I fear Grace is slipping away from us." (The latter led E. J. Kahn, Jr., of *The New Yorker* to write, "I had thought all along that the whole point of everybody's being over there was to acknowledge descriptively that Grace *was* slipping away from us.") In short, it wasn't the rush or public nature of events or the pressure of crowds that profoundly shook the Prince and his bride but the hostility and mischief inadvertently created when a small army of journalists had little or nothing to write about.

Admittedly, this sort of "coverage" often elicited disgust from the press itself, sometimes even from the purveyors themselves. Fred Sparks, for one, might have walked off with the hypocrisy prize for ending the above story with the promise, "I just won't read anything

‡ "Grace Faces Big Gamble," New York *World-Telegram* (January 9, 1956).

more about the Prince of Hearts and the Queen of Cinema." The *Herald Tribune*, published in Paris, aided him in his self-denial with a piece entitled "Positively the last cute story about Grace Kelly," while the Rome-based *Daily American* expressly snubbed its colleagues by running its coverage of the wedding in twenty-five words. ("Monte Carlo, April 18. The American actress Grace Kelly and Prince Rainier III of Monaco were married here today. No one stole the wedding ring.") A movie theater in Houston promised people it was "the one place where you won't see, hear or read about Grace Kelly."

None became more indignant about press manners and coverage than the Monégasques themselves, yet they too contributed a juicy morsel to the newspapers because of their National Council's wedding gift to the new Princess. That august body, having decided to give Grace a necklace, dispatched one of its members to choose something suitable. An elderly gentleman, he took his time, and $33,000, to make a down payment (of one third the purchase price) on a heavy, bejeweled monstrosity which only the majority of the Monégasque National Council could consider fashionable. Prince Rainier took one look at the ornate horror and pronounced it more appropriate for the dowager empress of China than his twenty-six-year-old Princess. He agreed with the minority councillors that this gift was not only entirely unappealing but could cause more sniggering about the Principality's taste. Another gift was quickly bought elsewhere for Grace, and back went the councillor to the jeweler with the jewel. But the store owner refused to hand over the money. A deal was a deal, he said; there had been no arrangements made for any return of merchandise. Cajolery and threats having no effect, the Council was obliged to take the jeweler to court, which of course meant the press got wind, and the guests, and Grace. She passed the matter off gamely, but nobody else did. "It was a really sordid affair," the Prince said.

Under the accumulated weight of these circumstances, it was no surprise to see visible tension in the faces of the bride and groom when they met for their civil wedding on the morning of April 18 in the throne room of the Palace. By now, Rainier had had at least four confrontations with photographers, one of whom had flung himself in front of the Prince's speeding Lancia. The man would have been run over were Rainier anything less than a crack racing driver with split-second reflexes. As it was, the episode deeply distressed him.

Not only the Prince but everyone in the throne room appeared on edge. Rainier twisted uncomfortably in a black morning coat; Grace, dressed in a rose dress of alençon lace and a Juliet cap, sat quietly, mirroring his nervousness. Rainier did not smile throughout the short ceremony, and he rarely even looked at Grace. They both replied with only the softest "oui" to the question posed by Judge Marcel Portanier.

(The *World-Telegram & Sun* produced what was unquestionably the richest typo in the compendious annals of the wedding when it printed Prince Rainier's response as "Qui.") The throne room was a large baroque chamber but still far too small to accommodate more than one hundred guests. The excluded four hundred mingled outside, some of them complaining quotably to the 99.9 percent of the press corps who also could not be permitted into the Palace. Dorothy Kilgallen's failure to land a place among the elect at the civil wedding perhaps induced her to compare (sight unseen) Prince Rainier's expression to that of a guilty man being questioned by police. She concluded gratuitously, "he does not immediately strike the average viewer as ideal husband material . . . Grace has tackled a whopper."

But it was not only journalistic obiter dicta that marred the atmosphere; the megaphones which the press provided anyone who talked to them caused conflicts among the guests and among nationalities to become magnified. With so little accessibility to the principals, reporters often preyed on the guests, many of whom had beefs and gripes of their own, and who certainly didn't know how to be quoted, let alone to be discreet. Nor did some of them seek to be. The severe space problem that arose in the civil wedding reappeared all too frequently. Not everyone could attend every event; and though great efforts were made to see that nobody was left out of everything, mistakes occurred. What shocked and hurt the bride and groom was how poorly their friends reacted to the inevitable glitches. In fairness to the visitors, their grumbles about the host's lack of generosity usually amounted to momentary flares of temper and were probably not intended to get back to the bride and groom, let alone appear in the newspapers. But they did.

Sometimes, the complaints were not spur of the moment. The subtle rivalries that had evolved in the States resurfaced when various personalities came back into contact around Grace and Rainier. A well-intentioned man, John Kelly, Sr., for example, had a bluff manner of self-expression and a sensitive pride. He obviously felt uncomfortable at being five thousand miles from Philadelphia, in a society totally foreign to him, where the shots were manifestly being called by a young man thirty years his junior to whom he was shortly going to have to turn over his daughter. Small wonder then, when speaking confidentially to some fellow American males, who just happened to be journalists, Kelly went out of his way to sympathize with their plight. The next day, on the front page of several major American dailies, Grace's father was quoted referring to his son-in-law's "autocratic air," which was, he said, "getting out of hand," so that he, John Kelly, would "have to have a talk with that young man." "That young man" happened to be the sovereign Prince of Monaco, whose subjects regarded their new

Princess's father as insolent and boorish when they got word of his remarks.

Nor did nuance of inflection and wry wit always come across in cold type. No less a well-liked man than the Very Reverend Father Francis Tucker appalled his adopted countrymen by telling American reporters that Prince Rainier was "a spoiled boy." The dust had not settled from this misfired "joke" than Tucker committed an indiscretion worthy of Ma Kelly when he adverted to Rainier's former love, Gisèle Pascal, during a sermon in his Monégasque parish.

In truth, the Prince was neither spoiled nor a boy, and although 650 years of Monégasque history indeed made him an autocrat, he was not particularly autocratic by the standards of his forebears. He was a ruler accustomed to ruling, not to managing the media, with whom he had had comparatively slight contact until late December of 1955. And he was growing dismayed, then desperate, as he watched his normally serene Principality turn into a madhouse, while his wedding—intended to be a dignified revival of "the richest ceremonial of the past" —degenerated into a clash of tempers (including his own), a wrestling match for pride of place.

The week of festivities was nevertheless not wholly depressing for the bride and groom. Individual moments of pleasure or profound feeling would be recalled by the Grimaldis for the rest of their life together, e.g., Grace's delight at the spectacular pas de deux which ballet stars Margot Fonteyn and Christopher Soames performed at one of the evening galas; or the small, private ceremony, following the civil marriage, in which Prince Rainier invested his Princess with Monaco's highest award, the Order of St. Charles. Then, too, some of the press's frustration was relieved when, toward the end of the week, a makeshift press office was set up under Morgan Hudgins (assisted occasionally by the garrulous and good-humored Father Tucker). Though issuing no regular communiqués, the office at least gave journalists a place to verify rumors and collect some news.

Nevertheless, the Prince of Monaco was overwhelmed and disgusted by the accumulated effect of all the tension and conflict. He tried to keep his feelings from showing, especially to his bride. Grace had never wanted the full production. On the boat coming over, she had commented privately to a friend about the irony in all the pomp and fuss that lay ahead. None of it, she said, beginning with the Palace-roomful of expensive presents, had ever remotely figured in her idea of a wedding. Yet she accepted this extravaganza as the requirement of state that it was. In the days following her arrival in the Principality, she had managed to remain in seclusion much more successfully than the Prince, with the result that while she heard about some of the contretemps and certainly sensed Rainier's eagerness to "get this over with," she still felt much of the excitement that a bride should feel.

The nuptial high mass, celebrated by the Bishop of Monaco, Gilles Barthe, was the grand culmination of the week of festivities in this very Catholic sovereignty. It took place late in the morning of the nineteenth of April in the Cathedral of St. Nicholas, the small, white stone, Gothic cathedral that dominates the rocky promontory that dominates Monaco. Inside the church, candles illuminated the high altar covered in white lilacs. Great golden baskets of lilacs hung from the chandeliers. The six hundred guests crammed into the Cathedral included a few international business or semipolitical celebrities (e.g., ex-King Farouk, the Aga Khan, Aristotle Onassis) but no heads of state or government, although several sent personal representatives—Conrad Hilton for President Eisenhower; Archbishop Paolo Marella for Pope Pius XII; François Mitterrand for President Coty of France, as well as personal representatives from the heads of state of Italy, England, and Spain. From the press's viewpoint the best-known guests were unquestionably the Hollywood contingent: Ava Gardner, the David Nivens, the Cary Grants.

The Prince had designed his own uniform for the occasion—a pastiche of French and Italian (which is to say Monégasque) military history. It included elements of an admiral, a Napoleonic marshal, and a colonel of the carabinieri. Grace's bridal gown was an extraordinary piece of design and painstaking labor that suited its wearer's physique, personality, and position. Manifestly regal and very old-fashioned, the ivory silk wedding dress had a bodice of 125-year-old Brussels lace, with a high scalloped neck and long sleeves. So well fitted was it, however, and so simple, that the classic features of Grace's beauty—her slender waist, long arms, curvaceous shoulders and neck—stood prominently in relief. The skirt was made of twenty-five yards of peau de soie and taffeta; both the veil and the petaled, crownlike coif were sewn with pearls. The total impression was one of girlish youth and beauty, yet tradition and gravity.

For Grace, the meaning of this event was religious through and through. She had joked that she was "half-married" after the civil ceremony, but in her own mind, her marriage's deepest significance and justification stemmed from its insertion in the Christian faith. This mass was, therefore, the most profound spiritual experience of her twenty-six years. Her attitude showed this from the moment she entered the Cathedral on John Kelly's arm. Protocol required her to precede Rainier to the altar and await him. When Kelly and daughter reached the altar, the Bishop discreetly indicated to Jack that he retake his seat. Again the bricklayer flouted custom, but this time with dignity. Politely, but adamantly, he communicated to Bishop Barthe that he would stand by his daughter until the groom arrived.* Where others, including her bridesmaids,† alternately smiled or looked graduation-serious, Grace's countenance throughout the sixty-three-minute ceremony bore a sternness and gravity that bespoke an intense inner experience and an unawareness of people around her, except for the Prince and the Bishop—and, it must be said, the occasional, annoying rustle of television cameramen in their aerie high above the main altar.

Grace and Rainier knelt on golden faldstools, close enough to clasp hands, as required by the ceremony, but they looked oddly uncoupled. The Prince was far less ill at ease than the day before, but his seriousness seemed a reflection of his consciousness of the external significances of the formalities, while Grace's was due to her deep inner feeling. In his charge, the Bishop exhorted Prince Rainier to temper authority with love and tenderness; Grace, to remember that physical beauty was insignificant and fleeting. ("He doesn't know Gracie very well if he thinks he has to say that," one of the bridesmaids said afterwards.) In the formal declaration of consent, Barthe adjured them to become "one in mind, one in heart, one in affection." The Prince and his bride vowed to "love unto death," but they made their responses so softly that a hushed congregation could not hear them. They did not smile, not even when Rainier had trouble fitting the ring onto his bride's finger (she finally had to assist him), and the only tenderness between them came late in the mass when Grace cast an occasional, loving sidelong glance at her husband. He did not return her gaze, nor did they kiss at the altar. Princess Grace's eyes teared when the boys' choir began to sing the Agnus Dei.

The pair emerged, arm in arm, from the Cathedral into a brilliant Midi sun that had broken through clouds and rain. They were smiling but subdued as they got into the open Rolls-Royce (a wedding gift from the people of Monaco) and made a rapid tour of the oldest sections of the Principality where most of the native Monégasques lived. The Rolls came to a halt at the little Church of Sainte Dévote where Grace knelt in the dust to ask the patron saint of Monaco (an early Christian martyr) to bless her marriage. This was followed by a luncheon reception at the Palace for six hundred people where the Prince and Princess cut a wedding cake that was taller than they were. Other activities filled the afternoon and were planned for the evening, but well before sunset, Grace and Rainier took their leave. They gave presents to their

* I am grateful to Sally Parrish Richardson for noticing this exchange (which eluded the press) and for communicating it to me. December 4, 1983.
† Her sister Peggy, Judy Kanter, Rita Gam, Maree Pamp (a Philadelphia friend of Grace's youth), Carolyn Reybold, Sally Parrish Richardson, Bettina Gray (the latter three were friends of Grace's from her modeling days). Grace's sister Lizanne, and her sister-in-law, Mary Freeman Kelly (Kell's wife) would have been bridesmaids, but both were expecting babies momentarily and could not come to Monaco.

bridesmaids and groomsmen (various pieces of gold jewelry engraved with the R-G monogram that would become so familiar). Then the car took them to the port where they boarded the *Deo Juvante II*—a wonderful old boat of English manufacture which the press, irrelevantly, insisted on contrasting with Onassis's fabulous *Christina.*

The Prince and Princess were so exhausted that they fell into a couple of deck chairs and couldn't eat the light collation that the crew had thoughtfully prepared for them. They just slept till evening. Encountering somewhat high seas on leaving Monaco's Bay of Hercules, the captain of the *Deo Juvante II* dropped anchor in a small cove off Villefranche, not far from the Principality, but blessedly, in the gathering darkness, out of shore sight.

$$\S \qquad \S \qquad \S$$

In later years, Grace, and particularly Rainier, could not speak for any time about their wedding without ruing the day. Indeed in the year following, they chose not to speak of it at all. Grace gave all the clippings to a secretary to put into a scrapbook for her; she couldn't bring herself to do it. Neither she nor Rainier looked at the book until 1958. Even then cheerful chats which originated in a happy memory of this or that event of the wedding week usually ended in lamentation. In talks with his authorized biographer ten years later, the Prince frankly called the wedding a "disastrous affair," and said how disheartened he and Grace had been by the unrelenting pressure and the lack of "intimacy, solitude, and dignity." He concluded, "I don't think I could go through it again. In fact, certainly, I wouldn't."‡ His wife was hardly less adamant. Grace lost ten pounds from the emotional strain of the month that ended at the Cathedral of St. Nicholas. She told a journalist several years later that the pressure before the wedding was bad enough, but the tension of the week itself was "quite unbelievable."

It was characteristic of Prince Rainier that, having lost his temper with nearly everybody in the crunch of those harried seven days, on reflection he nevertheless blamed himself for what went wrong. He and Grace would have preferred to get married "in a little chapel in the mountains," but as a state wedding was mandatory, he ought to have employed a "technician in press affairs and public relations." And in fact, Prince Rainier plugged this hole very soon after returning from his honeymoon. But as he would discover, the problems that arose at the wedding did not disappear just because the Grimaldis

‡ *Op. cit.,* p. 50. (Following quotes from Rainier from *loc. cit.*) *The Hollywood Reporter*'s review of the M.G.M. movie on the wedding *(The Wedding of the Century)* included the following line: "[The Prince] gives a vivid impression of impatience, uncertainty and of wishing devoutly the whole thing were over."

hired a press officer or two. In truth, no "technician" could have solved the problem of the wedding because the problem was not principally technical ("communications") but rather more old-fashioned, wounded pride and its satisfaction.

The wedding week, as Rainier was the first to point out, was no isolated mistake but "the disappointing culmination of all that had gone before." What exactly had gone before? The Prince of Monaco had come to America, fallen in love with the U.S.'s top movie star, asked her to marry him and quit films, and been said yes to. So far, so idyllic; but this thirty-two-year-old European prince, while well educated, was far from being the man of the world he would become. He had a strong, but subtle and reserved personality, and a Latin's temper and pride, *especially pride*. New to the United States, he was stunned then appalled at American ignorance of his Principality, particularly as that ignorance was often laced with sharp traces of sass and sarcasm directed his way for "stealing" Grace Kelly. Not everyone expressed himself as hatefully as reporters Fred Sparks or Dorothy Kilgallen, but to the Prince's sensitive ego, they weren't greatly different from Dore Schary when the Metro chief made his ill-conceived luncheon remark comparing Monaco's size to the studio's back lot. A few years later, the Prince would have passed that off with a witticism, but in 1956 he took it—and the thousand like it that he heard and read—personally.

The result was an attempt at what the French called *surenchère*—overbidding. Without fully realizing it, Prince Rainier returned home in February with vindication in his heart. "Graustark," as *Time* was forever calling Monaco, would throw a wedding that the world would not soon forget, beginning with the United States and its press. Unfortunately, Monaco was not the fictional Graustark, and it hadn't the capacity, the means, or, above all, the know-how to make good its Prince's bid. The matter of the ill-chosen wedding present was, in this regard, telltale. The Monégasque National Council was made up of men of an average age double that of their Princess-to-be; few of them had traveled farther from home than Nice or Marseille. It was unjust and naive to imagine they might encounter no troubles in coming up with the perfect gift for an American movie and fashion queen.

Overbidding, in short, became overreach. Many more people than John Kelly, Sr., remarked that the wedding was "a grand production. I felt I was in Hollywood watching them shoot a Cecil B. deMille film." This theme, indeed, was virtually a leitmotif of American and foreign reportage on the wedding. Yet the sad truth was that the wedding was manifestly *not* an M.G.M. production, but a misconceived and rather amateur attempt to rival one.

In fairness to Prince Rainier, he probably had only a slight idea of what was impelling him. Consciously, he knew that he must hold a

state wedding. But a state wedding was one thing—the Principality
had mounted those many times in the past (once, even, for an American—Alice Heine, the bride of Rainier's great-grandfather, Albert I).
But an extravaganza spreading over a solid week, with six hundred
guests, and live television coverage, was another matter. The Principality got swamped; it couldn't even adequately handle all the guests, let
alone the reporters. The Palace Chamberlain fainted under the strain
and had to be taken to the hospital. Security was overwhelmed, with
the result that several hundred thousand dollars in jewel thievery took
place (including to one of Grace's bridesmaids). Rainier was very upset
about this.

But the failure which distressed him most was moral, not logistical.
The "material" Monaco had to work with in mounting a state wedding
was, as its Prince stated at the start, "the rich ceremonials of the past."
Ceremonials arise from, and reflect, a nation's traditions and history,
its culture, and religion. In a Principality as old as Monaco, these were
complex, subtle, unbending, and, for Americans, unfamiliar realities—
precisely *not* the sort of plastic props and movable facades that DeMille
used in his movies. Monaco, moreover, wasn't Great Britain; not only
was its culture far less similar or accessible to Americans than England's, but its society was far, far less used to being on parade. It had
no experience with being cynosure of the world.

The result was a strenuous effort to turn a silk purse into a sow's ear,
or, putting it more delicately, to take a fine symphony orchestra into an
emporium (replete with Nadia Boulanger at the piano). Forced to play
to live television, a host of foreign guests, and fifteen hundred resentful
reporters, many of them utterly ignorant of Monaco, "the richest ceremonials" of the Principality's past got deformed, ignored, misunderstood, and badly underappreciated. The Prince complained again and
again that the wedding lacked dignity. Of course it lacked dignity; to
have dignity, the ceremonials would have had to be subscribed to, not
just by participants but, to some degree at least, by spectators as well.
But Monaco in early April was, as noted, a circus. Too many people
just gawked—whether by television, or from the streets. Even among
guests—at least those whom the press seemed to talk to—altogether too
many came to nitpick, or to be seen and to jockey for position.

Many guests, especially from America, were simply not people who
had the background to know what was going on or the sensitivity to
make the effort to find out. Guessing that few guests would have any
idea of the significance of the Order of St. Charles, the Prince planned
that ceremony as strictly private—and was right to do so. (Even then,
one of the bridesmaids complained that the red and white riband
didn't coordinate with Grace's dress.) The sister of the bride, when
asked politely for a message by an Italian radio commentator, figured it

was a joke, so she stepped to the microphone and spoke the one Italian word she knew, "spaghetti."* Another guest riffled a newspaper in the Cathedral during the mass, while several made cracks about the ornateness of Rainier's uniform without having any idea what its elements represented. Margaret Kelly wrote to her relatives in Heppenheim, Germany begging the humble villagers to suppress, or at least not publicize, their connection with her daughter; the fact that she wrote was immediately discussed in the press. So upper-crust hauteur mixed uneasily with arriviste anxiety, and "complete" coverage insured the embarrassing results.

Even the real aristocracy could not resist jumping on the bandwagon. An English lady, Lady Norah Docker, actually authored newspaper columns in which she scorned her host's yacht and derided him for not inviting the Duke and Duchess of Windsor to the wedding. One could hardly imagine her saying or doing such things at the Queen's coronation (although the Windsors were not invited there either).

In sum, a royal wedding secretly designed to awe the (American) inlaws, guests, and press with the pageantry and solemnity of ancient ritual wasn't good Cecil B. DeMille, but material for a George Kelly satire. Or it might have been the plot of a movie entitled *Anything Goes*, produced by The Société des Bains de Mer (S.B.M.), the company that ran Monaco's casino and tourist hotels, except that if the S.B.M. were running the show, the affair of the outmoded necklace would not have taken place.

The Prince could not, by any stretch, be blamed for all of this. Most of the truly embarrassing moments were not his or his government's doing; and certainly the press, by virtue of Grace's incredible celebrity, would have beaten most insistently on the door. But the door did not have to be opened *that* far. In his wounded pride, Rainier submitted to playing by rules and standards—and for audiences—that said "Hollywood," not the Principality of Monaco. A dignified state wedding might have taken place, a grand affair, to be sure, but one that spanned two or three days, not a week, and for three hundred guests, not twice that number. Monégasque security was famous even then for its strictness and control. No matter how importunate and ingenious journalists could be, they would not have entered the Principality in such numbers, or, even if they had, obstructed so much, unless the government tacitly cooperated. Press representation could have been limited to several hundred select reporters and photographers. M.G.M. need

---

* The French press couldn't get over the American taste for odd (by French standards) taste in gastronomic combinations. Even a correspondent as serious as *Le Monde*'s Jean Couvreur commented on Peggy Kelly Conlan's eating a dozen escargots and drinking a glass of milk with them.

not have made a film,† nor need live television have been called in so that thirty million people in nine countries could ogle at the goings-on from behind the very altar of St. Nicholas.

The result of the failed overbid was to encourage the foreign press in its miscasting of Monaco as "M.G.M., or Vegas on the Riviera." This may or may not have served the tourist business, but it definitely harmed the Principality in quarters where it very much depended on close relations—starting with the Vatican. Well before the wedding, the Palace had issued a communiqué proudly announcing that their Serene Highnesses would punctuate their honeymoon with one important piece of state business—a formal visit to the Pope. The communication basked in understated pride; the convocation to so early an audience was yet another mark of regard by a pontiff who had already dispatched his personal representative to the Grimaldi wedding. Then, only a few days before the joyous mass at St. Nicholas, Fr. Tucker took the Prince aside to inform him of a terribly disappointing message just received from the Vatican Secretariat of State. Under the circumstances created by the undignified pandemonium of the wedding, it would now be desirable for Prince Rainier and Princess Grace to postpone their visit to Pius XII—*for one year.* No single outcome could have brought home more penetratingly to Prince Rainier the reversal of his hopes and plans for the wedding.

And no one was more lastingly distressed by all of this than the Prince himself, as his remarks (public and private) over the years attest. The "disastrous affair" that was the wedding week ate away at him irremediably for two fundamental reasons. First, an honest, reflective man, Rainier was, or became, subliminally aware of his own partial responsibility for the events that befell the wedding and the Principality in those misbegotten seven days.

Secondly, the most goring irony of all had to be the Prince's recognition that the bride whose wedding was half-ruined—the apparent object of all the fuss—was the farthest thing imaginable from an egotistical Helen of Hollywood. Not only would Grace have preferred a smaller scale of celebration, she could have—had she been consulted— spared her Prince and Principality much grief. At twenty-six, she was

---

† *The Wedding of the Century* took a bath at the hands of reviewers. Bosley Crowther of the New York *Times* reviewed it together with another short on the Battle of Gettysburg. Based on the portentous commentary of the wedding film, he wrote, "it is difficult to know which event is the more important historically . . . The tone of the commentator's voice lead[s] one to sense that the rituals are almost too momentous for common view" (May 13, 1956).

Metro, while loudly disclaiming any desire to profit from its former star's enormous publicity, nevertheless waited until mid-April to release *The Swan* (the movie in which Grace marries a prince). It did not do well commercially. Dore Schary attributed this to the public's greater interest "in the real life story of Miss Kelly being married to a prince . . ."

not conscious of the deeper causes of what was happening around her, but had she collaborated closely in the conception of the wedding, she would probably have foreseen some of the problems. Of course circumstances entirely precluded her participation. Rainier would, at this early stage, never have asked Grace for her help; doing so would have appeared to him (not her) an admission of weakness. Moreover, the actress had been completely absorbed in her own, quite daunting round of celebrations and ceremonials in the United States.

The wedding provided a good illustration of the difference between the benefits everyone *figured* Grace would bring to Monaco and the real gifts she was to give the Principality. According to the American press, she was the "girl who saved the bank at Monte Carlo." In fact she became a caring, loving wife with an ability to intuit her husband's thoughts and inflect them helpfully with her own, a sensitivity to her new home, and her fierce desire to preserve Monaco's heritage.

But these gifts were not created nor given easily, quickly. Several extremely difficult and, at times, painful years had to be got through before Grace found her place in this strange, subtle, so easily misconstrued society that was Monaco.

PART THREE

LIFE

Elle voulait vraiment avoir une présence à Monaco.

—Prince Rainier III

Virtue does not culminate in effort but in ease, lest it become alienating.

—St. Thomas Aquinas

CHAPTER VII

THE SETTING: MONACO AND ITS PRINCES

One never stops discovering Monaco, for there exist several Monacos, and the truest one of them is perhaps not the one you know or think you know.

—Jean Couvreur, correspondent in Monaco for Le Monde *in the 1950s*

The Principality in which Grace was asked to make her home stretched narrowly for two miles along the Mediterranean coast. Monaco resembled a large softshell crab that had crept to the seashore: its dominant right (westerly) pincer was the high fortified plateau where the Prince's Palace stood; its smaller left (easterly) pincer was the promontory of the Larvotto; its mandibles, the hill of Charles adorned by the Casino and Opera. At its slenderest, Monaco was barely the breadth of a football field; at its widest, it ran 3,600 feet—roughly thirteen and a half New York City blocks. In 1956, the Principality occupied 375 acres, making it the smallest secular state in the world (the Vatican is 109 acres); but it would grow in size, thanks to enormous landfill projects, until it attained 480 acres, making it *still* the smallest secular state in the world.

Also the most densely inhabited. The population that turned out joyfully to greet the new Princess numbered twenty-two thousand souls, of whom fewer than 15 percent (roughly three thousand) carried Monégasque passports, the great preponderance being Italian and French citizens who worked and lived in the Principality. And yet, though populated by Frenchmen and engulfed on three sides by the great French Republic, Monaco was not French—especially if France is thought to be synonymous with Paris. Nor was it Italian, either Milanese or Roman.

Rather, Monaco, like its neighboring cities along the Mediterranean littoral and inland for nearly a hundred miles, was a part of an ancient, discrete culture known as the Languedoc—an ebullient, poetical, sensual, sun-loving "culture of the body rather than the spirit" (in the words of a local novelist). The Monégasque dialect was as old as French and Italian and developed from the same Latin roots, with the difference that, unlike Provençal, it never became a (written) literature.

Through fifteen centuries of colonization, the capital cities of Madrid, Paris, and Rome imposed their languages, economies, politics, and elite cultures on their Mediterranean provinces, but they never entirely drove out or subdued the vitality of the Languedoc—still less in Monaco, where political sovereignty always afforded a measure of cultural independence. Shrewd, adaptive, and devoid of illusions, the Monégasques learned to play by the rules of the north—indeed, as often as not, got the better of the northerners at their own games. Yet so long as the brilliant Mediterranean sun ripens the olives, and the mimosa blooms lavishly in spring, so long as Alp meets tideless sea, and sky and water compete in offering flawless shades of blue will a certain breed of Languedocian write and feel "I long for the Mediterranean . . . I feel in my bones that I belong in Monaco."*

§   §   §

Monaco, as Grace would soon discover, was a small place only in the newspapers. In life, the "postage-stamp domain" teemed with subtleties, shades, characteristics, distinctions, cleavages, and potentialities reflecting a thousand years of history; each needing to be known carefully, slowly, individually; all resisting casual interest. A broad overview of the Principality showed several distinct areas.

The best-known of these was unquestionably the hill that was simultaneously the geographic and economic epicenter of the Principality. For centuries called simply "Les Spélugues" for its caves and declivities, this "realm of the spelunker" became by the late nineteenth century one of the great gaming centers of the world. It also got renamed for the Prince who conceived the idea. At the time of Grace's arrival, Monte Carlo (or Mount Charles) was nearing its centenary of successfully bilking rich tourists; in the eyes of the world, if not of the Principality, Monte Carlo was the tail that wagged the dog: you said Monaco, you *meant* Monte Carlo.

But that was only the world's judgment, which a princess consort like Grace would be expected soon to see beneath. The steady thrum of political life in the Principality went on irrespective of the luxury clientele being sunned and burned at Monte Carlo. And the "first" commune of Monaco in the opinion of the people who lived there was undoubtedly the westerly plateau known bluntly and descriptively as "Le Rocher," the Rock. Here, in an immense burnt sienna and cream

* Caroline de Grimaldi, "Home," in the *International Herald Tribune*'s supplement on Monaco; April 1981.

fastness, the Grimaldi princes had lived since their thug of an ancestor, Francesco, had taken the fort by ruse in 1297. But the princes did not have the Rock to themselves, only the northern end of it. A densely packed medieval town, Monaco-Ville, stretched out just beyond the Place d'Armes in front of the Palace. Here dwelled the large "clan" that were the native Monégasques—families with lineages nearly as long as the Grimaldis', bearing proud names like Bellando, Crovetto, Palmaro, Simon, Auréglia, Boisson, Sangiorgio, and several dozen more. Men with these names had participated in the governance of the Principality since before Columbus arrived in the New World.

At the foot of the Rock, and to the east, lay the Condamine—the port proper, of Monaco. On this very narrow plain lived many of the newcomers to the Principality, though in many instances "newcomers" could count back three, four, and more generations of residency. The non-Monégasque population had been predominantly Italian until the Second World War, when the Fascist occupation made Italians (and Germans) rather unpopular, and certainly unfashionable, all over the Riviera. With the fall of the Axis, many of the more important Italian families re-emigrated to Italy, even those who had lived in Monaco for over a century. They were replaced by increasing numbers of Frenchmen, some of whom occupied positions of the highest importance— from the directorship of the corporation that ran the Casino of Monte Carlo to the Prince's own minister of state. There was also concentrated in the Condamine (as well as Monte Carlo) a fairly large permanent English colony, and, lastly, forty-two displaced Americans, whose median age was fifty-seven and who had no desire whatever to return stateside even though they admitted to a *New Yorker* reporter that no Yank, and certainly none of them, could ever be completely assimilated in Monaco.

There was, lastly, the Larvotto section of Monaco, to the east of Monte Carlo. Largely residential along the beach, but with some retail commerce inland, the Larvotto was far less densely populated than the westerly regions of Monaco, and, as such, beckoned to be, as the city planners put it, "developed."

§   §   §

This, then, was the visible geography—the exotic, luxurious Principality—that Grace came to live in in 1956. But invisible, and critical to understanding her life there, was a whole history that enframed her choices, her hopes, her achievements, in short, her identity as a princess. Without that history, Grace will always remain an enigma. When examined, the history makes Monaco less a rock than an iceberg: nine tenths hidden, much of it cutting.

The history of Monaco is long and tortuous but simple: it is the story of a small nation's struggle for corporate survival—and, more particularly, of one family's durability as its rulers. The two themes are inextricably linked; and, on balance, both have been brilliantly successful. One should attribute this success to the Monégasques' uncanny skill at transforming would-be adversaries into allies. Like many other small nations, Monaco has pursued the time-honored policy of playing off one large enemy against another—Guelf against Ghibelline, Spain against France, or France against Italy, France against world good opinion. More cagily still, Monaco has survived by luring outsiders *in*, providing outsiders pleasures and conditions that they cannot, or will not, provide themselves.

In earlier centuries, Monaco's battle was fought with diplomacy—the shifting politics of alliances and alignments—or, very occasionally, and in the last resort, with a display of armed might. But since the mid-1800s, the battle has been mainly one of economy and appearances, or profits and prestige. The first serious threat to the Principality's economic fortunes came in 1861 when Charles III was obliged to sell three fourths of his domain to France. Until that time, the Prince's holdings comprised, besides Monaco proper, two important coastal towns and their outlying lands. Roquebrune and Menton lay respectively four and five miles east along the coast from the hill of Monte Carlo. Menton, especially, with its growing, active population, was a lucrative source of customs, excises, and profits from citrus exportation, not to mention the Grimaldis' personal holdings in both communes.

But French nationalism and the facts of power politics obliged Charles to sell Roquebrune and Menton, at a fraction of their worth, to the consolidated French Empire of Napoleon III. The Prince had little choice; the alternative might well have been to lose both communes, and possibly Monaco itself, to the unified Italian kingdom. Exercising the small say given him, Charles opted for France. The Treaty of 1861, while overtly regulating the Roquebrune-Menton cession, contained secret articles that ratified the de facto French protectorate, which had replaced the Italian influence in Monaco.

A close friend of the Emperor Napoleon's, Prince Charles could finally breathe free that his sovereignty was assured. On the other hand, the loss in prosperity and prestige was enormous for the Grimaldis. Theretofore Monaco had been small but respectable—a domain measurable in square miles, smaller but on the order of San Marino or Liechtenstein. Now, with one signature, the Principality went from tiny to microscopic. A fortress and a small town hugging a steep rock and a few hundred acres of farmland were the stuff of derision: what the New York *Times* would call "Graustark-on-the-Mediterranean."

Fortunately, Charles III's enterprise and pluck were not fractional-

*Grace and Rainier at the announcement of their engagement,
Philadelphia, January 1956.
Credit: United Press International Photo.*

*The bride and groom at the wedding at the Cathedral of
St. Nicholas, Monaco, April 19, 1956.
Credit: Wide World Photos.*

Grace and Rainier, 1956; she is pregnant with Caroline.
Credit: The Penguin Collection.

The "infamous" news photo of "insensitive" Grace
at an amusement park with her children's nanny, Maureen King.
Credit: Sygma Photos.

*Grace and Onassis while he was still majority shareholder
in the S.B.M., 1963. Credit: Sygma Photos.*

*Rainier conferring with his closest adviser at the Monaco
Grand Prix, 1965. Credit: Sygma Photos.*

Grace and her brood: Albert in the foreground, Caroline
at left; baby Stephanie on the right, circa 1966.
Credit: United Press International Photo.

Grace and Stephanie, 1968.
Credit: United Press International Photo.

Grace and Rainier walking in the gardens behind the Palace.
Credit: Sygma Photos.

ized along with his holdings in land. Well before the Treaty of 1861, he came to the conclusion that the Principality's future lay in drawing wealthy outsiders to Monaco. The question was how. Together with his shrewdest councillor—his mother, Princess Caroline—Charles studied several possibilities at hand and presently arrived at the conclusion that Monaco's future lay in the gentlemanly pursuit of gaming. With the end of the French revolutionary era, casino gaming had reemerged as a favorite pastime among the European aristocracy, but then, as ever, betting basked in the heat of a certain formal religious, social, and legal opprobrium. Throughout Europe, it was permitted in only a very limited number of places.

The first thing Charles and Caroline had noticed was that the cities which fattened off the casino trade were almost entirely northern—middling towns in Belgium and Germany where the weather and the geography were, at best, forgettable, at worst, nearly impassable. The Principality had perfect climate and natural beauty, a glorious commingling of sky, sun, sand, and sea. Wealthy fashion had for some time now been turning back to "taking the waters"; why not, therefore, create a casino on the Riviera under the cover of a health resort? There would be no competition from Cannes and Nice or Genoa. In an excess of virtue, the bourgeois regime of France's "citizen king" (Louis Philippe) had banned gambling in the 1830s, and Napoleon III did not feel able to lift the ban. Casino gaming was also illegal in Italy. Monaco would have a free hand. La Société des Bains de Mer, or S.B.M., was born. The words mean literally Society of Sea Baths. However, like the Holy Roman Empire—which, Voltaire said, was "neither holy nor Roman nor an empire"—the S.B.M. was neither a society, nor a bath, nor did it have anything to do with the ocean. It was just a casino corporation masquerading under the name of a health spa.

As it happened, the S.B.M. was nearly stillborn. The fact that gaming was both highly popular and strictly limited to a few settings should seemingly have ensured that those happy places flourished. But they did not, necessarily. Gaming was treacherous to its would-be commercial domesticators. A thousand difficulties—beginning, but by no means ending, with a long run of house bad luck—could arise to ensnare the unwary and inexperienced. The least problem was overseeing the play, though that required gimlet-eyed scrutiny. A greater challenge in Monaco was getting visitors to the Principality—an altogether risky proposition (across mountainous terrain and bad roads) unless they came by boat. Then there was the endless expense and planning that went into putting up the visitors—i.e., feeding and entertaining aristocrats used to the very finest—while they decided whether, and how much, they would play.

The care and feeding of high rollers has always been an extremely demanding, tricky affair, then as now. For eight years, Charles and Caroline watched entrepreneur after entrepreneur try and fail to get the business of gaming to "take" in the unfamiliar setting of Monaco. Then they found their man. François Blanc came to Monaco from a brilliant tenure as director of the Bad Homburg casino. He had watched from afar while the S.B.M. floundered and gasped. In a luxury trade such as this, where taste and fashion were decisive, takeoff was crucial; toward that end, nothing should be spared, no economies made, no early profits anticipated. Where the scope and the hope were this great, so must the risk be. Having studied his predecessors' failures, Blanc tendered his offer to Prince Charles in 1863. The Prince granted him a fifty-year concession to run the Casino.

Under the lavish hand of François Blanc, followed (in 1898) by his son, Camille, and with the full collaboration of Prince Charles and his successor, the ensuing three decades saw arise on the hill across the Bay of Hercules from the Palace a vatican of sumptuous leisure. The Casino was itself a palatial edifice—an immense, ornate jewel box in the style that came to be known as *belle époque*. The elaborate gaming rooms occupied one wing of the building; in the opposite wing was an opera house designed by Garnier, the designer of the Paris Opera. At a right angle to the Casino stood the Hotel de Paris, a creation of such neobaroque splendor as to be the talk of Europe for the decade after it was built. Parallel to it, hardly a block away, was the sedate, elegant and regal Hotel Hermitage, modeled on the Winter Palace in St. Petersburg. Later, a large sporting club was built, and still later more hotels. By the turn of the century, the S.B.M. had made the hill—now renamed for Prince Charles, Monte Carlo—into *le dernier cri* of high fashionability, comfort, and culture—all for the purpose of drawing more people to bet more money, and then more money. *And people did.*

The Blancs' success was so astounding that the S.B.M. presently carried the Principality. Always Monaco's largest employer (three thousand employees by 1900, roughly a sixth of the population of the realm) the company soon became the Principality's banker; its annual contribution paid not only the Prince's civil list but most of Monaco's expenses. By the prewar era, the S.B.M.'s levy became all but synonymous with the state budget. Charles III endeared himself to his people, and raised eyebrows (and envy) all over Europe, by excusing his subjects from all direct taxes and rates. One result, however, was that unquestionably, for a certain leisured and frivolous class of titled tourists, the Casino and the Hotel de Paris were synonymous with Monaco.

That this process of synecdoche, where a part is taken for the whole, did not entirely engulf the Principality's reputation was largely the work of Prince Charles's son and heir, Albert I, who ascended the throne in 1889 and ruled until 1922. Monaco has been blessed with exceptional leadership for a century and a half, but indubitably its greatest prince was Albert. If Charles gave Monaco prosperity, his son brought it effulgence. Not since Henry of Portugal in the fifteenth century had a navigator-prince won more renown for a small realm than Albert de Grimaldi won for Monaco with his accomplishments in science and statecraft.

A young man of such fierce independence that his grandmother (Princess Caroline) scolded him for his "esprit de contradiction," Albert chose to enter the Spanish Navy for his military apprenticeship. The precedent for this action was distant, to say the least: Monaco had not enjoyed Spanish protection since the sixteenth century. Moreover, in view of the father's close ties with France, the son's choice might have precipitated a break, had Charles been so inclined. In the event, Albert did not dishonor his father. Within a year, he rose to the rank of lieutenant. Later, at the time of the Franco-Prussian War, he joined the French Navy, and, at a remarkably young age, received the cross of the Legion of Honor for his service.

The Prince was all of twenty-two when he developed a passionate interest in the comparatively fledgling science of oceanography. Where another wealthy young nobleman might have been satisfied to let an amateur's knowledge eventually give rise to a patron's largesse, Albert threw himself into the professional study of oceanography. Gradually, after several years of tutelage at the hands of the leading marine scientists of the day, he emerged as a colleague and an innovator. In his several specially designed yachts, over the course of a long career, Albert not only outfitted some of the most advanced oceanographic laboratories of his time, but himself invented several of the techniques and instruments used for measurement and exploration. The voyages of experimentation and discovery that Albert made, in the company of many of Europe's most eminent marine scientists, produced scholarly papers of the highest order. Some of the Prince's charts and maps were indeed still in use at the time of the Allied landings in North Africa, four decades later.

Albert was no less important or admired as benefactor. He founded in Monaco the awesome, palatial Oceanographic Institute, with its remarkable aquarium, museum, and library, and with separate research headquarters in Paris. In the late nineteenth century, the Institute became one of Europe's most creative and energetic scientific bodies, underwriting research around the world, publishing articles and books, holding conferences, and generally contributing to the secure foundation of modern oceanography.

Simultaneously, Albert developed an avid interest in fossils and the origins of man. He founded in Paris the Institute for Human Paleontology, which, in addition to maintaining programs in teaching and publication, undertook a number of major digs and investigations. It later opened a museum of paleontology in the Principality. The Prince himself took part in key discoveries in the Roches-Rouges caverns in the south of France.

Albert's intellectual achievement was honored the world over. In 1909, the British Academy of Science invited him to join its fold, replacing the renowned physicist, Lord Kelvin. Ten years later, at the time of the foundation of the International Hydrographic Bureau, delegates from several dozen nations unanimously chose Monaco as the site for I.H.B. headquarters "in recognition of the luster of the great oceanographic works of this Prince." In 1920, the American Academy of Science voted the Prince its gold medal.

Albert once said he believed the world needed fewer princes and more men of intelligence and learning. The fact remained that his intellectual renown would have meant less to Monaco if its acquisition had absented a prince from his duties to his principality. Such was not the case with Charles III's only son. When his father died in 1889, Albert immediately picked up a burden he privately described as "impossible and ungrateful." Given the deeply imperfect nature of diplomacy and politics, and the perfectionist, autocratic personality of the Prince, one can see how statecraft was, for Albert, inestimably more painful and disappointing than scientific work.

The more so because Albert's cherished project in foreign affairs was the pursuit of peace in an era bent on competition and conflict. A distinguished combatant in war, the Prince early on in his life became a pacifist. He was not unusual in this; the same era that witnessed the most formidable armaments race in European history also produced a would-be antidote in a group of clear-sighted, imploring Cassandras. Characteristically, Albert combined a personal and public, theoretical and practical approach to disarmament. He convened a peace congress in the Principality in 1902 and followed it with the permanent establishment of the International Institute of Peace which he charged with the study of the means of peaceful conflict resolution through arbitration.

More practically, the Prince occasionally intervened directly in European diplomacy. Calling on the close friendship he had developed over the years with the German emperor, William II, and the formal ties he had, as Prince, with the presidents of the French Republic, Albert again and again sought to defuse Franco-German rivalry and conflict. And again and again failed. War, when it inevitably came, found Albert melancholic, almost misanthropic. He spent the war on his yacht in the harbor rather than in the Palace because the former afforded more solitude. Monaco declared de jure neutrality, but in fact served the Allies with hospitals, convalescent centers, and recruits—among them, its crown prince, Louis.

Albert used the War to knit closer ties to France. The result was the Treaty of 1918, which updated and replaced the 1861 articles, and crystallized six decades of growing friendship between the Principality and the Republic. Its central great provision from which all other agreements flowed was this: France formally charged itself to guarantee Monégasque sovereignty and integrity "as if this territory were part of France herself"; the Prince, in return, undertook to exercise the rights of his sovereignty "in perfect conformity with the political, military, naval, and economic interests of France." The Prince could call on French military assistance at any time; and the Republic could, with the Prince's accord, billet soldiers in the Principality. In the matter of the succession, France's signal concern was to prevent the German branch of the Grimaldi family from occupying the throne.† The Treaty therefore stipulated that the crown could devolve upon no one who was not French or Monégasque and acceptable to the French government. If a vacancy in the succession arose—e.g., if the Prince had no natural or adopted heir—then the Principality, per se, would cease to exist; its territory would become an autonomous French protectorate with the name State of Monaco. In general, *any* disposition concerning the succession required prior French agreement.

For the rest, the 1918 Treaty continued in force the customs union, established in 1861, as well as common public services (post, utilities, roads, fire department, etc.). An official representative of the Prince was stationed in Paris and accredited by the Republic. France, finally, agreed to use its good offices in the international arena to facilitate Monaco's access to membership in world bodies and participation in international conferences.

Albert thus cemented the closest collaboration and friendship between the two nations, but the fact remained that Monaco was very different from France. Diplomatically close, it remained politically and economically independent and thus got the best of both worlds. The life offered in the Principality was in many regards quite preferable to what France (or any large nation) could offer—a fact that became penetratingly clear after the turn of the century. Seeds of discord lay buried in the envy with which French youths remarked on the absence of compulsory military service in Monaco, or French unemployed watched the flowing fountain of jobs and social services there, or French corporate elites cast longing eyes on the advantageous taxation policies of Monaco, or French speculators of all shades witnessed the

† Charles III's sister, Princess Florestine, married the Duke of Urach-Württemburg. As she was his only sibling, any cessation in the direct line of descent from Charles would move the succession to the German branch.

seemingly impregnable prosperity that the S.B.M. had brought to the fortunate Principality.

Well into the Depression, while around her waxed misery and want, Monaco led its charmed life. For six decades, tourism and gaming brought the Principality unexpected, unheard-of prosperity. The surplus from the S.B.M. cornucopia subsidized not only the Prince, his government, and Albert's prodigious scientific and humanitarian projects, but most of the public services of Monaco, as well as the Principality's lavish cultural life.

If Albert assured Monaco's political security and prestige, the realm's cultural flourishing in the *belle époque* and the twenties was largely the doing of one woman, Princess Alice, his wife, one of a long number of the Principality's activist, independent consorts. Alice Heine was a blond-haired, blue-eyed American beauty, daughter of a wealthy East Coast building contractor. In 1890 she became Albert's wife and strong collaborator. The Prince was in fact her second marriage‡; her first husband was a French noble, Armand, Duc de Richelieu, a fabulously wealthy man, who encouraged his wife to open a literary-artistic salon in Paris, but who, sadly, died five years after their wedding. Though only twenty-two when she arrived in Monaco, Alice thus had a thoroughgoing knowledge of the European social and cultural scene. Her temperament presented a contrast to Albert's—she was vivacious and witty; he, moody, reclusive, and increasingly melancholy—but she shared with her husband a tenacious determination to enrich Monaco's cultural ambience.

Surveying the scene, Alice recognized this effort could not be accomplished without the collaboration of the S.B.M. Both she and Albert had no interest in gaming and in fact shared a private distaste for the more garish sides of Monte Carlo, but both understood the crucial role that tourism and gaming played in underwriting Monaco's success in all fields. So, stifling her objections, Princess Alice played a vital role in extending the S.B.M.'s concession another fifty years. But she drove a hard bargain. The company had to agree to make an initial payment of $2.5 million directly into the state treasury, followed by another $12.5 million when the original concession ran out (1913). It further offered to pay nearly a million dollars toward the ongoing construction of the Opera House, and to contribute six thousand dollars apiece for each of twenty-four performances a season. All this was in addition to the

‡ As she was Albert's second wife. His first, ill-fated marriage was to an aristocrat, Lady Mary Douglas Hamilton, daughter of the Duke of Hamilton, ranking peer of Scotland. Only eighteen when she married the Prince and moved onto the Rock, Lady Mary could not stand the weather, the loneliness, or most of the people and customs of Monaco. Within a year (1870), she presented Albert with his only child and heir, Louis, and shortly after, she left Monaco forever. The marriage was annulled by the Vatican in 1880.

usual annual contribution that the S.B.M. made to the Principality, not to mention the ongoing "extras" that Princess Alice continued to extort for her endless cultural and charitable projects.

With this financing, and her own connections and taste, Princess Alice launched an enterprise (that continued after her) that promoted a town of fewer than twenty thousand people into something approaching a cultural Great Power. She brought one of the finest impresarios in Europe, Raoul Gunsbourg, to Monaco and gave him the Opera to run. The result was, just in one instance, a series of Wagner festivals previously unseen outside of Bayreuth. In order not to offend the French (in this era of Franco-German rivalry), Gunsbourg also created productions of the contemporary composer Jules Massenet's and helped to popularize his great, as well as a few of his lesser known, works. Finally, the impresario worked closely with Princess Alice in upgrading the theater of Monaco, bringing Sarah Bernhardt and the Comédie Française (among others) to the Principality for seasonal productions. Still later (after Alice's time), Gunsbourg was responsible for settling into residence in Monaco a troupe of emigré Russian ballet dancers under the direction of a man of singular temperament and genius named Sergei Diaghilev.

One major facet of Monaco still needed attention: its politics. At the turn of the twentieth century, the Principality was still Renaissance in its style and structures of governance. For a regime that had been overthrown by the French Revolution, the Monégasque principate had forgotten little and learned less. The Grimaldi princes restored by the Congress of Vienna (1815) revived most of the quasifeudal powers, prerogatives, and style of the old regime. They personally enacted all laws and decrees, collected and spent revenues with no accountability, and, in general ran the Principality as a patrimonial fief. The better princes like Charles III and Albert I took pains to avoid the appearance of arbitrary or despotic government, but their efforts did not always manage to conceal their authoritarian temperaments nor to placate local discontent. In one fundamental regard, Charles had only himself to blame for the loss of Roquebrune and Menton in 1861, for the communes' decision to become French was, in great part, a function of their wish to have the vote.

With the departure of the "radicals" of the two communes, the Principality settled down to its quiet feast of political reaction and economic clover, but by the end of the nineteenth century, even rump Monaco sprouted a crop of plaintiffs. The Monégasque opposition, which included a few of the oldest names on the Rock, maintained that it was antediluvian to see the Principality as the personal property of the Prince. States in the modern era, they said, were creatures of law and consent and right; Monaco, they said, needed a constitution. So far, so good. But concealed within this blameless rhetoric, as Albert well knew, was a rank vein of self-interest and oligarchical initiative. Consider the demography of Monaco: neither then nor at any time in the state's history did the Monégasques themselves comprise more than a quarter of the population, usually less. The call for self-government, therefore—however laudatory and overdue—was also a demand that 20 percent of the Principality, by reason of birth, be allowed to determine the political (and to a large extent the economic) fate of the vast majority, of people whose interest and stake in the state were no less great than those of the native Monégasques. In some instances, these "outsiders" had lived in Monaco for four and five (or more) generations.

Prince Albert, like his father, was keenly aware of this "hidden side" of the call for self-government. A hundred times he had received, read, and rejected petitions from committees and syndicates of nativist Monégasques calling for laws that would require the hiring of "citizens" in the best jobs of the S.B.M. or the state bureaucracy. To capitulate squarely to these demands would be not only cruelly unfair, but instantly destructive of the commonweal. The S.B.M., like all the institutions in the Principality, including even the higher reaches of government administration, quite simply ran on foreigners. The latter, beginning with Camille Blanc, were men of the highest professional caliber, irreplaceable within the limited pool of Monégasque citizens, many of whom, quite frankly, had educations in indirect proportion to the seniority of their lineage. In sum, Albert's reluctance to alter the status quo was not merely attributable, as his opponents sometimes maintained, to the "solitary and lordly ways of the sea captain on his quarterdeck, sole master after God."

On the other hand, something simply had to be done about the fact that at the turn of the twentieth century, Monaco's political structures had far more in common with Renaissance Florence than with the modern community of nations in which the Principality was eager to take its place. So Prince Albert impaneled a commission of three eminent French jurists and entrusted them with the task of drafting a blueprint for a modern Monégasque government. The result was the Constitution of 1911—a curious document antiquated at its birth. "Albert I, by the Grace of God, Prince Sovereign of Monaco," the preamble read, "concede to our beloved subjects this charter . . ." In language reminiscent of the Sun King, the "beloved subjects" were then vouchsafed details of the modern institutions Albert had in mind— from national and communal councils elected by universal male suffrage, and invested with the right of budgetary review, to a Council of State with certain limited, but independent executive powers. Thoroughly anachronistic in style, the document at least established Monaco as a public domain, not a princely appanage.

Except that it didn't last. World War I broke out three years after Albert's "concession," and the Constitution was suspended. Aside from the fact that circumstances in the neutral Principality did not justify suspension, that act alone set a very dangerous precedent, for it was quite unconstitutional. Nothing in the blueprint of 1911 indicated that once "conceded" the Constitution could be retroceded. Aware of criticism, Albert restored the Constitution in 1917, but with arbitrary "modifications" that he deemed necessary (e.g., the elimination of two of three communal councils; indirect, instead of direct, elections; fewer rights of budgetary review for the National Council, etc.).

The precedent of suspension became a running sore in domestic Monégasque politics for the next fifty years. Albert's son and successor, Prince Louis II, would, in his turn, suspend sections of the Constitution at the first sign of internal unrest (in 1930) and govern by sovereign ordinance—i.e., autocratically—for three years until public pressure obliged a return to constitutional government, but only until next time . . . And, six years later, with the outbreak of another war in Europe, Louis prorogued portions of the Constitution, including the right of assembly.

Monaco, in short, entered the second half of the twentieth century with basic questions of government by law and individual rights very much open. But the issues were not nearly so simple as the slogan "reactionary prince versus liberal opposition" would make it appear. Charles and Albert and their successors were certainly conservative men, princes accustomed to command and capable of the abuse of power. But not one of them wished to turn back the clock, and in the case of Albert's successors, there was a genuine eagerness to push Monaco further into modernity, even (if more cautiously) political modernity. From these rulers' perspective, the problem was not peremptory princely prerogatives, but the obscurantism and self-interest of a certain ancient caste of Monégasques who, if they got their way, would use the state like a pork barrel and plunge the Principality back into darkness. The autocracy of an enlightened prince was seen as the necessary bulwark against the medieval oligarchy that would ensue if a nativist National Council got hold of executive power.

Princes Albert and Charles were, in the end, profoundly unhappy men in their private lives. Charles long outlived his mother, Caroline, and his beloved wife, Princess Antoinette. He himself went totally blind, and died an eccentric and a recluse. Albert's marriage to Princess Alice had a good ten-year run but eventually even she could not tolerate his moods and need for unbroken solitude. After 1900 they became permanently estranged.

Nevertheless, the two rulers set standards of public service that could only awe successors. With his pleasure city on a hill, Charles III produced the greatest economic engine the Principality had ever known—Monaco's great *how*. And with his lustrous array of works of mind, conscience, and sensibility, Albert gave the world Monaco's persuasive *why*.

But the legacies were not equal, not by a far cry. The navigator-prince's accomplishments were intangible and fleeting compared to the gilded monument of Monte Carlo. The twenties, with its forced gaiety and forgetfulness, ushered in an era that more than ever mistook the Casino for Monaco. And thus resurfaced the old problem of derision: "Vegas on the Riviera," as a later generation would call the Principality. Concern for the realm's good standing understandably became something of an obsession for princes who lacked Albert I's unique talents for justifying his state's existence. "If the Principality and the dynasty endure another seven centuries, they will produce no greater sovereign than Albert I." The judgment, offered by Prince Louis at his father's funeral, testified to the burden Albert unintentionally laid on his successors.

And meanwhile, the S.B.M. coughed up its never-ending jackpot.

§   §   §

Between the giants of Monégasque history and Prince Rainier came Louis II. He was no genuis and no empire builder and had the stolid good sense not to tell himself he was. The basic problems he faced remained the same as his predecessors, and the same that faced Rainier when he married Grace Kelly. Louis was caught between the nativist Monégasques and the Casino—the Rock and the Wheel. The best accomplishment of his reign, with World War II to deal with, was survival.

A cosseted child, endowed with what his mother described as a "good, sweet, and open" disposition, Louis grew up in Baden with his Scottish mother, Lady Mary, long since estranged from Prince Albert. The son, indeed, only met his father in his eleventh year, when, as prince hereditary, he was obliged to move to Monaco to begin his training. Being suddenly torn away from the loving, warm, attentive environment of his youth and set down in a distant land with a remote, intellectual father proved a very painful experience for the ten-year-old boy. Albert made no move to draw Louis close to him, so the child was obliged to protect himself: he aped his father's coldness. The shell Louis built around his inner sweetness of character was a carapace of quiet, patient obstinacy and an irresistible insistence on independence.

He fled his father's realm as soon as he could and made for himself the only lasting home he ever knew: in the French Army. Louis entered Saint-Cyr, the French West Point, at sixteen, and emerged four years later with a commission in the cavalry and a fastidious affection for military getup. By now he had entered upon the title Duc de Valentinois, a title sometimes given to the crown (or, as they are termed, hereditary) princes of Monaco. Louis himself, however, had no interest in returning to Monaco. He therefore asked the French government to be posted with the Foreign Legion in Africa. For more than a decade, the young officer fought bravely and with distinction in numerous campaigns and lived up to at least one of his father's accomplishments by winning, precociously, the cross of the Legion of Honor.

He also met his first wife there, though one searches in vain through the histories of Monaco and her princes for any mention of Juliette Louvet.* This lacuna is no doubt attributable to the fact that Juliette was the daughter of a French-Algerian laundress, hence unacceptable to the Monégasque court or its sovereign as a consort to the Prince Hereditary. Albert firmly opposed his son's intention to marry, and his authority over the princely family was, if anything, even more supreme than over the Principality. He could, and did, refuse to permit Louis to marry Juliette Louvet.

But he married her anyway, in late 1897. Neither the fact that they were wed in a consecrated church by an ordained priest in a proper Catholic service, nor that Juliette bore Louis a daughter, Charlotte, made a whit of difference to Albert. In the eyes of this Prince whom Europe and America honored for his wisdom and humanitarianism, his son was a bachelor, and his son's daughter, a bastard.

Meanwhile Louis's tour of duty wore on. It was 1908, his thirty-eighth birthday, and his father (who was sixty), insisted Louis return home. He came back reluctantly. Albert, dependably, displayed indifference to his son's presence, but he did engage Louis's participation in the protracted and frustrating negotiations with the liberal opposition over the "concession" of a constitution. A Legionnaire major, recently returned from African duty, Louis was not the sort of man to display much sympathy for rarefied philosophical discussion and distinction-drawing, especially when he saw the goal was to diminish his princely birthright. Louis did not impress the constitutionalists and only irritated his father.

The outbreak of war in Europe was probably the only thing that prevented the re-eruption of hostilities between Albert and son. Louis jumped at the opportunity to flee; he re-enlisted in the French Army and was assigned to a staff post in the headquarters of the First, and later the Fifth, Army. The citations filling his dossier in the French military archives constitute a glowing testimony to Louis's love of the

* Léon-Honoré Labande, *Histoire de la Principauté de Monaco* (Monaco, 1934); Françoise de Bernardy, *Histoire des Princes de Monaco* (Paris: Librairie Plon 1960). There is also no mention of her in the authorized biography of her grandson, Prince Rainier III.

life of arms and his skill at it. He is commended again and again not only for "audace," "sangfroid," and "vigueur" under fire, but for intelligence and judgment. The end of the war found "Louis Grimaldi" a Grand Officer of the Legion of Honor (a higher grade than his father reached) and a full colonel. He was later promoted to lieutenant-general. Over their long history, there were Grimaldis who attained higher grades in the armed service of France (one made Field Marshal), but none who acquitted himself with more distinction.

But it was not Louis's war record that softened his father's heart, nor any mellowing of age. It was, rather, considerations of politics that now forced Albert to reconsider the question of his granddaughter's legitimacy. Louis had long since left Juliette, but refused to remarry. The year was 1919, the Prince Sovereign was seventy-one and ailing and had recently signed a treaty with France stipulating that if his house failed to produce an heir, Monaco would join the Republic. That provision cast warmer light on Louis and Juliette's daughter, Charlotte, now twenty-one. Was she Louvet or Grimaldi? Albert decided that *raison d'état* required her to be the latter, lest Monaco be without a ruler at the end of Louis's reign. A sovereign ordinance entitled Louis to nominate his own heir; he promptly chose Charlotte, and a subsequent ordinance named her a princess of the blood. Soon she married a poorer member of a great French noble house, Comte Pierre de Polignac, who, by decree (in accord with Monégasque custom) also became a Grimaldi Prince. Three years later, Albert died. The following year, 1923, Princess Charlotte gave birth to a male son, for whom she chose a name that had not been used for a prince hereditary in over five hundred years of Grimaldi history: Rainier.

As Prince Sovereign, Louis II was not the success that his father had been. Between 1922 and 1949, the Principality passed through some of the hardest years in its history, and Louis did his best, though the tests finally overwhelmed him. In this, he resembled most other European leaders of the era.

The first problem Louis faced, and made a start at solving, was the problem of the S.B.M. The destruction wrought by the War on European crowns and nobilities could not fail to affect an organism as parasitic on aristocratic fortune (and as attuned to aristocratic sensibility) as the Société des Bains de Mer. Whatever granddukes and archdukes were left now stayed away in droves, and for several years, profits took a terrible dive. Moreover, France had legalized casino gambling in Cannes and Nice, so that the S.B.M. no longer had the Riviera to itself. Gradually the twenties produced its own kind of wealth, class, and leisure, and Monte Carlo rapidly showed itself shrewder than the pack in luring in (and hanging onto) new business.

For starters, the S.B.M. teamed up with Elsa Maxwell (who regularly lost her honorific salary at the tables). At her instigation, the company built a blue-tiled swimming pool, flanked by a pink stucco hotel of Hollywood-Spanish design; it dropped a million and a half dollars completing a country club and another million on terraced tennis courts. The Monte Carlo Grand Prix—a serpentine round-the-Principality race of harrowing difficulty—was inaugurated. And later, the International Sporting Club opened, an immense white structure with more gaming rooms, a ballroom, restaurant, nightclub, and bar. As Miss Maxwell was the first to note, the "Society of Beach Bathing" now had everything except a beach. (Maxwell had suggested covering Monte Carlo's pebbly seafront with large sheets of rubber, covered over with sand. At the cost of considerable francs, it was learned that seawater destroys rubber.)

Without its beach, the S.B.M. sailed prosperously and fashionably into the thirties. Even in the depths of the Depression, albeit with an occasional year in the red, the machine turned over brilliantly. Louis II's problem was thus never (or rarely) with the S.B.M.'s take, but rather with its grip—its frighteningly strong hold on the life and the reputation of his Principality. Executive directors of the S.B.M. wielded extraordinary power in Monaco. Camille Blanc's successor was Sir Basil Zaharoff, a Levantine armaments magnate who had slyly acquired a majority hold on the company at the end of the War. For obscure reasons, Sir Basil entered into a feud with Prince Louis and had the audacity to call for his abdication. The incredible thing was not that he won his battle with the Prince Regnant but that he managed to conduct it—and for two years. Even then Zaharoff quit the field only because his wife had died and he was heartsick.

But uppity vassals weren't Louis's principal woe on the Hill of Charles. The thorn in his flesh was the same one that had nettled his father and grandfather: selfish Monégasque nativism hiding beneath the toga of constitutional liberalism. For some time Monégasque citizens had been employed by the S.B.M. far out of proportion to their numbers in the population; their spokesmen demanded much more, and, as always, framed the demands as calls for increased franchise and communal self-determination. Once, things even got indecorous. Louis was hissed in public, and in February of 1929, a few thousand demonstrators forced their way into the Palace demanding his deposition.

The Casino grew faint at even the mention of communal control of gaming and tourism; they sought to buy off the popular threat with constant increases in the S.B.M. contribution to state coffers. But that tack no longer took. The citizenry of Monaco were by now blasé about the infinitesimal size of their utility bills, or the absence of income tax and military conscription; and most of them didn't care a hoot about the "world class" cultural productions available in Monte Carlo. They wanted to have the golden goose.

Ultimately, the soldier in Louis moved swiftly and decisively. In 1930, he suspended the Constitution and ruled by decree. Monte Carlo must be delivered from the apparent threat of popular takeover, but Louis also recognized that the crown could not go on being hostage to the S.B.M., any more than the Principality could afford to depend so heavily on one source of financing, livelihood, and even, apparently, raison d'être. The government must take back from the S.B.M. public services and responsibility for the commonweal; Monaco must look for other sources of income. As Louis must have known, this was the project of more than one reign; and other events intruded to forestall planning.

The Second World War came late to Monaco, but stayed long and proved agonizing, for it ruptured the Principality's social cohesion. In 1914, Monaco declared itself officially neutral, but its internal sympathies were with France; in the Second World War, nationally heterogeneous Monaco was tormented by ambivalence and domestic conflict. Initially the problem was Italy, which under Mussolini, had cast its lot with "the enemy." By a considerable margin, Italians living in Monaco outnumbered Frenchmen.† When France fell to the Nazis, the French Monégasques writhed in indecision, hating the conqueror yet mistrustful of the Allies who had "abandoned" France.

The Italians of Monaco did no such agonizing. They knew exactly how they felt: they were proud, even pugnacious at being on what seemed the winning side. Their home country, led by the imperialist Fascist regime, now cast greedy eyes on the glittering Principality that only eighty years before had stood under Italian, not French, protection. Mussolini resisted temptation until 1943 before using a trifling pretext—in defiance of all international conventions—to dispatch a company carabinieri to occupy Monaco. They were greeted by cheers from the Italian colony, which, in collaboration with the occupying power, proceeded to set up a Fascist political bureau and to work closely with Italian secret police in hunting down Monégasques known for their prewar anti-Fascism. It was a time of the toad.

Things grew worse. With the Allied successes in Italy and Mussolini's collapse, Hitler sent his troops into southern France; they arrived in Monaco in September 1943. The Italian "protectorate" had managed Monaco in a loose fashion; the Germans brought efficiency and organization. A number of Jews, some of considerable wealth and standing, had taken refuge in Monaco after the fall of their home coun-

† The difference of 9,724 to 8,540 (in 1939). Monégasques numbered 1,761, which made them less numerous than the English community in Monaco, at least until most of the latter was evacuated after 1940.

tries. Left alone by the Italians, they became the object of dragnets and deportations at the hands of the Gestapo.‡ The rest of the population suffered from lack of food, electricity, gas, and water. Never dependably available after 1942, these necessities dwindled in supply to the point of severe hardship. Finally, in late summer of 1944, Monaco got its first taste of battle, as Allied planes and battleships bombarded German emplacements along the shoreline. Sections of the Condamine were seriously damaged or completely razed; several hundred casualties were inflicted.

Incredibly, one institution defied the bombs, proscriptions, and shortages. With only an occasional lapse, Monte Carlo continued to mount its spectacle of gaming, sport, opera/ballet/cabaret to a changing audience of Italian, German, or Allied soldiers. (All came in "civvies," though; uniforms had been strictly prohibited since the 1870s). The S.B.M.'s imperturbability, coupled with particularly balmy war weather and the opening of the Larvotto beach, constituted what one contemporary called "our flagrant paradox."* However bad the world got, somehow, *here*, things didn't seem so bad.

Through it all, Prince Louis comported himself morally well and politically badly. He remained with his people throughout the War and did his best to keep them united and hopeful. His own sympathies were entirely pro-French. He had watched with anguished horror as the beloved army of his youth crumbled beneath the Wehrmacht in six weeks. After the collapse of the Republic (and indeed, slightly in anticipation), Louis's loyalty shifted 100 percent to Marshal Pétain, his old colleague and friend. The Prince's unswerving support for Vichy thus placed him at cross-purposes with England and the United States, hence with those (minority) elements in his realm which favored an Allied victory from the outset. But it would be wrong to imagine Louis felt anything but contempt for the Fascists and hatred for the Nazis, or that he went out of his way to cooperate with them in the way Vichy did. On the contrary, in the matter of the arrests of the Jews and *maquisards*, Louis's police often, at risk to themselves, warned people in advance of the Gestapo's "interest."

As the tide of war slowly shifted, Louis's loyalty to Pétain was tested by his wish to share in the German defeat. That he nevertheless stuck by Vichy was in large part due to the influence of his strong-willed French Minister of State, Émile Roblot. Roblot's association with proto-Fascist elements in Vichy and his overoptimistic belief in a German victory became real liabilities as the War dragged on. Louis came

‡ Raoul Gunsbourg, a Jew, was obliged to resign his post at the Opera and go into hiding.
* Jean Drouhard, "1938–1945: Monaco et la grande tourmente," in *Annales Monégasques* (Revue d'histoire de Monaco), #7, 1983, p. 80.

under great pressure to dismiss him, but to do so would be to fly in the face of *le Maréchal* (Pétain) and risk a break with France. On the other hand, after the Allied landings in nearby Provence, Roblot's views and policies became a source of genuine conflict in Monaco.

No one resented the Minister more than Rainier, Louis's twenty-one-year-old grandson and heir.† A lonely and moody young man, the product of a broken marriage and an English prep school, Rainier Louis Henri Maxence Bertrand de Grimaldi had spent little time in his future realm when he returned to Monaco in 1944 from Paris where he had been a student at the École Libre des Sciences Politiques. What he found nauseated him. An opponent of Hitler's from the first day, Rainier was appalled at the hostile indifference that his grandfather's government showed the Allies, not to mention the mindless immorality of the "business as usual" policy at the S.B.M. But what infuriated the young Prince most was the Minister of State's defeatism and his ties to the Vichy sectarian right. When Roblot forbade all anti-Nazi and pro-Ally public demonstrations in Monaco, Rainier went to the Prince. What would it look like to have this man at the helm of government when the Americans liberated Monaco, Rainier demanded of his grandfather?

A soldier, not a politician, Louis had no answer to this question. He was heartsick at what was happening, but beyond visiting the scenes of destruction almost before the bombs and shells stopped falling, he did not know what to do. Leaving Roblot to run affairs, he sealed himself off from "politics" and spent his time culling through his collection of Napoleonana. He did not like his Minister of State, but he stubbornly refused to take the risk of firing him, and he very soon lost any taste for explaining himself to someone he saw as a hotheaded boy. Rainier stomped out of the Palace and shut himself up in his villa at Monte Carlo. The first moment he could, he joined the Free French forces under General de Monsabert (though not before informing the Allies in full about Roblot and his activities). Second Lieutenant Grimaldi fought so courageously in Alsace (during the Nazi autumn counteroffensive) that he won the Croix de Guerre and the Bronze Star and was later awarded the rank of Chevalier in the Legion of Honor.

† At the time of Princess Charlotte's legitimation (1920), it was quietly hoped, and probably tacitly understood that she, a laundress's daughter, would never, barring tragic contingency, actually sit on the gilded First Empire chair that served Monaco as a throne of state. She was a conduit of the succession, and she accomplished her lot in life by giving birth to two children, Antoinette (1920) and Rainier (1923). Charlotte herself may have wished for more, but in the end, she defeated herself—initially by making a mess of her private life (after innumerable public scenes, she and Pierre were divorced in 1929), and later with her pro-Mussolini sentiments, which by 1943 put Charlotte in very bad odor. After a certain amount of cajoling and stiff-arming, she consented to renounce the succession in favor of her son. Louis promptly named Rainier his successor (June 2, 1944).

§   §   §

A chubby-cheeked, smiling blond baby, a sweet-tempered, sensitive child torn from a father he loved and flung into a foreign school, so that by adolescence he had turned himself into a blunt, quick-tempered and emotionally constricted pugilist, with a taste for the military. Did Louis recognize in Rainier the same "protective" response to a broken home, uprootedness, and bitter loneliness that he himself had undergone in his youth? One does not know. Louis wrote no memoirs, while his grandson's are, in matters psychological, remarkable for what is left out.

Following Pierre's and Charlotte's divorce, a French court assigned responsibility for six-year-old Rainier to his father. The Comte de Polignac placed his son in an English school, St. Leonards-on-Sea (near the old battlefield of Hastings). Here Rainier got his first taste of corporal punishment, caning, which badly "shocked me," as he later told his biographer (adding, in an altogether characteristic attempt to put a good face on something that he has found genuinely disturbing, "Being caned is more of an occasion to have a good laugh, and fun, so there was nothing dramatic about it.") Insisting he had "no deep-seated grievance," the young prince progressed a few years later to one of the better British public schools, Stowe, where he was the only foreigner out of 560 boys. His first day there, he promptly ran away and was fortunate enough to be received back to tea by a kindly and understanding master. It "surprised" him, he said, to have to "fag"—i.e., bow, scrape, and serve—for the older boys, but he made the best of a bad thing, and, again, waved off a distasteful experience in manly fashion by supposing that "on the whole, it was very good." Husky and muscular, and rather aggressive, he became a good swimmer and a champion boxer at Stowe, but he also displayed a cautious interest in acting.

Yet if the young prince adapted to life at Stowe, as he had at St. Leonards, he was clearly lonesome and longed to spend time with his father, who lived in Paris. Later, he said, "When you are twelve years old you feel that the Channel is terribly wide." He was not permitted leave, however. Prince Louis, recognizing that his grandson would succeed him directly, presently took a dominant interest in his heir's formation. He got an order from an English court restraining Comte Pierre from taking Rainier out of school. Louis had some reason to take preemptive action; the Comte de Polignac had once tried to kidnap Rainier to keep Charlotte from taking him.

Eventually, perhaps in part because he begged to be, Rainier was sent to a place nearer his family and the world he knew. He entered the school of Le Rosey near Geneva were he stayed for three years, until he was seventeen. Back in a French-speaking environment, and able to see his parents periodically, Rainier came out of himself more. Totally unaffected and straightforward, he was liked by students and teachers. He kept up with sports—individual, not team, and especially boxing—but he also pursued amateur dramatics. Indeed Rainier's delight in stage grease, costumes, and all the artifices of appearance led one historian to wonder if the grandson didn't share the grandfather's love "for gussying himself up."‡

Reading between the lines, what emerges from Prince Rainier's portrait of his own youth is a lonely, unhappy young man. He developed pronounced talents both for concealing his distress under a bluff facade of "I'm all right, Jack" and for sublimating anger (at being pushed out by his family) in well-sanctioned forms of aggression—boxing, pranks, etc. Making do, or, to put a finer point on it, *appearing* to make do, became the identity of a hurt young man intent on not showing he needed affection. Good at being liked, he yet made few friends because, by his own admission, he trusted almost no one and granted intimacy almost never. As a young boy, the mistrust showed itself in a nearly paralyzing shyness, a severe handicap which Rainier fought to overcome. By the time he reached adolescence, he had molded himself into a social being akin to Oscar Wilde's "introvert posing as an extrovert," acquiring skills at introductions and chatter, but civilities never came easily to Rainier. The Prince was always a better, more relaxed observer than participant in the social scene. As such, he was acutely perceptive of human beings. He also displayed—perhaps remarkably in one who had been hurt—a ready willingness to forgive human weakness, beginning with the people closest to him, his family. None of them receives a whisper of reproach for shunting the boy off in private schools and not granting him more time.

War drew a premature end to Rainier's childhood, as it did to so many of his contemporaries'. He left Le Rosey in 1940 before taking his *baccalauréat* (or *bac*, roughly the French equivalent of a high school diploma) and returned to Monaco. He did not linger, however, for Louis insisted he proceed with his studies. So Rainier entered the French university at Montpellier, in the heart of the Languedoc. There he passed the *bac* and began college-level study. Later he went to Paris and entered the prestigious institution of learning known among its graduates as *Sciences Po* (École Libre des Sciences Politiques). In 1944 he returned to Monaco with the intention of starting his on-the-job apprenticeship in statecraft, but, to his credit, Prince Rainier broke with Louis over Roblot and his foreign policy and courageously went his own way.

‡ Françoise de Bernardy, *op. cit.*, p. 285.

From the perspective of what was best for the Principality of Monaco, as well as for the development of its heir, it would have been desirable if Louis II had abdicated or died in 1947 when Rainier was decommissioned from the French Army. The young prince had stayed as long as he could in the Army, serving in Berlin in the Economic Section of the French Military Mission, and eventually attaining the rank of colonel. He returned to Monaco in 1947 to find the Principality mired in neglect. Little had been done in desperately needed reconstruction, and less was planned. Louis II's final years in office were almost entirely absentee, in mind as well as body. The seventy-seven-year-old Prince Sovereign divided his time between the family estate, Marchais, and nearby Paris where he courted, and eventually married, a woman decades his junior, Princess Ghislaine. Louis fussed endlessly over his antiquities but ignored the business of state, staying alert, it seemed, only to keep his grandson—from whom he remained half-estranged—out of public affairs.

Immensely bored and even more frustrated, realizing the realm badly needed an active leader but denied an active role, Rainier threw himself fitfully into a joyless existence of perilous "fun." He took to downhill skiing on slopes and at speeds considered lethal. Skin diving, he several times came close to drowning himself with his stunts. Spearfishing with friends in the shark-infested Red Sea, the young Rainier shot at a fish and lost his arrow. In the clear water the men could see the arrow lying at the bottom of deep water. One by one they tried to retrieve it, but the pressure was too great at that depth, and none could hold his breath long enough. Then Rainier, having tried and failed, announced grimly, "I'm going down and get that arrow." He plunged in and stayed down so long that his friends became quite worried. Finally he surfaced, gasping and exhausted, but he had the arrow. "He is the type of man who, when he decides to do something, will do it if it kills him," a friend told a journalist.

Although he enjoyed hunting (especially going after killer boar in the desolate Basses-Alpes region of France), Rainier developed a love of animals. One evening, shortly after he acceded to the throne, he discovered a small pigeon with an injured wing that had taken refuge in the Prince's box of the Monte Carlo Opera. He took her back to the Palace where he had a veterinarian dress the wound. The Prince named her Carmen because he had met her at the Opera. And when she was recovered, he let her go. His affection for animals also showed itself in a rather particular craving for the company of large carnivorous cats (e.g., lions and tigers) as well as a wide range of less predatory animals, which he kept in his private zoo on the premises of the Palace.

But surely Rainier's most harrowing, life-endangering pastime was automobile racing. He took lessons from Louis Chiron, a Monégasque who had once been world champion. Chiron told a reporter that his pupil was quite apt, but he drove "a shade too fast perhaps." At this time, Rainier lived outside of the Principality, at nearby St. Jean-Cap Ferrat in a villa that he shared with one of France's best-known, and most beautiful, movie stars, Gisèle Pascal.

Rainier's activities in these years won him the reputation of playboy, but the charge was inapt. The opposite of fancy-free in character, the young prince was striving to fill his life with something; and danger at least imbued it with a kind of meaning. Polite and personable, he was too much the loner in these years to qualify for high status with the international set. He also could not be counted on to contain the contempt he felt for frivolousness, conspicuous consumption, and promiscuity. The few friends Rainier associated with, moreover—Roger Crovetto or Jean-Louis Marsan—were far too decent and serious fellows to endear themselves to callous voluptuaries of the Aly Khan mold. Rainier, in fact, chose to decline his invitation to the Aly Khan-Rita Hayworth wedding reception, although it was unquestionably *the* event of Riviera society in the postwar period, largely because he didn't enjoy the company of the people who would be there. Privately, the Prince enjoyed quoting Dorothy Parker's deadly quip about the chichi circuit, "Ennui all?"

And as for Gisèle Pascal, she was glamorous and famous, to be sure, but Rainier's association with her very quickly became serious and lasting. They lived together for several years, during which time neither one was reported dating anyone else. Despite the fact that she was a divorcée, the Prince might have married her, but it was discovered that she could not have children. Even then, Rainier considered abdicating in order to marry, but that act might well have ended the dynasty. Ultimately, and in anguish, he chose the path of duty, but he continued to wear the ring Pascal had given him for many months after they quit seeing one another.

§   §   §

In April of 1949, the aging Louis II became too infirm to continue with the charade of governing. He had no choice but to delegate power to his heir. A month later, the old Prince died—ironically, after so much time away, in his Palace on the Rock. Though publicly respectful, indeed protective, of his grandfather's reputation, Rainier came to the throne acutely aware of how demanding the job was and how neglected it had been in recent years. The example that absorbed and somewhat awed him was Albert I, the polymath prince who had died the year before Rainier was born.

Yet the new sovereign came to two sharp conclusions at the outset of his reign. First, he had no illusions that he could rival Albert's intellectual achievements. Secondly, he sensed that the times had greatly changed since the idyllic era before the great wars when moral and intellectual stature commanded rapt attention in the international arena. In his view, Monaco needed less idealistic initiatives than the founding of institutes for paleontology and peace. For openers, it needed extensive reconstruction of its war-damaged quarters; then it needed thorough reconstruction of its economic base and finances. All this would entail a dramatic reshaping of the Principality's appearance and even its geography. In sum, though mildly infatuated with Albert I's fame as a sailor and guardian of science and culture, Rainier had the sense to know that the times called for a Charles III.

To Rainier, however, this did not mean carte blanche for the S.B.M. Far from it. The new Prince, like his predecessors, personally disliked gambling, was forbidden by law from entering the Casino, and felt disdain for some of the gaudier practices (and tourists) at Monte Carlo. Beyond personal dislike, however, Rainier had reasons of state for a new policy. As every Prince since Charles III discovered, the S.B.M. was becoming something between the sorcerer's apprentice and, on bad days, Dr. Frankenstein's monster. If Rainier was sure of anything as he moved into the Palace, it was that the importance of the S.B.M. to the Principality had to be reduced, and that the means to do so was to establish rival sources of prosperity.

This was easy enough to entertain as a hypothesis, but sobering when one considered the reality. First, there was the problem of space: where would new industry go? To this, the Prince had an answer, albeit a bold and dangerously costly one. A careful scrutiny of the Principality revealed certain areas, and potential areas, where a new Monaco could arise alongside of the old. To the immediate west of the Rock, for example, lay several dozen acres of unused land and shallow, open water—the basin of Fontvielle. Here Rainier reposited high hopes. A pacific imperialist, he would colonize the sea. A Fontvielle district would literally arise out of the Mediterranean as bulldozers and trucks shifted thousands of tons of rock and earth. After Fontvielle, the Larvotto region, at the eastern extremity of Monaco, could be extended with landfills, the Prince believed. The combined result would be Rainier's great economic monument of light industry, corporate headquarters, high-rise residences, and tourist attractions.

Very well, but where would "rock and earth" in sufficient quantities to make a pedestal for this "new Monte Carlo" come from? Rainier proposed an audacious answer. Long an eyesore (one of few) of the Principality, the Nice-Genoa railroad bisected Monaco north of the Rock and the Condamine. Princes before the present one had talked of "burying" the railway, but the cost-to-benefit ratio of a two-mile tunnel in solid rock had never seemed persuasive enough to galvanize the more timorous elements of the Monégasque government. Rainier, a great believer in technological solutions to all problems, was convinced the job could be done, and done on budget.

Before embarking on projects of this dimension, however, the Prince had to set his house in order, and this was not easy. When a new sovereign mounts the throne, it is understood he will want his own advisers and staff. In a realm as rigidified by seniority, precedent, and protocol as Monaco, however, such shifts take time and patience. Rainier III had neither, particularly for men who, in his estimation, had poorly run Monaco during the last ten years. Louis II's Cabinet and Household,* however, had come to wield great power in recent years; Rainier described them as "a sort of supergovernment." In a bold move, the Prince retired or reassigned the fossilized lot of his grandfather's advisers. Such high-handedness proved to be a mistake for a leader who needed support and consensus for great enterprises. The enemies Rainier made early in his reign remained to thwart him.

In fact opposition to the tunnel scheme—and hence to the new Prince's whole vision for his Principality—arose from the outset. Discontent centered among older, native Monégasques who sat on the National Council. Bold in matters of constitutionalism and the franchise, these forces were timid about massive "bricks and mortar" enterprises. Some of them, of course, simply opposed *any* change on principle; Monaco was what it was and mustn't change. Yet even those who welcomed development had objections to Rainier's plans, and not merely to their immense cost. The heart of the matter was political power over public works and the profits to be made from wielding it. Under the Constitution of 1911, legislative initiative could come only from the Prince or his government, headed by the Minister of State. The National Council had the right to debate the budget, which it could reject, but only as a whole, not piecemeal. In order to cut the railroad tunnel, it would have to reject the entire annual budget. In sum, as things stood, the tunnel and the reclamations would be princely undertakings that would elude control of the National Council, which was to say, they would not be economic plums reserved exclusively for native Monégasque interests.

The forces on the Rock were thus set on a collision path. Rainier could not be budged from his belief that Monaco's best hope for the long-term future lay in systematic economic development, beginning with the tunnel and the landfills. He hired expert consultants to study the project, and he created a governmental commission to work with

---

* The Cabinet consists of five or six personal advisers to the Prince, including a chief, a secretary-general, a secretary, and individual staff members corresponding to the several parts of government: finances, domestic policy, etc. The Prince's Household is nonpolitical, it includes his aides-de-camp, the head of protocol, chamberlain, chaplain, etc.

them in drafting a formal report recommending the best means to the desired goals. The National Council, while not objecting wholesale, intended to profit from this venture in several ways—from extending its own constitutional role in government to extending its members' fingers into Monaco's economic pie. While less powerful than the Prince, the Council had its time-tested instruments of persuasion. Besides the budget veto—a rash move usable only in the final resort—the councillors had the ability to swallow up initiatives in a quicksand of study and deliberation.

Rainier, at twenty-six, simply wanted to get on with it. The subtle kabuki of parliamentary infighting that loomed left him incomprehending and fuming with impatience. By temperament he was an absolutist, by training and blood, a prince. Persuasion, compromise, and loving skill at the game of politics were what were called for, but they were not at all the fortes of young Rainier III—at least not yet. He would learn.

In the meantime, there was the business of day-to-day governance to wrest the Prince's vision from his tunnel. On questions large and small he acted with a brisk decisiveness that took the breath away when it didn't offend. The orchestra at the Hotel de Paris was ordered to stop playing that damn legionnaire's song every time the Prince entered (as it had for Louis II); the lethargic Palace Guard was given a month to lose the bulbous bellies that broke over their unpolished belt buckles. (A practitioner of physical fitness, Rainier couldn't bear to look at the Guard in Louis's time.) The Prince immediately brought back his father from the exile to which Louis had unofficially condemned him. The Prince de Polignac became an active exponent of his son's reforms and projects. He organized the Monégasque invitational golf and tennis tournaments and became an active president of the newly founded Literary Council that had its headquarters in the Principality's legation in Paris.

This Council was near to Rainier's heart. Early in his reign he had voiced his profound admiration for Albert I and his intention not only to maintain that Prince's legacy (entailing a costly renovation of the Oceanographic Institute) but also to build on it. The Literary Council was such a venture. So was the cash prize—Le Prix Rainier III—that it awarded annually to a body of work in French selected by the Council. (The Council shone briefly under the honorary presidency of the wonderful writer Colette, but thereafter it got weighted down with members of the irrepressibly stuffy French Academy. As a result, the Prix Rainier III often went to somewhat "safe bets," e.g., Troyat, Julien Green, Giono, Bazin, de Vilmorin, etc.)

For a while it almost seemed as though the Prince would get sidetracked by the S.B.M. In the year of Rainier's accession, the company hit the nadir of its postwar slump, posting a $600,000 loss and a 75 percent decline in visitors. Deficits were very rare but not unprecedented in the company's annals; what was new and worrisome was that the S.B.M.'s leadership seemed to have lost their imagination at the same time as their rivals in Cannes, Nice, and Deauville had finally learned how to run a casino. The Cannes Film Festival, for example, had "arrived" as a Major Event in the Riviera season; by comparison Monte Carlo looked stuffy and archaic with its insistence on white ties and a waiter behind every chair.

Appearances were deceptive; in truth, the S.B.M. was stepping back only to leap ahead. Edward G. Robinson had barely time to mutter his famous observation, "What this place needs is a real crap table," before the Casino's emissaries returned from Reno with a half dozen of them, not to mention the intention of paneling sections of the Casino with slot machines. Soon the novelty of the new hotels along the Promenade des Anglais (in Cannes) wore off, and most of prewar society loyally "returned home," as Elsa Maxwell put it. They brought with them a new crop of high rollers—the "exes" (i.e., ex-King Farouk; ex-Emperor Bao Dai; ex-King George of Greece; ex-King Peter of Yugoslavia) and a host of Hollywood players led by Errol Flynn.

The man most responsible for breathing life back into the S.B.M. was a Greek who had first looked upon Monte Carlo from the sea in 1923, while traveling steerage on a ship bound for Buenos Aires. He was seventeen and was fleeing his native Smyrna which had been sacked by the Turks. He told a journalist many years after, "Every time I see the lights of Monte Carlo, I think how beautiful they looked that night as we passed—to me and to a thousand other seasick and homesick exiles." Having made his fortune, indeed several times over, he happened to return to Monaco three decades later. Noticing that the old Winter Sporting Club was derelict, he offered to buy it as a headquarters for his fleet of tankers. He was informed curtly that the building was not for sale or even for rent; he asked why and was given no answer. That triggered his interest. Directly, and through "anonymous" foreign (mostly Panamanian) companies, he quietly acquired a controlling interest in the S.B.M., at which point he let the world in on his latest purchase.

When news arrived on the Rock that Aristotle Onassis was majority stockholder in the Société des Bains de Mer, Prince Rainier was cautiously pleased. He did not know Onassis personally, but he knew *of* him enough to realize that the imitative lemmings of the international set would now have a new leader to follow. On the other hand, Onassis was even then known for the rapacity, wile, and (not least) the bull-headedness that underlay his bonhomie. Few tycoons of international business were more accustomed than he to doing things their way.

Onassis was aware of the peculiar and vital ties between the ostensibly private S.B.M. and the public purse of Monaco, and he arrived in the Principality trailing lavish, self-effacing statements of "loyalty" to "the Sovereign Prince." But the truth was, he had his own empire to run, in which the S.B.M. figured as one, not-so-major component.

He also had (or would develop) particular notions about Monte Carlo and its exploitation that were not those of the Prince, or consistent with Monégasque history. But these collisions also lay in the future. For the nonce, the Greek magnate and his two Christinas (wife and yacht) made sensational additions to Monégasque society and economy.

In the early years of his reign, Prince Rainier had reason to be optimistic and pleased with himself. The severe damage the War had wrought in Monaco—both physically and morally—was all but completely repaired; relations with France were in fine condition (Rainier had charmed President Auriol when he visited him in Paris in 1950); and the Principality's economy was attaining its old stride. Yet this agreeable young leader was anything but as sure of himself as he seemed. Beneath the smile and the acquired civility was a lonely and restless man who, it almost seemed, so mistrusted people that his closest friends were quadrupeds. He alarmed his subjects with his lingering yen for auto racing (and was very nearly killed, along with his mechanic, in the 1953 Tour de France), as he exasperated some of them by not finding a wife. He himself was in no hurry. Only too keenly aware of what unsuccessful marriages his predecessors (and parents) had made and how that ruined their personal lives, Rainier intended not to follow suit if he could possibly avoid it. He knew he would need a woman more willing than Gisèle Pascal had been to put away her own career and assume the mantle of activist Princess in the tradition of Caroline, Alice, and his sister Antoinette. But he also knew he needed a woman sensitively attuned to his own deeply repressed, but aching emotional needs, a wife who would complement him by filling out his very definite shortfalls—a partner in the full sense.

§   §   §

In the same month that the Prince was introduced to Grace Kelly, a crisis broke in the Société Monégasque de Banques et de Métaux Précieux. Both occurrences set off chains of events that shaped the rest of his reign.

The Monaco Banking and Precious Metals Society had overinvested in a consortium set up to exploit Monte Carlo's commercial radio and television station. In the summer of 1955, it suddenly declared bankruptcy. The collapse—or *krach*, as it was called—of the Precious Metals Society (P.M.S.) initially appeared to wipe out a large number of investors in the Principality, including many native Monégasques. But what made the event catastrophic from Rainier's point of view was that the P.M.S., even more than the S.B.M., was a semiofficial creation. The Prince's government had major deposits in the bank. Several of the Prince's closest associates, including a friend and member of his own Household (Roger Crovetto), occupied positions in the Society or subsidiary companies.

On closer inspection, things turned out to be less serious than they had seemed. The P.M.S.'s assets were greater than realized, and a group of French companies appeared on the horizon willing to help bail out the P.M.S. in return for a large share of stock in the holding corporation that owned the transmission stations on Mount Agel, above Monaco. In due course, the Prince's government felt compelled to step into the remaining breach and guarantee current deposits in the bank connected with the P.M.S.

But if the economic injuries were contained and eventually redressed, the political damages to Prince Rainier proved severe and long-lasting. In Monaco, the one accusation that is absolutely fatal to a sitting Prince is corruption. The price he pays for nearly absolute political power is Calpurnia-clean hands. In the wake of the *krach* of the Precious Metals Society, no one accused the Prince of venality; but he was badly scored for mismanagement. His political opposition in the National Council, many of whom had invested in the P.M.S., wasted no time in capitalizing on the scandal. The Council launched an immediate inquiry that resulted in the demand for suspension of three of Rainier's associates, including Crovetto, from positions in his Household. Characteristically, the Prince dug in his heels, dismissing the Council's demand out of hand. But the pressure on him grew until, a few days later, he issued an enigmatic and prolix communiqué accepting the resignation of Crovetto "in order to ensure the maximum of impartiality and objectivity in the examination of the situation created by certain financial engagements undertaken by the Public Treasury."

The political struggle waged on through 1955 into the winter and spring of 1956. The Council demanded further resignations and even an indictment, all resisted, then admitted, by the Prince, acting through his Minister of State. But this was superficial skirmishing; as always, it came down to fundamental questions of political power and economic control. The opposition demanded to know how this young Prince could undertake herculean techno-economic labors like a railroad tunnel and land reclamation schemes if he and his government couldn't even manage the P.M.S. The only way the National Council would seriously entertain major new budgetary expenditures was if

Prince Rainier agreed to constitutional reforms that would strengthen the powers of the Council to control public finances in *all* their facets.

Surprisingly, the Prince agreed. Changes in the Constitution must be made, he said.

Then, he and the opposition turned to the happier matter at hand: a state wedding.

CHAPTER VIII

LA PRINCESSE MALGRÉ ELLE 1956-63

I fell in love with Prince Rainier, no matter how it might all turn out. What followed was a good deal more difficult than I had thought.
—*Princess Grace*

"Nuages, c'est pour la France" (clouds are for France) was one of the first expressions Grace learned when she returned from her honeymoon. She would smile and refrain from explaining that, personally, she *liked* clouds because they sometimes brought rain, and she liked rain. What she didn't especially like was sun, day after day after day of it. She used to complain of the monotony of the climate in Los Angeles, but the weather on the Côte d'Azur—three hundred days of sunshine per year—made southern California's seem dappled by comparison.

And yet the physical beauty of Monaco arrested Grace at the very start. She wrote her mother that she couldn't even count all the shades in the sky at eventide, and she asked a writer friend how many ways there were to write "blue" to capture the tones of the Mediterranean as it deepened off the Rock. The serious walker in her took a decade just to take inventory of what was available in the Principality and the mountains behind it and arrive at a ranking of favorite paths and their correspondence with mood. But it was the lover of growing and blooming things, who had never been indulged, who forever won Grace to this fertile crescent that was the Principality of Monaco.

She presented herself to Monsieur Kroenlein, Director of the Jardin Exotique, within a fortnight of taking up residence in the Palace. She just walked into his office without any preparatory fuss and confused the gallant Monégasque for just an instant as he realized she expected him to shake, not kiss, the proffered hand. Something had been puzzling her, she said politely. Why were the rare varieties of desert and subdesert succulents for which the Garden was so well known not drowned by the amount of rain they received in a temperate climate like Monaco?

The botanist stared at the dazzling ex-movie star for just the briefest second, then explained that the steep rock slopes and escarpments on which the plants clung not only ensured that most of the water drained away but exposed them maximally to sunlight. But wouldn't *"Son Altesse"* prefer to have him illustrate his answer *"sur place,"* Monsieur Kroenlein inquired, not knowing the English phrase for "on-site." She would. Thus began a quiet friendship between the scientist and the Princess that endured through hundreds of hours and thousands of miles of walking through the countryside of Monaco and Provence, looking at flora and fauna, picking flowers, discussing geology, geography, climate and their effect on growing things, and did Monsieur Kroenlein think she would have any luck with planting Iceland poppies in the Palace Gardens? (He did and was wrong.)

More than once in these early years Grace would say to Rainier that she thanked God there were oases like the Exotic Gardens where she could take refuge from other sides of life.

For instance, protocol. The word had almost no meaning to Grace until it enveloped her existence. On her return from the honeymoon, Grace began to see a good deal of Count Fernand d'Aillières, the Chief of Protocol attached to the Household. D'Aillières's life turned on the punctilious unfolding of ceremony and ensuring that the much-derided, minutely observed etiquette of precedence and address was followed *au pied de la lettre* (to the letter). It pained him deeply that Prince Rainier had democratized protocol at court since his accession. Nevertheless there were just a *few* details that Grace would be wanting to remember. The Princess, for example, must never appear in public except on her husband's arm or unless accompanied by a lady-in-waiting. She must sign her name "Grace de Monaco," not Grimaldi; in her correspondence, as indeed in all state documentation, pronouns referring to Her (or Him) were capitalized, in the fashion of European (but not English) courts. Women would curtsy when presented at court; but a curtsy was not a full *révérence*, which in turn must not be confused with the English bow. Grace would be called "Her Serene Highness," which in writing could be abbreviated to H.S.H. People could correctly say simply "Your Highness" in conversation; the French was *Votre Altesse*. Straight *Altesse* was also acceptable, but "Highness" was not, nor was "Princess." English people would probably say "Ma'am," said the Count, and this, while technically incorrect, had evolved into accepted usage.

Grace concentrated hard, trying to take it all in. And on it went.

D'Allières said he wished to help Grace sort her way through the maze of honorifics that made her, as consort to the Prince of Monaco, one of the most titled crowned heads of Europe. It was simpler, he said, if you approached it historically; titles were usually granted by allies and protectors of the Monégasque rulers, or acquired through intermarriage. Grace was a princess, thus, because Rainier's forebear, Honoré II had ingratiated himself with the French Regent who, in 1612, elevated him from *Seigneur* (Lord) to Prince of Monaco. Grace was "Serene," or more correctly *Serenissime* (most serene), because an ambitious sixteenth-century in-law had extracted that somewhat rare Venetian sobriquet from the Spanish King who also happened to be the Holy Roman Emperor and protector of Monaco. Grace's son, if she had one, might eventually receive one of the realm's most prized titles, Marquis de Baux, for which he could thank Cardinal Mazarin, who had induced Louis XIII to honor Honoré II thus. Though she would then lose Baux, however, Grace would still be a Marquise—and a Countess and Baroness—because her husband's eighteenth-century kinswoman, Louise Hippolyte Grimaldi had married Jacques de Goyon-Matignon, who held these titles for, respectively, Estouteville, Torigny, and Saint-Lô. And if Grace felt she needed reconfirmation in these monikers, she was, in addition to the above, twice a Duchess, once a Princess, and twice more a Countess, Baroness, and Marquise— all thanks to Honoré IV's thoughtfulness in marrying a descendant (and sole inheritor) of Cardinal Mazarin.

Then, of course, there was the Grimaldi family coat of arms. H.S.H. was told she must not confuse this with the escutcheon of the Principality; the latter was merely a heraldic sop to nineteenth-century nationalist sentiment, but the former was a legitimate armorial bearing, which to be described properly required the listener to know that "dexter chief" meant upper left-hand corner or that "gules" was the color red. Coats of arms give historical information, Count d'Aillières told Grace, or sometimes misinformation. The two monks in the Grimaldi crest, for example, were not actually monks at all, which could be seen from the detail that they are not "discalced," that is, not shoeless, as proper monks should be. The "monks" represent Francesco Grimaldi and a kinsman who dressed up as Cistercians in order to penetrate the Palace and take the Principality in 1297 (at a time when the Grimaldis had no title).

And this wasn't the half of it. Grace would quickly have to learn the key dates that marked the unfolding of any Monégasque prince's calendar, each event having its own customs and obligations: the Principality's national holiday; the Prince Sovereign's birthday; the anniversary of his reign; the feast day of Monaco's patron saint (Saint Devota) and all the other many holydays (Ascension, Assumption, All Saints, Holy Week, etc.) that were *officially* observed in Catholic Monaco. Then there was the social-charitable calendar that started with the opening gala kicking off the winter season and ended with the great Red Cross Ball. The sports calendar, culminating in the obnoxious automobile rally that turned the Principality into a racetrack, could not be overlooked; the Princess would at least have to attend these "sacred" events even though she could depend on her husband to handle the "rituals."

And this was just the ordinary calendar; Grace would have to be thinking about the special events that loomed ahead—e.g., the tenth anniversary of Prince Rainier's reign, Monte Carlo's centenary, and so forth.

Now then, did Her Highness wish to hear the list of charities, institutions, and committees that *she* would be expected to head or serve on?

§   §   §

It was overwhelming, the more so as Grace took her duties and her lessons as deadly seriously as Count d'Aillières and his confreres intended they be taken. But she simply could not assimilate it all quickly. She hardly even knew a smattering of French when she arrived. There were, of course, people to help her—secretaries, servants, ladies-in-waiting—but often they became part of the problem. The elderly Countess Bacciochi, for example, was as sweet-tempered as a grandmother, but other than regale the Princess with stories she had heard about the court of Emperor Napoleon III, she was of slight help to the young American. She didn't understand.

Nor, for that matter, did Madge Tivey-Faucon, a much younger woman than the Countess, who was Grace's first personal secretary and (eventually) lady-in-waiting. Australian by birth, "Tiv" had been a friend of Gisèle Pascal's. The Prince hired her as his English-language secretary, then assigned her to the new Princess. Useful in some regards—Madge was perfectly bilingual—the woman had so entirely assimilated what she imagined was the outlook and sensibility of "the aristocracy" that she met many of Grace's needs, reactions, ideas, and humor with subtle condescension or incomprehension. For example, Tiv felt certain Grace's parents "think of us as barbarians" because they would occasionally send their daughter "CARE packages" containing (among other items) Kleenex and soft American toilet paper. She was scandalized by Grace's "bourgeois" American friends who greeted her with a loud "Hi, Gracie!" (thereby "destroying in one blow," Madge wrote later, "the careful staging of protocol"). And naturally Tiv was deeply unamused when the young Princess brought her a multicolored feather duster as a joke. Grace, she felt, was naively, perhaps fatally, American; what else could explain why Her Serene Highness wished to wrap her own Christmas presents? Or that she spent so little money on clothes, or took so long to understand that princesses should wear hats? Like the businessman visiting Paris in Henry James's *The American*, Grace could not help feeling out of place with Tiv's eyes on her.

In the immediate princely family, Grace fared only slightly better. Her greatest friend and supporter was the gallant and elegant Comte de Polignac. Rainier's father was enchanted with his son's bride and constantly went out of his way to show it. He spoke excellent English and did his best to guide (and humor) Grace through the labyrinth of protocol and public appearances. Better than Rainier, Pierre intuited what an excruciating torture it was for Grace, speaking little French, to walk into a room of twenty-five strangers—of whom the youngest was probably a decade (often more) older than Grace—and try to play the part of Princess Consort to a group of guests and subjects who were expecting to meet "this American movie star."

Princess Antoinette, Grace's sister-in-law, was personally friendlier to Grace than the newspapers speculated, but she remained distant. The problem was not that the new Princess usurped what Antoinette regarded as her terrain, rather that Antoinette had long before resigned it and now felt bad. Throughout their youths, and early into Rainier's reign, the brother and sister had been close—in part, no doubt, as an antidote to the pain of a broken home. When Rainier acceded to the throne, his sister made an efficient and charming hostess presiding over galas and charities. Presently, however, she began to show signs of what might be called "the Princess Margaret syndrome" —i.e., a taste for the lifestyle, parties, and some of the handsomer males of the international set. Rainier growled about her choice of friends, but he didn't really get annoyed until she became deeply involved with Monaco's tennis champion, Aleco Noghues, a playboy of whom Rainier entirely disapproved. When Antoinette eloped with Noghues to Genoa, it drove a stake between brother and sister that remained for the year or two Antoinette stayed married to the athlete. Divorced from him in 1954, she returned somewhat penitently to Eze, near Monaco.

By the time of Grace's arrival, brother and sister were publicly polite. Antoinette had not, of course, been invited to live in the Palace where she had lived in former years, nor was she offered a post at the Monégasque Red Cross where she had once been vice president. But the Prince did make available to her a house in Cap d'Ail, on the western border of the Principality, and invited her to most official events. Any gradual return to the old closeness was nipped in the bud, however, when Antoinette began seeing a lawyer, Jean-Charles Rey, who happened to be one of the leaders of Rainier's political opposition. Unfortunately, and probably against her will, Antoinette herself then became linked with the opposition.

Princess Charlotte, Grace's mother-in-law, lived rather to herself and thus (as George Kelly described Craig's wife) was left to herself. She made her residence on the lovely Grimaldi estate, Marchais, near

Paris. Here she tended a changing menagerie of paroled convicts whom the French judiciary had nervously entrusted to the fifty-eight-year-old Princess's care and responsibility. Charlotte, for her part, was untroubled by doubt. She had returned to college late in life, had taken a degree in social work, and now was certain that she knew more than the state about rehabilitation. (Her self-assurance notwithstanding, the French police had more than once been called in to deliver the Princess of one, "René la Canne," known as "the Swagger Stick" among his confreres, but an unsalvageable convict to the French constabulary.)

The one support to which Grace might have turned for real strength was himself a frail reed. Prince Rainier was the center and purpose of her life. That single certainty was her rudder on very high seas, but it didn't make navigating easy, just possible. Rainier, as Grace learned—for she'd had to marry the man to spend any time with him—was still somewhat an emotional cripple. The scars of his childhood would fade only *very* gradually, with great effort and patience. The fiancé who sailed out in his yacht to meet the S.S. *Constitution* was not a man who could show or receive emotion readily, let alone admit need. Grace differed from him in this regard, reflecting perhaps her happier childhood experiences with love. Though far from effusive or casually demonstrative, she unstintingly gave affection, confidences, reassurance to her family and closest friends, and expected them. But in these matters, her husband had to be led. His natural tropism was toward solitude. After he was married, he worked at curbing this inclination, but success sometimes only presented Grace with a husband who was alone while he was with her—quiet, moody, and *not* interested in discussing what was wrong. So the Prince's emotional greening would take place slowly, and in privacy. (Fortunately Grace shared Rainier's intense distaste for any public demonstration. And "public" meant a third party. Never once did eagle-eyed Tiv, the ubiquitous secretary and lady-in-waiting, catch the couple exchange so much as a kiss. She did see them hold hands in the car when they thought nobody was looking, however.)

Whatever Rainier's limits, Grace could not be the center and purpose of the Prince's life. The Prince loved her deeply but his commitment to Monaco was second nature to him, more ineradicably etched in his conscious and conscience than even he realized—for he was forever grumbling about how he would have preferred the life of gentleman farmer or animal trainer.

Finally, more commonly, Rainier was more of a crotchety old bachelor than he appeared or suspected. Though only thirty-two, he had become very set in his ways—a tendency no doubt encouraged by his being an absolute monarch. Rainier undoubtedly saw himself with the easygoing, tolerant self-regard of a Professor Higgins who had "let a woman in his life." The truth was that he (like Higgins) had very strong ideas about a whale of a lot more subjects than he realized. It was *his* world Grace entered, and though Rainier was forever encouraging her to "do what she wanted," that license had a funny way of expiring cold when she crossed certain thresholds—even the one that Rainier would have been expected to carry Grace across, had they lived in the States.

The Prince must have told Grace a dozen times while they were courting how he would leave refurbishing the Palace in her hands. And yet the young Princess arrived on the Rock to find that Rainier had taken it into his hands to redecorate even their private apartments, not to mention the 190-odd official rooms of the Palace. She cast one summary look at his selections, then resolutely called in a top American decorator and worked with him to redo things her way. The Prince submitted, but far from magnanimously. He and Grace snapped and growled at each other about colors and arrangements, Rainier wailing loudly to the pictures of his ancestors, "Never in the history of my family have we had a decorator!" But in the end he quite liked Grace's choices. (Though that didn't automatically extend her right to monkey with arrangements in the formal apartments. The only occasion when anyone remembered hearing the Prince raise his voice in real anger to the Princess was when he learned from the Governor of the Palace that Grace had thoughtfully placed white chrysanthemums in vases around the guest suite where a foreign dignitary and his wife would be staying. "For God's sake, in Europe these are the flowers of the tomb," he yelled at her. "Take them out of here!")

Not surprisingly, too, Grace and her Prince had some differing ideas about what constituted fun. Rainier had a Kelly love of sports, water, and danger—regards in which his wife had stopped being a Kelly long ago. The Prince adored taking the *Deo Juvante II* out every chance he could. Grace gamely went along, but that amount of exposure to sun and waves often sickened her. (Indeed she got seasick more than once on the honeymoon cruise.) Her favorite times on "her" boat were calm, overcast days when she could sit with a book under a large floppy hat. (Rainier soon sold the yacht in favor of one he hoped might please Grace more. She eventually arrived at a tepid enjoyment of sailing, but nothing like her husband's burning zeal for it.) Rainier soon came to love Grace's poodle; from the first night, Oliver slept at the foot of their bed. But Grace never reciprocated by developing much affection for her husband's jungle menagerie. She was glad *he* liked them; and she admired his way with feral creatures. But it was an admiration she preferred to show at a distance, for such animals frightened her to the touch. Even the Prince's beloved female chimpanzee, Tanagra, terrified her. For a long time, Rainier strove to interest his wife in Tanagra.

He talked on and on one day about how rare it was for a wild chimp to breed in captivity until the Princess grew bored and snapped, "All rightie, I'll knit her something."

In sum, Grace faced the formidable demands before her largely alone.

§   §   §

The job of Princess was exceedingly hard to learn because it was so undefined. In New York and Hollywood, the model and actress had always known exactly what was expected of her—what to wear, where to stand, how to look, what to say. Even at the height of her phenomenal success, it was rare indeed that Grace herself selected a project; nearly always, circumstances presented it to her, and she was dutiful. She had worked bloody hard, of course—rising early, tolerating endless importunities and inconveniences, taking few breaks or vacations, etc.—but her days, like her life, had very clear definition. It was so different in Monaco. Ostensibly the job of Princess was immeasurably easier than that of actress. Given secretaries, servants, court, staff, and ladies-in-waiting, what was there left to do? The answer was everything or nothing. Had she wished it, Grace *could* have chosen to be a Dresden-doll-of-a-princess who made nice at court and state functions and spent her time spending money and traveling. This option was never entertained—by Grace, Rainier, or the majority of inhabitants of the Principality. That left the other alternative: everything. In this case, the job required immensely more imagination and initiative than acting, which was, after all, a performing art only. The job of Princess certainly required talents for performance and display, but at base, it was an art of creation—usually behind the the camera: initiating, devising, persuading, advising, helping, preparing, and always, to be effective, remaining self-effacing.

But where to begin? From the moment she arrived, Grace began hearing of the accomplishments of Princesses Caroline and Alice ("she was *American*, you know") and even Antoinette. Yet if anything was sure, it was that their examples were useless for instruction: their achievements had been the product of the commingling of individual personality, historical mood, and immediate circumstance. Endlessly to hear of the achievements of Alice's role in establishing Monaco cultural radiance was, in short, to hear nothing very useful to the task at hand. Out of *her* era, *her* place, and *her* talents, Grace would have to draw the materials simultaneously to write her own script *and* play it. It was a very demanding order that could only be met slowly, over the course of years of false starts, discouragement, and finally self-denial and self-transcendence.

Fortunately there was at least one vital and immediate task that needed no special conceptual skill, while it also afforded the Princess a year of grace. The first principle of a hereditary monarchy is to survive. The news of Grace's success at conceiving heirs was announced with much fanfare in midsummer of 1956, and her success at producing one, the following winter. While Monégasques were less stricken with anxiety about the succession than American newspapers kept reiterating, the sound of twenty-one cannon shots from the Rock on January 23, 1957, did occasion much celebration in the Principality, and even a pause in the day's occupation at the Casino. The Grimaldis' daughter was named in honor of the "renowned Princesse-Mère" of Charles III—Caroline. She would be addressed by her Swiss nanny, quaintly, as "Madame," the New York *Times* reported, adding Grace's intention that "little Madame" would nevertheless "be spanked whenever she deserved it." In a ritual dating from the dawn of hereditary monarchy in Monaco, members of the government were ushered into the Palace to see the baby and to receive formal attestations that she was indeed the daughter of the Prince Regnant and heir to his throne. From all over the world, felicitations poured in on Grace and Rainier. Pius XII sent a special apostolic blessing.

In Philadelphia, relentlessly true to form, John B. Kelly, Sr., said, "Oh, shucks, I wanted a boy."

He got his wish. Fifteen months later, Grace gave birth to a son who replaced his sister as heir to the throne. Shortly before Caroline's birth, the Prince and Princess had announced that if the child were a boy, he would be named Grégoire (Gregory). In the intervening months, however, Rainier prevailed on his wife. When their son was born on the fourteenth of March 1958, he was named Albert—in honor of the great Prince-Navigator. (He also carried the names of Rainier's father and grandfather, Pierre and Louis.) Again the congratulations flowed in, though the American press caused a minor contretemps. In their eagerness to claim Albert (and indeed Caroline) for the United States, several newspapers wondered if the children weren't American citizens, as well as Monégasque. The Prince predictably rose to the bait and insisted they were "Monégasque and nothing else."*

Princess Grace gave birth to Caroline, naturally, without anesthetic, in a room at the Palace which had been specially converted for the confinement. She breast-fed her babies. The world greeted these choices with surprise bordering on amazement. Not going to a hospital was, of itself, remarkable in an era that uncritically revered doctors and pandered to their convenience by going to hospitals for events that weren't medical. Grace's decision to go through natural childbirth was

---

* In fact, U.S. law permits all children, living abroad, who are born of at least one American parent to claim American citizenship, though they must do so by a certain age.

regarded as "bold" and "brave." But what elicited mild stupefaction was her breast feeding her babies. Women, particularly women of her social and economic station, and *particularly* young beautiful shapely women, simply did not do it. Breast feeding was painful; it misshaped the breasts; it played havoc with eating, sleeping, and socializing habits; and it could be embarrassing because the exposure of naked breasts risked giving offense or causing comment.

Grace was amazed at the amazement. To her way of thinking, breast feeding was the natural thing to do. As she and her sisters and brother had been breast-fed by Ma Kelly, so she would breast-feed Caroline and Albert. It was "wholly normal and right—I never considered anything else," she wrote later. Grace would one day develop a whole philosophy and psychology around breast feeding, but in 1958, she hadn't yet intellectualized the issue. To her then, breast feeding was the complement to natural childbirth, even a kind of willed attempt to prolong gestation with physical closeness. Both were intrinsic acts of motherhood—the first ways (and among the best) that a mother could show love for, and solidarity with, her child. Anesthetics and bottles and wet nurses were, from Grace's perspective, so many interlopers between mother and child. Any eluding of the cherished responsibilities, Grace saw as potentially very damaging not only to the baby, who needed a serene, loving birth, but to the mother who had shirked her responsibility, and indeed, by extension, to the family whose unity was subtly breached. In sum, Grace never thought herself "bold" or "brave"; the alternative—foregoing breast feeding—would have required far greater boldness, if she'd entertained the thought.

Still, the outpouring of murmurs and disbelief disappointed Grace. She interpreted them—not always fairly—as simply euphemisms for irresponsibility and selfishness on the part of women "too busy to be bothered" with motherhood. The seeds were sown in her that would one day, under the impact of "sixties' consciousness" and the women's movement, blossom into a full-blown crusade.

From mid-1956 through the spring of 1958, Grace was thus preoccupied with what American newspapers called "rescuing Monaco from becoming French." Her pregnancies were, in fact, rather more debilitating than her childbirths, for she was afflicted with everlasting colds and sore throats. Grace nevertheless began to chart the terra incognita that was Monaco and her job as Princess. The first chance to make an important contribution of her own came as early as the Grimaldis' trip to the United States in the fall of 1956, only four months after the honeymoon. After the debacle of the wedding, Rainier was won to the idea of hiring public relations assistance, but it needed Grace, with her hard-earned knowledge of the press's interests and forcefulness, to insist that the forthcoming trip to the States would be a disaster without PR coordination. Moreover, only Grace could have introduced the Prince to one of the loyalest, most competent retainers and friends they would have, Rupert Allan. Allan had by then left his job at *Look* and was associated with the PR firm of Arthur Jacobs & Company. Thanks to Rupert's friendship with Grace, Jacobs secured for his company the PR work of the Grimaldi U.S. trip, to which he promptly assigned Rupert Allan.

Despite her awkward, easily fatigued state, Grace insisted on presiding over the first of many Christmas parties for the young children of Monaco. All Monégasque children between the ages of three and twelve were sent personal invitations; no parents allowed, except the Prince and Princess. Six to seven hundred small guests—some weeping, some swaggering—duly arrived in four shifts and were shown into the throne room where clowns, magicians, a movie, refreshments, and individual presents awaited them. Afterwards, a crew of four servants required three hours and untold buckets of detergent to wash the sticky fingerprints off the wood paneling and brocaded walls and furniture. In later years, Grace would say that no activity in her leisure time or on vacation competed with this "obligation" for the delight it brought her.

The following year, the Princess accepted an invitation from the United Nations High Commissioner for Refugees and made her first sally into the international arena. She made a speech on CBS advocating the placement of some thirty-nine thousand neglected World War II refugees languishing in camps and the closing of the camps. The speech was memorable for the lapidary last line: "If you wish to know how you can help, don't hesitate to write me. My address is Monaco."

Being confined indoors much of the time, Grace concentrated on imposing her mark on the Palace and its routine. But gently. There was already in place a staff of two hundred, directed by a *régisseur* (manager) who guarded his turf. As diplomatically as she could, the new Princess gave her opinion and made her wishes known to Monsieur le Régisseur. A new efficiency and economy were needed, she felt. Toward that end, she would henceforth expect to meet daily with the *régisseur*, she would decide the menus, oversee the budget ("If it gets too high, I hear about it," she told a journalist), and even make certain decisions about important personnel changes. Then she turned to the job of carving out a home in this gloomy labyrinth.

The Palace had been a major headache for Rainier since his accession. Begun in the twelfth century, it seemed to have been in decline ever since. The roofs hadn't been touched since the death of Charles III and now required complete overhaul, while the rest of the interminable, semiderelict edifice required four carpenters, two plumbers, two locksmiths, six electricians and several masons just for maintenance.

But the Palace had superb potential; some of the public salons, if well restored, would rival their counterparts at Versailles and the Schönbrunn. Rainier, enraptured by this prospect, could barely contain his impatience to get on with that job, horrendously expensive as it was. He already had a scheme in mind for opening the state rooms to the public and charging a small admission price. With the annual number of day visitors to Monaco approaching a million, the sums would mount quickly. Grace advised him to give half the take to a special fund for the relief of the poor lest they be scored for selfishness; the Palace was their personal residence, after all. She was right; a small storm of criticism broke anyway but nothing like what it might have been.

She also convinced the Prince to put in a swimming pool in the Palace gardens, swimming being one of the few sports she truly liked. Characteristically, however, Grace simultaneously urged Rainier to build a large indoor pool for the Principality. Partly, this would benefit the inhabitants of Monaco and, partly, prove valuable for winter tourist business. The Prince adopted her idea and a public swimming pool, —glassed-in, heated, and with steam rooms—presently arose on the beach of the Larvotto. A few years later, he finally convinced the S.B.M. to install a pool for its guests.

The Princess, however, was distinctly less interested in the history and restoration of the Palace than in making the private apartments "homey," as she put it. Rather precipitously she decided to close down her New York apartment in the fall of 1956; she thus had five rooms of furniture to distribute through six private apartments in the west wing of the Palace. The decorator who helped her distribute it, as well as make the best of the small, dark rooms available was, again, George Stacey, who had collaborated with her on doing over the Fifth Avenue flat. The two now became good friends. Under their combined touch, the homey enclave that emerged was very comfortable—but far from luxurious (Madge Tivey-Faucon, that ever vigilant neoaristocrat, described it disdainfully as "modest suburban").

Grace, in the period she gave birth to Caroline and Albert, also managed, inter alia, to inaugurate a boulevard in the Principality renamed for her, open a radio station, have lunch with Francisco Franco, entertain Sir Winston Churchill, dine with Ike and Mamie, be received by Pius XII, and take tea with Elizabeth II (to whom protocol required she curtsy on presentation). She also held down the vice presidency of the local Red Cross.

The pace of her public life picked up considerably in the late spring of 1958, beginning with the blast that removed the first ton of rock for Rainier's beloved railroad tunnel. His Highness was to have pushed the plunger himself but in the event, he unexpectedly deferred to his wife. He would do this very frequently in the next few years as a sign of his esteem and affection for Grace and as a means of enmeshing her ever more fully with his princeship. (The occasion that meant the most to the Princess took place at West Point in 1959. It is the custom that visiting heads of state may grant amnesty to cadets in the brig. Rainier ceded the right to Grace. She later spoke of her pleasure at being able to pardon what she called "the wayward cadets.")

In September of 1958, the hospital of Monaco opened a new wing while simultaneously renaming itself in honor of Princess Grace. If the directors thought that Grace would be "proud and touched," they were right. If they expected she would go on her way with a smile, they were wrong, for Grace developed a zealous—some felt almost an aggressive—interest in the institution that bore her name. Several visits to the place convinced the Princess that much could be done to improve the quality of the patients' lives. The rooms, she felt, were antiseptic and cold, devoid of any human touch that would reassure people and make them feel more at home. The medical staff protested what-was-the-point: patients either left the place or died; the administration thought the furnishing of any "color" a useless expense. Grace weighed in nevertheless; she brought flowers, wall pictures and hangings, and other "signs of life" to the rooms to prove her point. She patiently (and not so patiently) nagged the directors to heed her arguments; she offered to help raise the small amount of money necessary to "decorate"; she chose the colors and decorations herself. And eventually she got her way.

A similar scenario was replayed at the Monégasque Home for the Aged. Grace visited it and was appalled at how the gray depression in the faces of the residents matched the grayness of the establishment. The old people would hardly budge except for meals. More was needed here than flowers and some imaginative play with inexpensive decorations. These people were not transients who would leave the establishment soon; they were here till they died and they desperately needed dependable human contact. So the Princess established an Assistance Center made up of volunteers (including herself) who would make regular visits to the Home. When volunteers didn't turn out in number, she leaned on the Red Cross until they found a way to help. And shortly after, when she became honorary president of the Girl Guides of Monaco (here again, proving to be more participant than honorary), she used her position to secure young Guide volunteers for her center.

"She brought us heart," said one elderly lady.

For her pains, Grace got two promotions from her consort. Rainier named her to replace him as President of the Monégasque Red Cross and he named her to succeed him as Regent in the event of his death. Grace would rule Monaco for Albert until he attained his majority.

Both were important appointments. Though recently founded (in 1948, by Louis II), the Red Cross was far and away the most important eleemosynary organization in a Principality that took international charity very seriously. As for the Regency, it signaled that Grace had won a measure of trust—not just the Prince's but, reluctantly, the government's. And trust was something the suspicious and parochial National Council did not grant easily, especially to ex-American movie actresses. Both appointments hearkened the end of the beginning of Grace's apprenticeship as Princess.

At this time, too, she hired a new collaborator who soon, in vintage Grace-fashion, became valuable to her as a friend as well as helpmeet. A tall, comely brunette, Phyllis Blum had graduated from Vassar about the time Grace Kelly was getting hot in live television. She had worked temporarily for the Prince and Princess, assisting Rupert Allan with PR during the 1956 U.S. trip. In the fall of 1958, Grace needed a secretary; Madge Tivey-Faucon had been promoted to lady-in-waiting. Allan recommended Phyllis, who got the job. The two gradually became friends, for Phyllis was as scrutable and artless as Nellie Forbush in *South Pacific*, and she had the rock-hard inner decency and values that Grace looked for first in the people near her. She was also a youthful American girl very much like the friends whom Grace badly missed. The Princess did not push her friendship onto Phyllis, nor pry into her life, but she communicated that she cared and took a genuine interest in her. When, after a few months, Grace uncovered a pranksterish sense of humor lying just below Phyllis's businesslike facade, the friendship was sealed.

Phyllis's invaluable asset was that she spoke frankly to a young Princess surrounded by courtiers, servants, and supernumeraries of all types, many of whom made a profession of euphemism, deception, flattery, and the concealment of incompetence. Blum had no axe to grind and no ambition (or chance) to hold any other job than the one she had—English-language secretary to the Princess of Monaco (who also had a French-language secretary). As a result she was a great help to Grace in spotting obstructionists and troublemakers.

Like Jamesian innocents, however, they often mistook their mark. What neither Grace nor Phyllis understood—because they were too young and too American—was that the problem was not always lethargy and incompetence but different work styles. The Princess and her secretary would arrive at meetings of the Red Cross with notebooks full and pencils sharpened, ready to get right to business and slice through any knots that appeared. Things didn't work that way in the land of the *langue d'oc*, still less so in a "society" charity where many of the people present were there voluntarily. The ladies of Monaco did not view meetings of the Red Cross as exercises in efficiency, nor did they see the organization itself primarily as a business. The Red Cross symbolized for them a kind of social solidarity and interaction that was to be enjoyed for its own sake as well as for the good it did. They thus regarded the young Princess and her bushy-tailed secretary as abrupt and insensitive *girls*. Gradually, Grace would learn that the way to get more out of the staff and volunteers at the Red Cross (as elsewhere) was to engage them in their fashion—ask about the family, make a little small talk, perhaps drop a small pearl of gossip—and in that way win them to her intentions. It would become a fruitful, reciprocal interaction—Mediterranean conviviality superimposed on Yankee initiative. But not for some time yet.

In these early years, Grace frankly had more consistent luck with roles where she was on display, although the attention garnered wasn't always the sort she (and Monaco) wished, nor, in any case, were formal appearances Grace's favorite use of her time. Nevertheless, it went with the territory. Prince Rainier took the United Nations very seriously and saw to it that Monaco took an active role in various subsidiary UN affiliates—UNESCO, various scientific organizations, the World Health Organization. When the WHO chose Monaco for the site of a major conference in 1959, Prince Rainier was at great pains to show his realm to its best advantage. He and Grace held several elaborate receptions and do's. These were ideal for their full attendance and the amount of newspaper coverage generated, but, frankly the delegates were rather more keen on seeing "Grace Kelly" than on talking with the Prince and Princess of Monaco about topics related to world health.† Grace's celebrity, in short, was not a thing that had to be lived down, but it did have to be built upon.

Grace in these years came off better in one-on-one encounters than with groups; in personal interaction, her *a priori* fame faded before the human reality. This was never truer than in the Grimaldis' state visit to Paris in October of 1959. No relationship approached the importance to Monaco of that with France, as Grace was all too aware. Rainier had previously been received by Presidents Auriol and Coty, but not with anything like the pomp and circumstance planned for the forthcoming visit to Charles de Gaulle. "The presence of Princess Grace at [the Prince's] side will undoubtedly give more splendor to this latest expression of Franco-Monégasque friendship," wrote *Le Monde*. Although this meeting was far from Grace's first encounter as

† Sometimes, frankly, looking became ogling. On the Grimaldis' state visit to Rome, Grace wore an impeccably cut, but short, dress of pink satin. After dinner at the Quirinal Palace, Grace was sitting talking with Signora Gronchi, wife of the President of Italy, with her dress well above her knees. She received so many admiring glances from the ministers that Madge Tivey-Faucon was mortified. "There was no way to attract her attention without being too obvious," Tiv wrote, "so I stationed myself in front of her."

Princess with a head of state, she reacted as if it were. The prospect tormented her. She could not eat or sleep well for days in advance of the visit. She had her French secretary draw her up a précis of de Gaulle's war memoirs, which had just been published, and she studied it.

In the event, things went perfectly. With good guesswork, Grace eluded disaster at the outset. As she and Rainier mounted the steps to the reception salon of the Élysée Palace, Grace was blinded by the flood of spot- and flashlights. Always poor at recognizing people at a distance because of her nearsightedness, Grace later told Phyllis, "I headed toward the tallest form and prayed it was de Gaulle." It was. That night, and during the three days of the official visit, Grace's improving French served her well, as did her knowledge of the General's war exploits and of French history and culture. The President of the Republic would not be so "taken" by an "Aphrodite américaine" until the appearance a few years later of another beautiful young consort who spoke better French and had also prepped herself in French history, Jacqueline Kennedy. In subsequent days, Grace visited hospitals, nurseries, and factories, demonstrating such an informed and lively interest in them that one magazine said "it momentarily made people forgive her for being the most beautiful," while Agence France Presse put out a story detailing Grace's accomplishments in these areas in Monaco. *France-Dimanche* summed up the trip as the victory of a wife who has succeeded . . . in raising her husband ever higher, the victory of a princess who has contributed to reaffirm the prestige of her prince."

By the time the Princess returned home, none of the press was referring anymore to "the former movie star, Grace Kelly." When Jacqueline Kennedy made a similar sensation in Paris, her husband publicly quipped, "I'm the man who accompanied Jacqueline Kennedy to Paris." Rainier, but for sensitive Monégasque pride, might well have spoken likewise.

Though relieved when it was over, her "first de Gaulle visit" lingered long with Grace. She would never boast of her "triumph," as the newspapers did, but she showed her pride in her nearly total recall of (in Phyllis's words) "every single detail of cuisine, decor, and couture as well as where she went and what was said. She was like an excited little girl who knows she's done well."

Grace followed the trip to Paris with literally a riotous *succès* two years later when she and the Prince made a state visit to Ireland. The journey bore great personal meaning for Grace who visited many of her Kelly ancestors in their homes, shared tears and embraces with them, and invited several dozen to visit her in Monaco. Grace visited the little whitewashed stone house in County Mayo where her grandmother had lived, and she wept publicly when she heard a crowd sing "Kelly, the Boy from Killann." She and Rainier later bought the land that had once been owned by her Kelly grandfather, and they restored the little white cottage.

§　§　§

Grace's work in Monaco and her trips abroad amounted to less time and demand than meets the eye. In truth, by choice and proud admission, Grace's remarkable singlemindedness in these years was concentrated on child-rearing. No one, including Phyllis Blum, could keep Grace focused on affairs of charity, culture, or state if Caroline or Albert happened to be around—as they nearly always were. Even Rainier, previously something of a workaholic, now spent time in the nursery away from his desk, playing "horsey" with Albert and "Grand Guignol" (monster) with Caroline. By intention and design, the children were at the center of their parents' lives; they accompanied them nearly everywhere—including to Paris to see the de Gaulles or to Dublin to meet the De Valeras. Asked by a reporter if winning the Oscar was the most exciting moment in her life, Grace replied without thinking, "No, it was the day when Caroline, for the first time, began to walk and she took seven small steps by herself, one after the other, before reaching me, and throwing herself into my arms."

The choice to center her life—and even, to some extent, the Prince's life—on her children was another of Grace's "remarkable American innovations" that confounded the world in which she lived. Children at the very top of European society were seldom seen and rarely heard; they were brought up by governesses and tutors and packed off to boarding schools at young ages. Grace, of course, never had the slightest intention of doing things thus, but Rainier might well have. One of the very first subjects that she raised with the Prince while they were getting to know one another and falling in love in Philadelphia and New York was his thoughts about raising children. Fortunately, Rainier was a man who had learned from the pain of a terribly lonely childhood; he had every intention, he said, of ensuring that his own children were not "strangers, relegated to the opposite end of the house." As a result, his ministers and secretaries no longer raised their eyebrows when, in the midst of a meeting, a small person walked into the room and climbed upon the Sovereign's knee, or when the Prince's personal phone rang, and a little girl's peremptory voice demanded of "Daddy" why he hadn't come home yet, it being five o'clock.

The Grimaldis had no conscious systematic philosophy about how to raise Caroline and Albert (and later Stephanie), and yet a coherent approach to child-rearing emerges from their actions. Love was to be expressed by the quantity and quality of time that the parents passed with the children. The children were respected as people, but in so far as possible they were not treated as "princes." Grace especially had a phobia about spoiling them or overtly imbuing them early on with a sense of being different or better. She also avoided "infantilizing" the children with baby talk and precious or gooey nicknames. (What diminutives she did occasionally use with them, she kept strictly private. Only after her mother's death did Caroline mention, in passing, that Grace sometimes called her "Caroline-Câline," a sweet rhyming French pun that means "Caroline my little cuddler/wheedler.") If anything, Grace sometimes wondered if she was being a bit too severe, but she would banish such thoughts when she remembered how indulgent her husband could often be.

The choice of governess was thus considered crucial. Rainier had had what he called a "nana," an Englishwoman named Miss Marshall whom he loved very much (and who is buried in Monaco), but he did not wish a spinster as governess to his own children. He felt that older, unmarried women were "frustrated mothers" with an unconscious tendency to spoil children. The woman he and Grace selected, therefore, was young and had a stated intention to marry one day (as indeed she did). Her name was Maureen King, and she hailed from Rugby in the English Midlands. Having previously worked for the French playwright Jean Anouilh,‡ Maureen spoke good French, which commended her to the Grimaldis. (The children were raised bilingual. They could be spoken to in French or English; the only rule was that at any given moment, only one language be spoken so that the children wouldn't confuse which was which.) She also had a wonderful disposition, good sense of humor, and an odd, infectious laugh, which Caroline began imitating almost immediately. Maureen in fact became close to the whole family, if not an intimate friend. Rainier dubbed her "Killer" because of her alleged appetite. (He "insisted" that she ran up a food bill higher than Grace's hospital fees at the Swiss clinic where they went for the Princess's appendectomy in 1959.)

If child-rearing was a most serious business, it generally happened in a pleasant, lighthearted way. "Killer" King proved just as intolerant of "any nonsense" from the children as Rainier had hoped, but there was relatively little need for discipline. The rules and routine were clear to the children and internalized by them. By European standards, Caroline and Albert were, if not exactly spoiled, then overindulged *à la américaine*. Grace, for example, could not resist Caroline's tears and would sometimes make herself and Rainier late for an engagement because she refused to depart until her daughter was consoled. Madge

‡ Some years later, while on holiday in Switzerland, Grace asked Maureen to invite the Anouilhs, who happened to be in Gstaad as well, for drinks. She had played in *Ring Around the Moon* in stock theater and wished very much to meet the author.

Tivey-Faucon, with her unforgiving eye for any breach in decorum, found Caroline altogether too undisciplined and rambunctious, but then Tiv's philosophy of child-raising differed antithetically from her employers'. Certainly, nobody hovered over Caroline and Albert with constant do's and don'ts or nagged at them for inspecting things or being occasionally disorderly. On the other hand, any sign of selfishness in the children was noticed and rooted out. Grace and Rainier, in short, were vigilant in matters of character and decency, while somewhat more lax (at least by European standards) about good manners.

Of the two children, blue-eyed Caroline had by far the stronger personality. She was a little Gallic terror—imaginative, uninhibited, and unpredictable. Grace spent days teaching her how to curtsy properly. The former Queen of Spain, Victoria Eugenia, was coming to Monaco, and it mattered to Grace that Caroline do her stuff well for Albert's godmother. Caroline had been bobbing politely all over the Palace that morning. She got to the train station and curtsied to everyone she met —except, naturally, Victoria Eugenia, who overawed her. "Caroline no want to," she said. Grace did not scold her in the slightest.

Albert, or Albie, as he grew to be called (if not yet by his mother), had a quieter, subtler personality than his sister. He was also much shyer of people. Though both were very affectionate children, Albert more completely duplicated his mother's hypersensitivity and his father's hidden need for love than Caroline. Brother and sister both displayed a precocious awareness of other people's feelings, and both developed senses of responsibility at a young age. Caroline, at three, for example, helped her mother with the children's Christmas party. Both children, especially Caroline, were good and conscientious pupils—in part, no doubt, because their parents believed intellectual development almost as crucial as character, hence were very demanding about lessons and marks.

§   §   §

Life for Grace and Rainier follows a fairly regular routine in these years. They arise around eight-thirty (they sleep in a double bed) and without dressing go immediately to breakfast in their private dining room. Here, around the oval mahogany table that Grace had shipped from her Fifth Avenue apartment, they find Caroline and Albert sitting beside the scrubbed, ruddy-faced Maureen. The kids reflect her chipperness and humor; no one hesitates to participate in the chatter. They are all morning people.

Breakfast done, the Princess rings for her personal maid, Nicoline, who has worked in the Palace for thirty years (many of them assigned to Princess Charlotte). She arrives promptly and helps her mistress dress—probably an English tweed if she is going out during the day;

slacks if she is not—but the Princess does her own hair. Then she goes to the library where she receives the *régisseur* of the Palace, an elderly man of solemn dignity, who dates back to Albert I's reign. Grace has had to win him very gingerly to her way of running things. Menus planned and sundry Palace business attended to, Grace will go to the nursery and spend a good hour with the children.

Here, around eleven, Phyllis Blum will find her and announce that the post office has dropped its usual haul of fifty letters (and much more on special occasions).* Reluctantly, Grace leaves the children to Maureen and departs with Phyllis for her office in the Saint Mary Tower, one floor below her husband's. Once concentrated on her work, the Princess enjoys it and moves along efficiently. Most of the letters fall into standard categories—"Grace Kelly" fan mail (which continued to the time of her death), requests for photos of the family, expressions of goodwill, requests for information or recipes or advice, etc., all get read by Grace, who verbally tells her secretary how to reply. Occasionally, the Princess will personally answer a letter in her big looped handwriting (as she does mail from her family and friends); and every so often, a human story will unfold in a letter that touches Grace deeply and elicits her help. The vast majority of mail comes from women, which suits Grace just fine. She says she knows "how to talk to women." By one o'clock, Grace may have finished the mail, *if* she has been left alone by the children—a fifty-fifty proposition. In any case, they are there to see that she comes to lunch.

"Lunch" does not begin to describe the elaborate meal that draws Mediterranean families together for five courses over two or three hours (including the siesta). It is not only the principal meal of the day but the best opportunity most families have to be together. Grace has found *le déjeuner* hard to adjust to—in part because she doesn't like to eat so much in the middle of the day. Mainly, though, she greatly misses her New York custom of lunching with girlfriends at the Algonquin or a restaurant. If there are guests, *le déjeuner* may be held in the formal Palace dining hall, with footmen behind every chair (a bit of protocol that Grace sees as a useless waste), but also with Caroline and Albert very much in attendance. Afterwards, the Prince and Princess will perhaps take coffee with the principal members of their Household and maybe a cabinet officer or two.

In the afternoon, Grace will attend meetings of the several organizations she heads, or she may have appointments with people in her office. She will try to save time—especially on the rare days it is raining—for a walk in the Palace gardens or on the Chemin des Douaniers

---

* The day after Caroline's birth, Grace and Rainier received seven thousand letters, and for several weeks thereafter, the mail stayed at five hundred letters per day.

along the beach. (The Prince gets his exercise in a violent hour of squash with Georges Lukomski, his all-purpose equerry and chum.)

Late afternoon is another of the children's hours. The family, with or without the Prince (according to his work), assemble in the library. Here reigns what Tiv calls "indescribable disorder"—toys, papers, magazines, books, photographs, flowers, and knitting strewn about. This was the room that was transformed into the maternity ward where Caroline and Albert were born. The Princess still feels it is theirs. As Albert and Caroline go to bed before the adults have their evening meal (at nine—standard in the Mediterranean world), they will say their good-nights now. Grace usually tucks them in and says prayers with them.

In the evening, there may—very occasionally—be a formal dinner in the state dining room. Then the men wear white tie and medals, the women are in formal gowns, and there is a footman behind every chair. If there are simply a few guests coming, possibly friends of Grace's from the States, the meal may be held in the private dining room. Rainier would just as soon dine *en famille*, but his wife greatly enjoys the chance to entertain friends, or even, as she gets more used to it, visitors or state guests she doesn't know well. After dinner, if the party has "jelled," Grace may suggest moving to the garden or even taking a dip in the swimming pool. On Mondays and Thursdays, they will move to the modern projection room (known as "the playroom") that used to be the Palace stable. The cinema equipment was the wedding present of the whole Kelly family. Rainier likes Westerns; Grace prefers to keep up with the latest American movies. They compromise. Afterwards, the Prince may become fascinated with the fancy electric train he has installed for Albert. (If protocol is being observed, which is not usually the case, nobody may sit while he fusses.)

If the family has dined alone, Rainier may put on his favorite Al Jolson songs or some Negro spirituals. Grace will eventually replace these with the latest Stan Kenton records that her mother had sent over, and the two may end the evening dancing cheek to cheek. Rainier tires quickly at night; indeed, when he has worked hard, or is under pressure, sleep has a way of overtaking him—occasionally even with company or at the opera. (Tiv hyperbolized when she later wrote that the musicians of the Monaco National Orchestra were "aware that he can rarely last out the first bars, in spite of nudges from the Princess," but it is true that Rainier's energy level begins to decline with the sun.) On retiring, he will generally go right to sleep while Grace will read till past midnight. She needs her sleep. If she stays out late at a party, she will take a nap the next day.

The Palace routine obtains from November through May, with breaks in midwinter (usually to ski in Switzerland) and spring (shopping tours in Paris), as well as state visits which happen when they happen. (Grace's presence in the Prince's life makes him more invitable than formerly.) During the long Mediterranean summer, however, and on occasional weekends the rest of the year, the family retires to their country home on top of Mont Agel. Misnamed "le Ranch" by the inhabitants of Monaco, Roc Agel is a two-story Provençal villa with a red tile roof, wooden window shutters, and the Moorish arches endemic to a region comparatively near to North Africa. The slender justification that the locals have found for dubbing Roc Agel a "ranch" is the presence of horses and what the English press (and Grace) call a "paddock" (corral). But the real reason is everyone's eagerness to show the American Princess how "with it" everyone is in American usage.

When Grace first saw Roc Agel, she despaired of ever making it livable by American standards. Then, when she got immersed with the French contractors, she despaired even more. "I had a terribly hard time convincing them I wanted what I wanted . . . There were a few very unhappy moments." From their perspective, however, one can sympathize: this woman wanted four bathrooms! (Actually she wanted five, and settled for four.) And closets in every bedroom, not to mention off the vestibule. These are needs from which gossip, even legends, are spun in the Monaco of the 1950s. It would no doubt reassure everyone to learn that the decor throughout is Grace's favorite French eighteenth-century provincial except that no one outside the family and the immediate circle knows what Roc Agel looks like, for Grace steadfastly refuses to describe the place as she and George Stacey have redone it. "Preserving its privacy is a kind of fetish with me," she tells a reporter who inquired. (She later confides to another interviewer that one of the bedrooms is furnished with pieces from Toulouse-Lautrec's home, adding, lest he misconstrue the room as gloomy, "in spite of that artist's odd personality, that room is very sweet and pretty.")

Life at Roc Agel is much less formal than in the Palace. The driver and guards have their own quarters. A servant or two might be on hand, but probably won't be. "Killer" is there, of course, but she is a member of the family. Grace often does the cooking (she vacillates from American—especially barbecues—to Provençal recipes she has learned); Rainier putters in his machine shed, fixing things (that occasionally don't need fixing). Grace takes long walks, returning with more flowers than even she knows where to place. She prefers it here, especially in the summer, for the wind high up on the mountain cuts the relentless heat. Sometimes, even, a cloud appears.

§   §   §

The life described seems idyllic. Most of the press thought it so. So did many of Grace's friends and all of her Philadelphia family. But it was not, by a wide mark. The tension and unhappiness and pressure below the surface of Grace's and Rainier's life were constant and increasing.

There was first of all the ongoing standoff between the Prince and his domestic political opposition. Grace had learned of this on their honeymoon. The truce that the marriage might have afforded was largely spoiled by the disaster that was the wedding, and by the infighting and accusations that followed. Rainier next hoped that the arrival of an heir would substantially knit the wounds. His public announcement in August of 1956 that Grace was pregnant contained a special paragraph for Monégasques: "I ask of you to put your confidence in the choices I have made for the future of Monaco, in the assurance that the Principality has not existed nor survived nor will continue to maintain itself, except by the Sovereign Prince in the plenitude of his intact powers." The National Council knew exactly what that meant and didn't buy it. The marked increase in self-assurance that Grace brought to Rainier now manifested itself as aggressiveness toward the opposition. The Prince both ignored his vague promises to inaugurate constitutional reforms and pressed ahead with his tunnel. The sensational growth of tourism (up 75 percent between 1955 and 1961) coupled with the S.B.M.'s return to prewar brilliance and profit provided Rainier the financial backing he required to launch his enterprise. The Council would have had to veto the national budget, precipitating open war, to stop him—an act it could not yet bring itself to do.

The tunnel, once started, however, proceeded at a snail's pace; the job was much harder, hence costlier, than anyone had anticipated. The Prince talked himself hoarse trying to defuse the redoubled opposition; he kept reminding his opponents of the economic bonanza that would take place when the railway was underground and its present site liberated for development, but conservative, tradition-bound Monégasques remained wary and worried. The opposition, led by two extremely adept lawyers, Louis Auréglia and Jean-Charles Rey (the latter soon to be the Prince's brother-in-law), kept up constant pressure for constitutional reform. Auréglia, especially, proved a canny parliamentarian; by the end of 1958, he succeeded both at uniting the National Council (of which he had been president in the previous term) against the Prince, and—a tougher job—stiffening its backbone for a test of wills.

The trigger was not the tunnel, which was a fait accompli, but Rainier's request for a steep increase in the subsidy allocated to the Oceanographic Museum. In part the monies were needed to pay the large salary of the new director—Jacques-Yves Cousteau. International opinion had considered Rainier's appointment of the world's most famous sea expert a major coup for Monaco, but the National Council balked. One of the inventors of the Aqualung, who also helped develop the individualized bathyscaphe, Cousteau arrived at his desk with a long list of demands (new laboratories, aquaria, programs, etc.), all of them expensive. The Council ignored the Prince's arguments that the Museum was a "vital, living part of our national heritage that must be sustained and built up, whatever the cost" or that Cousteau's projects would more than pay for themselves in renown, new tourists, and possibly other new sources of revenue for the Principality. Rainier III hadn't Albert I's domestic prestige or international renown. Auréglia convinced his confreres that the time had finally arrived to challenge the Prince. On the grounds that important new allocations could not be acquiesced in until constitutional reforms were granted, the Council held up the 1959 budget.

Whether or not a man as contemporary in his thinking as Rainier actually thought himself sovereign by divine right is unlikely, but as an embattled Prince, he knew where to grab hold of weapons, ideological and otherwise. He was no more inclined than his predecessors to try to untie this parliamentary knot, so he cut right through it. On the twenty-ninth of January 1959, he took to the airwaves to announce to startled inhabitants of Monaco that he was suspending the Constitution, dissolving the National Council (and the Municipal Council), and abrogating the right of political assembly or demonstration. For precedent, he cited Albert I and Louis II, and he couched his strategic justification in divine right language. Tactically, however, he portrayed his action as defensive: the Council, with its demands for reform, was attacking "the plenitude of my princely powers," and with its budgetary obstructionism was "paralyzing the administration" of Monaco. He promised that his measures were temporary; a new, and permanent, Constitution would presently be "conceded" to the Principality.

The reaction was swift and strong. The President of the National Council joined with Auréglia to call Rainier's action "a coup d'état." Others called him a "dictator," a "reactionary," a "destroyer of liberties." The Prince defended himself proficiently in the ensuing battle of image. Far from admitting to "reaction," he portrayed himself as the modernist, fighting for the health and wealth of his country against a backward, parochial, self-interested opposition. Rainier's best argument was to hurl the democratic spear straight back at the Councillors, as Albert I had done so cogently. Who, if not the Prince, would speak for Monaco's great majority of noncitizens? Their interests in, and love for, the Principality were in most cases as great as the natives, while their cumulative, not to say individual qualitative, contribution to Monaco's commonweal was far greater. The Prince drove home his point about the regressive and undemocratic attitude underlying the opposition's cries of "rights" and "law" by noting that they had opposed extending the franchise to women—something he had favored from the time of his accession.

The nub of Rainier's case, however, was enlightened self-interest. The opposition, he said, wasn't just selfish, but stupid. Else why would they display such indifference to the Oceanographic Museum, which had been in decline until he convinced Cousteau to take it over? Or why were they such obstructionists of Monaco's development? The Council replied that *it* wanted authority to oversee that development, but how many of them were even qualified to sit in corporate directors' seats, he asked? How many of them, for example, had come up with a single idea for the economic, cultural, or intellectual-scientific flourishing of Monaco? Only the Princes and their advisers had ever done so, he said, answering his own question. In interview after interview, he pointed out that many Councillors hadn't been farther than La Turbie (a neighboring village) in ten years, that they were, in general, poorly educated and parochial in their thinking. They represented, in sum, a blind and rapacious minority of the population that, since the middle of the last century, had been aching to despoil the wealth of the Principality by getting their hands on its generators. If they did, they would destroy everything.

Some powerful arguments these were, but the opposition was not bereft of their own. Some of their spokesmen (as opposed to their followers) were far from the troglodytes of the Prince's caricature. Louis Auréglia, in particular, was an extremely articulate and erudite practitioner and theorist of the law. Unfortunately, he had little taste for polemics. His response to the suspension was flawlessly reasoned, but recondite and restricted to academic circles. Even his column in *Le Monde* on the subject was impenetrable to any but the most assiduous. Nevertheless his logic was unassailable. The Prince had solemnly promised and repromised reform, he said, while never granting it, nor even defining what he had in mind. In his action of January 29, he flagrantly broke the law of the land, for the Constitution of 1911 made no provision for suspension. Moreover, there was no need of it. The Constitution offered him recourse with an obdurate Council: he could dissolve it and call for new elections. If he did not, Auréglia implied, it was because he had no faith in his case with the public and no interest in democratic procedures. In acting as he did, Rainier reposed shamelessly on tradition and might—on eight centuries of sovereign princely authority. Auréglia might have added, though he was too modest to do so, that he and several of his colleagues were eminently qualified by education and outlook to run the government, oversee the economy, and contribute to Monaco's cultural and intellectual life, but they had never been asked because they weren't blind believers in autocracy. At no point, however, did Auréglia or his colleagues defend themselves against the charges that they ignored the non-Monégasque majority in the Principality, and that they had opposed the franchise for women. They did not even refer to either issue.

Through it all, Grace stood staunchly by Rainier. They traversed the crisis together; although she took no public role, she was his closest partner and consultant. It spoke well for her that she had achieved enough respect in Monaco that none among the opposition took any shots at her. But if she supported her husband, it was not blindly nor in ignorance of the subtleties of the issues or the battle. Grace understood why Rainier acted as he did, but as an American, she frankly realized how unappealing her husband appeared mouthing divine right rhetoric, suspending the Constitution, and abrogating various individual liberties. Privately, she was at considerable pains to explain to her American family and friends the complexities and exigencies that (she felt) compelled Rainier to suspend the Constitution. If he had taken a beating in the American press (which he had not),† she would possibly have gone public with her role of "interpreter."

Grace also played an important role in Rainier's defense by pushing him hard on the issue of the women's vote. The Prince and Princess shared a traditional view of the differences between the sexes; Rainier had been offended by the Broadway production of *West Side Story* because, as he told a journalist, "you couldn't tell boys and girls apart." (He added, with pride, "Princess Grace understands the value of femininity.") Their conservatism, however, did not extend to politics. Grace believed unhesitatingly in women's right to vote. Rainier believed in it, too, but less actively. He had made faint allusions to the desirability of extending the franchise before he met Grace, but his strong advocacy of it after 1956 was very much her doing—partly by word, and partly by the power of her example.

Finally, Grace did her husband another service. While supporting him, she kept at him in the matter of granting a new Constitution, even though it was quite clear that once this happened, he would have to give up the trappings and some of the substance of his feudal and absolutist power. As in the women's issue, Grace's role here was one of supplement and gentle goad. Rainier was prepared, as part of his project to develop Monaco, to "modernize" the facade, and even the structures, of governance. Although he seized the initiative in economic matters, in politics, however, he needed reminders. Grace of course wasn't the only reminder; but she was one of the most effective.

The immediate aftermath of the suspension was a time of great

† U.S. reporting was generally benevolent or neutral toward Rainier, though unable to resist the impulse to trivialize *any* happening in "Graustark." See, for example, P. E. Schneider's piece, "Graustark Becomes a Boomtown" in the New York *Times Magazine,* February 15, 1959.

strain for Rainier and Grace. In so small a polity as Monaco (with at most a thousand eligible voters) an acrimonious battle like this poisoned civil society. Auréglia, Rey, and their allies amounted to a major section of the immediate community surrounding the Palace. With them now at odds with the Prince, life was hardly made any easier for the Prince's new consort. But Rainier was thicker-skinned and certainly more used to political infighting than Grace, for whom this kind of pressure was a new experience. The wives of Rainier's dissidents worked in some of the same organizations as the Princess did; Antoinette, the sister-in-law with whom Grace had succeeded at maintaining friendly relations, soon married Jean-Charles Rey and drifted back into her old status of *persona non grata*. Grace lost some needed friends.

The domestic crisis, which exploded with the suspension, gradually returned to the smoldering status quo of the pre-1959 years. The opposition recognized there was nothing it could do; in Monaco, the Prince called the shots. Until Rainier granted a new Constitution and reconvened representative bodies, there were no forums in which the former Councillors and their allies could act. And, in the meantime, political meetings were technically illegal.

There was, however, emerging on the horizon a new, external crisis for the Principality that would both dwarf, and eventually resolve, the conflict of 1959, as it drove the Prince and his opposition into a common front.

Like a pot that finally comes to a boil, Monaco and France had been feeling the heat of economic conflict for a long time before the great crisis of 1962. The contention was not mainly, as it is sometimes painted, a personal antipathy or eruption between de Gaulle and Rainier. Quite the contrary, the two men had similar political temperaments and got on very well together. The thirty-nine-year-old Rainier was never less than reverential toward the aging General or respectful of France and the Franco-Monégasque tie. De Gaulle for his part completely approved of Rainier's action of January 29, which so loyally emulated his own coup of the year before when he overthrew the Fourth Republic and established Gaullism in France. (The new French Minister of State in Monaco, Émile Pelletier, was a staunch Gaullist. At the time of the suspension, Pelletier unflinchingly backed the Prince, saying publicly that France "can only approve the strong determination of Prince Rainier to put an end to internal difficulties harmful to the interests of the Principality." He would never have dared to say this unless instructed thus by the Élysée.) In short, the trouble was not problems between individuals but issues (largely economic) between states.

Monaco's "differentness" from all of her neighbors was never more apparent than in the economic arena, especially during periods of prosperity, which for her seemed synonymous with status quo. With the start of the railroad tunnel, Rainier III irreversibly launched his reign on the path of development. While the results of this policy were long term, even as early as 1960–62, the first significant consequences of his "bricks and mortar frenzy" was becoming manifest in Monaco. Two "skyscraper" apartment buildings—the "Sun-Flower" and the "Chateau-Périgord," twenty-three and twenty-six floors respectively—had already shot up to astonish all Monégasques (and infuriate a few). For the next two decades, anywhere one looked in Monaco, he saw cranes, building sites, and Italian work crews.

And this was only the half of it. Something had to occupy these new buildings. Rainier's great and novel offensive, which also got underway at the turn of the decade, was an organization called the Monaco Economic Development Corporation (MEDEC)—a kind of superdeluxe chamber of commerce which set out to coax new business into the Principality. Co-conceived by Rainier himself, in collaboration with a young American ex-Foreign Service officer named Martin Dale (formerly Vice Consul at Nice), and a French lawyer from Algeria, Yves Laye, MEDEC encountered a phenomenal response from American, British, German, and, most especially, French businessmen. The great attraction, of course, was the absence of personal or corporate income tax or of land and inheritance taxes. In the twenty-two-month period from 1960 to October 31, 1961, 103 corporate entities established themselves in the Principality, while several hundred permits to conduct business in Monaco were given out to foreign companies. In the same period, the volume of business done in Monaco rose 40 percent.

It was both the nature and the degree of this prosperity that drew critical regard from Paris. France had tolerated Monaco's success over the years because it was so exclusively tied to the S.B.M. and that company's elite, inimitable activity. But now the Principality was competing on the open market to attract business of all sorts, and it did so very favorably because of the advantage of its unique tax policy. From the French perspective, Rainier was now breaking the Treaty of 1918 which (among other provisions) specifically held that the Monégasque Prince not act against French economic interest. The most flagrant example of his doing this was the extraordinary influx of *French* companies into Monaco—whether from metropolitan France or from former French colonies (Morocco, Indochina, Algeria, etc.). The latter provenance, particularly North Africa, raised a secondary bone of contention that angered de Gaulle personally. The heartland of right-wing anti-Gaullism lay in North Africa among the Caucasian French citizens who felt de Gaulle had "abandoned" them when he pulled France out of Algeria. It rankled the General no end to see some of his most implacable foes escaping French taxes and control by ducking into Monaco's easy port of access.

A fuse was needed. It arose when Rainier blocked further French investment in his television monopoly. The Prince was already smarting from increased French influence over Radio Monte Carlo (which had begun to happen with the 1955 *krach* of the Precious Metals Bank). It now infuriated him that French state-held companies were angling to gain control over Monégasque television (whose programming was disseminated all over North Africa as well as the Midi). He issued an ordinance blocking the further sale of the company's stock on the Paris Bourse. The Élysée was flabbergasted—how dare Rainier use political power to prohibit French economic investment while simultaneously competing with France on the world market? De Gaulle ordered the French Minister of State in Monaco (Émile Pelletier) to insist that Rainier rescind the ordinance. Pelletier telephoned the Prince late in the evening of January 23, 1962, and requested an immediate audience.

During that meeting, Rainier lost his temper and set off the fuse: he fired Pelletier as his Minister of State, upbraiding him for not championing Monaco's case with General de Gaulle, and announcing to the press next morning that Pelletier had misserved French as well as Monégasque interests. The Minister returned forthwith to Paris and told the President that Prince Rainier was "anti-French." The explosion duly followed. In April, the French Minister of the Economy (Valéry Giscard d'Estaing) transmitted to Prince Rainier notification that in six months' time France would abrogate the current tariff convention between the countries and thereafter expected the Principality of Monaco to "align its fiscal policies with those of France." In the event it failed to do so, there would be "juridical consequences."

For the Grimaldis, the strain now imposed made the 1959 crisis seem trivial. With the domestic conflict smoldering, Rainier faced the fight of his life with his own forces divided. He rescinded the offensive ordinance prohibiting the sale of Monégasque television stock on the Bourse, and he wrote several contrite epistles to de Gaulle offering a number of concessions, professing his very genuine devotion to France —as evidenced by his valorous war record. But he insisted (with remarkable frankness) that the demand for alignment of Monégasque taxation with French, if met, would "fatally compromise" not only the state's sovereignty (which France was sworn to uphold) but its raison d'être. He received no answer. De Gaulle was simply intending to let the clock run until Rainier met his terms. The most informed, serious newspapers like the New York *Times* and *Le Monde* wrote that the Grimaldis were facing "one of the most serious tests in their long history" and surmised what would happen if Monaco refused to meet the French terms. The word abdication came up. In lesser periodicals, speculation was rampant about what would happen if Rainier lost his throne.

The arrival of the French *Diktat* coincided nearly to the day with Grace and Rainier's sixth anniversary. It also coincided with the culmination of Grace's most painful personal crisis since she arrived in Monaco—a crisis that distanced her from her husband at the time he needed her most.

§   §   §

I'm ashamed to say how insensitive I was to Grace's loneliness in those early years. I projected my myth of a fairy-tale marriage onto her.
                                        —Judy Kanter Quine ‡

The seemingly smooth years of 1956–62 were in fact shot through with undercurrents that sapped Grace's happiness and periodically threatened her equipoise. There was, first of all, the ache of homesickness. It did not diminish, despite the good face Grace put on things in her letters and to the people she worked with daily. Rainier would inquire sometimes if she were lonesome, she would reply "maybe, a little," and they would talk about it. She missed her friends more than her family, she said, adding "friends, one chooses; family, you're born with." She missed most what she called her "hen parties" with Judy and Maree and Rita and Prudy and other girlfriends. But Grace didn't talk at length; she was too aware of how sensitive Rainier was underneath the "princeliness." She tried to take care not to hurt him. But he was aware, at least subliminally, of how badly she needed a girlfriend, and he wished he had communicated this awareness to her.

They did not lack for visitors. In these years they were thronged with guests—the Kellys, of course, who came several times, but also a large host of friends: Rita Gam, the Nivens, Frank Sinatra, Bob Hope, Jay and Judy Kanter, the Cary Grants, Edith Head, the Hitchcocks, Ava Gardner, Jessie Royce Landis, and many more. They came and stayed in the Palace, and Grace seemed to delight in their company, plying them with questions about show biz, but also proud to show off her own "biz" in Rainier and the children. Rainier alternated between welcoming everybody warmly or barely tolerating their presence, depending on his mood, the outside pressure on him, or his curious insecurity vis-à-vis Grace's Hollywood life which sometimes surfaced to cast a pall over things. Cary and Betsy Grant arrived for Easter of 1961, for example, and Grace went to Nice to pick them up—an honor usually reserved for Mrs. Kelly Sr. She happened to be photographed

‡ Interview with author, April 14, 1983.

kissing Grant, and the Prince happened to see the cut the next morning on the front page of *Nice-Matin*. That set Rainier off. For the Grants' stay, he remained distant and sulky. Grace knew enough not to confront him; she remained, in Tiv's words, "cool—her usual attitude during her husband's moods."

But visitors couldn't take the place of daily friends. Rainier encouraged Grace to make new friends in Monaco, but it was hard for her—not just because she wasn't yet comfortable in French, but because her role here forbade ready access to the psychological and social conditions of friendship. Then, too, the Principality did not teem with people her own age. (Monaco, it used to be said, was a place "where grandchildren go to tell their grandparents goodbye.") They indeed had some Monégasque friends—Maurice Donat, Rainier's physician, and the good Count d'Aillières, who had a beautiful young wife—but few, and in the last resort, they were the Prince's friends, not Grace's.

Finally, Grace's problem was larger than lonesomeness.

In the winter of 1960, word came that John Kelly, Sr., was gravely ill, with cancer, as it turned out. Grace flew home to be with him in the spring; it was clear she would not see him again alive. Returning on the plane, Grace was temporarily overwhelmed by the sort of emotion she was so careful not to show, especially to employees (albeit her secretary Phyllis was becoming a friend). The secretary realized it was the first time in two years of working for Grace that she had seen her in a black depression. She also sensed that the feelings gripping the Princess were more complex than grief and harder to deal with. Indeed, Grace was having to face the conflicts and feelings she strove so hard to deny and suppress. The frustration at never being able to satisfy Jack Kelly, never being quite the daughter he wanted her to be precipitated a kind of desperation in Grace now that she knew Pa was dying. "She told me she wanted so much to be loved by her father," Phyllis said. "Talk about being a goody-goody; there was nothing she wouldn't do for him. But she could never get what she needed in return." The frustration sometimes gave rise to anger—anger at those barbed comments of Jack's that had a way of dropping out at Grace's moments of greatest pleasure and accomplishment, reminders that there, on Henry Avenue, from whence she most desperately sought understanding and appreciation, they would never be forthcoming. But anger, in a woman like Grace, instantly touched off guilt. And so Grace would soon take back or modify what she had said to Phyllis, or she would spew forth a defense of his "values" and "character." It was clear to her secretary that Grace was caught up in profound ambivalence, anger as well as love.

John Kelly died barely a fortnight later, in June 1960, leaving a humorous, caustic, self-opinionated will that was the delight of reporters and city editors, a mild insult to his sons-in-law (expressly excluded from sharing in the estate), and a monument of selfish hypocrisy. "My wife and children have not given me any heartaches," wrote this man who had caused them so much grief with his indiscreet philanderings and withheld approval. Then he commended "character" to them as greater than "worldly goods." The will was also a disappointment to anyone who thought Kelly an immensely wealthy man: his estate was valued at $1,193,062.99, of which Grace shared around $200,000, minus inheritance taxes.

Grace returned briefly for the funeral. When she got back to Monaco, she was distant, even to her husband. Rainier sensed she was still dealing with the emotions occasioned by Jack's death. "She was oversensitive to [the Kellys]. They mattered terribly much to her—more, it certainly seemed, than she mattered to them. It's not that she wasn't loved; she knew she was. But though there were strong family ties with the Kellys, there wasn't a lot of heart."

As a child, Grace had her mother to turn to. Now she did not. Margaret Kelly was a rock for all her children, the mainstay of the family, and certainly far less perverse and undependable than Jack in showing approval and love. But if the frustrations with her mother were less galling and primordial than with her father, they were present. Margaret's authorship of the series for Hearst "struck Grace a terrible blow. She just didn't understand how her own mother could do something like that" (Rainier). She recognized that Ma Kelly hadn't had bad intentions—a conclusion she would have been far less sure of with her father—but that did little to mitigate her embarrassment and shock at seeing this ill-informed exposé at the hands of her own mother. Since then, their relationship had not been the same, though Margaret came to Monaco fairly often (with and without Jack). Caroline's birth brought a degree of reconciliation between mother and daughter, but it is unlikely that Grace yet felt she could truly trust Ma as she once had.

Jack Kelly's illness and death, with its unresolutions and lingering, splayed emotions, left Grace vulnerable and suspicious. She hadn't been home a week from visiting her father's sickbed when someone passed on a rumor to her that in her absence Rainier had been seen at a Monaco nightclub dancing with Zénaide Quiñones de León, Grace's Spanish lady-in-waiting. The truth was that on May 31, Rainier had celebrated his thirty-seventh birthday while Grace was in the United States. (He made the trip to Philadelphia for the funeral in late June.) He invited a group of friends, including Zénaide (as well as Madge Tivey-Faucon) to join him and had danced with all the women. Unsurprisingly, the rumors would not die down (Monaco was a small town in that regard, too); more surprisingly, Grace let them get to her, even though her husband and everyone who had been present that night told her the truth. Grace was uncharacteristically indecisive about what she should do—and was half appalled at herself for her suspicions and jealousies. But in the end, she could not master her emotions, and Zénaide had to go.

These events were followed by the death of her beloved pet, Oliver. The poodle was killed before Grace's horrified eyes by a dog in a neighboring chalet while the family was on a skiing holiday in Schoenreid (Switzerland). Grace was for a time inconsolable. Oliver had been not only her constant companion and delight but a tie with her past. Rainier thoughtfully replaced the animal within forty-eight hours with a similar black poodle brought from Paris, but "Chester" obviously could not then, or ever, take Oliver's place.

"I am easily influenced by climate, by moods, and by the people around me," Grace told a journalist around this time. The summer and fall of 1961 saw the mistral, the Riviera's hot, eye-stinging wind, more unrelenting than ever. The winter, on the other hand, had more days of sunshine, fewer of clouds and rain, than usual. The combination was Grace's least favorite. She mentioned to Rainier the irony in what some in Monaco had been calling "Princess Grace weather." At the time of the wedding—a rainy season in Monaco—Grace had publicly "prayed" for sun on the day of the nuptial mass. She got it; the clouds literally "departed for France" during the cathedral ceremony, and the rest of the day was brilliant sun. Thereafter, the appearances of sunshine when rain was present or expected was "Princess Grace weather"—pleasing to everyone, except Princess Grace.

By the end of 1961, Grace began to sense a painful truth: though her life was busy and full in Monaco, it left her in some profound ways unfulfilled. For all that existence in Hollywood had frazzled her, abused her, infuriated her, it had given her a quality of personal satisfaction (from her work) that was precious. For five years now, she had taken life at the other extreme—from careerism to domesticity. She told a reporter that she did not "look on myself so much as a princess as a woman married to a wonderful person and having a baby. That is what makes me happy." But did it last? Grace flung herself into the demanding job of wife and mother and found it interesting, preoccupying, alternately frustrating, pleasing. She had a myriad of other reactions—but never felt that singular sensation that is personal artistic fulfillment at the highest level.

Her film career remained a delicate subject with the Prince. Grace Kelly movies were still not shown in Monaco. At the time of the wedding, Rainier had banned them as part of his attempt to nip commer-

cialism.* Thereafter, it seemed that the few Monégasque theater own-
ers censored themselves, for Grace's films were not shown in the
Principality in these years. Except at the Palace. The Grimaldis owned
copies of only three of Grace's films, *High Noon, The Country Girl,* and
To Catch a Thief. The last had scenes that Rainier enjoyed (the Riviera
panoramas, the fast-driving sequences), but when it was shown in "the
playroom," none of the Palace staff was invited. It was not deemed
suitable for them to watch scenes that showed Grace seducing Cary
Grant.

There was no question that Grace faced more often than "Are you
ever going to go back to acting?" Through Albert's birth, her answers,
while occasionally evasive, were negative. As these words to William
Arthur of *Look* illustrate, "My [acting] career was the central focus of
everything I did. Now, my life centers around my husband . . . My
hopes for the future center entirely around this family. What I want
most is to make a real home for my husband and my children."

By the next year, however, a subtle change was detectable. In an
interview with Pete Martin, a writer whom she knew from her Hollywood days, Grace lapsed into significant silence when Martin observed, "I'm curious why anyone would expect you to drop all you
have here . . . and go back to the rigors of moviemaking. It must be
wishful thinking." (He wrote: "She looked at me, smiled sweetly and
said nothing. I found myself hurrying to the next question.")† In the
fall of 1959, she told a reporter "I miss acting," then added, "but I do
not miss Hollywood." Thereafter her answers to "The Question" were
marked with more and more ambivalence, though never, of course,
anything approaching a straightforward yes. Meanwhile, the Hollywood friends who visited her at the Palace were struck by the new
intensity of her interest in every detail of current show business.

Her husband was struck, too. Speaking of this era, Prince Rainier
told his biographer (in 1966) that there were "times, you know, when
the Princess [was] a little melancholic—which I quite understand—
about having performed a form of art very successfully, only to be cut
away from it completely."‡ Years later, however, he conceded that
while Grace had grown claustrophobic living in a small city of twenty
thousand and missed her friends greatly, "the hardest thing for her was
to give up her career." He called it her "nostalgia for acting." "We
would talk about it from time to time," he said. "What she missed was

---

* One year later, Rainier won an injunction against Barclay Records which wanted to
issue a record called *Sérénade à une Princesse*—a collection of title themes from Grace's
movies—in a jacket bearing the shield of Monaco and a portrait of the Princess.
† "I Call on Princess Grace," *The Saturday Evening Post,* January 23, 1960.
‡ Peter Hawkins, *Prince Rainier of Monaco: His Authorised and Exclusive Story* (London: Wm.
Kimber, 1966), p. 118.

creating something herself, alone. When I replied, 'well you are creating things here,' she would say, 'yes, but not alone.' "

The truth was, the Prince did not "quite understand" with the genial evenness of his tone and his words to Peter Hawkins, his biographer. Nor was "nostalgia" the word to express the urgent desire that had rekindled itself inside his wife after 1959. Time and again, Rainier and Grace had some hot confrontations over the question of her returning to films. Initially, her interest surprised and hurt Rainier. He would remonstrate with her that "stardom" (a word they both disliked) was, gratefully, a thing of her past; it had only brought her loneliness and exhaustion. Yes, she would agree, it had brought some of that, but it had brought pleasures, too—satisfactions which only in their absence took on the true, vital importance they had to her. As Grace had fought with her father, so now she did battle with her husband, hesitantly and fitfully at first, but with increasing determination.

Rainier, for all his Mediterranean temper and stubbornness, was no Jack Kelly. Recognizing that Grace was deeply sincere and motivated in her arguments, his love for his wife gradually gave birth to sympathy with her plight. He even told a reporter as early as autumn of 1959 that "it would depend on the subject of the film and the people connected with it." The reporter, Robert Musel of UPI, couldn't believe his ears. He wrote, " 'You mean,' I said slowly so there would be no mistake, 'there are actually conditions under which the Princess conceivably might return to making movies?' " Rainier repeated his original answer.* But if the husband said these words, the Prince showed himself very reluctant to live up to them. He remained obstinate because he understood the Principality better than Grace did. She had arrived in Monaco an internationally acclaimed American "movie star." His countrymen had very deep-seated prejudices about what it meant to be both American and a movie star, and neither bias melded readily with the Monégasque ideal of Consort to their Catholic Prince. Grace herself knew how critically her "performance" was judged in the early years of her marriage. Only slowly was she winning the trust of the inhabitants of Monaco. But she could lose that trust, Rainier said, and the surest way to do so would be to return to acting, never a particularly honorable profession in Europe and sometimes associated with the oldest. Moreover, she was in a sense Crown Princess until Albert reached the age of twenty-one. If anything happened to the Prince—including abdication—she would have to reign. Her position was thus vital to the dynasty at a time when it was imperiled for both domestic and foreign reasons. How could she risk her own, the Prince's, and even her son's future?

* New York *World-Telegram*, October 6, 1959.

But the scripts continued to arrive, and, try as she would, Grace couldn't stop herself from periodically pitching one of the more attractive offers to her husband. In 1960, she made a strong case for her playing the Virgin Mary in *The Kings of Kings*—a part offered her by her old employer, Metro. How could anyone object, Grace demanded to know, if she played so innocent and sacred a role? For one thing, some of the more conservative Catholics in Monaco might think it sacrilegious, the Prince answered. More problematically, though, most Monégasques would interpret *any* role as a signal that Grace was "going back to Hollywood." He wouldn't relent; she declined the offer. But doing so hurt her; she became incommunicative and pensive for days on end; and that, in turn, hurt the Prince. Their arguments about filmmaking punctuated many an evening and gradually wore down the prince in Rainier.

In this process, Grace had a powerful collaborator: Alfred Hitchcock. Hitch was one of the very few among Grace's movie crowd that the Prince genuinely liked and respected. He and Alma had visited the Palace several times. In the course of a number of earnest dinner conversations in the winter of 1962, Hitchcock convinced Rainier that Grace desperately needed to get back into acting—a conclusion that the Prince was rapidly coming to himself. The director had a fine role at hand for the Princess, but of course she would not do it without her husband's accord.

Eventually, reluctantly, Rainier gave way, hoping against hope that somehow the news that Grace would star in a film could be got past the Monégasques without uproar. In his biography, Rainier not only insisted that the decision was entirely his but accused himself "of talking her into it; almost literally pushing her along because I thought it would do her a lot of good."† It was consistent with Rainier's chivalry and his love for his wife that he would assume the blame. It was also entirely implausible that Grace had to be talked into it. On the contrary, it is hard to imagine how, by then, Rainier could have refused.

On March 18, a brief communiqué from the Palace stated that at the end of the coming summer, the Prince and Princess would depart on vacation for the United States where "Her Serene Highness" would play the lead role in Alfred Hitchcock's new film, *Marnie*, a mystery based on a novel by the English writer, Winston Graham. It ended with an emphasis on the limited nature of the venture: "Her Highness will return to Monaco with her family in November."

The news produced an immediate "explosion of joy" in the Hollywood "trades" and in much of the American press. It produced an explosion of disbelief and disapproval in Monaco. The general reac-

† Hawkins, *op. cit.*, p. 119.

tion, as *Le Monde* and other French papers culled it, was that "the Princess's place is not in Hollywood, but in Monaco beside her husband and children and among the people who have adopted her." The Monégasque reaction never varied greatly from this theme; the volume simply rose, despite all "explanations" from the Palace, until silencing it became Grace's (and Rainier's) only thought.

But the speculation that now began ululating everywhere else, in the United States as well as Europe, could only be called bizarre. Two days after the initial release, for example, the Palace had to issue a denial that in returning to filmmaking, the Princess was trying to bail out her husband from financial ruin. To clinch that point, the next day the Palace announced that Her Highness's salary for *Marnie* would be donated *in toto* to a foundation to help needy children and promising athletes in Monaco. Grace herself tried to justify this by referring to cases of where "priests [became] involved in secular pursuits in order to make money for their charitable and religious works." Grace later told Rainier's biographer that she had been very displeased at being obliged to make public "use" of a private intention that she had conceived at the outset. She did not believe charitable acts, particularly financial gifts, should be announced. "[It] was a matter for me alone.")

These were simply the rumors the Palace saw fit to try to scotch. The ones it ignored included "news" that Pope John XXIII had written to Grace, entreating her as a "Catholic princess" not to return to the stage (the Grimaldis' chaplain called this "preposterous"). The French press concocted a marvelously recherché hypothesis that (naturally) related *Marnie* to the ongoing Franco-Monégasque crisis: the Princess was returning to acting, it was said, as a way of flaunting protocol, which was, in turn, a sign to Charles de Gaulle that a Princess of Monaco (hence a Prince) could do what she (he) wanted. (An alternate French surmise: Madame de Gaulle disapproved of movie acting, so she pressured her husband to pressure Rainier to rein in Grace lest Monaco be seen as a comic-opera annex of Hollywood.)

But it was the reactions of her own people that meant the most to Grace, and to discover them, she had only to open the papers, for they were filled with interviews with disapproving Monégasques, whose statements bore out their Prince's assessment of the local mentality ("I'm afraid the simple image people here have of a Hollywood actress is Mae West," he told a journalist at this time). A florist wondered, "How could we call her Her Serene Highness if she becomes a movie actress again? She would have been slighting our country." A dockworker recoiled at the thought: "What about her kissing the leading man? That would really be the end!" A lingerie saleslady said Grace was a "sweet, lovely, aristocratic person" who had won much affection in Monaco, but "I could no longer [respect] her if she [goes] to

Hollywood." A taxi driver replied indignantly to a question from an American reporter: "Would *you* like it if President Kennedy and Sal Mineo shared top billing?"‡

Grace was stunned, then staggered, by the outpouring that inundated her personal hopes and plans. She spent ensuing weeks agonizing over the uproar that greeted the *Marnie* communiqué; it dominated most of her waking hours. The Prince had to have been far less surprised; he knew all along what a risk was being run. He had simply been hoping that the fact of doing the film over a holiday would pacify anxiety that Grace was "going back to Hollywood." Typically, he construed (in his biography) the *Marnie* disaster as a failure of public relations—the Palace didn't word the release properly nor provide enough explanation of it (his own fault for not briefing his staff fully). But he must have known that it wasn't form but substance that distressed his countrymen. One of his own secretaries confessed her dismay at the thought of seeing "our Princess kiss another man on the screen."

In his heart, the Prince in Rainier not only expected and understood the criticisms, but ruefully agreed with them. It would *not* do for a Princess of Monaco to play the role of a neurotic, frigid, unscrupulous thief in a film that included explicit sex scenes (and a rape). But Rainier the husband had come this far out of compassion and love for his wife, and he was prepared to back Grace to the end, even though for him it might very well be the end of his reign.

The *"Marnie* affair" erupted simultaneously with the collapse of Franco-Monégasque relations and the arrival of de Gaulle's ultimatum. Newspaper coverage by and large strained to adduce the most outlandish linkages between the events (e.g., Madame de Gaulle's intervention) while overlooking the simplest and truest: the events were "linked" in the paroxysm of strain and pain they brought to two people. Unfortunately Grace's and Rainier's directions diverged: her satisfaction would redound against his interests. If the Princess stuck to her agree-

‡ The Monégasques did not *quite* have the monopoly on wounded indignation—not while executives drew breath in the Thalberg Building at M.G.M. Joseph Vogel, Schary's successor as head of production in Culver City, wrote a personal letter on March 23, to "HSH Princess Grace of Monaco" in which, in the most respectful terms, he told her that "news of your return is most welcome, but your intended employment by anyone other than Metro-Goldwyn-Mayer is equally disturbing" and went on to make a moral case that her loyalties, and services, should lie with Metro. To Hitchcock, Vogel was more forthcoming. As M.G.M. saw it, he wrote the director on March 28, Grace's contract with Metro still had four and a half years to run, hence represented "an important but unused asset of this company." In both letters, Vogel somewhat shamelessly enumerated what he thought Grace owed Metro. Hitchcock let his lawyers reply for Grace and himself. M.G.M., they averred, had no legal case. Grace's contract ran for seven years, hence terminated in 1960. Metro's legal staff advised Vogel et al. that they were indeed on thin ice maintaining that Grace's contractual obligations to M.G.M. could somehow be "frozen" in perpetuity until/unless she finished her contract. (Metro Archives; "Grace Kelly" dossiers.)

ment with Hitchcock, it would perhaps fatally undermine domestic unity and tranquility in the Principality at a time when Rainier desperately needed them. His political opposition in the dissolved Council had not yet seized on the *"Marnie scandale,"* but it was only a matter of time. Yet if the Prince did not conciliate them, and *fast*, he would have little to face de Gaulle with in the looming autumn confrontation.

The situation was Corneillean in shape and solution: personal fulfillment balanced against the good of the state, with both principals reacting basically unselfishly. Having fought hard for his or her own way in previous months, in the moment of crisis, each offered to sacrifice for the other. In the event, Grace "won" the right of self-denial. It could not have gone any other way unless she was prepared to endanger the reign. Grace gave a short interview to *Nice-Matin* in which she stated she had abandoned the *Marnie* project for two reasons: first, Hitchcock had advanced the shooting date into 1963 when it would not be possible for her family to be with her during the shooting; secondly, "I have been very influenced by the reaction which the announcement provoked in Monaco." A journalist wrote, "It was one of the few revolutions in history fought by commoners to keep their monarchs *on* the throne."*

Even in the flood tide of the *Marnie* hue and cry, Rainier and Grace had their gazes riveted to the French crisis. As in the constitutional crisis, Grace figured as her husband's closest confidante and firmest supporter; he made no decisions without consulting her. Grace had nothing like a worked-out political theory, but she had the democratic reflexes of an American who had grown up in the highly political atmosphere of immigrant (Irish) Democratic politics, and she was stubborn in her loyalty to opinions that she regarded as basic to her sense of democracy (e.g., the right to vote for women, the superiority of constitutional government, the guarantee of individual rights and liberties). She also had something of her father's talent for rapid and shrewd assessment of people, to which she brought a very un-Kellyan willingness to listen and learn. Far sooner than he imagined it possible, Rainier saw that Grace understood the subtleties and idiosyncracies of Monégasque politics.

Most useful to Rainier, however, was his wife's remarkable capability (acquired and honed in her Hollywood years) for understanding what people wanted and how they perceived—i.e., through the media. Admittedly, Grace totally misjudged the *Marnie* reaction, but only because her regard was fixated on her own needs and wishes. When her husband's interests were at issue, however—particularly if, as often happened, they involved anything to do with the United States—

* Leslie Lieber, *This Week Magazine*, August 10, 1962.

Grace (even before their marriage) displayed a superior ability for accurate appraisals of popular and media perceptions and for making suggestions on how to improve those perceptions (or at least not offend them). Rainier recognized these abilities and depended on them. In their first trip to the United States after the wedding, he was very nervous about a public address (his first in America) to the Overseas Press Club. Grace not only helped him write it, she sat nervously behind him while he delivered it and tugged unobtrusively at his coattail to slow him down when he spoke too quickly.

In the Franco-Monégasque dispute, Grace understood the impossibility of giving way on the matter of tax alignment. In a much-quoted line, Grace cited the words of the French marshal, MacMahon, at the siege of Sebastopol in the Crimean War: "j'y suis; j'y reste" ["Here I am; here I stay."]. Nevertheless, she felt that Rainier had made a mistake in losing his temper and firing Pelletier the way he did. (She would often beg him to control his temper in public.) His splenetic burst had only played into de Gaulle's hands. She now urged the Prince to be conciliatory in his approaches to de Gaulle. But conciliation didn't work. With de Gaulle not even deigning to reply to Rainier's entreaties, it became clear that the October confrontation would take place. If it did, and if abdication became a necessity, Grace assured Rainier she would reign as Regent until Albert came of age. But in the meantime, there was much that could be done to effect unity at home by rallying Monaco to the Prince's colors.

Toward this end, Grace was strong in her advice to Rainier to grant a Constitution so that elections could be held and the Municipal and National councils reconvened. The Prince had promised to do so at the time of the suspension, as he had promised reform before that. He even assigned the drafting of one to the Crown Council, a body that depended entirely on the Prince. Nevertheless, Rainier personally wasn't eager to see a document emerge, and he had an aversion to pressing the Council to all haste. Whatever they came up with, he knew, would not delight the ghosts of his ancestors lying in their tombs in the Cathedral of St. Nicholas. Grace, however, was not enamored of the trappings, the cant, or the power of "divine right" monarchy. She expressed her views forthrightly—so much so, indeed, that Rainier was moved to give her a framed cartoon from *The New Yorker* depicting a bedroom scene where the queen is telling the king, "Don't pull your divine rights on me, Buster . . ." Rainier adored it, especially the word "Buster," which he would repeat aloud.

As it happened, necessity, not counsel or conscience, authored swift action. As the Crown Council could not do its work of constitution writing in pace with events, the Prince reconvened the National Council on his own authority. He expected the worst from the return of

Messrs. Auréglia, Rey, et al. and was pleasantly surprised. The tug of patriotism and self-interest outweighed the importance of parochial squabbles for the Councillors, who rallied to the Prince in his test with the French. Rainier promptly deputized a contingent of them to negotiate for Monaco with the French Ministry of the Economy.

Before these discussions could bear fruit, however, the deadline of the six-month ultimatum arrived. On Saturday morning, the thirteenth of October, the inhabitants of Monaco awoke to find that a thin blue line of customs officials had replaced what Colette once called the "frontier of flowers" between France and the Principality. The officials slowed down traffic between the countries, harassed tourists with inspections and imposts, and raised the price of postage, and beyond that, events did not go. But rumors did. Rumor had it: that French parachutists would land in the Casino square; that French warships would fire from the harbor; that de Gaulle would cut off telephone, lights, gas, electricity, and railroad service in the Principality; and even that the "force de frappe" (France's nuclear arm) would "knock Monaco out cold," whatever that meant.

Hot air, not a mushroom cloud, resolved the conflict, however. The complex and protracted negotiations going on between Giscard and the Prince's representatives eventually produced a compromise very favorable to Monaco. The credit went to the Principality's crafty and patient diplomats. What *Le Monde* termed Louis Auréglia's "Nestor qualities"—garrulity, phlegm, and his brilliance as a jurist—now worked on his Prince's behalf, just as they had once been Rainier's nightmare. But if Rainier's domestic political foes tasted the delicious irony of saving the Prince's hide (as well as their own), the price they paid was the commonwealth of their French countrymen in Monaco, who lost their economic immunity. Auréglia, Rey, et al. had no choice; the only way France would permit the Monégasque barque to float was by throwing the Frenchmen overboard. The key provision of the convention that emerged obliged French citizens and corporations that had moved to Monaco within the past five years to pay all French taxes. In one fell swoop, over half the population of the Principality came under French economic sovereignty. On the other hand, Monaco retained its independence and its right of economic self-determination. In fact, the convention had the effect of reducing the French presence in Monaco in favor of other, "immune" nationalities.

With due respect to Auréglia's skill as a negotiator, an important consideration that kept the French from winning more was the force of world opinion, which Rainier, with his display of lonely courage, played on more skillfully than de Gaulle. To realign Monaco's taxes systematically, the French, given Rainier's intransigence, would have had to force the Prince out, hence abolish Monaco's sovereignty—a reckless and unjustified act, given Rainier's willingness to turn over French citizens to French fiscality. To its credit, France respected the 1918 Treaty. Nevertheless, Monaco's "differentness" would continue to annoy certain French (and American and English) pundits.

At the same time as Monaco brought order to its most vital foreign relation, it restored tranquility at home. The Constitution of December 17, 1962, has no preamble making it the "concession" of a divinely sanctioned, omnipotent Prince. The document boldly proclaims Monaco "a sovereign and independent State," a hereditary and *constitutional* monarchy, and a "state of law tied to respect for liberty and fundamental rights." The Prince doesn't even enter the scene until Article 3, where he is endowed with executive authority. In the next Article he loses half his old legislative authority to the National Council; and in Article 5 he hands over judicial power to the courts and tribunals. There are ninety-seven other articles (including one giving women the vote) but they are basically only amplifications of the first five. They amount to a thoroughgoing alteration of the political face of the Principality.

The world did not see it that way. The press, for example, murmuring over the old-fashioned nineteenth-century style liberalism of the language and provisions, generally criticized the Constitution for being "still very autocratic." But their viewpoint was parochial (French, American, British) and missed the Monégasque reality. The powers of the Prince remain ample in part because he continues to be the arbiter among nationalities, the protector of the non-Monégasque majority from the ancient minority dwelling in Monaco-Ville. In short, the Constitution of 1962 is a revolutionary political document: it brought Monaco from the seventeenth into the nineteenth century.

It was also irreversible and inalienable, as the Constitution of 1911 obviously was not. In acquiescing in its promulgation, Rainier III stripped himself and his successors once and for all of the style, and some of the substance, of absolutism.

The turn of 1962 was a happier New Year for Monaco than any of the preceding ten years. The Principality's domestic and foreign trials were past; the tunnel was complete; the landfills proceeding apace; real estate booming; tourism breaking records; and the S.B.M. reaping its usual rich harvest. There was, indeed, only one problem unsolved: Grace's.

§   §   §

From earliest childhood, Grace knew to put on a good face. Though keenly intuitive and compassionate about other people's suffering, little was more distasteful to her in herself than self-pity. If you were hypersensitive, you didn't let people know that a blow had been received. The hubbub over *Marnie*, followed by the loss of the picture, brought Grace to her lowest point since she'd come to Monaco, but she kept it to herself. To the Kellys, especially, she put on a smile and made a joke. Her regular letters to Ma (which got passed around the family) or her occasional notes to her sisters struck only glancing blows on topics like loneliness and career frustration and said virtually nothing about any tribulations with Rainier. Peggy told biographer Gwen Robyns, "If she was homesick, she never complained. Never once . . . Grace is not one to complain . . . it is not in her character. Besides, she could always see something funny in even the dreariest of situations."† Even Phyllis Blum, who worked with Grace daily, saw only the obvious crises (such as her father's death) while missing her friend's abiding inner frustration and unhappiness. Phyllis was not a person inclined to peer deeply into people's hearts, but she was far from an insensitive person. Grace simply gave her few clues to her inner condition, and on the rare occasions she did, she followed it up immediately with a denial or a light joke. She told a journalist from *Look* in February 1963, "I'm always very pessimistic. I'm a gloomy type. Things are never as black as I think they are," then added immediately before the writer could say anything, "but then I have happy surprises. What [birth] sign are you?" Madge Tivey-Faucon was more perceptive (because more critical) of her mistress, and noticed the frequent tears which Grace attributed to head colds.

Only the Prince was aware of the discomfiture belying the pleasantness. Years later he would regret that he hadn't reached out to Grace more helpfully, but by then he would be a far stronger, maturer Prince and man than the besieged ruler and constricted young husband of 1956–63. He could not, in any case, have done much to lighten Grace's burden. Her problems were deep-rooted and intensely personal; the heart of the matter was her need to create a satisfying identity for herself in this new milieu. The path to doing this would be long and winding.

And constantly eventful. Grace had a fresh crop of troubles following the resolutions of the *Marnie* and Franco-Monégasque crises. First, she lost her trusted secretary and friend, Phyllis Blum, who left to marry an Englishman, Julian Earl, the nephew of Somerset Maugham. Grace wept through the wedding in St. Paul's Chapel in Monaco (reminding herself, perhaps, of her Uncle George's heroine Edith Espinshade). She was happy for Phyllis, she said, but rued about not being able to replace her.

Then came another, more painful loss. The only really good news in 1962 for Grace and Rainier was that she became pregnant again. They

† Robyns, *op. cit.*, p. 182.

both took great joy in the prospect of a third child; Grace wrote the happy news to her family, a few weeks before it would be publicly announced. Before then, Grace suffered a miscarriage, on June 25. She and Rainier were acutely disappointed.

Then came the Tivey-Faucon affair, flattening Grace with another *scandale* just about the time she was recovering from *Marnie*. Beribboned, bemedaled, pensioned, and thanked, Tiv retired as first lady-in-waiting in early 1962 and moved to Paris where she opened a small gallery. She did something else: she wrote a series of articles about the Grimaldis for *France-Dimanche*, parts of which were later translated and sold to the Anglo-American press. Billing herself quite properly as "the woman who knows best the secrets of the Palace of Monaco," Tiv spilled every bean she had saved, from the commonplace to the exotic. Grace drank Metrecal; Rainier ate "American hotdogs"; they both liked "peanut butter and maple syrup sandwiches." Jack Kelly, while staying in the Palace, "received the first lady-in-waiting" [Tiv] in his bathrobe!! He also set up a small business, making a large sum, peddling first stamp issues of the wedding to his American friends. Rainier thought it funny to scatter fake dog shit around the house and garden; Grace was unamused, and indeed mortified when friends and official guests came across it. Virginia Darcy stayed in Monaco a long time after the wedding and "was constantly combing the Princess's hair as if she were still a film star on a movie set."

And so it went, page after page of mildly titillating but hardly scandalous revelations. Grace couldn't believe her eyes when she saw the articles. They crystallized for her all the resentment, gossip, and misunderstanding she felt she had been a victim of since arriving in Monaco, culminating in her loss of the *Marnie* role. Yet though Grace took Tiv's articles as an act of treachery, there was in them no trace of real animus. On the contrary, she made it perfectly clear she had come to like and respect Grace, whom she initially feared wasn't good enough for her beloved Prince. "The iceberg legend" about Grace, she wrote (implying she once believed it), was entirely false. The Princess, she had discovered, was refined, compassionate, intelligent, conscientious, and endowed with (for Tiv) an overly active sense of humor and taste for practical jokes. For an outsider who did not enjoy her mistress's friendship, Madge was also remarkably aware of Grace's deeper feelings. "The Princess is a shy, self-conscious, introverted, oversensitive human being. Inwardly, she suffers," Tiv wrote.

In sum, one finally believes Tiv's initially incredible preface: "I am [writing these articles] as an act of service to the Prince and Princess, and I beg their forgiveness if they are upset." The "service" she was trying to do emerges gradually. Grace, Tiv urgently believed, was stubbornly remaining too American, and she was dragging her adoring husband, the Prince of Monaco, into committing the same error. The Monégasques would not forgive her for alienating their Prince with barbecues, hotdogs, and *enfants gâtés* [spoiled children]. The unmistakable, if implicit, conclusion: Grace must not only understand the Monégasque reality but locate and find herself *in it*.

§ §   §

Undoubtedly Grace's greatest accomplishment in these years was her role of wife (it was too soon to judge her as a mother). "A woman must be a genius to create a good husband," Balzac wrote. Grace was perhaps no "genius," but she had taken Rainier great strides toward becoming emotionally alive. In his response to Grace's love, he discovered abilities and needs deep within himself that he had suppressed all his life, even with Gisèle Pascal. Unquestionably, Rainier was a happier man—hence a fitter father, husband, and Prince—thanks to Grace's unswerving devotion. Articles about him at this time never failed to note the blossoming of the man's humor and human warmth, not to mention his increased attention to work and diminished interest in physical peril. With new, more regenerate sources of meaning in life, Rainier had no need to create artificial ones. (His love of auto racing was transformed into a passion for collecting cars of all types, particularly antiques.) Their love for each other and their mutual devotion to the children brought the Grimaldis joy, satisfaction, and a quality of daily life that was seriously impaired only at the peak moments of the external crises.

The bond that united Rainier and Grace hardly went unnoticed or unsung. "They are a symbol of love in a world full of hate," wrote the editorialist of an American newspaper. "Their romance and marriage are a refreshing antidote for us all." When these words were brought to Rainier's attention, he was deeply touched: "It's a wonderful thing to have written about us, a really wonderful thing. I feel most humble, and I am certain the Princess shares my feeling. It is something I pray that we will always live up to."‡

There remained, of course, ongoing problems and challenges in the marriage (aside from the external turmoil). Legion among these was Rainier's temper, which he still could not control properly. Grace returned home one evening from the coiffeur's with her hair cut shorter than she'd ever worn it. Absorbed with his thoughts, Rainier took an hour to figure out what was different about his wife. But when he understood, he reacted abominably, shouting at Grace and flinging his glass of bourbon to the floor. Grace never shouted back; she simply couldn't. In an altercation, she could argue and stand her ground stub-

‡ William Arthur, *loc. cit.*, *Look* (December 1957).

bornly, but before a display of raw, irrational temper, she had few resources. If mollifications didn't work, and work quickly, she fell into silence—not as a ploy, but because she was hurt and (sometimes) intimidated.

Rainier's temper was something they both knew about and worked at overcoming. The greater problem with the marriage in these years was far less apparent to either partner. Ironically, concentrating so hard on her marriage, Grace misperceived something fundamental about Rainier—which was that he was first a prince, and only then a husband and father—and in doing so, she subtly misguided both herself and him.

Tiv, strangely, was right in her view that something was askew in the Principality of Monaco, though wrong in thinking it "Americanization." Rainier's newly found taste for peanut butter was but a minor and amusing manifestation of a more serious underlying problem: uxoriousness and its consequences for a reigning prince. Remarkably, Rainier's love for Grace and his joy at the inner life they were creating under her gentle evocation were so great that they subtly inflected his self-perception and judgment. Despite his background, training, and experience in office, Rainier to some extent bought into Grace's belief that, at bottom, they were "normal people" like everybody else and accepted her priorities that children and mate came before all else. One result was the *Marnie* disaster, which could have been avoided if the Prince in Rainier had not bowed to the husband.

An even more serious consequence fell on Grace. In indulging his wife in her domestic preoccupation, Rainier was helping her to mislead herself as to who she was and what she must do to find deep and lasting satisfaction in her new life. In public statements like "I don't look on myself so much as a princess as a woman married to a wonderful person and having a baby," Grace was hiding from reality. As first Lady-in-Waiting Tivey-Faucon well knew, Grace and Rainier were *not* "just folks," with a bigger house and more servants than the neighbors on the block. He was a ruler with not only great power, but vision and extraordinary projects, making his responsibilities to his people all the heavier. Grace, in turn, was not only a Princess-Consort; given her abilities and Rainier's obvious wish to collaborate with her at the closest level, she should in key regards be a *co*-sovereign. She should not spend as much time as she often did in the nursery, or the private apartments, pining away for her old career, and impatiently anticipating the visits of her American friends and family.

In her appreciation of Grace's multifaceted talents, Tiv clearly felt that the Princess wasn't *only* the mother and wife she thought she was. In any case, the *Marnie* affair exploded that myth even if the Tivey-Faucon articles didn't. A fine mother and wife, Grace was also a superb artist who could not practice her art. She must, therefore, find a way, if possible, to redirect her gifts. It was never a question of becoming *less* of a mother or wife—unthinkable propositions—but of Grace's slowly disabusing herself of the myth that domesticity was sufficient either for Grace Kelly *or* Grace de Monaco. It would take time, but 1963 was at least the end of the long, painful beginning.

Significantly, Grace told a reporter at this time that the book she most enjoyed was Bette Davis's memoirs, *The Lonely Life*, because "She is objective about herself, a quality I like in people. This is what an actress has to be, and not many are." If Grace had turned her own considerable objectivity onto herself, how might she have evaluated her record as part-time princess in these years? By most standards, of course, she was assured that she was doing well. Certainly the American press tended to award her high marks. Grace, however, did not agree. She would later comment wryly, "My apprenticeship was overrated." Indeed, the more irresponsible society writers sometimes credited her with the ludicrous accomplishment of financially "bailing out" Prince Rainier. Not only was he *not* in any trouble, he was a considerably wealthier person than his wife and her family combined. It was easily overlooked in view of Grace's celebrity that she was far from rich. She had nothing but the money she saved from her M.G.M. salary and bonuses and her share of Pa Kelly's estate. It all amounted to less than the Prince's civil list for a year ($300,000, though that had been raised by $108,000 when he married). His private fortune ranged into the millions; he owned a Rolls-Royce, Mercedes-Benz, Imperial, Jaguar, Citroën DS, Lancia, Willys, and a Chevrolet station wagon.

The more serious journals credited Grace with bringing a certain cachet or glamour to Monaco that paid off in many ways, most notably increased tourism. At its most hyperbolic, this view alleged that Grace was "The Girl Who Saved the Bank at Monte Carlo." Other than its wittiness (a paraphrasing of the old hit song, "The Man Who Broke the Bank at Monte Carlo"), this claim was patent nonsense. The S.B.M. may have become an overbedizened old whore, but she was still successful at trafficking in international celebrities, as she had been for eighty years. Thanks to Onassis, Monte Carlo was booming when Grace arrived. Indeed, the Greek's star-drawing power (Churchill, Callas, Garbo, etc.) would have been hard to top. If it now boomed a little louder in the next six years, Grace would have been the first to agree that, at most, she had only brought a few more coals to Newscastle. The claim, in any case, missed the crucial point: in Grace's eyes, the increased glamour accruing to Monaco due to the Grace Kelly Phenomenon was no "accomplishment" at all. She created nothing; it cost her nothing.

Similarly, while the press (in Europe as well as America) praised the new Princess for being a wonderful "ambassadress" for Monaco—particularly during her visits to other countries—Grace herself was aware that much of the attention really amounted to flattery accorded to her beauty and movie glamour, and this meant far less to her than to everyone else. The state visit to the Élysée was an exception here and was one of Grace's proudest moments.

Young and new at her job, preoccupied with other activities, when Grace thought of herself as a princess, it was more as Rainier's consort or private adviser than as his collaborator. Thus, Grace personally conceived little beyond children and initiated little beyond overhauling the private apartments in her first half-dozen years as Princess. It was Rainier, not Grace, who, in addition to his political wars and economic development, undertook the restoration of the magnificent public rooms of the Palace. He, not Grace, proposed having the National Orchestra of the Opera of Monte Carlo give a series of open-air concerts in the Court of Honor at the Palace; and he, not she, arranged for musicians of the reputation of Kubelik, Rampal, Menuhin, and Casadesus to take part so that Monaco once again became the talk of the European musical scene. The Prince, not the Princess, established a Music Prize to match the Literary Prize, and he alone saw to the costly resurrection of the quality and prestige of the Monégasque Opera. Even the International Festival of the Amateur Theater, held in Monaco in 1957, with the participation of the United States (and fourteen other countries) was Prince Pierre and Princess Antoinette's doing, not Grace's. As late as November of 1966, a sharp-eyed observer (Barbara Walters) could write, "You feel his presence in every corner of Monaco. You do not feel the presence of the Princess as much."*

By 1963, Grace had only one serious innovatory accomplishment to her credit: the International Television Festival. Inaugurated in January of 1961 (in part as a way of competing with the Cannes Film Festival), it was a fine success, with entries from a dozen nations, including the U.S.S.R. Yet it was Rupert Allan and his associate Nadia Lacoste, not Grace, who arranged for Yul Brynner and Gene Kelly to represent the United States.

None of this is to denigrate Grace's early years in Monaco, only to judge her in the light of *her* talents, *her* aspirations and standards, and *her* subsequent accomplishments. What might have sufficed to fulfill and do honor to another woman did not fulfill Grace nor resound to the glory of an artist who, in fifty months had climbed to the heights of her profession. Monaco had known better princesses than her in Caroline and Alice (the latter being, indeed, younger than Grace when she became Princess). "During the first years of my marriage I lost my

* *Ladies' Home Journal*, November 1966.

identity because I didn't have ways of recharging my batteries that I had depended on before. I tended to let my husband and his life and work absorb my personality. This was wrong. I had to find ways of finding myself in this life."

Grace herself thus summed up (for a reporter, many years after) her situation at the end of 1963. A strong personal identity was the stock-in-trade of a great princess, as a great actress. Having failed to find a complete identity in domesticity, and having been obliged to forget once and for all the hope of returning to acting, Grace the artist now had no choice but to begin to express, to impose, herself in new ways.

She would find, curiously, that the effort benefited, not harmed, her marriage, for in striving to become a better Princess, she would discern and appreciate the Prince in Rainier. Grace often quoted Kahlil Gibran *(The Prophet)* in these years: "When love beckons to you, follow him though his voice may shatter your dreams as the north wind lays waste the garden. He is for your growth . . ." With *Marnie*, Grace had the exquisitely painful experience of both realizing how meaningful a dream (acting) was to her, despite her early attempts to downplay and suppress it, and seeing the dream completely shattered before her eyes. Growth, as she began to grasp it, would consist in finding another, more suitable one. Ultimately the only road to a truly shared life with a conscientious ruler devoted to his people was collaboration. And so, slowly, she began to set the broad molds of the partnership in princeliness that would eventually become her "présence" in Monaco.

CHAPTER IX

THE FOUNDATIONS OF "PRÉSENCE" 1963-70

One of the curious questions of modern public opinion is why the world's imagination continues to be intrigued by a certain tall, slender, thirty-two-year-old blonde, who is married, has two children, is nearsighted, plays the piano, loves dogs, hot jazz, and practical jokes, hates the sun and crowds and small talk, adores rainstorms and long solitary walks and serious novels, and has for six years contributed absolutely nothing of any world-shaking social, artistic, political, or economic importance that would justify the amount of attention she gets.

—*Maurice Zolotow*, Cosmopolitan *(December 1961)*

Grace had hoped and believed that once out of the movie business, her celebrity would gradually diminish. It did not. On the contrary, Princess Grace remained, if anything, *more* publicized than Grace Kelly—one of the seven most popular women of the fifties and sixties (along with Marilyn Monroe, Princess Margaret, Brigitte Bardot, Elizabeth Taylor, Jacqueline Kennedy, and Queen Elizabeth). The presence of the press was less inhibiting in Monaco, where in winter (the "off" season for tourists) Grace could walk in peace with her children. But the moment she left the Principality, hell broke loose. On the Grimaldis' Italian trip of 1957, the paparazzi turned out in such swarms as to require large police detachments to surround Grace and Rainier. Later, in Corsica, the Prince cut short their vacation because the police weren't able to provide enough "insulation." For example, a pair of English tourists coolly walked over to Rainier and asked him to remove his sunglasses so they could get a more recognizable snapshot of his face. In New York City, six mounted policemen stood guard from morning to late night just to hold back the crowds in front of the Grimaldis' hotel. In Ireland in June 1961, Grace was frequently brought to tears by the mob scenes that greeted them wherever they went. Between overzealous fans and overactive police, one hundred casualties were sustained in Dublin alone on the day of the Grimaldis' arrival.

Grace's popularity caused problems in other ways. Little mortified her more than the pique she brought friends and acquaintances by unintentionally upstaging them. Rita Gam's wedding was a small harbinger of what Grace was in for. Accompanying no less an international celebrity than Maria Callas, Grace not only drew more attention but did so in Milan, the home of La Scala. At the wedding of Princess Sophia of Greece to Juan Carlos of Spain in 1962, Grace got noticeably more cheers than the bride and groom, not to mention King Olav of Norway, Queens Ingrid of Denmark and Juliana of the Netherlands (both well beloved), King Paul and Queen Frederika of Greece, and the parents of Juan Carlos, Don Juan, Pretender to the throne of Spain, and his wife the Countess of Barcelona. *Good Housekeeping* trumpeted this as "one of the signal triumphs of Princess Grace's career," overlooking that Grace herself found the experience excruciating and hard to live down. Divas and royalty were not Rita Gam in their willingness to forgive.

One might ask, with Maurice Zolotow, *why*. What was the source of such tremendous interest when a new Grace Kelly picture hadn't been released in years and wouldn't be? On the list of Most Popular Women, only Princess Margaret of Britain matched Grace in possessing a celebrity that was unattached to any particular position or occupation. In Margaret's case, fame was explicable—tied to her rebelliousness, her affairs, marriage (and later divorce), and, generally, the whiff of scandal that accompanied her, at least in the press. But the opposite was true for "square" Grace. If no scandal, then what? The Consort to the Prince of Monaco rated mention in the *Bottin Mondain*, the listing of the French aristocracy, and little more.

The label "ex-film star" explained some of Grace's popularity—especially in Europe where the masses had only in the last decade or two begun to see Hollywood movies and idolize its heroes and heroines. Grace's films had introduced her to the European public well before they met her as Princess. Her beauty was as noticed on the Continent as in the States. Here, too, some of Grace's roles *(Rear Window, To Catch a Thief)* had titillated by suggesting hidden capacities for passion and a taste for excitement, while others *(High Noon, The Swan)* evoked interest by pointing to mysteries of sadness and poignancy underlying her famous reserve.

The French and Italian crowds were not turning out in such force to see Lisa Fremont and Amy Kane, but the actress whom they seemed to reveal. Grace's film record, in Europe as in America, led audiences to ask the basic question: *who is this woman?* In short, the Grace Phenomenon was now translated into romance languages, and the protean, endlessly debated question of "figuring out" Grace absorbed as much printer's ink on Fleet Street, in Rome, Paris, Milan, and Frankfurt as it did in the United States. True, by 1963, there were some answers to the question, yet despite Grace's departure from Hollywood and her choice of "the traditional values," it was still clearer who she wasn't than who she was. Her persona remained a mystery.

Some chose to do it for her. If there was anything new on the journalistic front, it was the appearance of a malicious streak in writing about Grace and Rainier. Sometimes it could be attributed to inadvertence or to the European misunderstanding of American ways. In April of 1959, rumors ran rife in many continental publications that Grace was "gravely ill." It was reported that she lay in a Swiss hospital being treated by American specialists flown in to try to cure her "rare intestinal disease." Cancer was the diagnosis hinted at. The truth was that Grace had checked into a Swiss clinic to have her appendix out, and her Philadelphia doctor (an old family friend) flew over to do the surgery. She would have had the operation in Monaco but the surgical wing of the hospital was still under construction. Ironically, the choice of an unobtrusive Swiss clinic had been motivated by a desire to avoid publicity.

Far more often, however, the mistake was due, not to misunderstanding or inadvertence, but to outright scandal- and gossip-peddling. Rainier banned *France-Dimanche*, a weekly French picture-feature tabloid, after it printed scurrilous nonsense alleging that Grace was jealous of the Kennedys and disdained by them. From time to time, he would do the same with German or Italian publications that stepped grossly beyond truth in their "reporting." Nor was it only the European or English press who indulged in rumors and innuendo. The Americans were never far behind. Thus, King Features, a respected syndicate, printed a piece in the fall of 1956 entitled "The Invisible Princess," maintaining that Grace "hid" in the Palace, that Monégasques were "completely disillusioned" with her, that Rainier married Grace for her money and for what she could do for Monaco, and other such myths. Two years later, the *World-Telegram*, a respectable New York daily, ran a piece speculating that Grace would return to films "to bolster the finances of her husband and his country." Journalism of this ilk was commonplace in the history of the Grimaldis' marriage.

But its very ludicrousness often rendered this sort of rumormongering less painful to Grace and Rainier than the highbrow malice and literate sarcasm that they periodically encountered in both the American and the European press. Unquestionably one of the most savage blows came at the hands of Philadelphia columnist John Cummings who, in an *Inquirer* article dated November 29, 1963, accused Grace and

Rainier of selfish, heartless insouciance at the time of John Kennedy's assassination: "While her native land was in deep mourning for the slain President, Princess Grace was on an outing in a Monaco park. A photograph shows her in a shooting event on that tragic weekend." Obviously penned in a white rage at what Cummings took to be the Grimaldis' insensitivity in not coming to the President's funeral, he gave free run to personal animus and sardonic invective: "As reigning heads of a dice table, it would appear natural enough for the Rainiers to establish diplomatic relations with Las Vegas . . . ; Before sulking in their mansion on the Mediterranean they should have consulted with their 'prime minister' and 'Ambassador at large,' Aristotle Onassis," etc.

Grace read Cummings's jeremiad with tears of rage, hurt, and frustration. Like her husband, Grace was extremely sensitive to what was said about her, her family, and Monaco, and (like him) never developed a thick hide. She replied to this "unfounded and cruel attack on my loyalty to the country of my birth and my sentiments regarding the atrocious assassination of the late President." In a letter printed in the *Inquirer*, Grace pointed out that she and Rainier had declared a week's period of mourning in Monaco and had a special Requiem Mass sung in the Cathedral. Their relationship with the Kennedys, she said, had always been more of a personal than an official one (Monaco had no diplomatic ties with the United States), so she and Rainier had expressed their condolences privately. As for the offending snapshot of the Princess shooting an air rifle at an amusement park, Grace wrote, "The photograph published with your article was taken on Thursday, November 21, the day before the tragedy when I accompanied my children and a few friends to a local fair." She added, "I was hoping to win them a prize at the shooting gallery."

Reasoned responses did little good, however. There was something about Grace's manner—her mask—that had always put off a minority and always would. But during the Hollywood years, their sarcasm had been confined to scandal sheets or to occasional quotes in essentially admiring pieces. The marriage to Rainier and her promotion to Princess, however, insupportably annoyed a certain brand of hard-nosed, liberal iconoclast among the better writers and reporters. A writer of the stature of Robert Massie (author of *Nicholas and Alexandra* in 1967) wrote a nasty piece in *The Saturday Evening Post* on what he called Grace's "state visit" to Philadelphia (in 1963) "to promote another dynasty—the Kellys. In royal circles this is known as *noblesse oblige*, which, loosely translated, means 'Rub my back and you may wind up with some scratch.' " Massie then described Grace's "smile that seemed to have been fixed into place by a plasterer" and the "meaningless chant" that were her amenities. Again, a stereotypical example of a kind of reaction that Grace (and sometimes Rainier) would always elicit but never refute: it dealt not with facts or even gossip, but simply attitude.

To some extent, witty sarcasm was undoubtedly an irritated reaction against the obsequious treacle in Grace's praise that often passed for straight reportage. One need only consult the *Philadelphia Bulletin*'s coverage of the Grimaldi visit to East Falls to understand Massie's anger. "Her Serene Highness, Princess Grace of Monaco," the *Bulletin* wrote, "dressed in a startling beautiful turquoise Givenchy gown, honored us today with her witty and brilliant introduction she gave her famous brother." Between the syrupy society page copy and sharp satiric response, there often seemed to be too little middle ground.

The popular uproar and journalistic outpouring created by Grace's comings and goings quickly became a burden to herself and her family. "If I could have one wish granted for only one thing that we do not have now," the Prince told a friendly journalist from *Look* in 1957, "it would be for privacy." As this was a futile wish, Rainier and Grace sought to accomplish the next best thing—the reduction of misinformation. By the turn of the sixties, it had become all too clear that occasional use of press officers like Rupert Allan to handle state visits was no longer sufficient. The Grimaldis needed a full-time staff. The person whom Grace and Rainier settled upon was Nadia Lacoste, the daughter of a Rumanian emigré to America. The same age as Grace, she had gone to Wellesley College then worked a few years in the M.G.M. publicity department before coming to Paris in 1952. She came to know Rupert Allan, who highly recommended her to the Prince and Princess. Having proved herself to Grace and Rainier in part-time PR work for several years, she eventually became the effective Minister of Information for Monaco and for its ruling family. Lacoste's appointment was unusual for Rainier, surrounded as he was by male counselors and councillors. A journalist of long experience on the Riviera commented that "Lacoste had to be doubly good before getting a position that the Prince unquestionably regarded as a man's job."*

What the journalist overlooked was that Rainier's best adviser on public relations was a woman, his wife. Lacoste was good, but she had excellent help. Grace herself had by now developed an even shrewder grasp of the press and its manipulation than her employee. For a few years, the media's access to Grace and Rainier had been haphazard and a bit whimsical. Journalists, especially feature writers and photographers, got through if they knew someone, ideally Grace or Rainier or

* Paul Ress, at that time stringer, later correspondent for *Time*. Interview with author, May 25, 1983.

Rupert Allan. On this basis, *Look* magazine (Allan's former employer) enjoyed exceptional privileges. Its photographer Howell Conant—a personal friend of Grace's from Hollywood—even accompanied the Grimaldis on vacation to do photo features.

By the early sixties, however, a more formal set of procedures was needed, and the "minimization of misinformation" evolved naturally into "the management of information." Between them, Nadia Lacoste and Grace attempted with some success to institute the kind of control standard in government and to publicity departments everywhere— including Culver City, California, where Grace and Nadia had learned their lessons at the knee of M.G.M.'s Howard Strickling. With Grace a uniquely "hot item," and rumors and myths about her billowing up like smoke, access to hard facts—and to Grace herself—was highly prized and could be bartered for measures of control that the fourth estate nominally did not grant—notably the right of preview. An interview with Her Serene Highness might be arranged if a writer turned over his copy for an "errors check" before sending it in. Similarly a photographer could do a photo feature if he were willing to permit Lacoste (or Grace herself) to select the prints that would be published, or at least to exercise a veto of certain unflattering shots. The process— especially the negotiations and ingratiations—had a sordid side. But it was necessary to the Grimaldis—from their view, a rearguard counter-operation mounted in self-defense.

In fact, this policy worked only partially. Reporters from major daily newspapers and most of the newsmagazines generally (though not invariably) stuck to the rules issued from their own headquarters: no preview whatever. But that left a broad array of feature journalists, aspiring correspondents, stringers, free-lance writers and photographers—all in competition with one another, and hence in supplication to the newly created Office of Tourism and Information, headed by Lacoste. As the years passed, Nadia developed ever closer ties with journalists and an ever more nuanced hierarchy of the "trustworthy" and "untrustworthy." The effect of it all was limited, however: beyond major publications and free-lancers, whole sections of the press—the scandal sheets and "personality" publications—were impervious to reason or barter.

§   §   §

There is no doubt that Rainier III will one day appear in the long history of his country as one of its hardiest innovators.

—*Jean Couvreur,* Le Monde *correspondent in Monaco*

The management of information about the princely family was only the lesser half of Lacoste's job; disseminating news about the "new Monaco" was her greater *raison de'être*, and involved her closely with Rainier's ongoing political struggle. With the conclusion of the Franco-Monégasque crisis and the granting of the Constitution of 1962, Rainier focused all of his considerable concentration on his development schemes for Monaco. The American head of MEDEC (Monaco Economic Development Corporation) had departed in 1962, partly as a sop to the anti-American President de Gaulle, but also because the Prince was not entirely pleased with him and preferred to take up the reins with his own hands. The authority still remaining in those hands was ample, if no longer total, in the new Constitution. Despite the changes it brought, the National Council did not win control over the S.B.M. or economic policy in general; the Prince himself would continue to husband the gaming golden goose and to oversee what was variously referred to as the "urbanization," "modernization," "development," or "ruination" of Monaco.

Those who said the last stressed (among other things) the cost of the railroad tunnel. Finally completed in 1964, it went three years over schedule and 500 percent over budget (costing five billion francs). "Graft and corruption" hollered the opposition, but could prove nothing beyond the simple truth that neither Rainier nor his advisers nor the finest engineers in Europe had foreseen how hard Monégasque rock was, and, by comparison, how weak human flesh and technology. In any case, the anger soon melted away in the Riviera sun; the development and real estate which the tunnel's completion entailed repaid its cost many times.

The tunnel was merely the start, however. Development was Rainier's great dream, by which he meant attracting to Monaco foreign corporations engaged in industry and commerce. For him, realization of the dream was the hope of the Principality. "We'll become a museum, otherwise," he would tell Grace and Nadia Lacoste when they had discussions about PR strategy. "There won't be any future for young people in [Prince] Albert's generation, no reason for them to return here after university."

Development had another motivation, too, though one not to be discussed in glossy brochures. In addition to providing jobs and hope for the young, new industry would accomplish something equally concrete and political: it would reduce the importance of the S.B.M., and more particularly of gambling, to Monaco's finances and to its identity in the eyes of the world. Louis II had taken some steps in that direction; at the time of his demise, gambling profits accounted for only 10 percent of the Principality's budget—the great majority of which came from indirect taxes, taxes on consumers, largely foreigners and tourists. However, the question of the S.B.M. was delicate. The gradual reduction of gambling's fiscal and "cosmetic" significance for Monaco must in no wise entail harming the S.B.M. itself. Far from it. Despite the Grace Phenomenon, Monte Carlo was *still* the major draw of tourists, and tourism—even Rainier had to concede—would always be Monaco's principal industry.

The Prince had actually given considerable thought to tourism, and here, too, he had a strategy. Studying the records kept by the S.B.M., two trends emerged—one opaquely, one clearly. First, if one were inclined to worry—as people in the gaming business invariably were (and are)—one might work up concern over the fact that while the Casino's "take" hadn't fallen off nor even leveled out, its rate of growth had diminished perceptibly from its twenties heyday. Like his princely ancestors who supported the Casino with personal disapproval and a guilty conscience, Rainier was inclined to read the statistics pessimistically, believing they pointed to the imminent collapse of gaming profits. The Prince was reinforced in this by the proliferation of successful, competing casinos in Cannes and elsewhere, ignoring the opposite deduction, i.e., that the gambling impulse was growing and pervasive.

Subsequent history proved Rainier's fears needless. But it bore him out in another conclusion. Though gamblers still abounded, the Casino's clientele—hence Monégasque tourism in general—was undergoing a radical "sociological" transformation. Gone was the halcyon era when Sir William Hapgood, the English cotton magnate, was refused admission to the Casino annex because he wasn't wearing a white tie (so he went back to his suite and put one on). In the sixties, there were fewer of Sir William's class and sumptuary capability to go round, while not many of the good knight's middle-class successors at the gaming tables knew what a white tie was, let alone owned one. Monaco, like everywhere else, was witnessing the "democratization" of wealth and the "bourgeoisification" of taste and style.

Accordingly, Rainier was convinced that a new strategy of tourism was in order. Without losing its appeal to the very rich, the Principality must try to attract a more popular tourist. As it stood, Monte Carlo, with its imperial baroque buildings, its gloved ushers, its hushed voices and dress codes, was rather forbidding to someone not in the habit of ringing for his valet on rising. Reforms in style and pricing would help to make physicians and executives feel more at home here. Rainier never had it in mind to radically alter the Casino, the Opera, or the "classic" hotels (the Paris and the Hermitage). Nobody, least of all he, wanted to risk losing Charles III's legacy. Rather, he wanted to build a new "Monte Carlo" in and around the old one, not replacing but augmenting it.

Such intentions meant bricks and mortar: new hotels, several beaches, and lavish new sports, entertainment, and gambling facilities —all built, laid out, and managed as tourists might expect in the best resorts and hotels of Miami or Cannes. In Rainier's view, all this was possible: the completion of the railroad tunnel provided the landfills in the Larvotto whereon the new "Monte Carlo Bord-de-Mer" could sit; the landfills of Fontvieille opened up an "industrial" region where new corporations could set up shop; the high-rise dwellings sprouting up all over the Principality could house the newcomers or simply take advantage of the real estate boom. This, then, was Rainier's Grand Design— in scope, vaster than Charles III's, and with an impact on Monaco no less revolutionary.

By 1964, only one man stood in his way.

Aristotle Onassis had something like a child's fondness for the S.B.M., whose controlling shareholder he became in the early fifties. He in fact called the company one of his two "toys" (the other being his yacht, the *Christina*), though this by no means kept him from taking it very seriously—when he felt like it. Conventional wisdom had it that taking over Monte Carlo was merely a beachhead for a full dress invasion that would come when he headquartered his vast fleet of tankers and commercial empire in Monaco. Throughout the fifties, Rainier was disinclined to think this a good idea (Onassis was too big, too unpredictable). By the early sixties, moreover, the de Gaulle government resolved his lingering ambivalence by firmly vetoing what *France-Dimanche* called "Monaco's becoming 'Aristotelian.'"

Nevertheless, Onassis remained head of the S.B.M., and Rainier and Grace maintained cordial, if not intimate, relations with him. It is doubtful that they would have become intimates; aside from a love of the sea and the habit of command, Rainier and "Ari" had little in common, while Grace—though never "disapproving" (as some of the press put it) of Onassis for his ostentation or his occasional vulgarity— wasn't especially charmed by him either. She and her husband simply enjoyed the man's humor, intelligence, and zest, and for the rest, didn't judge him.

In the early sixties, Rainier still looked on Onassis as a valued partner. He had wasted no time exhorting the Greek about his schemes for Monaco, and he received the solid impression that Onassis was behind him 100 percent. As if to prove it, Onassis effected a series of small reforms and refurbishments at the Casino and the Hotel de Paris that advanced the Prince's design by modernizing slightly the wrinkled old face of the S.B.M. Until the completion of some of the landfills in the early sixties, however, the company was not called on to play its vital role in the recasting of Monégasque tourism.

In the meantime, the Grimaldis and the Onassises stayed friendly, entertaining one another as often as the Greek was in the Principality.

That became less often in the late fifties, when Onassis divorced his wife. Grace had been fond of Tina (who quickly remarried, to her ex-husband's profound misery) and privately sympathetic to her plight as the wife of a sometime tyrant and egotist. Nevertheless, when Onassis started appearing regularly with Maria Callas, Grace was invariably cordial and available. Indeed, the artist in her was in awe of the great diva. In July of 1961, the four took a cruise on the *Christina* to Palma de Majorca. But the newspapers made life difficult with stories about "Her Serene Highness" being "scandalized" by the Callas-Onassis duo, or alleging that she had "adopted the Vatican's disapproving line." Once again, such assumptions showed only how out of touch with Grace the press could be. Grace was too much her father's daughter to be "scandalized" by any human actions in pursuit of romance; and still less was she apt to adopt squinty church moralism. But as she never made her feelings plain, the misunderstanding persisted.

In any case, the issue, as in the Franco-Monégasque confrontation, was not personalities but policies. What became frustratingly evident to Rainier by 1963 was that his "partner" in the all-important S.B.M.— "the state within a state," as the French newspapers called it—had jumped ship. Not only was Onassis *not* carrying his large share of the responsibility and cost of the Grand Design (the S.B.M. was expected to put in the beaches and some of the new buildings), but he seemed to be drifting into outright opposition. In a famous meeting, he casually told Rainier that he thought gambling should be abolished in Monte Carlo because it was "immoral." The Prince couldn't believe his ears and replied with words to the effect that the magnate made a poor ethics professor.

Whim and hypocrisy aside, the heart of the matter seems to have been that Onassis had reconceived his view of the S.B.M.: it was no longer a "toy," no doubt because the friendly world in which it had so figured—his happy life on the Riviera with Christina and his children —no longer existed. Instead, the company now seemed a lucrative real estate venture—a source of land development, construction, speculation. Onassis occasionally intimated this to Rainier, only to be testily informed that such a view ran flagrantly contrary to the Prince's own thinking, not to mention a hundred years of Monégasque history. So, an astute politician, Onassis helped himself to the language of Rainier's local opposition—which raved about the cost and purpose of modernization. In their view, Monte Carlo was a monument to be cherished and maintained, not altered. The paradox was quickly noted: "Onassis, self-made and with a reputation for ruthless thrust," wrote an English writer in a book on Monte Carlo, "seemed obsessed with preserving Monte Carlo's Edwardian image of gilt and crystal chandeliers at the Hotel de Paris and the Hermitage. By contrast, the heir to eight centuries of tradition veered more towards corporations like 'Holiday Inns' which had put out tentative feelers to erect a new hotel complex for package tourists and business conferences."† In truth, there was no "paradox," just political maneuvering on the part of a canny entrepreneur. Onassis, as most were aware, would have chucked the "gilt" overboard in a moment if his plans called for that. But nobody, including Rainier, could be certain what the Greek's plans were, or even if he had any, for he spent almost no time in Monaco anymore and confided in nobody. The "divisions" of the S.B.M., meanwhile, were badly needed in Rainier's battle. Running out of time, he was also running out of patience.

Grace knew of Rainier's plans for Monaco even before she knew much about Rainier. The Prince's vibrant enthusiasm and laboriously worked-out designs had struck her during those long, intense Christmas discussions in Philadelphia as among his most attractive traits. She could marry a man with a dream and with the intelligence, perseverance, and power to realize it. The dream was, moreover, very American in scope and presuppositions, which was not surprising even though the dreamer hadn't visited the United States before December 1955. The midfifties were still a postwar period for many Europeans. American economic thinking, as American power and influence, held a commanding presence in Europe, not least in the minds of many of its young leaders. Entranced with the ideals of modernization and efficiency, Prince Rainier would have been eager to adopt American ways even if he hadn't married Hollywood's biggest star (whom he had delighted and stunned with his knowledge of American slang). Indeed, far from seeking a bride, as the press depicted him, Rainier came to the States in the autumn of 1955 wanting to meet and court businessmen, study their corporate methods, and, ideally, return home with many useful suggestions, connections, and even deals. In all of this, there was nothing that a red-blooded daughter of J.B. Kelly, contractor and bricklayer, wouldn't instantly understand and admire.

In seven years in Monaco, Grace had not only seen and learned a great deal but had also developed many thoughts of her own. Despite the fun Grace Kelly had had playing roulette one day on a trip to the Casino while filming *To Catch a Thief,* Grace the Princess rapidly acquired her husband's wariness of the S.B.M. and his distaste for "the Monte Carlo image." Some of its activities and practices indeed revolted her—for example pigeon shooting, a pastime beloved of wealthy English landed aristocrats. One fired a shotgun at pigeons (imported from Spain) whose tails and one wing had been clipped so that they

† Stanley Jackson, *Inside Monte Carlo* (New York: Stein & Day, 1976), p. 220.

flew an erratic course and were very hard to hit. Indeed most escaped, but many did not, and their dead and dying bodies were often to be seen scattered about the sundecks of the Monte Carlo hotels and Casino.

Rainier never particularly liked pigeon shooting, but Grace was truly appalled by it. Aware that princes did not directly intervene in the running of the S.B.M., she nevertheless lost no opportunity to register her strong dislike. As it happened, her protests coincided with complaints of many patrons of the Hotel de Paris who—in a postaristocratic era—did not tolerate pigeons flying into their rooms or dropping on their heads or luncheon tables. With such grumbling from the so-called "Kipling set," the management abolished the custom. The new Princess was instantly credited by pun-conscious journalists with delivering the "coup de grace" to pigeon shooting, although its termination was hardly her doing. On the other hand, Grace was largely responsible for the decree requiring the Casino to close on Good Friday evening, a time when the most sacred and beautiful religious rituals of the year unfolded with medieval pageantry on the streets of Monaco-Ville.

Grace strongly favored diminishing the S.B.M.'s importance to Monaco, and understood both the need for the industrial and commercial expansion of the Principality and the necessity of constructing a new bourgeois tourist base to supplement the old elite one. She hoped that the influx of corporations and their personnel would open up "little Monaco," making it a more exciting, cosmopolitan place to live. In her view this could provide more subsidies for, and participation in, the Principality's cultural and charitable life, her own special preserves.

Grace was encouraged to take a large role in realizing her husband's Grand Design. Publicly, the two of them so often voiced their belief in male dominance in marriage that one got the impression that Rainier made more of the decisions and acted more independently than in fact he did. The truth was that, from the start, he saw the two of them as a team. In every facet of his work as Prince he consulted Grace, listened to her, and often submitted to her. Indeed, he might have given her a public voice even in politics and economics if she had wanted it. She did not. *He* may have seen themselves as Albert I and Alice; *she* needed time to grow into that.

At the very least, Rainier pressed his wife into the role of spokesperson or "interpreter" for his "new" Monaco, especially to Americans. He did so in part because he was proud of Grace and aware of the effect her beauty and presence had on people, and in part because he believed he was poor at public appearances. Here he was twice wrong. In Europe (as opposed to the United States), Rainier was in fact far more articulate and engaging than he realized, while Grace both wasn't as persuasive or as comfortable at public appearances as her husband thought she was. Lacoste, for one, was aware of this; so was Grace. The two of them urged Rainier to be his own "interpreter" to the world. Not only did he know Monaco and his own plans far better than Grace did, but his public image rang truer than hers.

This was evident in the television special, *A Look at Monaco*, that Grace and Rainier did in 1963. CBS flew in a team to do the shooting in color (the crew often forgot themselves and referred to Grace as "Your Highness, honey"), and the result was a good hour collage of Monégasque history, geography, current society, and the personalities of the reigning couple. They both came off well, but Grace had to find and play a role, while Rainier was just himself. His combination of warmth, humor, intelligence, and enthusiasm were very appealing. Grace's best and most personal imprimatur on the film came in directorial suggestions—notably her insistence over the producer's spineless frettings on filming the scene at the orphanage where the little girls are sitting on their potties, chatting amiably with one another while doing their business.

Almost the same scenario replayed itself a few years later when Grace did a documentary on Monaco for ABC. "I play Ed Sullivan," she told a New York *Times* reporter, meaning that she MC'd a variety program from various parts of Monaco, doing short monologues and introducing the several talents who did musical numbers. Unfortunately that wasn't the only way in which Grace was reminiscent of Ed Sullivan. Again she was nervous about being herself on camera, and in her anxiety occasionally adopted wooden or affected postures. She even kept it up with the *Times* interviewer, whose admiring piece contained the quite friendly observation that he'd never before known anyone to pronounce "both 't's in the word 'rotten.'"

Typically Grace herself put her finger on the problem with her performances in these (and one or two other) documentaries: "It's more difficult not to play a part, and to stand up there alone, as just yourself," she told a *Look* editor. "I couldn't do any real acting," she told the *Times* writer, "which is inhibiting, and I feel a bit stiff just being myself." Indeed these hostess parts must have seemed difficult, inhibiting, and unfair to Grace. As a small girl, she had chosen acting as a means of fleeing her world, *getting out of herself*, and now here she was in her mid-thirties, a fine actress deprived of further practice of her art, being asked to appear on screen *as herself*. What was she to do?

Grace's solution was to fall back on the mask she had invented as a teenager, then honed as a young woman. It had served her well in Hollywood, but in large measure because she didn't have to wear it every moment she was in the public eye. For one thing, she had parts to play in her movies; and for another, sometimes, with the right re-

porter, she took off her mask and showed him or her the "Gracie" that
her friends and family knew. But in foreign Monaco, alone, frightened
and unknowledgeable, Grace was in a tougher bind. She had no roles
to act, but she did have a heavy burden of public responsibilities. Grace
might have tried to "reinvent" herself altogether, as her Uncle George
had done in becoming the crisp, fashionable patrician playwright. But
it was late in the day, nor had she the heart and motive, for *that* degree
of self-fragmentation. Instead, when she was nervous, Grace became
the caricature "princess" that the Hollywood press was forever saying
she was, and her critics were always lambasting her for pretending to
be. She became detached, cool, elegant, impassive, with the stilted
semi-English inflection and the *soignée* diction. These mannerisms, coupled with the nearsightedness which kept her from recognizing people
until she nearly bumped into them, produced the "image" that doomed
Grace with anyone unable or unwilling to look beneath it. Small wonder that she and Nadia Lacoste took pains to protest to Rainier that he
was better at public appearances and should do them more often.

   In fairness to Grace, she was not wed to her facade. No less a scruti-
nizer of human foibles and raiser of defenses than Barbara Walters
came to Monaco in 1966 to see for herself. Remarkably, with such a
formidable, aggressive interviewer, Grace remained relaxed and the
two got on well. The result was a triumphant "there-I-told-you" piece
in the *Ladies' Home Journal* (with only one surprising error: Walters
called Grace "Main Line") in which the author assured readers "There
is no remnant of the impression writers have had of her in the past—
that she is acting her finest role. Grace Kelly *is* Her Serene Highness.
. . . I did not feel there was a single affectation about her. She is a
serious and sensitive woman who can appear aloof."

   The first major public event that Grace took part in in Monaco was
the Monte Carlo centenary in 1966. Publicly, a celebration of one hundred years of Charles III's Casino, it was privately a celebration of
Rainier's defeat of Onassis. As his grandfather Louis II had bested the
Levantine arms merchant, Basil Zaharoff, Rainier had finally outma-
neuvered the Greek shipping tycoon, though in both instances victory
came with comparative ease because the foe was elsewhere engaged.
Once again, Rainier proved himself to be simultaneously a courageous
taker of public stands and a wily infighter—as Auréglia, Rey, and de
Gaulle could attest. In the final conflict, when Onassis spoke to journalists (which he did infrequently), he came off sounding testy and
personal, while Rainier took the high road of a policy debate. In interview after interview, he harped on Onassis's absenteeism, his reneging
on pledges to update the Casino and Hotel de Paris or to support the

cultural life of Monaco, and the incongruity of the Greek's plans with "the historic traditions of Monaco" (read Rainier's own designs).

Behind the scenes, the Prince worked to secure his alliances for the impending public confrontation. He had already decided on a tactic to defeat Onassis: the state would eradicate his foe's control of the S.B.M. by diluting his stockholding with the creation of six hundred thousand additional shares—to be owned by Monaco. But this was a "radical" tactic that smacked of socialism and Rainier had his work cut out bringing around the National Council to his side. Far from ignoring its members, as he might have done several years earlier, the Prince confided in them, reassured them of his intentions (i.e., not to put Monaco on the road to state ownership of private property), and asked for their support. He and Grace made a state visit to see de Gaulle in April of 1966, apprising the General of Rainier's strategy and trying to win him over to his side in the struggle with Onassis. The French President approved.

In June, Rainier sent a bill to the National Council asking for the creation of the new shares—a step he (and Lacoste) were at pains to present as short of "out-and-out nationalization [which] would have given us a liberal image we did not want, either politically or economically." Onassis tried to fight the measure in the Monégasque Supreme Court, and he managed to rally the support of a few National Councillors who were leery of state ownership. In the end, however, the Prince's alliances held, and the Greek sold his shares (at close to 1000 percent more than what he paid for them in 1952).

It had taken him every one of the seventeen years he had been on the throne, but now, in late summer of 1966, the one hundredth anniversary of the foundation of Monte Carlo, Rainier III was finally uncontested master in his own house. Grace was credited with planning, and even executing, many of the beautiful decorations of the 1966 celebration, and with initiating and planning the myriad cultural events of that gala year. She was even praised for fighting her winning battle with the "modernizers" (including, from time to time, her own husband) to preserve and restore in all its finery the *belle époque* style of the buildings on Monte Carlo.

All these deeds were rightly put to her account, but her most significant role between 1964 and 1966 was unquestionably the behind-the-scenes encouragement and advice she gave Rainier in what could well have turned out to be a dangerous duel with Onassis. Perhaps, as the press and Rainier (in his biography) believed, the Greek fought haphazardly because of the bittersweet personal memories (of love and marriage lost) that Monaco held for him. But "the little princeling" Onassis had disdained had also become a lion, whom even the canny Greek didn't care to tangle with, especially in his own den. On his own, Rainier had been somewhat inclined to like and trust the "peasant" in Ari, but Grace saw through that instantly. She played a singular if covert role in the battle—keeping Rainier aware of the real nature of the Greek, and ensuring that he held his temper with the press and kept the debate to issues. She advised him to work with the parliamentarians on the Council, who made Rainier impatient, and she helped him charm de Gaulle—a man with whom he had been eyeball-to-eyeball only a few years earlier.

The yearlong centenary celebration to climax these maneuvers was a marvel of planning and display. Grace threw herself into the big and small of it—opening a ball with the Duke of Edinburgh; inaugurating with Rainier the Prince Pierre Foundation (to oversee the Literary and Music Prizes); working with Cecil Beaton on the official centenary poster; welcoming Van Cliburn, Birgit Nilsson, Joan Sutherland, Zizi Jeanmaire, Jean-Louis Barrault, and Madeleine Renaud (all of whom, and many more, performed in Monaco); and organizing the International Ballet Festival, whose first performance saw Fonteyn and Nureyev dance *Romeo and Juliet* in the courtyard of the Palace. Grace also went room by room through the Hotel Hermitage with the newly appointed director-general of the S.B.M. "advising" (read "haranguing") him on color schemes, wall and bathroom fixtures, the arrangement of furnishings, and generally fighting a dogged rearguard action with cost-conscious management to enhance the quality and authenticity of the Hotel and its decor. Finally, Grace and her Garden Club saw to it that the floral decorations at the centenary figured among the most noteworthy features of all the events and displays that drew saturation attendance, comment, and reportage. A busy year, and so far her best.

§   §   §

Father Tucker once told Grace that the duties of a Princess-Consort could be compared to the two parts of the Roman mass: the "proper" and the "ordinary"—i.e., the work of special events associated with certain times of the year, and the ongoing work of day-to-day. The Monte Carlo centenary was "proper"; so were state visits (and state guests), inaugurations, speeches, and launchings, the Christmas parties, the Grand Prix auto race, the Television Festival, the charity galas, the National Feast Day (Saint Devota's Day), and a dozen other events. They all had to be planned and executed in the high style associated with *any* public happening in the Principality of Monaco. Grace used to sigh and ask Rainier unroyally, "Can't we do a couple of things half-way around here?"

Then there was the "ordinary." For Princesses of Monaco, the ordinary began with the Red Cross. In European society, the RC was not just *a* charity, it was *the* charity—not only in terms of social cachet (in a world where charity was inextricably associated with high society), but in sheer public use and import. A crisis occurred, from flood to war to famine, the Red Cross was there, the first line of recourse. And not just in crises; the RC was regularly involved in very diverse eleemosynary activities—from infant care to assistance to the aged.

The Monégasque Red Cross, founded by Rainier, had had a short but happy history when Grace took over. In a decade it had become one of the more active chapters in Europe, raising money, blood, and volunteers at a rate considerably beyond what could be expected of a state the size of Monaco. Just to be competent, a president of the national chapter of the Monégasque Red Cross must preside over the board meetings and over the August fund-raising gala and use her prestige to secure subsidies, various forms of patronage, and volunteer participation. Finally, but not least, to be competent, the president must speak the local language fluently enough to plead, beseech, scold, and exhort "en français."

By the early sixties, Grace's French was coming along better than she subjectively felt about it. She told a reporter in mid-1961, "French will be a constant struggle," by which she meant that a perfect French accent was unattainable (as indeed it is by 99.9 percent of foreigners). In truth, Grace's command of vocabulary, idiom, and diction was quite sound thanks to her actress's ability to memorize and her ear for dialogue. And although Grace's American accent plagued *her*, it was not unpleasant to natives. Rainier, for one, ceased hearing it. (When Father Tucker one day commented on Grace's accent, the Prince snapped at him, "She speaks better French than you do." To which the quick-witted old cleric replied, "My Lord Prince, I always knew that love is blind, but this is the first time I realized that love is deaf.") In sum, by the early sixties, Grace had learned enough of the French language and the congenial Mediterranean way of doing business to function competently at the Monégasque RC.

To be more than competent, a president of the Red Cross had not only to be willing to increase the hours logged at meetings but also to be imaginative in broadening the RC's scope with new programs and finding the funds to support them and the personnel to man them. Grace was making headway here. She institutionalized (via the RC) the service of visitations to the elderly that she had initiated in 1958–59 not just at one residence but for all the elderly and shut-ins in Monaco. Also under the auspices of the RC, she founded the Résidence Cap-Fleuri, a splendid home for the retired. When Grace found there was no day nursery for working mothers, she worked through the Red Cross to found the "Garderie Notre Dame de Fatima," and then personally saw to the decorating of the building (down to the huge animal cutouts she brought from the United States and Caroline's favorite teddy bear, which her mother "gave" on her unwilling daughter's be-half).

The most noteworthy Red Cross activity was the great August gala, where most of the funds for the year were nabbed in one fell, fastuous fusion of *haute couture, haute cuisine,* and *haut monde.* Far from Grace's favorite Red Cross activity, this gala was nonetheless her and her husband's one big, dependable concession to the international café society that the uninformed press constantly associated them with. Neither enjoyed such circles, and they rarely attended their functions unless charity were involved. Typically, however, once Grace knew something vulgar had to be done, she did it *à outrance.* True daughter of Margaret Majer, who justified even an exposé on her celebrity child's sex life with the argument that it raised money for her beloved Women's Medical College, Grace went after the rich and status-conscious with a vengeance. Normally, the S.B.M. almost never dared to importune Her Serene Highness to use her Grace Kelly connections to snag a Hollywood "name" for a Monte Carlo function. But to fill the RC's coffers, Grace pressed all her old friendships (and acquaintances) into service in order to ensure that both the program and the audience in the Hotel de Paris, site of the August gala, were studded with celebrities. Not that the Nivens, Grants, Sinatras, and Sammy Davises, Jr., et al. considered it a burden to come to *the* ball of the Riviera season, but their schedules might not have permitted a "holiday" in Monaco if Grace weren't on the phone to sweetly "persuade."

In 1963, Grace the mother infused her "ordinary" work as princess with another activity: she agreed to become honorary president of L'Association Mondiale des Amis de l'Enfance (the World Association of Friends of Children), or AMADE, an organization dedicated to fighting what it called "les fléaux" (the scourges) of childhood: poverty, mental and physical illness, and deprivation. AMADE carried on its fight by helping national organizations directly concerned with these issues. Unlike the UN, it had a minimum of bureaucracy and "politics" and simply quietly went about its work, sometimes making direct deliveries of milk or medicine or whatever was needed. Having taken an active part in founding the Association, which existed independent of the UN or governmental authority hence needed to be self-supporting, Grace felt obliged to accept the honorary presidency when it was offered. Yet, as with her later involvement with the La Leche League, she did not construe her work for AMADE as the obligation of a princess but of a mother—the direct extension of her love for Caroline and Albert. She did good work for AMADE. The Association held its 1967 general assembly in Monaco during the course of which a motion against violence on television was debated and passed (Grace firmly on the side of its passage). A year later, the motion came up before the

General Conference of UNESCO and was passed. In 1970, Grace presided over the founding of an Italian chapter of AMADE, giving one of her rare public speeches in a French noteworthy for its elegant poignancy: *"L'AMADE est née de ce sursaut d'angoisse, elle est née sans autre force que la volonté de réussite de ses créateurs. Son berceau est dans le plus petit pays du monde. Mais elle entend, de frontière en frontière, couvrir progressivement la terre d'un réseau de vrais amis de l'enfant."‡*

Charitable work seriously pursued admits of as much creativity as any other labor—maybe more. Grace didn't just join organizations; she invented them. Reflecting on her own interests and the myriad of needs and causes that regularly came to her attention, Grace early realized that she needed an institution of her own to express her own charitable instincts as well as "catch" some of the cases that fell between the auspices of other organizations. In 1965 the Princess Grace Foundation was born into humble circumstances. With no other headquarters than Grace's office in the Saint Mary Tower, no staff but Grace (and whatever time she could scrounge out of her hardworking secretaries), and a tiny endowment (Grace had no personal fortune at her disposal), the PGF yet had the energy and imagination of its founder. Herself a crack (but slow) knitter, creweler, and maker of needlepoint, Grace had noticed from her earliest days in Monaco how rich the Principality was in amateur craftsmen and artisans. But they had no outlet. Through her Foundation, Grace purchased a small boutique in one of the narrow serpentine streets in medieval Monaco-Ville on the Rock (not for proud Monte Carlo, this), and stocked it with the best of the local output in home ceramics, pottery, sewing, painting, knitting, jewelry, etc. Included in the inventory was some of her own work, notably a design for a scarf that sold like hotcakes with tourists. Perhaps because Grace set demanding standards for the quality of goods permitted in the Foundation-sponsored Boutique du Rocher, sales were good from the outset, which no doubt delighted the contributing artists (of all ages). It also delighted the local population in general. No accomplishment of Grace's in Monte Carlo or Paris or the United States was, for her subjects, anything other than what was expected of a glamorous ex-movie star. But this boutique was Monaco's first sign that "l'Américaine" was becoming "Monégasque."

A certain sign that she was "européenne" was Grace's admiration, friendship, and (through the Foundation) her support for Josephine Baker. Creator and finest practitioner of "le jazz hot," this Black American dancer-singer had left the United States in the twenties to become

‡ "AMADE was born from this spasm of anguish; it was born with no other force than its founders' will to succeed. Its cradle is the smallest country in the world. But we fully intend to grow, from frontier to frontier, until the earth is bound with a network of the true friends of children."

one of America's most famous expatriates. As a performer, Baker's combination of style and sophistication set off a sensation on the Continent. She was earthy yet regal; adept in several languages; stage-plumed in high fashion; yet anchored in her Black American culture; and she electrified audiences. The tawny, long-legged, wide-eyed performer had a career that spanned forty years; she was still doing her act on the best stages of Paris when she was past sixty.

The poet Langston Hughes wrote of Baker's "rhythm, warmth, and her impudent grace," but what got to Grace of Monaco was her largeness of heart and soul. The entertainer's actions offstage surpassed her talents on. While showing audiences in Occupied Paris how to dance the Black Bottom, she was also working as an effective spy for the Resistance, and at the same time mothering twelve adopted children of diverse national and ethnic backgrounds. After the war, she won a reputation for her commitment to brotherhood and humanity, using her fame and her money to assist a large number of causes and people. Indeed her generosity outstripped her funds; when Grace came to Baker's aid in 1969, the entertainer was bankrupt and had lost her home in the Dordogne Valley. With Grace's help, Baker and her motley brood were settled in a Riviera villa near Monaco. That same year she performed at the Red Cross Gala, and in subsequent years, as well as becoming a friend of Grace and Rainier, she made it a point of honor to repay their loans. She also did them a big favor. When, in a fit of pique, Sammy Davis, Jr. canceled his engagement to perform at the 1972 Gala only a few hours before the show, "the Black Venus," aged sixty-seven, not only filled in but rounded up Bill Cosby, Desi Arnaz, and Burt Bacharach to join her.

Besides the boutique and diverse charity, the Princess Grace Foundation had one other interest that ate up increasing amounts of Grace's time but was never something she regarded as work: ballet.

If the word "Monaco" had any association in Grace Kelly's mind before 1955, it was in connection with the "other" great love of her youth apart from the theater. For a period earlier in the century, Monaco was synonymous with great ballet. After several visits, the Ballets Russes of Serge Diaghilev—perhaps, then, the world's finest company, but unquestionably its most daring, glamorous, and controversial— took up permanent residence in Monte Carlo, from whence it dominated ballet for a quarter of a century. And not just the ballet. Tyrannical alchemist of several arts, Diaghilev made of classical dance "a total art form," "a universal language," bringing (or summoning) to Monaco choreographers of the talent of Fokine, Balanchine, and Lifar; composers Stravinsky, Prokofiev, Debussy, and Ravel; artists Picasso, Cocteau, Matisse, Braque, and Rouault; fashion designer Coco Chanel, and dancers Nijinsky and Karsavina. Until Diaghilev's death (in 1929), an endless stream of masterpieces premiered on the stage of the Salle Garnier at the Monégasque Opera: *Specter of the Rose, Afternoon of a Faun, Petrouchka, The Blue God, The Blue Train,* among many others.

Even after the great impresario's death, Russian ballet stayed alive and shining in Monte Carlo for a generation. René Blum, Michel Fokine, and Serge Lifar assured the continuation of the Ballets Russes into the late forties. Eventually, however,—partly due to Monaco's depletion in the war, partly to the migration of the "classical" tradition of émigré Russian ballet to New York—the Monte Carlo company came to an end. The world's great companies continued to visit Monaco in the fifties (though with decreasing frequency), but the local light was out.

If Grace wanted to accomplish anything as Princess of Monaco, she wanted, *somehow,* to relight that flame. But this was an undertaking as large as Rainier's tunnel—larger, perhaps, because any rock will finally give way to enough blasting, while the creation of a world-class ballet company required more than funds. In any case, Grace hadn't anything approaching the subsidies necessary to think about "buying up" enough great dancers and choreographers to recreate the Ballets Russes de Monte Carlo. She sensibly realized that the way to found a great company of dance is to create an environment for it. Monaco had a unique tradition, of course, but frankly it was fraying at its satin cuffs when Grace came into her own as Princess. The appearance of Fonteyn and Nureyev at the centenary was a coup for her, but the cost incited nearly as many grumbles from locals as its brilliance won international acclaim. Grace would have to prepare the ground very slowly and carefully.

And the first thing to do, as any choreographer or artistic director would agree, was to found a ballet school. But to do that, you needed a teacher. Here, Grace was in luck. In 1952, a ballet instructor named Marika Besobrasova had opened the "École de Danse Classique" in nearby Beausoleil. Russian by birth, the ballet mistress had, with her family, fled what she called "the red tornado" and come to settle in Nice. Here she studied dance with several of the former staff of the Imperial Ballet and was eventually engaged by Blum for the Ballets de Monte Carlo. In a few years, she switched to teaching, and by the fifties, was known as one of Europe's finest mistresses of ballet, with students of the reputation of Jean Babilée, Etchevery, and the Golovines. Nevertheless, the Riviera of the era was not a center of classical dance, and Besobrasova's school had a hard time paying the rent on the floating series of studios that were its address. "Madame B," as her students called her respectfully, needed a patron.

What was to become one of the better collaborations in the modern

history of the ballet began one day in the spring of 1963 when Grace
appeared in Besobrasova's dilapidated studio to enroll five-year-old
Caroline for ballet class. The daughter enjoyed the lessons greatly, but
no less than her mother enjoyed *her* enjoyment, and in her pleasure,
Grace paid closer attention to "Madame B." What she saw impressed
her. Besobrasova, by her own proud declaration, was not a teacher or
even a professor but a master for whom the ballet was an *ascesis,* a way
of living. Conversely, one didn't simply instruct pupils in the geome-
try of graceful movement; one formed the whole person with a view to
dance. On the other hand, Grace did not fail to see the rest: Madame B
was almost ruthlessly tough and demanding on students; she was tem-
peramental and dictatorial with colleagues and subordinates; she suffered fools atrociously; and she had every bit of oversensitive vanity
that a granddaughter of the Commanding General of the Romanov
Imperial Guard might be expected to have (and a little more). In short,
a lousy bet as a fund-raiser.

But she happened to be a genius at running a school and training
dancers. Grace saw this presently, and so she overlooked the rest. She,
Grace the Princess, would see to the fund-raising and ego-salving;
Besobrasova would turn out dancers. On this rock, Monaco would re-
build its cathedral of the ballet.

The women talked. Grace's dream of refounding the Ballets de
Monte Carlo was also Madame B's, not surprisingly. Understanding
that its realization lay years, even decades, off, the two yet set immediately to work to recreate the fecund environment of dance that would
be the long prelude to the rebirth of a ballet company. While the Princess Grace Foundation stepped in with increasing funds for ballet
scholarships, Besobrasova turned her considerable clout in the ballet
world to getting guest dancers for Monaco at comparatively "reasonable" fees. The Nureyev-Fonteyn coup at the Monte Carlo centennial
was a tribute to the combined hard work of both women. Shortly
thereafter, Grace launched the International Festival of Ballet in
Monte Carlo, which, in the ensuing years, brought back to Monaco
many of the leading world companies that had long since deleted the
Principality from their tours. In 1967, with the Prince and Princess's
solid support (and her Foundation's help) Madame Besobrasova formed
a small touring company called the Ballet of the Monte Carlo Opera
and made a short but brilliant foray through Italy with dancers Carla
Fracci, Rudolf Nureyev, and Juan Juliano.

Meanwhile the school grew in numbers and quality; the Foundation's benefactions permitting it to import the best students from all
over Europe and the United States, not simply southern France, as
before. By the turn of the sixties, Besobrasova's reputation was established internationally—in no small part because Nureyev had become

one of her devotees, faithfully showing up in her master's class whenever he was on the Riviera, and sometimes sending for her when he
wasn't. But the "School of Classical Dance" still desperately needed a
permanent headquarters appropriate to its excellence and, above all, to
its dream. Grace assured Madame B over and over that they would find
a way. "Patience. That's what Princess Grace taught me in those
years," Besobrasova said a long time later. "I learned patience from
her, and I shared her dream."*

§   §   §

Have you ever looked into the heart of a flower?
—*Princess Grace,* My Book of Flowers

The paradox that led Grace to found the Garden Club of Monaco in
1968 was this: in a land lush with blooms, famous for its provision of
roses and carnations the world over, few people seemed to care about
flowers, or, as Grace sometimes said, "I don't mean care about flowers,
I mean *care about flowers!*" She had visited any number of flower shows
up and down the French and Italian Rivieras, but they were all commercial affairs where a "product" was "wholesaled" to "dealers" and
"shipped out." Grace came at things from an entirely different, perhaps even 'opposing,' tradition: the Anglo-American garden club,
whose devout members looked on flowers as far too important to serve
as a mere living; they had to be a way of life.

Again it was the occasion of the centenary that solidified Grace's
intentions. Nearly every one of the fifty-two weeks of that protracted
celebration had to be filled with something original. Well what could
be newer on the floral Côte d'Azur than a flower show, including an
arranging competition? Conceiving, announcing, and even planning
what was to become the first annual Flower Show were not half the
battle, nor even a third; they were at most a tenth. Grace was stunned
at the amount of cajoling, pleading, shaming, hand-holding, and re-
monstrating required to get entries (virtually all women; at this early
stage in the show's life, the exigencies of Mediterranean macho would
have forced the local men to take hemlock rather than enter a flower
show). But she flung herself into it, and fortunately, her example early
on won a valuable ally to her cause. The French wife of the Minister of
State of Monaco decided this was a wonderful idea and provided great
help in rallying (by sweetly stiff-arming) a score of ladies from up and
down the Riviera. But though willing, these Gallic torchbearers of
floriculture were not yet knowledgeable, so Grace brought in Countess
Malvasia, a well-known flower arranger from Bologna, to provide ele-

* Interview, May 23, 1983.

mentary tuition in the art of arranging. Everyone now settled down to work on her arrangement.

And then it happened. In Grace's own words: "Through working with flowers we began to discover things about ourselves that had been dormant. We found agility not only with our fingers but with our inner eyes in searching for line, scale, and harmony. In bringing out these talents within ourselves, we gained a dimension that enabled us not only to search for harmony in an arrangement, but also to discover the importance of carrying it into our lives and our homes."† The show itself—a great novelty to locals—was an early hit of the Monte Carlo centennial (Grace herself designed the official poster in calligraphy). Perhaps not surprisingly, however, the show was something of an anticlimax for the participants themselves, who had registered their important gains in the doing.

The experience decided Grace to try to institutionalize this "spirit," if that were possible, but it took two years and much effort for the Garden Club of Monaco to be born. Grace and her handful of loyalists from the first show understood what it was all about, but few others did, and they required conversion. Until they were converted, it sounded strange to hear the Princess making extravagant claims like "I feel that every city, every town, every village should have a garden club. It is as necessary for the lifeblood of a community as a library, art gallery, [or] museum." That was a very Anglo-Saxon thing to say; the locals, surrounded by flora all their lives but never seeing it ("I mean *really seeing it*"), required time to catch on. To quicken the process, Grace took the future Garden Club members on trips around the Riviera to see a few of the gardens there—some of them magnificent examples of architectural design, others, rare collections of exotic blooms. She showed them the Palace gardens, and of course, Monsieur Kroenlein at the Jardin Exotique gave them many a tour of his unique domain.

But things still took their Mediterranean time, and Grace would get impatient. This wasn't an international ballet troupe; this was a simple garden club. She apprised Rupert Allan of her frustrations one day: "So [after all this preparation] we chose a steering committee to lay the groundwork for the club. I met for an hour in the morning with these ladies and then I had to return to the Palace for other meetings. I called several of them later that evening, however, to see how their luncheon meeting had gone. 'Oh, charming, wonderful. A delightful afternoon at Madame So-and-So's,' I was told. 'But *what did you decide?*' I finally blurted out trying to hide any trace of exasperation. 'Decide? Decide

† Princess Grace of Monaco, with Gwen Robyns, *My Book of Flowers* (New York, 1980), p. 10. Subsequent quotes on flowers from *Ibid.*, pp. 10–15.

what?' they said, 'Were we supposed to decide something?' " And so it went. But in October of 1968, the Garden Club of Monaco came into happy existence and, with subsidies that Grace cadged from the government, undertook the annual May Flower Show, including a competition in arranging. They also took trips around Europe and beyond and brought in guest speakers.

The first of these was a woman after Grace's own heart, Julia Clements (Lady Seton) from England. She brought tears and deep smiles to the ladies as she described how, at the nadir of World War II, she raised the spirits of her countrywomen with flowers. Grace paraphrased Clements's speeches to the women of England: "Instead of longing for things that they could not have, they should look around for something positive . . . something that would bring color and expression into their lives. 'Why—it's flowers,' she cried. 'Flowers we have in our gardens and countryside in greater abundance than almost any country in the world. Why don't we all become artists with flowers?' " Grace concluded the story with words that shed as much light on her own intentions and character as on Clements's achievement: "And so through this one woman's *cri de coeur* began a whole new awakening and experience for thousands of British women."

A few years later, this Anglican Apostle of the Flowers demonstrated her remarkable apostolic skills very vividly for the Garden Club of Monaco. At the time of Rainier's Silver Jubilee, the women decided to decorate various important buildings in the Principality. But the pastor of the parish church of St. Charles in Monte Carlo was an old-time priest who didn't see that flowers had any place in a church, save perhaps some lilies in two vases on either side of the altar at Easter. The cleric was so stubborn that Grace herself, in a private convocation at the Palace, failed to persuade him to permit the club to decorate his church. Then Lady Seton visited the man, and, in her own inimitable way, entranced him with a depiction of how floral decorations in English churches had inspired something like a minor national reconversion. The priest said "yes."

> *People [say] such foolish things . . .*
> —*Princess Grace (in an interview in* Playboy, *1966)*

In sum, the foundations of Grace's "présence" in Monaco were not merely a lot of energetic activity, but activity from a center, with an immediate purpose toward an ultimate end that transcended the activity (or organization) itself. Grace was not able to explain her "philosophy" coherently in the sixties—she was still young, doing what, for her, "came naturally"—but her work may be seen historically as of a piece. In its many facets it carried Grace's particular stamp: external enterprise, to be truly worthwhile, had finally to refer back to the internal person and his or her moral, spiritual, or intellectual improvement. A profound but hardly a new philosophy—in doing for others, we do more for ourselves—Grace nonetheless applied it her way.

Curiously, in these still-early years, her actions often spoke her views more persuasively than her words did. It would take Grace time to learn that it wasn't necessary—indeed it was ill-advised—for the young Princess of Monaco to hold forth on every subject. Grace's words perhaps more uncritically reflected her time and place and the prejudices of her position than they would later.

Her Serene Highness never in her life sounded more self-opinionated and off-the-cuff than in an interview she gave to *Playboy* in 1966, which a French newspaper summarized under the headline, "Grace of Monaco Holds Nothing Back." Following a lengthy introduction by the editors (porous with errors), Grace proceeded to scatter obiter dicta like confetti, holding forth, variously, on de Gaulle (she disliked his anti-Americanism, but without putting it in any context), the Americans in Vietnam ("Well, *someone* has to be there"), the French Communist Party ("[They're] too well organized to suit me"), Red China in the UN (she was against it but in the next breath agreed "it is difficult to ignore a nation of seven hundred million people"), and Franco ("Some countries at certain times *need* dictatorships").

A lamentable performance, reminiscent of Ma Kelly at her more dogmatic or of a character from a George Kelly play, yet typical of what happened when Grace made pronouncements on every question posed rather than admit ignorance and (more importantly) shape the interview to her own interests and knowledge. On semi-political social issues, Grace often did no better. Here she would sometimes sound like a fogy, which she was not. She said she opposed women wearing slacks in public; she also opposed miniskirts, although she tried to make a joke of it by saying they did not suit her personally because she hadn't pretty knees (untrue). She told one magazine writer that she personally had undergone a transformation on the subject of women's independence. Having been a "thoroughly modern Millie" in her show biz years, she had now learned that a woman's real place was in the home. A dozen times she must have insisted on what an old-fashioned (or "European") marriage she and Rainier had—he the decision-maker, she the obedient wife. But the best line of all was when Grace told an interviewer, "Girls should learn to cook, sew, and make clothes," and then added, "They should learn sports."

A few writers (those who knew Grace or had read and thought about her life) demurred politely at the outrageous contradictions of some of these statements, noting that she herself hadn't liked sports as a child nor had she ever led the life of housewife confined to her kitchen and nursery. Had they known more than any journalist could have, they might have added: "nor do you permit your husband to make all the decisions [nor does he try]." But most journalists understandably just wrote her words down and printed them. As a result Grace got a reputation, especially among liberal political correspondents, for being either her husband's political shadow (he being considered a right-wing capitalist autocrat) or—among the more forgiving—an apolitical young "old prude."

Yet the truth was that in the Prince's case, the labels were inexact (and certainly historically insensitive), and in Grace's dead wrong. As John B. Kelly's daughter, she was far from a conservative blueblood. More liberal than her husband (who nonetheless listened to his wife and could frequently be brought round by her), Grace followed Moné-gasque politics carefully and "tilted" in the progressive direction when she chose to. She also campaigned for John Kennedy among the American colonies in Europe in 1960. To be sure she was an outspoken anticommunist, but then so were most Democrats of her era and background (especially Irish, big city Catholics like the Kennedys). But even here, Grace did not let strong views prevail on friendships, as it did for many. She maintained her ties with the screenwriter Carl Foreman, whom she had met during *High Noon*, after he was blacklisted for being a Communist and had taken refuge in London. Grace and Ava Gardner appeared in restaurants with Foreman at a time when that sort of gesture of solidarity had endangered many a career, even of the famous.

What it came down to was that Grace, especially at this time, had a genuine interest in politics, but not a great deal of knowledge. She was still unsure of herself in the position of princess, feeling she had to "pronounce" on all political questions just because she held a semipolitical post. She had a keen nose for what the Romans called *cui bono?*—who benefits?—as well as for the politics of the press and appearances, but little grasp of conflicting ideals and national and class perspectives. Grace subordinated the political dimension of life to her understanding of the moral and spiritual, and, at her best, infused political issues with moral-spiritual concerns, but in the sixties, she hadn't lived or thought enough to do this consistently well. Not surprisingly, therefore, when Grace addressed political questions, *per se*, in these years, she often sounded unreflective and foolish, just as when she addressed social issues she sounded waspish and Victorian.

When, more rarely, Grace verbalized the political consequences of some of her social interests (AMADE, breast feeding, the woman's role), she could be insightful and systematic, even if one did not agree with her. She was appalled at the amount of sex and violence on television—a complaint that would prove prescient and justified in another decade, but was still comparatively overlooked when she started mentioning it. Similarly, she voiced her disgust with the pornography proliferating in magazines at the newsstands. (Her diatribes were not hurled at publications like *Playboy*, which, she felt, had redeeming intellectual and sometimes artistic content, but at the growing number of "hard-core porn" magazines.) She was fearful of pornography's effect on children, she said, but she also worried about its impact on society in general—*not* because it would create licentiousness, but because "This trend, if it goes on, will probably lead us back into a terrible kind of Victorian prudish period."

A similar "twist" lurked behind her protests against movies like *Dr. Strangelove, Advise and Consent,* and *Fail Safe*. It was assumed she opposed them outright because they were critical of American politics. Undoubtedly Grace's political views were not those of the films' makers, but her opposition was highly specific. As books, she said, the latter two ran from good to excellent. As films, she personally thought little enough of their technical quality, but that was not her point, she said. Her point was that the movies were suitable for release in America, *not in Europe*. Their effect there was disastrous: "Europeans look to America for leadership," she said, and these films disillusion them because the parody and humor are the insiders' kind and are missed altogether by the average film-going European, who naively believes these are factual portrayals. (Grace wrongly blamed greedy producers for exporting them to Europe, when in fact it was the Europeans who demanded them and lapped them up.)

One may not agree with Grace's views but grant that they are thought-out, reasonable, and consistent with her life and position. Sometimes, too, Grace was capable of pulling out real surprises. In the *Playboy* interview, for example, the questioner touched on birth control, and Grace got out the start of a reasoned stand that ran at serious cross-purposes with her Church. Typically, however, she politely followed her interviewer on a ridiculous tour of the political horizon, rather than probe in depth a few issues. Worked-out political statements and positions would never be Princess Grace's forte. What she could hope to do was to continue thinking about the "linkages" that related breast feeding, motherhood, flowers, AMADE, etc. to larger political and social spheres in ways people did not generally consider.

§   §   §

Grace sometimes would tell journalists that she admired Queen Victoria for having nine children, and then, while the look of amazement was still fresh on their faces, hasten to add, "Oh, I don't mean that *I* will have nine children." But the fact is, she was probably tempted, for Grace (unlike Victoria) loved having little ones around—her own, preferably, but anybody's might do in a pinch. (She was many times a godmother and tremendously popular with her young cousins, nieces, and nephews.) As she did not baby or talk down to children, she did not tire of them easily; they were people to her, little people, and now, as before, as ever, they were the joy of her life.

The third "little person"—the all-time apple of the family's eye—joined the Grimaldis on the first of February 1965: Stephanie Marie Elisabeth. She arrived early. Grace had driven to Villefranche to meet her mother's plane, then had lunch with her when the labor pains began. An easy birth, like those of her sister and brother, Stephanie greeted the world in the same library-cum-delivery room that Caroline and Albert had known; indeed her arrival was so swift that "Killer King" had hardly had time to collect her siblings before Stephanie was lying in the crib next to her mother. Albert, aged seven, sat counting the cannon shots, delighted when they stopped at twenty-one ("*I* got a hundred and one!" he informed everyone). Perhaps because a fairly large age gap separated Stephanie from her brother and sister, she aroused none of the intense, conflicting emotions in Caroline and Albert that might otherwise have surfaced.

It would be hard not to make the children's infancy and youth sound idyllic. Their nursery was a large bright room, whose one entire wall was a window looking out onto the Palace garden, and whose other walls contained a copy of Picasso's *Happy King*, a Jean Cocteau poster of a fish in a top hat, and a slew of family photographs. The room was a veritable menagerie of stuffed animals and toys. Above each child's bed was a simple gold cross. They had equally delightful rooms at Roc Agel. Maureen King was a good and a beloved nanny, who tolerated less mischief from the children than beloved nannies usually do (or Rainier wouldn't have kept her on). King spent less time alone with Caroline and Albert and held less solitary authority over them, than was normally the case in wealthy European families, for Grace throughout the sixties continued to steal every possible moment she could from her many tasks to be with her children. And when she couldn't come to them, she brought them with her—not without amusing results. At a reception for de Gaulle in the Legation of Monaco in Paris, Caroline was presented to the President of the Republic, whom she had been carefully tutored to call "Votre Excellence." In the nervous crunch, the nine year old got confused and fell back on her last formal presentation—to Cardinal Tisserant. She called the General, "Votre Eminence." King wrote later, "It was the only time I ever saw a great grin spread over the usually stern face of General de Gaulle." On another occasion, Caroline met Sir Winston Churchill on an airplane and was so charmed by his gallant attentions that she did him the signal honor of permitting him to cradle her favorite doll, Poor Pitiful

Pearl. There, for the rest of the flight, meekly sat the Vanquisher of
Hitler, stogy in one hand and Poor Pearl in the other.

With one notable exception, the relationship between Caroline and
Albert was very close. For a period, Caroline got into the habit of
biting her brother. Stoical, or frightened, Albert never complained,
but Nanny King noticed the teeth marks on his body and told Caroline
to stop. She did not; King took up the matter with Grace, who got
nowhere with her daughter. Finally Grace sat Caroline down, said to
her, "You must not bite your brother. It hurts." She then bit her Caroline firmly on the arm. The demonstration worked. This apart, the
eldest child was loving and sweetly maternal with her younger brother
and baby sister. Caroline was, indeed, calling Stephanie "our baby"
even before she was born. Both she and Albert remained sensitive and
considerate as they grew older. Caroline insisted that the children of
the Palace staff be invited to a birthday party because "I didn't invite
them last year [and] they must have been very upset." Albert, on winning a swimming competition and receiving the medal, noticed a little
girl crying because she hadn't won one. With no fuss, he walked over
and handed her his medal.

Grace, in 1965, described Caroline as "gregarious, outgoing, terribly
frustrated if she can't do something immediately and do it well." She
might have added, "and do it her way"—already Caroline was showing
her father's stubborn streak, with the result that Grace, much more
than once, took her over her knee. Intellectually, Caroline was not only
the keenest of three intelligent children but the most interested in her
schoolwork. Initially she and Albert received tutoring (with a few
other children) at the Palace; then, while still in elementary school,
Caroline was enrolled at a convent school on the Rock (Les Dames de
St.-Maur) where she was addressed, by Grace's request, as "Caroline
Grimaldi." Always, her grades were good, her interest (particularly in
languages) high.

Albert, Grace said, was "gentle and shy and very neat and methodi-
cal." They took him to the circus one day and he sat with his nose in
the program until Rainier, who adored circuses, practically forced him
to watch the entertainment. But the little prince was more interested
in making sure that the circus performers did precisely what the program said they would do. Like Caroline, Albert was put into a local
school so that he wouldn't suffer the homesickness and feelings of
abandonment that Rainier remembered and dreaded for his own children. He, too, did well, but perhaps more in conformance to his parents' wishes than because he had Caroline's zeal for the life of the
mind. In contrast to his sisters, Albert was shyer (but not weaker) and
far, far more self-controlled. He early developed a slight stutter which
did not go away and which worried his parents. Like the girls, he was

deeply loved, but unlike them, he remained a bit of a mystery. In many of his traits—conscientiousness, politeness, reserve, consciousness of duty, self-control to the point of suppressing emotion (especially when hurt), an underlying fortitude and hypersensitivity—Albert was, in looks as in disposition, reminiscent of the preadolescent Grace Kelly.

Stephanie was very young in these years, but from the earliest age she recapitulated (and redoubled) many of Caroline's traits. Although shyer than her sister at first meetings, she, too, had a very strong character that sometimes erupted in flashes of willfulness or stubbornness. Grace would later say she "gave up" swatting Stephanie for her infractions; "I could have beaten her like a gong without making her give way." On the other hand, Stephanie had a genuine loving sweetness and vulnerability that could melt any heart (and, not quite so often, get around any injunction).

The children lived an ordered life. During the week, they rose early, came home for lunch, did their homework, and, except on weekends, watched no television. They also said their prayers, went to weekly mass and to Sunday school, and progressed through the various levels of Church formation. Less weight was attached to their being stout Roman Catholics, however, than to knowing the Christian God and his life, way, and commands. Undoubtedly, there were high premiums placed on accomplishment, conformance, and duty, but these were far from so exclusive or pervasive that they stifled individuality among the Grimaldi children (or even induced great anxiety in them).

Although Rainier took an active role as father and delighted in it, there could be no question but what Grace played the more formative part in their offsprings' lives in these years (and perhaps later). "Daddy" represented the family unity—togetherness, fun, trips, games, sports. "Maman," although she adored these things (and anticipated them with more impatience than anybody), unconsciously cultivated her children as individuals. She was intensely close to each child; with each she made a separate peace and pact. The contents of that "pact" were elusive. When asked by the press what she most wished to imbue her children with, Grace invariably replied "character." What she meant, presumably, was the stentorian morality of J.B. Kelly, whose word she so self-consciously cited—a sense of family pride and honor, loyalty, civic duty and service, individualism, accomplishment. These were noble virtues, of course, but somewhat of the storefront sort. What Grace's actions (and Rainier's as well) in fact conveyed to their children were examples of qualities of a different nuance: decency, consideration, sensitivity, charity (in the largest sense), humility, self-awareness. Like any qualities, these had their weaknesses, their excesses, their potentially damaging transmutations. Kelly's could lead to vanity, a double game and double standard, or could deform or break a sensitive child's identity on the anvil of parental expectation. Grace's qualities—particularly when combined with the consistency and elevation of her behavior—had the potential of sinking deep wells of self-reproach and guilt in children who felt such values, and indeed their own, to be at odds with instinct and desire. Every action has an equal and opposite reaction, and Grace's, no less than her father's, could nurture seeds of rebellion.

§   §   §

A man isn't so badly off at all when he's married to a woman that's in love with him. I think that's what they mean by "home."
—*George Kelly*, The Deep Mrs. Sykes

In the years after Stephanie's birth, the work of princess began profoundly if quietly to transform Grace's identity and to restrict her hallowed home life, but it did not bring her the conscious satisfaction that the role of mother and wife did—not by a long shot. Grace talked freely, even loquaciously, about her children, of whom she was proud, but she said nothing about her relationship with the Prince beyond the oft-cited notice that her marriage "is entirely European. Here the man is definitely the master of the house and there are no two ways about it." This statement, coupled with the occasional retort to a foolish question—"No, I never see anything fairy-talish about it [the marriage]"—obscured the truth far more than revealed it. Indeed, it led the speculative and mean to suspect that she was unhappy with Rainier but resigned to life with him.

Nothing could have been further from the truth. Yet nothing was more private, hence unavailable for public utterance. Grace and Rainier had their problems, of course, but the years brought them closer together and deeper in love. During her pregnancies, Grace was particularly attentive to him because her mother had once warned her that "men are likely to feel neglected when you're expecting or when there are babies around." Indeed he would joke that if she were knitting him something, she *must be* pregnant, for otherwise the item would be for some friend or family member in Pennsylvania. When Maureen King left their service (in 1965), she gave in to the temptation to write a memoir, which, although it was laudatory and previewed by Lacoste, cannot have pleased her intensely private former employers. In it she described watching Grace and Rainier walk "hand in hand in the garden, . . . a picture of vibrant happiness," or finding them sitting together on the sofa in the salon, where they "reminded me of young lovers."

Lovers, the two were also friends. Despite all the differences in background and taste, they *liked* being together. Rainier had few intimates among the people around him (whose motives he had learned to reflexively mistrust) so he sweetly pressed Grace into the role of pal as well as wife and consort. She accepted with relish, for she, too, now had no one else. The Prince would even accompany her shopping, where he would goad her into spending more than tightfisted Grace was inclined to; and she would put up with his sailing in the succession of yachts that replaced the *Deo Juvante II* (all named after the kids—*Albecaro I & II, Carostephal, Stalcia*). When bowling lanes made their appearance in Monaco, they both learned to bowl, so they could do it together. Some anniversaries, they would throw a party, but just as often, Rainier would drive Grace to the Hotel de Paris in his Lancia. They would take a quiet table for two in a corner of the terrace, and dine, dance, and toast each other with champagne—all by themselves. Grace was a fine dancer; so was Rainier, but he was self-conscious. He refused to do the samba and rumba in public.

They also went through trials together. In the summer of 1967, with Grace nearly four months pregnant, she, Rainier, and the children voyaged to Montreal to see Expo 67, where Monaco had a small, but beautiful pavilion. The popular impact of their visit may be seen in the New York *Times*'s coverage, which opened with the sentence, "Despite an attendance of more than 22,000,000 to date, including Queen Elizabeth and Prince Philip, nothing happened at Expo 67 until the arrival today of Their Serene Highnesses Prince Rainier and Princess Grace of Monaco." The two presided over a glittering reception—a celebration of Monaco's National Day at the fair—and the next day were preparing to visit Quebec City when Grace became ill and had to be put to bed. The next day she lost the child. The whole family was bitterly disappointed, but Grace for a time was nearly inconsolable. She had so badly wanted "a companion" for Stephanie, who, she felt, was too removed from her siblings in age. Besides, three children was *simply not enough*, and Grace, heading toward her thirty-eighth birthday, very much feared this would be her last chance.

There was other pain in these years, which husband and wife bore together. Grace was almost as saddened as Rainier by the passing of his father, Pierre de Polignac (in 1965). The old Count had given Grace unswerving support and sympathy from the very first; the two had forged a special friendship as deep as any that Grace enjoyed with her older women friends. The jewel she loved most in her collection was a present from Polignac—a magnificent, opulent drop pearl the size of a plum encircled with tiny rubies and topped by a diamond crown. Part of its deep significance to Grace was that the pearl had belonged to her illustrious predecessor, Princess Alice, and when her father-in-law gave it to her, he had whispered, "You will be her worthy successor."

And, like any happy couple, the Grimaldis fought together. Rainier was gaining on his temper, but certain topics, people, and situations set him off. A dress a mite too décolleté or tight-fitting might provoke a "Don't you wear that again!" from him. (Curiously, though, he urged her to get a bikini—*de rigueur*, he insisted, for Riviera sunbathing. Grace finally did, but never got the courage to wear it at the public beach.) More seriously, the two had divergent notions, not so much on the modernization of Monaco, which Grace accepted as a necessity, but on some of that policy's personnel, elements, and consequences (intended and unintended). As we shall see, Grace usually submitted to her husband's wishes, but not always, and *not* without a fight.

In personal matters, despite his Americanophilia, Rainier could not for the life of him get used to what he called "U.S. informality." Here he meant everything from the way Grace's friends argued with (or, worse, contradicted) their husbands in public, to their arrival for a visit, virtually without notice, with uninvited guests in tow.

A more ticklish subject was Grace's family. Rainier deeply admired Ma Kelly, although he understood his wife's anger and anguish at the time of the publication of the infamous series on her "romances." He had also fully appreciated his father-in-law's virtues and accomplishments, but without holding any illusions about J.B., nor feeling any need to whitewash or idealize him, as Grace manifestly did. Rainier had been aware at the start that he was an outsider in the Kelly midst —not altogether accepted by them—so he remained graciously reserved during his biennial visits to East Falls with Grace, just as he graciously welcomed Ma, Lizanne, Peggy, and their families to Monaco (and overlooked the obvious differences between their social style and the European).

However, very gradually Rainier's feelings chilled as he watched what he saw as the growing gap between his wife's treatment of her family and their treatment of her. He had always recognized that Grace altered herself slightly when she was with them. Hypersensitive to her family's reactions to her, and ruthlessly teased by her sisters, she went unnecessarily (to Rainier's way of thinking) out of her way to be "just one of the girls" when she was in Philadelphia. It was as if she felt the need to belittle herself, her successes, reputation, and position —and for what, Rainier asked? As the years went by, the Prince came to believe (as did several of Grace's closest friends) that the Kelly family's feelings about her were inflected with more than a little envy, resentment, and—in some of their cases—a desire to turn their relationship to her to personal advantage. Slowly, this started to needle Rainier, who occasionally and gingerly suggested to his wife that she was being a bit of a chump. Grace's psychological conflict and ambivalence about her family ran very deep, but on the surface her defensive/ protective mechanisms were in very good repair, and Rainier could get nowhere with Grace unless he was willing to precipitate a major fight, which he was not.

In sum, as it entered its second decade, the Grimaldi marriage was sound, sustaining, and affectionate. Nothing showed this better than Grace's and Rainier's teamwork in all phases of life. The conclusion of the *Marnie* affair had righted the one potentially serious imbalance in the relationship (and in Monaco's governance, for that matter), but the price paid was terribly steep. The self-suppression of Grace's artistry could not be swallowed easily or quickly, no matter how energetically the ex-actress flung herself into her duties as Princess. If the marriage lacked anything, it was ample opportunity for Grace to probe and air this frustration. Brisk and realistic, she and Rainier were strongly inclined not to talk about things they couldn't do anything about. She certainly did not blame Rainier for her problems; on the contrary, if she blamed anybody it was her stubborn self for not bowing more philosophically to reality.

Grace was haunted by her past. Wherever she looked "the Hollywood myth is still potent," as a *Times* reporter wrote in 1968. With these words, Mark Shivas meant that people continued to come to Monaco because Grace was there. A dubious thesis, that, albeit popular in America; Monégasque tourism figures did not vary with Grace's physical presence in the Principality, nor did they in any way decline in the seventies when she lived much of the time in Paris. In any case, she was invisible to all but the tiniest fraction of a percent of tourists. Shivas would have been on the money to say that the acting myth was still potent in Princess Grace. Despite her desperate awareness that it was a "myth," she could not subjugate the aspiration, dream, and the excitement that would wildly dart out of her heart when, say, George Kelly visited the Palace (as he periodically did), or when she saw a production of *The Show-Off* in California (on its way to a 1967 Broadway revival), or when producer Sam Spiegel sent her the script of *Nicholas and Alexandra* with a letter beseeching her to consider the part of "Sunny" (the Empress). Spiegel said it was perfect for her, which it was, but Grace said she just could not take it, or even seriously consider the proposition. But her heart fluttered.

And so the journalists would keep posing the Question, and Grace would concede readily that "Oh, certainly I do miss acting . . . I love acting. I loved my job as an actress," but then sweetly point out that she loved her life of mother, wife, and princess more, and she couldn't have both. She wasn't lying, but like a great ballerina, she was totally concealing the strain and the pain. Nevertheless, the tension was visible, as she searched to lose one identity and take on another. Grace was stiffer in her middle years in Monaco than she had been before, stiff in the ossified princess mask she often wore that was so much less "faith-

ful, discreet, and superlative" than her old Hollywood mask; or stiff
with the "opinions" she would hand down to the press on "women"
("For a woman today, there aren't as many challenges to one's creative
instincts as before").

§   §   §

Q. *What are you smiling at?*
A. *I'm thinking of the persistence of habit.*
                                                —*George Kelly*, The Fatal Weakness

Just before her fortieth birthday (November 12, 1969), Grace received a feature writer whom Nadia Lacoste no doubt enthusiastically
let through. Roderick Mann, author of many a piece on Grace, might
have been president of the journalists' branch of the Grace Kelly/
Princess Grace Fan Club for the burbling reverence he displayed to
"Her Serene Highness." His attitude was the polar opposite of the red
hot animus of John Cummings, but his questions betrayed no less misunderstanding of Grace than the Philadelphia columnist's (and manifestly evoked her irritation). "I have admired Princess Grace since, as a
reporter, I covered her fairy-tale wedding to Prince Rainier on April
19, 1956 . . . She has remained a feast for the eyes in a world where
the menu is not noticeably meager," wrote the genial Mann in *Ladies'
Home Journal* (May 1970). Then, after describing her clothes and appearance, he asked Grace, how did she stay so young and beautiful? He
wrote: "She seemed slightly impatient. 'Honestly, I've never thought
of myself as a great beauty. I think I'm quite nice-looking, but that's
about it. Frankly, I've always hated being known for my looks. I'd
much rather be known for my ability. One of my few regrets is that I
wasn't able to develop more fully as an actress. I stopped acting before
I could do that. But that was my choice. I just hope I've developed as a
person instead. That's what's important to me—to fulfill my role as a
wife and mother and princess . . . not whether I'm beautiful, but
whether I have more character than I used to."
  Well, how *very interesting*, but couldn't Grace tell people how she
managed to "hold back the cruelties of the calendar?" To Mann, "there
was no denying the way she looked." With what must have been an
interior sigh, she answered the question with good grace, but not without a mild, self-objective reproof, "You say I've got a trim figure? It's
not true. I'm rather fat actually." (True enough; Grace by 1969 had put
on some ten to fifteen pounds over her Hollywood weight). Mann then
wanted to know, "Wouldn't it be difficult, anyway, to diet at the Palace,
where the food is just placed before you?" ("Not if you're determined
. . ."); then he wondered if she ever cooked herself ("Sometimes I do. I
have sudden splurges of domesticity [especially on vacation].") What

exercises did the Princess do? How did she feel about "rejuvenation treatments—facelifts"? ("It takes a lot of courage to . . . change your appearance. The very idea of surgery scares me stiff. Anesthesia, too; I get such a feeling of claustrophobia. I wouldn't have it even when I had my babies. I don't approve of it anyway in childbirth—I think the babies suffer. No, I don't really think I'd do anything—unless one day I found my face had fallen down around my knees.") Did she use much makeup? How about wigs? What about clothes? What was good fashion and beauty advice for a mother to give a daughter? ("Beauty is to be natural . . .")

Among the elements of Grace's regrets at reaching forty were questions like these, and the articles they gave birth to. Mann's was no specialty piece for a diet, fashion, or coiffure magazine, but supposedly a portrait of Grace at the start of her fifth decade on Earth. The "fairytale," "society," and "glamorous" images that her former countrymen stubbornly clung to weighed on Grace, for they trivialized her while neglecting totally her hard efforts to create a new identity for herself, a "présence" in Monaco. Misunderstanding in the Principality she counted on; but such willful misunderstanding by Americans who insisted on projecting onto her their own fantasies—*that* annoyed. Or annoyed when it didn't wound and enrage. The natural counterpart and consequence of a Roderick Mann was the vitriol of a John Cummings or the crafted snide asides of a Robert Massie. Yet in part, all this was Grace's fault. The assaults of the crowds, the press, and the paparazzi had so upset her and Rainier that they built a rampart and "purifying" mechanism in Lacoste and her PR office. One of the results was the court writer.

Another relic that got trundled out with dependable regularity was the query, "Are you happy?," often reinforced by the emphatic, *"really* happy." In this era, Grace gave conflicting and revealing answers. To *Playboy* in 1966, she defined happiness as "being at peace with yourself, not anxiously seeking for something, not being frantic about not having something"—an appropriate definition for a woman just emerging from several years of frenzy, culminating with denial. The interviewer then asked, "Are you at peace with yourself?," and again Grace gave an honest, candid answer, "Well, I understand peace." What would she need to achieve peace? "Well, I have many unfulfilled ambitions in life . . . God willing, some of them may be realized."

One year later, Grace sat through an examination by the intense, inimitable Barbara Walters, who also hit on the "happy" question. She replied carefully at first. "I've had happy moments in my life, but I don't think happiness—being happy—is a perpetual state that anyone can be in. Life isn't that way." Then perhaps thinking of her answer to *Playboy* twelve months earlier, she added, "But I have *a certain peace of mind,* yes. My children give me a great deal of happiness. *And my life here has given me many satisfactions in the last ten years.*‡ Was it just Grace's mask talking—the persona who felt it "wouldn't do" to have people think she wasn't at peace with herself—or had Grace actually begun, in that jam-packed, unforgettably busy and successful year of the Monte Carlo centenary to find *some* peace of mind in becoming Grace de Monaco?

‡ Emphasis added.

CHAPTER X

PRINCESS EMBATTLED
1971-80

The first time Grace played baseball since the East Falls gang "drafted" her was when the sailors of the U.S. warship *Constitution* came ashore in Monaco by princely invitation. But this time she *wanted* to play. Her Highness never looked less serene than on the diamond that afternoon with the delighted servicemen. In Barbara Walters description, "the usually sedate regent [was dressed] in a T-shirt, denim skirt, bobby socks, sneakers and baseball cap having the time of her life running the bases."

And yet even as she savored her heritage, Grace was losing her national identity. "I'm no longer entirely American but not yet entirely Monégasque," she would say. Many of her subjects added to her confusion by sweetly going out of their way to try to speak English to her (and in France, waiters and shopgirls did nothing but), while in the United States, "I seem to evoke everybody's broken French," Grace said ruefully. She was never one to court or even follow fads and fashion, least of all in the America of the sixties, when it took her years to find out that Haight-Ashbury wasn't a person. But she was sometimes saddened by her loss of roots, confiding to a journalist, "You know you've lost touch when you no longer understand the jokes in *The New Yorker.*" Rainier delighted in certain elements of American style, and she tried to acquaint him with U.S. slang. But her cherished additions to his vocabulary—"buster," "catawampus," and "See ya later alligator"—weren't even "hep," let alone "hip." "I guess I'm just a square," Grace conceded, and no one argued otherwise.

The irony lurking behind this cheerful superannuation was that the realm over which Grace co-reigned was fast becoming the last word in "American modern." By the midseventies, the "fief supported by a casino" which Rainier had inherited from his grandfather was a constitutional regime with a thriving mixed economy, a nearly doubled population, and a revised skyline and coast that conservative old Louis II might have gagged over—if he'd recognized it. To give Rainier III his due, few monarchs in European history have hung on against odds so varied and great to consolidate a triumph so complete.

Also unrecognizable to Louis would have been the Societé des Bains de Mer. "The Sleeping Beauty" had very definitely awoken when its Prince-savior arrived to snatch her from the wicked Greek warlock, but the life to which he brought her was considerably more bourgeois than a fairy tale permitted. The new hierarchy of the old company— now owned by the Monégasque state in collaboration with a consortium of European banks—was a team of Franco-American "whiz kids," trained at the Harvard Business School and the École Polytechnique, and with experience in some of the leading American banks and corporations. The new head of the company, Marcel Palmaro, had previously been head of the foreign department at the investment house of Lehman Brothers. Under their unlavish hands, the cut crystal, sterling-encased dispensers of fine confiture, traditionally set on each table at *petit déjeuner*, had been traded in for uniform metal containers of predetermined, rather chintzy amounts of clear jelly. Nor were flowers and fruit automatically provided in the suites of newly arriving guests at the Hotel de Paris. The wiser part of "rationalizing" turned out to be rationing.

In the lingo of the new accountancy the "benefit" far outweighed the "cost." For the first time in its history, Monaco was touristically "in season" all year round, not just winter. Over a thousand new hotel rooms—in buildings owned by Loews and Holiday Inn, among others —were available at attractive prices that, together with new beaches and pools and a packed social calendar of galas and "special events," made Monaco a twelve-month member of the international tourist circuit. Even more novel in old Monte Carlo than summer visitors were the trendy new cabarets and nightclubs, owned and operated by the elite of disco management in Europe, where the *jeunesse dorée* [gilded youth] of "le tout Paris" twisted and shouted and shocked the elders whom they rivaled for spending. The S.B.M. itself got in on the act and opened a Western-style "saloon," followed by an American "salon" in the Casino, which now became the only gaming room in Europe boasting a full array of Vegas games, including slots. They were so popular they amortized themselves in under four weeks.

Another welcome newcomer who made his appearance in Monaco in the late sixties and seventies was the conventioneer. And actually, as Rainier reminded his advisers, he wasn't altogether new. Dating back to Albert I, Monaco had been the site of tony conferences and gatherings of scientists, jurists, and scholars. Rainier hoped to replace these with classy conventions in the American sense, and he had his 160 consulates around the world open a skillful canvass of the "right" business firms and professional organizations. To prove its seriousness, Monaco built the finest conference facilities on the Riviera. The result was rewarding; by the end of the decade, the "Palais des Congrès" was booked months in advance.

These new facilities, attractions, and policies—disseminated to all the right markets by experts—coincided with international inflation in the early seventies to remake the face of Monégasque tourism. Honorable members of the upper-middle and even middle-middle class, individually or in professional groups, who would previously have never given a thought to taking a hotel room in the posh Principality, now "rewarded themselves with Monaco," as an advertising slogan put it. What the hoteliers called "overnight tourism" shot up 75 percent in seven years. Day tourism rose 200 percent in the seventies. Cousteau's Oceanographic Museum, for example, drew an estimated hundreds of thousands of visitors a year, paying not only for the director's "outrageous salary" and the "exorbitant costs" of renovation, but also decisively proving wrong those National Councillors who had objected.

The most hidebound, timorous traditionalist could not even argue that the Principality had lost its mainstay: the "Old Guard" of international society, whose "decline and disappearance" had been mispredicted for decades. True, the croupiers were now generally the only people wearing black ties on Monte Carlo. But the class that, in former times had "dressed for dinner," *still* came for dinner—in leisure suits. Niarchos had never left, while Onassis and his new wife (Jacqueline Kennedy) returned occasionally, and Ari resumed his friendly personal ties with Grace and Rainier. ("It was a business disagreement," the Prince told the press—which was quite true.) Gianni Agnelli also turned up, and instantly became legendary and beloved for distributing chips to losers around his table so they would stay and keep him company. Further company was provided by the Burtons and a large Hollywood contingent, the Duke of Westminster, and, after 1974, a growing number of Arab sheiks whose sumptuous habits, especially gambling, stupefied everyone.

The new face of Monte Carlo was only the beginning of the change. What Rainier called "ocean-stealing" opened up landfills in Fontvieille, Monte Carlo, and the Larvotto nearly a whole square mile of new Monaco. On it stood buildings that gave the skyline the appearance of Miami Beach. Tens of condominium high rises were either completed, underway, or in blueprint, with apartments going for $500,000 a throw. Traditionalists saw it as a vulgar "concrete slum" for *arrivistes,* but the Prince and his advisers had their eye on the added revenues in turnover taxes. They were also well pleased by the success of their "industrial plan" which brought to Monaco (mostly in Fontvieille) manufacturing corporations in cosmetics, printing, clothing, ceramics, precision engineering, plastics, machine tools and brewing. There also arrived approximately seven hundred other "companies"—corporations in name only, without facilities or personnel, occupying a rented apartment or office, only too happy to pay a local registration tax and other minor fees in order to escape taxation or scrutiny in their home countries.

The benefits that the Principality reaped from these several developments were numerous and generally popular. To start at the top, the state budget for 1973 (a typical year) was not only balanced but five million dollars in surplus of income over expenditures. Unemployment was nonexistent; the average per capita income in Monaco was enough to provide automobiles for one of every two adults, the highest ratio in the world. Residents of the Principality also enjoyed one of the finest state-subsidized health care services in Europe, excellent schools, and high social security benefits and pensions. No less an avowed critic of the Prince's policies than Charles Soccal, the only member of the French Communist Party to sit on the Monégasque National Council, conceded to *Le Monde* that Monaco's largest employer, the S.B.M., was good to its workers. Beyond this, Monaco was virtually crime-free; there was not even a noticeable drug problem among the young. The various security forces in the Principality were efficient and omnipresent; it was literally true that a woman wearing as much jewelry as an empress could walk alone through the streets at midnight and have nothing to fear.

Finally, the major advantage of the new status quo was that it realized the dream of the last three princes: despite prodigal S.B.M. good fortune, as well as the fact that several new casinos were open and flourishing in Monaco, gaming now accounted for only 2.5 percent of the Principality's total revenues. Gaming receipts alone for 1974–75 hit thirty-two million dollars—roughly the equal of the combined revenues of all French Riviera casinos—but still less than half the amount raised by the sale of postage stamps, and a mere fraction of the various sales and customs taxes. (Nevertheless, the S.B.M.'s taxes were still enough to cover the $1.8 million that the state treasury paid out for the upkeep of the Palace and its staff of nearly two hundred, as well as the Prince and Princess's civil list, now up to $600,000 per year.

In short, the "new" Monaco was a veritable tableau.

Or was it a *trompe l'oeil?* The sight behind the stage of Monaco's tourist display was less gratifying. As a critic noted in *Le Nouvel Observateur*, "The Principality is bulging at the seams, so they've pushed into France everything that isn't profitable or attractive—warehouses, cemeteries, utilities . . . and the old people's rest home." Of far greater concern, but lessened visibility, was the truth behind the boom. Who *were* all these "corporations" that registered in Monaco, subletting apartments as "headquarters," but never showing up, let alone doing business or constructing plants? Who owned many of these high rises? Companies, it was alleged, that no one ever heard of, holding

Grace and her daughters in the late sixties.
Credit: Sygma Photos.

The Grimaldis in 1973. Credit: Sygma Photos.

Rainier, Albert, and Grace performing one of Grace's favorite duties as Princess: handing out presents at the annual children's Christmas party, 1973. Credit: Georges Lukomski.

The Grimaldis on a skiing holiday in Switzerland, 1976.
Credit: Sygma Photos.

Albert, formally garbed as Prince Hereditary;
Rainier in the personal uniform he designed for himself;
Grace wearing the Order of St. Charles, 1976.
Credit: Sygma Photos.

*The Grimaldis, their daughter Caroline, and new son-in-law,
Philippe Junot, 1978. Credit: Sygma Photos.*

Grace making a bob to the Queen Mother at St. James's Palace, 1978. The other poetry reader is Richard Pasco of the Royal Shakespeare Company. Credit: Geoffrey Shakerley

Mother and son in Provence shortly before Grace's death;
Albert had graduated from Amberst College the previous year. 1982
Credit: Sygma Photos.

Husband and wife, 1982. Credit: Sygma Photos.

*The family exiting from the Cathedral of St. Nicholas after the
memorial mass, one year later, September 14, 1983.
The former Bishop of Monaco (Barthe) who married Grace
and Rainier is at left. His successor,
Archbishop Brand, is at right. Credit: Skyline Features.*

property on behalf of people only *too* well known but eager to escape detection.

And as for the businesses and businessmen who publicly alighted in Monaco, some of them brought only infamy, not prestige, to the realm. Rainier was always saying that the industry he wanted for Monaco had to be "the right sort"—small scale, nonpolluting, beneficial to society, and honestly run. In view of some of what actually arrived, Rainier's words were charitably called "normative" by some observers, and a "travesty" by others. Maugham had once called the Principality "a sunny place for shady people" but Monaco in the late sixties and early seventies threatened to become a permanent address for shifty corporations. Entrepreneurs like the Arab Adnan Khashoggi and the American expatriate, Sam Cummings, who made millions of dollars in the armaments trade gave Monaco such a reputation that when Rainier once asked a visitor what he would think if his company received a proposition from a corporation based in the Principality, he replied, "I'd think twice."

There were other problems. Some of the new industry in Fontvieille, for example, caused serious pollution. Moreover, the right to strike was severely limited in Monaco; the state was a generous but stern father where labor was concerned. Workers obeyed the law and did as they were told, or they got out, but they did not strike or agitate. Management unquestionably had the advantage in disputes. Then, too, the price paid for a crime-free Monaco was, in the opinions of some, a police state. With three hundred uniformed officers and plainclothesmen "securing" thirty thousand residents, Monaco undoubtedly had one of the highest constabulary-to-population ratios in the world.

The police and the judiciary, moreover, were as tough as anywhere in Europe—and far better paid, quartered, and respected. A visiting college professor was hauled into a local precinct on a minor traffic violation. He lost his temper and shook a fist at a portrait of the Prince, for which action he drew a stiff fine and a twelve-month suspended sentence. The police also practiced "preventive" or preemptive procedures; ill-dressed or disheveled or suspicious-looking people were detained, then hustled out of Monaco. (And if they were formally banned from the Principality, the ban applied to the entire French Riviera.) No hitchhikers or migrant workers, let alone hippies, were to be seen on the Principality's antiseptically clean streets after dark. The New York *Times*'s John Vinocur described hypersensitive Monégasque security as "Mississippi-in-the-mid-50's mentality," adding, "The theory behind all this is to eliminate the appearance of anything, down to a kid with a backpack, that would get the rich consulting their Nice Airport schedules."

In short, the "under" side of Monaco was high-rise eyesores, noisy and car-clogged streets, gas fumes and pollution, overcrowding, a dearth of parks or libraries and bookstores, and a quiescent, socially homogeneous, wealthy population. For a minority of detractors, the Principality was redolent of covert oppression and decay; its "traditions" and "history" were simply the window dressing of chicanery and corruption; its cultural and social calendar, an imitation of art, the forced gaiety of uneasy people with something to fear and something to hide. Monaco's reality was its economy and its police force. A Mediterranean Hong Kong.

§   §   §

Q. *Why did Princess Grace participate in a modernization policy she didn't always agree with?*
A. *Faithfulness to me, devotion. She was fulfilling that part of the [marriage] contract without perhaps liking it so much.*

*—Prince Rainier**

Some of the European press actually blamed Grace for the "Americanization" of Monaco, simply because she *was* American and because Rainier so readily acknowledged that he discussed "everything with her." What the Prince neglected to add, however, except occasionally and with heavy euphemism was that in the area of modernization, "we disagree very frequently." "Some nostalgics, including myself," wrote Stanley Jackson, "may have regretted that too much pink stucco has been replaced by concrete."† Unquestionably, the "nostalgics" included the Princess Consort, although "from the closet." There was an extraordinary irony in Grace and Rainier's personal developments; at about the time that he was calling himself a "corporate chief executive responsible to both shareholders and workers," his wife was accepting what it was to act and appear like a princess.

It had not always been thus. For a number of years, she strove hard to be "one of the folks" even in Monaco. She too readily befriended people or confided in them, not understanding that they didn't see her as she saw herself. For example, despite Rainier's repeated warnings that it wouldn't work, Grace initiated a policy of inviting Monégasques to dine informally "en famille" at the Palace. The meals were painful for her and for them; the silence and embarrassment and forced civility would have been a topic for mirth, if Grace hadn't been so earnest. She had learned the hard way that her subjects were not going to stop regarding her as profoundly different from them, nor stop expecting her to act like a Princess, just because doing so clashed

* Interview with author, September 12, 1983.
† *Inside Monte Carlo*, (New York: Stein & Day, 1976), p. 259.

with her American sensibility and personal modesty. And further-more, they didn't especially *enjoy* dining intimately with princes be-cause "ici, ça ne se fait pas" ["here, it isn't done"].

Grace learned and adapted. She'd always had a convert's devotion to the Principality and zeal for its history, but after Stephanie's birth, her family and friends, and even the odd journalist, noticed that what had formerly been a toleration for protocol and ceremony now—in the light of experience and reflection—became a genuine interest. Rainier, for his part, was willing to loosen up on the pomp and flummery of the court. He did so, but his reforms were followed with no great sigh of relief from Her Highness. Now, when he was "too tired" to go to a gala or wanted to finesse an appearance, it was Grace who "doesn't bully me into anything, *but is able to make me understand why it's neces-sary.*" (Emphasis added.) David Halberstam described Grace in the New York *Times*, as "perhaps even more serious than he."

Armed with this hard-won sense of time and place, Grace became a purist. Her central belief was that finally Monaco's greatest asset—and more, its raison d'être—was its traditions and history. All that contrib-uted to maintaining and magnifying them, even if just to support them financially, was good; anything that sullied or detracted from them, bad. She always understood the rationale behind Rainier's Grand De-sign, and she certainly shared his hope for the Principality, but she was on guard. Tourism, for example, was necessary, she agreed, (a great ballet company cost money), but tourism—especially the "wrong sort" —could also become a threat. As early as 1966, Grace went on record opining that Monaco must "never become another St.-Tropez . . . Monte Carlo must remain elegant and old-fashioned."

In short, it became a question of balance, a battle of "trade-offs." How far did one proceed with means before they began to diminish ends? Rainier did not theoretically disagree with any of Grace's beliefs, but his immersion in the vast undertaking of his Grand Design weak-ened his grip on final goals. Frankly, his policies led to excesses and unintended consequences that upset him and totally disgusted Grace. Fortunately for Rainier and for Monaco, however, nothing diminished Grace's devotion to Monaco or even to her "idea" of Monaco. But it did entail for her the frustrating, enervating experience of fighting an extended rearguard action, winning a bit of ground here and there, yet finally conceding, yielding, retreating. It was a two-decade unequal tug-of-war between the Prince (with his advisers) and solitary Grace— he, pulling in the direction of development; she, reacting ever more heavily toward preservation. Because of their love, their mutual re-spect, and, at base, their agreement on ends, this was a regenerate tension, but tension it was, nonetheless.

The "traditions" of Monaco very much included, in Grace's way of thinking, the realm's appearance. Since prohibiting the high rises was out of the question, Grace fought to keep them restricted to certain regions in order to maintain the historical purity of others. In this, Rainier was mostly on her side. The Rock wouldn't be touched, nor would sections of the Condamine, while most (but, sadly, not all) of the best examples of *belle époque* architecture in Monte Carlo would remain. Grace had threatened to "nail myself to the door [of the grand old Hermitage Hotel] if they tried to raze it," as some of Rainier's advisers wished to do. These concessions won, Grace threw her troops into the battle to protect "her" buildings. To the great annoyance of directors, managers, accountants, and even decorators, she insisted time and again that they be maintained and restored exactly to her finical standards. She successfully fought against the overuse of the color gray (in new buildings as well as the restored ones). On the other hand, she lost the fight to exclude billboards from Monaco. But when she lost, her adversaries heard about it—sometimes even in public statements from the Palace. As early as October 1965, Grace began speaking forthrightly of the problems she was having with the modernizers. She told reporters that she "deeply regretted" they hadn't followed all of her advice in the matter of preparing for the upcoming centenary of Monte Carlo. She went as far as to offer a "personal opinion" that some of the newer buildings in Monte Carlo clashed with the "spirit" of the place. Typically, however, having registered her complaint, she did not press it, but proceeded briskly to discuss her plans for the centenary.

By the seventies, Grace was concerned about considerably more than high rises. Tourism, perhaps because she didn't like nosy crowds, always found in her a very timid friend. She understood, she told Rainier, the need to open the sluice gates wider, but her "understanding" never resulted in Grace's relaxing for a moment her vigilant guard over the "sort of people" who visited the Principality. The newly opened Monaco Tourist Office in New York, whose job was to throw the net far and wide, stopped looking to Grace for help, for they knew it would rarely be forthcoming. Caroline Cushing, the capable director of tourism who advanced the Prince's plans in the United States in these years, said, "Prince Rainier was very interested in attracting American businessmen to Monaco, especially conventions—for example, the Young Presidents Organization [consisting of chief executives under forty]. He was available when we needed him for speeches and appearances. But Grace would come only if it were absolutely necessary. On the whole she would turn down my requests."‡

A number of the people closely associated with the "new" Monégasque tourism privately saw Grace as a snob who couldn't be both-

‡ Interview with author, April 12, 1983.

ered with "mere businessmen." In this, they were wrong. Grace was no snob, though it was perhaps easy to mistake her for one, especially when she was beset by the breathless hard-sellers now working for the S.B.M., Loews, and Holiday Inn-Monaco. Grace simply would not construe even touristic Monaco as just a beach, a casino, some restaurants, discos, and a few hotels. If tourists wanted that, they could go to a dozen other places—Deauville, for example, or Cannes. But if they came to Monaco, it was for something more—the special events like the Grand Prix and the circus, of course, for the museums, the Exotic Garden, and the changing of the guard at the Palace, or for the array of fine arts performances (Grace even pitched in and transformed the International Festival of the Ballet into a broader, fuller Festival of the Fine Arts that took in all the arts and went year-round). Tourists came for all that, but there was still something more, to Grace's way of thinking. They came finally for the tone, the authenticity, the distinctiveness that only eight centuries of discrete history could produce. *That* was what risked being breached and traduced by an inundation of insensitive outsiders.

Accordingly, Grace worried as she watched her beloved Monaco win itself a new and worsened reputation for financial corruption and skullduggery. The Casino was one thing; all the princes since Charles and Caroline had got used to rationalizing that (though it no more needed apologizing for than a liquor license). But the allegations now being bandied about in the press and in the cafés about corruption in Monaco, with its dozens of "nominal" corporations like floating crap games, *this* was new, even if the allegations went largely unproved. As for the presence of people like Cummings and Khashoggi—not here on vacation or in retirement, but actually conducting (in the former case) the business of arms trafficking in offices on the Boulevard des Moulins —*that*, Grace could hardly abide. But she could do nothing about it in the short run. She begged the Prince to apply the brakes, to apply more stringent criteria in granting licenses to companies to do business in Monaco. Sometimes he would reply that the smoke in the press was far greater than any fire in the Principality, and that no investigative reporter had ever adduced much more than speculation and accusations. But for Grace this kind of negative publicity was nearly as damaging to her idea of Monaco as the facts themselves, and finally Rainier had to agree with her. Gradually, some of the excesses of the early years of the Grand Design—from literal pollution to the more figurative kinds —were isolated and partially eradicated.

These were of course strictly private discussions between husband and wife. Publicly, Grace either ignored certain things that were taking place in Monaco, or she would try to explain and defend them. Occasionally her arguments were well taken. Defending businesses that relocated to the Principality to escape high taxation, she told a New York *Times* reporter in 1978, "You can't get around the fact that the world is full of tax laws that discourage energy and all kinds of creative activity." Other times her words missed the point, perhaps intentionally. The *Le Monde* correspondent in Monaco asked Grace to comment on much-publicized strikes by croupiers and toilet room attendants in Monte Carlo, and she replied evasively that in her experience there were good dealers and johns-keepers, and bad dealers and johns-keepers. Still other times—perhaps when she felt the face-saving effort was just too great—Grace came right out and conceded (as she did to John Vinocur in the late seventies) that "Yes, we have a number of parasites, [corporate] rats who've come out of their sinking ships. It's not my family's way, but you must realize that these people are in New York and Paris, too."

$ §   §$

Reality does not penetrate the universe where live our beliefs; as reality did not give birth to beliefs, so it will not destroy them.
                                              —*Proust*, Swann's Way

Replies, retorts, and concessions accomplished little enough, however, because finally most of what the Grimaldis and the Monégasque government were responding to was a deep-seated attitude of hostility far more than a bill of particulars. The patent animus that Monaco, and Monaco alone, could sometimes arouse suffused the writing of even the best foreign correspondents. John Vinocur—a journalist fully aware of the line between opinion and news—wrote a long piece on the Principality in the New York *Times Magazine* (June 18, 1978) which is an instructive example of what the Grimaldis had to face. He described the Casino as "a room so ornate, so gilded and eleganted-up that it could have been an imitation of itself as played back through the prism of the M-G-M people who designed Princess Grace's wedding dress 22 years ago." Why so angry (and "ornate") a conceit over a rather splendid example of Second Empire architecture, designed by the architect of the Paris Opera?

The author quickly supplied an answer. Monaco, Vinocur said, "is a zone of advanced decay," "a remarkable capitalist pustule," a "world center of what de Maupassant described then as abjection, arrogance, pretension, covetousness and greed . . ." Then, by unmistakable implication, Vinocur scored the signatories of the 1975 Helsinki Agreements for permitting Rainier to add his signature. He cursorily reviewed the Prince's career. Rainier, he said, had manipulated Onassis into "refloat[ing] the country's economy, and then successfully conspired to ease him out of the way . . ." He married Grace to gain

"Hollywood respectability" to increase tourism, and to "create a de facto alliance with the United States." He "surrender[ed] to Charles de Gaulle." Grace and Rainier "take themselves quite seriously" and both "seem to share with some intensity a dislike for anything that brings ridicule to Monaco." For her part, Grace had "an American impatience with nuance and subterfuge which passes in Monaco as extreme honesty." She was "also terribly literal and does not like to be made fun of." Vinocur wrote of Monaco's "play[ing] at sovereignty" and he described a statement averring that the percentage that gaming profits contributed to Monaco's revenues was 3 percent as "the princely party line." He derided a local television show, initiated by the Prince and Princess, that displayed lost dogs so that they might be recognized and reclaimed. He criticized parts of Monaco for new buildings that "crush[ed] the scale of things, block[ed] the sun," and made parts of the Principality look like "Lefrak City," in Queens. Finally, he asserted that Monaco's security forces had made the Principality into "a live-in safe-deposit vault/bomb shelter."

But where was truth amid all this rhetoric? One may not share Vinocur's dislike of neobaroque architecture and still agree with him that the Prince's Grand Design had ruined the appearance of Monaco. Granting a certain license for metaphor, one may also agree that the Principality's police forces were rather pituitary. But for the rest, the reasonable reader would require more proof to justify nouns like "abjection, arrogance, covetousness," etc. He would need to have it explained why the signatories at Helsinki were wrong to include Rainier in their number, especially given the credentials of the rest. He would very definitely need to know why Grace and the Prince were wrong "to take themselves quite seriously," or what was exceptionable in the "intensity" of their dislike of ridicule of Monaco, or in Grace's impatience with subterfuge, or her wish not to be made fun of. In sum, the reader would need to know *why* the Prince and Princess of Monaco should regard themselves, or the world should regard them, with John Vinocur's loathing? The sarcasm and rhetoric present here point to profound, thoroughgoing corruption and evil, yet if the yoke of accusation is easy, the burden of proof is not light. The author's recap of Rainier's career amounts to an almost Orwellian reversal of the truth ("Hollywood respectability"; "surrender" to de Gaulle; "manipulation" of Onassis).

Vinocur was by no means alone in his fury. One of the finest journalists in Europe, Pierre Viansson-Ponté—a man who, had he lived, would have almost certainly been named editor-publisher of *Le Monde* —penned a less sardonic, but intensely earnest, moral condemnation of Monaco, attacking the presence of "the new Croesuses" (by which he intended mainly Arab sheiks like Khashoggi) and their conspicuous spending, playing, and losing while people starved in the Third World.* Why did the French editor stop with Monaco, however? What about Cannes or Deauville, Atlantic City or Brighton, Las Vegas, Palm Beach, Newport, or Beverly Hills; what about any other place on the globe where the "haves" disported themselves—and did so with *far* less conscience, charity, and culture than the Principality of Monaco? Or if questionable entrepreneurial and corporate ethics were the issue, then how did Monaco differ morally from any one of the major economic centers of the Western World, or from Liechtenstein, where dozens of international corporations had found a home? How about the assets hidden in numbered accounts in Swiss banks, or the corporations headquartered in Panama and Liberia? The French arms trade was one of the most active; as was the United States and the Soviet—all far greater than Sam Cummings's business. If a low standard of political ethics excited Viansson and Vinocur, then the scandals rocking the Paris of Giscard and the Washington of Nixon merited the kinds and degrees of disapprobation reserved for Monaco. *Why Monaco?*

Unless it can be answered with massive and systematic evidence (altogether missing in these, or any such similar, articles), the inquirer is left with an attitude, a loathing which must itself be explained. What about Monaco caused this kind of venting? The talented writer, Anthony Burgess, who settled down in the Principality in the late seventies, told a journalist "Monaco suggests an immorality to the puritanical north which is not there." He went on to argue that the scrupulosity of a Vinocur or Viansson concealed resentment and envy. The beauty, leisure, wealth, and sheer success of Rainier's realm "get under the skin of some people" who, rather than analyze their own overreactive spleens, "have to believe something is deeply wrong and decadent here." In short, it was the old point that kept resurfacing in Monégasque history. What set the Principality apart from the world was not some strange and extraordinary moral failure, but Monaco's all-round success at being what it had been for a century: *different*— small, rich, beautiful, mild, cultured, independent.

"It *is* a midget country," wrote Rainier's biographer, Peter Hawkins, "and some misguided people will always find humor in midgets."† That was one way to look at it. Another was to take a more impersonal view and see the Principality as standing rudely in the path of the homogenizing drive of large nations. Monaco was hateful because it went its own way; for example, it had low taxes. But it had low taxes because it could afford to. Rainier capitalized on the diminutive size of his realm in the same way and for the same goals, as other rulers

---

* "Une été fou," *Le Monde*, August 29–30, 1976.
† *Prince Rainier of Monaco*, p. 195.

capitalized on their might and measure. Was he wrong to do so? Monaco had every right (and indeed was well advised) to expand its economic activity beyond the S.B.M. and elite tourism. It went too far and paid a certain price in pollution and unsightliness; it had an overvigorous security force; corruption and skullduggery were alleged (if not demonstrated); and some of its new citizens didn't have pew-sores on their knees. But how did any of this justify the kind and degree of moralistic abuse heaped on the realm and its rulers?

There was, finally, another reason for Monaco's being singled out while all around her conducted their perfidies and affairs with prosaic invisibility: Grace. More than Rainier, she attracted caricature, misunderstanding, and saber-toothed spite. For some, the Princess was too good to be true, therefore she was phony. This required real effort at misconstrual, however. John Vinocur reported with a poker-faced seriousness the following conversation between Grace and her elder daughter:

> "*[Caroline's] tone is assertive and usually fits in with the reports about the 'strong-willed princess' who has always got her way.*
> '*Am I strong-willed?' she asks her mother.*
> '*No, no, not at all, darling,' Princess Grace says.*
> '*I never get my way, do I?'*
> '*No, never, never,' her mother says, beaming with good nature.*"

The thought initially occurs that Vinocur wrote this *cum grano salis*. He was there in the room, after all; he *had* to have been aware of the intended facetiousness of the exchange. But he did not write it that way, nor does it read that way. On the contrary, in the context of the rest of an article where (besides the things said about Rainier) Caroline is described as "bored," "tough," "assertive," "not tolerant," and "not beautiful," and Grace is called "a phone-in princess" and relentlessly made to appear insouciant and arrogant à la Marie Antoinette, the report of the mother-daughter conversation is damning. It makes Caroline look spoiled and manipulative, Grace seem naive and indulgent, and their relationship appear shallow.

Other treatments did not help either. A group biography of *Those Philadelphia Kellys* appeared in 1977. Though author Arthur Lewis offered a probing and pungent portrait of many of the family, his picture of Grace was skimpy and highly tendentious. Lewis did not meet with Grace (and made no attempt to do so), so he depicted her largely with materials gathered in an interview with Ms. Leslie Bennetts, "a sharp-tongued blond reporter"‡ for the Philadelphia *Bulletin*. Bennetts ap-

‡ Ibid., p. 278. Subsequent quotes from pp. 279–82. (Ms. Bennetts is now with the New York *Times*.)

prised Lewis at length of observations gathered on Grace in an interview she gave her in Monaco:

> *"It's so funny,"* Leslie told me, *"you come up to this Palace and you see what looks like some little pink thing on top of a cake. And those soldiers outside in their funny, funny uniforms! They take themselves so seriously. There's a changing of the guards and they're all carrying bayonets. They also take their security very seriously . . .*
>
> *"[Grace] is quite beautiful although not breathtaking. Not the way she was when she was twenty-five, when she really was exquisite. Now she has age spots on her hands but she* is *a beautiful woman . . .*
>
> *"As to her personality, she had less warmth and less spontaneity than anyone I ever talked to . . . she is an awful stick. With Kell [whom Bennetts also interviewed] I always had the feeling—it's really funny—that he really knows only a certain number of things to say. Grace is exactly the same way, although I think she's brighter than he is . . . No matter how unusual a question, she reverts to something familiar and noncontroversial, something that doesn't require thought . . . She appears to have no political opinions whatsoever . . . She's strictly for garden parties and charity balls. Her life revolves around the rituals of her position . . . She has this stilted, vaguely bastardized French. It's the damndest thing you ever heard, in this incredibly affected voice . . . Grace was very cordial but in a completely surface way. I think she's a woman of very rigid opinions, one who doesn't question a lot of things. It's beyond me how someone can grow up in America and feel comfortable having other people bow and curtsy and scrape to you and call you, 'Your Highness.' But this doesn't faze Grace in the least. She won't confess 'getting off on it.' I don't know if she does or doesn't enjoy that kind of thing. But it would make most Americans profoundly uncomfortable, the undemocratic set of rituals they go through over there. It's a preposterous little postage-stamp kingdom. But she loves it; I think she loves all the trappings of royalty. And I don't think she thinks about the political, social, and moral implications of anything. She didn't talk about her mother or Kell or anything except in the most bland, innocuous, and totally uninteresting way. It was really a very boring interview."*

What had happened here? Given Grace's experience with the press, her knowledge (thanks to Lacoste) of Leslie Bennetts's reputation for biographical vivisection (including a brutal profile of Kell), and especially given Bennetts's manner—alternately aggressive, confidential, and guilefully informal—Grace hid behind her mask. Lacoste thought she'd have done better to decline the interview, but Grace felt an obligation to Philadelphia callers (especially from the *Bulletin,* whose usual coverage of Grace sinned in the opposite direction—syrupy). Short of pretending to be the kind of person and princess that Bennetts manifestly wanted her to be, Grace could not have hoped for more than this wanton burlesque. It upset her even more that a book author like Arthur Lewis would include such testimony uncritically, and without verifying it himself, in his biography.

Meanwhile a large branch of the press continued to deal in its own speculations and willful misrepresentations. A hue and cry was raised in several British papers when Grace wore a white gown to Princess Anne's wedding. She was trying to "upstage" the bride, columnists said, blissfully unmindful of the dozens of other women guests who wore white and off-white. (Grace's dress was in fact cream-colored. She had intended to wear a blue gown but hadn't a hat to go with it and couldn't buy one in time.) Grace was angered by these reports in a way that Bennetts or Vinocur's words couldn't get to her, because in this instance someone else's feelings, Princess Anne's, were involved. Despite the many compliments Grace received at Westminster Abbey, including from the royal family, she worried that the Princess would take umbrage at her on reading the accusations in the press. So she wrote a letter of explanation to the newspapers. Anne was not angry, and indeed the Grimaldis' very friendly relations with the Windsors continued unaffected. Grace's greatest fan was Lord Mountbatten of Burma, uncle of the Duke of Edinburgh. When asked by a reporter whom his grandnephew, Prince Charles, might marry, the Earl of Burma replied that it was too bad that Grace of Monaco was not available for she was induplicable. His quotation was printed, albeit not with direct attribution.

There was little that Grace and Rainier could do to alter or stem jaundiced reportage. She remonstrated with letters when something outraged her unusually; and he, from time to time, expressed his anger with lawsuits and bannings, but these measures hardly dented the trend. Lacoste and her staff (up to three full-time press officers) did their best to protect their employers, but their means were limited. Nadia could disseminate facts, not alter prejudice or ferret out animus. To erect too much of a rampart around the princely couple was to court other risks—being called inaccessible, or accused of playing favorites, which the Grimaldis sometimes did with certain photographers and writers. In other words, the disquieting problem of the court writer remained at the forefront. The result was paradoxical: hostile intelligence sometimes served truth better than uncritical mediocrity. Dorothy Kilgallen's coverage of the 1956 wedding, as snide as it occasionally was, came closer overall to catching the Grimaldis' own experience than the smarmy, misleading book that a writer-friend of Grace's rushed into print practically before the bride and groom returned from their honeymoon. Gant Gaither's *Princess Grace of Monaco: The Story of Grace Kelly* had not pleased Grace with its society column prose and depth, and its author's infatuation with celebrities and flaunting of ties with them. The book indeed drove a stake between Gaither and Grace that required a number of years to be removed.

The experience of being pilloried and pejoratively caricatured by many writers weighed so heavily on Grace and Rainier, however, that they gradually came to feel warmer toward court writers. In the mid-seventies, Nadia Lacoste brought word that an English writer, Gwen Robyns, was intending to furnish the world its first complete biography of the Princess. Robyns, who had already written nearly a complete manuscript, was complaining of the same problem of "stonewalling" that anyone who wrote about the Grimaldis encountered if they didn't present themselves and receive formal approval by the press office. None of Grace and Rainier's friends would consent to an interview.

Grace had felt a biography was very premature (she was only forty-five), and in any case, looked forward to writing her own book one day, but Lacoste urged her to receive the author. If Grace cooperated, Robyns had agreed to permit the Palace to preview her work and make requests for alterations. Lacoste, in brief, argued for co-optation. It was rare enough, she assured Grace, that the Palace got the chance for this degree of control. Grace met Robyns, liked her personally very much ("She's a cozy lady," she later told Phyllis Earl), and induced a few of her friends to receive the Englishwoman. The biographer, in her turn, vetted the manuscript, deleting anything remotely negative or that she feared would give offense. The result was a bland, chatty, unstructured and unrelievedly upbeat life story that left Grace intellectually and emotionally unmoved, but sighing with relief that nothing injurious was done to her family, Monaco, or herself.

Sadly, the same defensive reflex that now welcomed and sought out the court writer, journalist, and photographer on the Rock also led Grace and Rainier to see hostility where it didn't exist. Caroline Cushing, Monaco's tourist representative in New York, several times advised Grace to receive Charlotte Curtis, a society writer for the New York *Times*. Grace finally consented to Curtis's attending a poolside luncheon that the Grimaldis threw for some of the VIP's in Monaco for the forthcoming Red Cross Gala. In separate pieces* on the luncheon and the ball Curtis produced perfectly straightforward society reporting (who was there, how they were dressed, what was served), and indeed the article on the Gala amounted to an enthusiastic review. But the short piece on the luncheon was interlarded with trite, off-the-

---

* The New York *Times*, August 11 and 12, 1969.

cuff quotes of Grace. Of themselves, they neither condemned nor flattered her. The luncheon was a social event, not an interview, and Grace moved among many guests, but without that context being specified, she sounded marginally trivial or flighty ("I don't have to do anything if I don't want to, but I'm not that kind of girl . . ."; "Frank Sinatra said I was the squarest person he ever knew . . ."). Princess Caroline, finally, was depicted as the twelve-year-old tomboy she probably was that day.

Grace overreacted to this harmless piece and blamed Cushing for not vetting it—which, of course, Cushing could not have done with a *Times* reporter. Living in New York, and not being privy to the near-paranoia on the Rock and in Lacoste's press office, Cushing simply hadn't realized how gun-shy Grace was or that a "bunker psychology" prevailed in the Palace. To her mind, the luncheon piece was unexceptionable, while Curtis's article on the Ball had excellent PR value, for the *Times* often neglected Monégasque social events.

In sum, it was a measure of Grace's profound mistrust—occasioned by innumerable episodes of savage misrepresentation by some of the press—that an artist of her standards would have let herself sink into fretting over one, fairly neutral society column. Under siege, she became hypersensitive and withdrawn.

§   §   §

You could say she worked from the inside out. Once she had her immediate family around her, she could then move outside the palace into our larger 'family.'

—*Prince Rainier*

The process of Grace's becoming both Princess and Monégasque was continuous, but if a moment could be singled out to symbolize her full acceptance of Monaco and vice versa, it would perhaps be Rainier's Jubilee, the twenty-fifth anniversary of his accession to the throne. Certainly the Prince felt the 1974 celebration was as much for Grace as in honor of himself. The event itself very much bore the Princess's stamp. Having instituted the custom of Thanksgiving dinners in the hotels of the Principality, Grace thought a Texas-style barbecue would be in order for the entire citizenry of Monaco (4,529 people), assembled on the soccer field of the Louis II Stadium. Grace wore for the first time the "official national costume" (red and white striped skirt; white bodice; embroidered black silk apron; ornamental straw hat with flowers); Stephanie and Caroline came, more or less similarly garbed. The Jubilee was a great success—in Caroline's words, "one huge family party." Indeed, nothing better highlighted Monaco's status as an old Genoese clan more than a modern nation than these periodic assemblies of "the whole family." The political opposition linked arms with the Prince to celebrate "national harmony"; everyone gorged himself; the men (including Rainier) played pétanque while the women sang folk songs; and late in the afternoon, Grace and Rainier opened the open-air ball. For years after, Grace liked to quote the eighteenth-century Prince de Ligne who, when asked if he'd rather be Tsar of All the Russias or Prince of Monaco, said he'd prefer the latter job because "the Prince of Monaco knows all his subjects and calls them 'tu' whereas the Tsar knows none of his."

Nothing special to report, yet that was the whole point. Clans are, by definition, clannish—and none more so than the Monégasque. For over a decade and a half, Grace had had to wait to truly belong to this "family," but now she finally fit in; she was "home." She continued to visit and love the United States, of course, and she remained a source of "American ideas" in Monaco. She chaired the Monaco-U.S.A. Foundation, and she dreamed one day of opening an American branch of the Princess Grace Foundation. Yet by the midseventies (if not sooner), a subtle, all-important difference pervaded her activity in the Principality where she was no longer "la Princesse américaine," but simply "la Princesse." Only one final, highly symbolic act remained to be done. Very quietly, without fanfare or announcement, Grace gave up her American citizenship and became exclusively Monégasque. How could an adopted daughter of Saint Devota better demonstrate her total commitment to her people than by "burning her boat"?†

None of which was to say that Grace invariably got her way from her loving and beloved subjects. On the contrary, not long after the Jubilee, the National Council handed her one of her biggest disappointments of the decade: they refused to vote funds for the creation of the Ballet de Monte Carlo. Grace took the blow hard, deploring the Council's shortsighted miserliness to Rainier, her close friends, and anyone else who would listen. She had a point. Besobrasova was doing brilliantly. Her École de Danse Classique was now nearly on par with the Royal Ballet School in London or the school of the Paris Opera Ballet. Several of the École's dancers had won major competitions (including the most prestigious Prix de Lausanne). Marika herself had been several times invited to oversee productions at several of the lead-

† According to Christian legend, Devota—a young Corsican girl whose family had been killed in the Roman persecution of Christians—managed to elude her attackers. Together with a faithful servant, she set sail in a small boat and, guided by the Holy Spirit, arrived safely in what is now Monaco. There she burned her boat so she would not leave. On her feast day, part of the Monégasque ritual involves the burning of a small barque on the shore in front of Saint Devota's Chapel.

ing world ballets—notably *Paquita* for American Ballet Theatre in
1971.

If Grace couldn't yet found a company in Monaco, however, she
managed to find a home for the École. Perhaps the single most beautiful villa in Monaco was called the "Casa Mia"—a large, three-story
Florentine loggia of rose terra-cotta and stone, set into the west hillside
of Monte Carlo, overlooking the bay. Built in the thirties by Paris
Singer (of the American sewing machine family), the Casa came on the
market in the early seventies and was quietly purchased by the Prince.
He generously turned it over to the Princess Grace Foundation which
subsidized some renovations and redecoration at Grace's direction.
Then, in 1975, Rainier put it at the disposition of the ballet school, now
renamed Académie de Danse Classique Princesse Grace. Meanwhile,
Grace pulled herself out of her pique at the National Council and
returned to the ongoing battle to found a company. "Patience," she
reminded Besobrasova.

The work of princess continued to dominate more of Grace's time as
the demands of child-raising gradually diminished. The Monégasque
Red Cross under her leadership established itself as proportionally perhaps the most active and generous in the world. It expanded some of its
facilities beyond the limits of the Principality and, in collaboration
with the Rotary and Lions Clubs, set up homes for battered and abandoned children in Bouyon (France). The RC of Monaco also played
outstanding roles in supplying aid to disaster-stricken areas in Yugoslavia, Turkey, Peru, and Pakistan. Grace's most singular contribution,
however, was in making the Red Cross a living expression of more and
more Monégasques. Her appeals, and her example, rallied not only
wealthy residents, but also a great many middle-class residents of Monaco to give their time and money to the Red Cross. Also the young:
the junior branch of the RC, which Grace established, was remarkably
active and full. The Princess's direction of, and presence at, the Gala
had long since established it as a European, not merely Riviera, social
event. Indeed, already by the late sixties, Gala attendance hit its ceiling
with the number of people that could be accommodated (one thousand)
and was being oversubscribed.

Thanks also to Grace's eventual involvement, the Monaco Television
Festival gradually established itself as a more stylish, better-run affair
than the Cannes Film Festival, and with judges, guests and entries of
comparable quality. (One of the judges in 1977 was the distinguished
American TV director Martin Manulis, who had known Grace briefly
in her live television days. Yet she walked right over to him and said,
"Marty, there's something I've always wanted to ask you, why didn't

you hire me that time for the 'Philco Playhouse' script?" Came the reply: "Because you weren't right for the part, Grace."‡)

The Garden Club was certainly one of Grace's most brilliant blossoms in the seventies. After a slow beginning, it burst into life with Grace as its first president. The club's speakers were leading figures in floriculture and landscape gardening from all over the world; its members took annual trips to places as distant as Japan. No major, and few minor, public events took place in the Principality where the Garden Club didn't leave its flowery trace. The annual Flower Show drew entries from up and down the Riviera and beyond. At Grace's suggestion, it was organized around a central theme that changed each year ("Monte Carlo Flora," "Orchids Throughout the World," "World Rose Show"). Equally popular was the separate International Flower Arrangement Competition, which Grace also organized around varying themes—"Fire and Ice"; "A Fairy Tale"; Signs of the Zodiac; "Virtue or Vice," etc. The contests became so intense and serious that it was necessary to subdivide the competition into categories so that amateurs wouldn't have to take on florists.

Grace even accomplished the next-to-impossible: she got men to enter. Rainier, naturally, had been prevailed on to offer himself as a scapegoat to lead his confreres to new horizons. He entered under a sort of pseudonym—using one of his more obscure titles—and won a prize. After that, he entered regularly. So did a number of men. Grace herself, under the crush of other obligations, had reluctantly to pull back from active involvement in the club. She missed it greatly, she told one of its members, her friend and fellow American expatriate in Monaco, Jane D'Amico. D'Amico replied that it was a testimony to the club's tenacity that it now grew independently of its gardener.*

The Princess Grace Foundation's Boutique du Rocher did so well in attracting both contributors and customers that a second store to retail homemade arts and crafts was opened, this one in Monte Carlo. The P.G.F. became even more active in seeking out and helping individual cases of need that didn't qualify for aid from other sources—including, among many other examples, scholarships for poor students. The Foundation also did little works that Grace but no one else thought important enough to merit funding: e.g., a choir to sing in a small church or an old people's home at Christmas Eve; Christmas presents for the children of foreign laborers working in Monaco; and frequently flowers for this or that public building or church.

‡ Interview with author, November 3, 1983.
* Interview with author, September 13, 1983.

These are simply the peaks of a formidable range of activity that Grace undertook in the seventies. They look out over a vast correspondence that required two full-time secretaries; a packed calendar of appearances, speeches, inaugurations, launchings, and sundry ceremonies —such as setting the first brick of a retirement village for veteran French actors, co-hosting a posthumous tribute to Josephine Baker with Jacqueline Onassis, presiding with Lord Mountbatten at a fund-raiser for colleges in London. It also entailed constant travel on behalf of the twenty-seven organizations—as diverse as the Irish-American Cultural Institute and the Medical College of Pennsylvania (formerly Ma Kelly's beloved Women's Medical College)—over which Grace presided, or on whose boards she sat. Finally, there was a host of regular and special duties at home: hosting "American Week" at the S.B.M., decorating and furnishing (with George Stacey) the private apartments in the new wing of the Palace, and finally Grace's ever-favorite: the handing out of Christmas presents to the children of Monaco, a job she shared with her own family.

There was, however, one thing Grace of Monaco did *not* accomplish in these years, but which she came to love almost as much as ballet and theater. In 1975, Rainier created the International Circus Festival, which took place every December. Grace never missed a show.

§   §   §

PENNY: *Now, Mother, you* must *admit that Vernon is a bit naive when he starts talking about life and marriage.*
MRS. ESPINSHADE: *I'll admit nothing of the kind. I think he simply has a bit of* heart *left in him, that's all; and a few ideas about faithfulness and moral obligation—and a few other things that probably do make a person seem a bit incredible these days.*

—*George Kelly,* The Fatal Weakness

Newsweek once noted airily that "Princess Grace, now 44, is into enough causes to make the Sugarplum Fairy look cynical." Cute line, but inapt. Grace's stands—her "crusades," as Rainier called them— were far too unpopular to suit the Sugarplum, or any other, Fairy. There were many, especially in feminist circles, who might have associated Grace's opinions with the Wicked Witch of the West. As time wore on, and pressures grew upon her and her family, Grace retrenched—literally, behind Lacoste and figuratively, behind her philosophy of life.

Grace's thinking was provoked by the subject of breast feeding. In 1971, she received an invitation to deliver the keynote address at a convocation of an international organization called La Leche League (literally: "The Milk League," in Spanish), of which Grace was an honorary member—indeed *the* honorary member. Originally of American origin, despite the Spanish name, the La Leche League propagandized on behalf of breast feeding and was, by the early seventies, so widespread as to defy national labeling. At the time of Caroline's birth, Grace had already offered the simplest, most straightforward defense of breast feeding—its psychological and physical benefits to the infant —in response to the muted explosion of surprise that greeted her act of feeding "naturally" her newborn daughter. Now she expanded on it.

"I will not be the first," Grace told an audience made up mainly of young mothers with infant children and a smattering of young fathers, "to compare life to a never-ending relay race, a handing on by us of the torch of life out of the past to be carried into the future by our children . . . The act of breast feeding, the giving of food and security from within our own persons, is an integral and vital moment in the passing on of that torch." The family unit was the only vehicle in which the "torch" could be carried, Grace said, and breast feeding was a splendid way of shoring up family unity at a time when it was under attack. In her view, no single force threatened the family more than cries for individual liberation which led to acts that only shredded families without assuring personal liberation. Breast feeding was not simply a metaphor but itself a didactic weapon in the eternal fight to preserve the family: "And one of the foundations of togetherness is the manifestation of nature itself and the way in which its miracles are performed. When other and older children in the family can be witness, unashamed and unembarrassed, to one of the greatest of these miracles, the feeding of a sister or brother from the person of its mother, they will have come a long way in winning protection from the miserable so-called 'freedoms' which, in our times, are being imposed upon the young."

Besides sustaining the family unit there was another reason that justified breast feeding, Grace averred. "A Jesuit priest, Father Lyons, once made a remark I haven't forgotten. He said, 'We have been deluded into thinking that knowledge is a substitute for discipline.' No age has ever tried to avoid discipline as much as ours. For his use of the word 'knowledge,' think of any alternate you will. Call it science, pediatrics, formulas, fads, theories, not to mention lame excuses based upon complaisant medicine, which will often condone sheer laziness and unwillingness to give . . . Breast feeding calls for discipline on the part of the mother. Sometimes, at the beginning, it can be both painful and discouraging. There is help of many kinds for these, but the greatest of all in overcoming them is the determination of self-control sparked by concern and responsibility for the child." The effort was worth the risk, Grace said, for it paid off in benefits to the mother as well as the child. In her view, it promoted a general familial "well-being that comes from the natural act of unselfishness."

Nevertheless, no mistake should be made about the order of priorities and benefits: "The breast-feeding mother is living for the happiness of another besides herself." This was never harder to do than currently, Grace said, for she was aware that "the frantic life of today has swept up women to the point where [for any number of factors] they feel that there is no time for this vital, natural function." Working women, in particular, experience "difficulties which cannot be ignored. But they can be overcome, and speaking for myself, I think I have been reasonably successful in doing so . . . At the beginning [of my children's lives] there were no compromises; state had to wait upon mother. And if, in my free time, I had to work a little harder to make up, that work became a pleasure for the sake of the newborn." The commonly heard phrase "doing their own thing," Grace said, raised only impatience in her because "that thing involves the kind of self-indulgence that turns [women] from what is right and natural . . ." When the contemporary woman says she cannot "relate to" breast feeding, she is couching the avoidance of her responsibility in trends and euphemisms. "What better 'thing' of one's own can one do than share in the creation of new life, thereafter integrating it into a loving and wholesome family?"

In August 1976, Grace and Rainier made a dual appearance in the Family Life Conference of the International Eucharistic Congress, held in Philadelphia. The theme—is there hope for the Christian family?—was abstract and ideological, providing Grace no anchor or referent in her experience, but she struggled to clarify and hone her thinking. A common ground of faith and morals was of course vital to raising children, she noted, but it was only the start. Parents should teach not with words but the examples provided by their lives. This was easily said, she conceded, but harder to do. "The role of wife and mother is probably more difficult today than ever before," she said, in part because women, whether by choice or need, spent many more hours away from home. Society itself fostered aspirations in women that were not necessarily bad of themselves, but which had the unfortunate effect of focusing women away from their husbands and children.

Concerning the raising of children, she repeated that the quality she wanted most to instill was what her parents tried to instill in her: "character." In a world obsessed with self-gratification, character would necessarily entail *"measure"* and "self-discipline." In her view these were damnably hard qualities to instill in children of the television generation, for they were constantly bombarded with contrary stimuli and influences. Nevertheless one had to try, and Grace told her audience straightforwardly that this job was "mainly the mother's," if only because the circumstances of life gave her far more contact with the children than the father had.

As a teacher, Grace was far and away more effective when she taught by example, not talk; but when she did talk or write, she was at her best when she gleaned eternal values and lessons from humble acts and activities seemingly far removed. Breast feeding was her most systematic application of induction, but her *Book of Flowers†* was another fine example. It is not only a brilliant and comprehensive illustration of innumerable possibilities of floral arrangement, but a thoughtful reasoning from-hobby-to-life, in which the author discovers in working with flowers several of the values (harmony, patience, balance, occupation) that life requires. The same underlying pattern that is discernible in this book is what shone in Grace's work as an actress, her insistence on breast feeding, her fascination with ballet, or her accomplishment as an artist with dried flower collages (see below, Chapter 11): extraordinarily rapid assimilation of technique followed by the sifting—almost the ransacking—of technique for "lessons." The harder the technique, the more lessons to be gleaned. But always the final lesson—the lesson of lessons—tended to be the same: self-control or self-denial, even more than self-knowledge, is the royal road to a meaningful life. In losing oneself (in technique, commitment, love), one finds oneself.

Grace was, in all ways, a better teacher than critic or prophet. It was perhaps unfortunate that throughout the seventies she continued to feel it a duty to "sound off." On the other hand, she was far less closed-minded in debate than many of her opponents, and she certainly heeded what the other side had to say, particularly the feminist line. Grace's views, even in the midst of battle, were not reflexively reactionary. One never knew when she might grant worth in an opponent's position. For example, she informed the La Leche audience that the culture of permissiveness and the "new" freedoms had the positive value of sweeping away "many absurd beliefs and old wives' tales" about breast feeding and the family, thus clearing the air for the real debate on matters that former generations "were at pains to conceal."

In short, Grace was not an old conservative who blindly rejected the sixties and seventies' calls for liberation, freedom, self-fulfillment. She heard and understood these calls—had even, she took pains to point out repeatedly, given in to them herself in going to Hollywood. Nevertheless, at every level, Grace finally had to resist the spirit of her age, which she (and many others) saw as narcissistic. Psychologically, the call to liberation ran directly counter not only to the conventional morality she had imbibed from Ma and Pa Kelly, but also to many of

† New York: Doubleday, 1980.

the coping and defense mechanisms (sublimation of desire in work; hyperconsciousness about one's image; suppression of emotion; self-lessness) that she had developed in the course of holding up under the conditions of life in her youth on Henry Avenue. Once only had Grace shared the liberationist dream and acted on it by becoming an actress. But the internal discomfort she inflicted on herself (with help from Hollywood) was eventually intolerable.

To the personal, professional, and psychological rejection of "libera-tion" Grace added one more: the spiritual. As a serious Christian, she applauded any human being's release from various forms of social and psychological bondage, but she worried more about the spiritual emp-tiness and sinfulness that the "liberation" seemed to her to bring in its wake. The rigid and exclusive concentration on the self, which Grace saw as the necessary outcome of the spirit and "movements" of the sixties, undercut a person's ability to love—at least to love in the only (Christian) sense that had any meaning to Grace: charity, self-sacrifice, altruism. When she looked around her, Grace saw the flourishing of selfishness and the loss of those values by which she had always lived.

The result was that she felt impelled to inveigh more and more often, forgetting her oft-quoted dictum that "Examples speak louder than words," forgetting that even at the moment of her finest speech— the La Leche convention in Chicago—the people who saw her there remembered her actions as much, if not more, than her words. Rupert Allan, who accompanied her to handle publicity, was struck anew at her "way" with the mothers and infants. "The babies were all over that hotel; *I mean everywhere,*" he said, "squawking, mewling, playing, feeding, getting into mischief. Grace not only didn't mind it, she adored it. She must have had her picture taken holding fifty different babies. She would have gladly adopted a half-dozen if the mothers had been willing."

But in her criticisms thrown off to the press, Grace made less of an impact, sounding alternately fuddy-duddy or waspish, but sometimes blatantly contradicting or even misrepresenting herself. It was one thing to champion "squares," as Grace did in an interview with John Bainbridge of the Philadelphia *Inquirer:* "What we need today are more square people," she said, "more people who are dependable in the old-fashioned way." But it was another thing entirely to claim, as Grace did to Joyce Winslow of *Holiday* magazine in 1977, that "Some women may be able to cope with politics but most cannot. In the Mediterra-nean lifestyle, men are the heads of families—and that is not ques-tioned." She then told Winslow that *she had not favored Monégasque wom-en's getting the franchise in 1962!* Nothing better reflects the hostility— perhaps even anxiety—that the women's movement evoked in Grace than this confabulation.

But then Grace in the late seventies was doing battle on the home front as well as in the public arena. The problems she was having with Caroline (see following) and their dénouement rigidified Grace's public stances and closed her mind in ways no political foe could have done. Self-objective and certainly self-critical to a remarkable degree, Grace momentarily lost her grip on these abilities. She no longer brought to her own ideals and positions all the scrutiny she brought to her adversaries'; she did not consider that "squares" and the "old-fashioned" might evolve their own variations of "egotism, cowardice and laziness."

Above all, Grace embattled hadn't the opportunity and peace of mind to reflect on the darker sides and potentials of her cherished "self-discipline," or to realize that it could traduce itself as certainly as "liberation" could and become a shackle too easily labeled as "character." Grace may have considered how self-discipline was both a profound strength but also a form of self-suppression that had wounded her. It is unlikely, however, that she sensed how deeply the wound went, having undesirable and unforeseen effects—notably in her relations with her elder daughter. Grace's choice to sacrifice her acting career she bore nobly for a higher end; but it was not the isolated decision Grace believed it to be and had an impact on her family in the subtle ways it inflected her behavior.

Publicly, her oft-stated messages were useful reminders that hedonism and self-indulgence underlay some of the calls for "personal fulfillment" in the Culture of Narcissism. Privately, it was no less true that mothers who preached and practiced "self-discipline" could nevertheless, under pressure, impose standards and expectations on their children that made it into an intolerable fetter. There were indeed "forces threatening the [Grimaldi] family," but they weren't all external.

§   §   §

In the fall of 1974, Grace gave a long and candid interview to a writer from *McCall's* about her problems as a mother. The clearest note to rise from her words was that structure was as pervasive in the Grimaldi household as love. The children (Caroline was 17, Albert, 16, Stephanie, 9) were accorded respect and independence; they wanted for nothing, least of all parental attention. Their world was exciting, comfortable, filled with travel, adventure, and a vast array of interesting (often famous) people. But their lives were also sheathed in a latticework of rules, standards, responsibility, authority, discipline, and expectations—both external and internalized. Grace jokingly referred to herself as "Coordinator of Domestic Affairs," and there were surely times when her children, particularly her oldest, felt "coordinated."

Few American or European children would have envied the unvarying strictness of a day that began sharply at seven and was governed, hour by hour, with school, private lessons, homework, sundry responsibilities (sometimes of state), and almost no television. They were close with their parents and with one another, and humor and occasional pranks (especially on vacations) broke the regularity. Nevertheless, they did not—as they were well aware—have life easy. The Grimaldis' concern about the dangers of "permissiveness" was not simply rhetorical; they practiced what they preached—right down to spankings.

Though Albert never needed one. In many ways reminiscent of the impeccable hero of Britten's opera *Albert Herring*, the young prince was saved from being tiresomely good by an active sense of humor and an occasional display of temper. Still, he was an ideal young man: fine athlete, dependable friend, reserved and soft-spoken but with opinions and judgment. He finished secondary school on the Rock and took his baccalaureate at the Lycée named for his great-great grandfather, Albert I. He went to summer camp in New Hampshire where he occasionally visited friends of his parents, who found his manners and consideration far beyond anything they were used to from teenage children.

Constantly referred to as a chip off the maternal block, Albert yet had much in common with Rainier—beginning with the fact that, given a choice, he would not have chosen the métier of prince. Albert, like his father, was a very private person, with no innate drive for power or taste for what the French call *faste* (pomp, luxury). Like both parents, he was painfully shy, sharing with his mother the irritating (because mistaken) reputation of being cold. But in his teens, Albert brought himself out to others, as Rainier had done at Stowe. Unlike Grace, who took occasional refuge in her mask, Albert adopted his father's casual technique of winning people to him with natural bonhomie and warmth. Still, he would never be a dominating or extroverted personality. Indeed only his stern sense of duty would make him Prince Sovereign one day.

According to Oscar Wilde, "Women grow up to be like their mothers. That's their tragedy. Men don't, and that's theirs." The writer would have found little cause for alarm in the Grimaldi son. The unspoken bond between Grace and Albert was the central, definitive fact of the young man's psychology. It arose from a sameness, not merely a similarity, of underlying emotional structure and response, perhaps because both were (in Grace's words) "middle children sandwiched in between strong personalities." Caroline was *like* her father, and Stephanie resembled both parents. But although Albert in many ways recalled Rainier, *he was Grace*. It was a credit to parents and son that they sensed this, appreciated its strength, and worked carefully to avoid the corollary danger of Albert's becoming a mama's boy. Rainier was strong and close to his son, in no way distant or rejecting. Albert was not therefore left alone to become submerged in mother love.

As Prince Hereditary, he had to be properly prepared. For his higher education, Albert chose Amherst College in Massachusetts. Curiously, no cry arose in France that he should study at a French university, nor did Rainier push Albert toward Oxford or Cambridge. The American "tilt" was still in force in Monaco, and from the time Albert was fourteen or fifteen, it was assumed he would go to college in the States, the only question being where. Harvard naturally was discussed, though Rainier in earlier years had thought the place "a bit left wing." Princeton was for a long time a strong contender. Finally the young man judged the pressure and competition there as too intense, and he opted for Amherst. After graduation from Amherst, he served for a year in the French Navy on the warship *Jeanne d'Arc*. Grace dreaded having Albert gone again and doted on his furloughs, but she knew what harm could be done by an overprotective mother, and she resolutely (and successfully) fought the possibility.

Stephanie followed her older sister to the convent school of Les Dames de St.-Maur on the Rock, as well as to ballet class at Marika's Académie, though her greater love—indeed passion for a few years— was gymnastics. (Nadia Lacoste even taught Stephanie a few words of Rumanian so she could impress her heroine, Nadia Comaneci, when she met her at a Nice gymnastics exhibition.) Less intellectual than Caroline and less thoughtful than Albert, Stephanie was more artistic than either of them, fond of drawing, painting, and clothes design. An impulsive and whimsical child, she argued passionately, could be willful to the point of intransigence, and sometimes drove her mother to distraction. But Stephanie was also a child of the purest emotion and held Grace's adoration even when she exasperated.

The seventies saw Caroline, the "honeymoon baby," grow from a little girl into a woman, in the course of which she underwent one of the greatest testings of her—and her mother's—life. The decade opened with the princess enrolled at St. Mary's, a strict Catholic school near Ascot in England, from which she graduated in 1973 with the English equivalent of a high school diploma. Her command of French, English, Spanish, and German ran (in that order) from perfect to good. What was more, she could even converse in each language about its classic literature, with which she had a sound beginner's acquaintance. She also played the piano and flute, and, though she loved rock and pop, had an appreciation of classical music. Yet she was only sixteen and not prepared to enter the advanced École Libre des Sciences Politiques in Paris (her father's alma mater), where entrants had to hold the French high school diploma. Caroline was adamant about wishing to prepare for her "bac" in a Parisian lycée, and her parents, particularly her father, didn't feel they could oppose her in the matter. After her hardworking years in Monaco and in rural England, Caroline had earned a stint of life in the exciting French capital. The question then arose, however, under what circumstances would Caroline live in Paris?

Rainier's feeling was that their daughter should live in the family's elegant townhouse on Avenue Foch (near the Étoile) with an adult chaperone or lady-in-waiting and a small staff of servants. His wife was not nearly so sanguine or decisive. Indeed, where her children were concerned, Grace leaned to the overprotective. Rainier was as aware as she of the obvious threats which their children faced (notably kidnapping), and took security precautions. Even in Monaco itself, members of the princely family were constantly attended by plainclothesmen, while outside the Principality, more elaborate measures were often followed. But Grace still fretted; in fact she was capable of victimizing herself with subjective fears and dreads about the children's lives and well-being that nothing could eradicate or palliate.

It wasn't only Caroline's physical safety Grace feared for, it was her emotional stability in the face of the innumerable stimuli, temptations, and exasperations that life in Paris would throw at her. Caroline's sophistication in matters of "lifestyle" was nil; thus far, her exposure to life was limited to the inside of a palace and a convent school. Grace would never have put it so (even to herself) but at bottom she had less trust in her daughter's ability to adapt to metropolitan life than even strict, straightlaced Ma Kelly had shown in her. Grace, after all was said and done, had moved into the Barbizon alone. Ma, moreover, had let Grace (and her sisters) exchange the hothouse of a convent school, Ravenhill Academy, which they disliked, for the more liberal Stevens School, while Caroline had had to stay at Ascot.

On the other hand, if Grace moved to Paris, the husband-and-wife team that was the core of the family would be divided. She and Rainier recoiled at paying *that* price, the more so as Caroline felt certain she could handle herself. Plans were made for a lady companion to go with her to Paris. But even with the decision ostensibly made, and Caroline pleased and excited about it, Grace could not quiet her anxieties. Rainier tried to calm her because, for in addition to everything else, Grace was wracked by a guilty conscience. In her heart she half knew she wasn't trusting her daughter as she should have. Her words to the press at this time betrayed her inner conflict and ambivalence, as she searched for a pretext to reverse the decision. On the other hand, Grace bragged to journalists about Caroline's intelligence and talent and conceded readily that in intellectual ways "she is more mature than I was at that age." Then in the next breath, she would add hastily, "but in other ways [she is] more vulnerable." Having never before harped on her daughter's position as princess, Grace now noted time and again, "Caroline is not a normal girl. Her father is a reigning prince, and because of this people will be watching, looking, seeking her out. It's happening already."

Nevertheless, the consideration that initially prevailed was Grace and Rainier's distress at the thought of being separated from one another. Caroline would get her chance to live apart from her family. Together with a female companion, she went to stay with close friends of the Grimaldis in Paris. The experiment might have worked, for Caroline worked hard and got on well with her new "family." The misfortune that brought an overattentive mother back into her daughter's life was the constant presence of so many reporters and photographers. They turned up in such numbers in front of the house as to disturb not only Caroline but everyone else in the house. It was unfair to expose any family friends, no matter how close, to this sort of pressure.

A revised plan was now decided upon, not entirely to either daughter's liking. The family would divide; Grace and Stephanie would accompany Caroline to Paris for at least a semester while she settled into a very new life. The teenager would commute to classes at an exclusive, conservative parochial school on the outskirts of Paris and live at a new larger townhouse that the Prince purchased on the Avenue Foch not far from the old apartment. Later, they would see. If all went well, Grace and Stephanie might return to Monaco.

All did not go well. The external pressures visited on beautiful, lively Caroline now that she was eligible and proximate quickly never let up. Worst by far was the press. Grace and Rainier had had their problems with reporters, but 1974 ushered in something new. With the launching (and success) of *People* magazine, the dissemination of gossip and "newsless news" was no longer mainly the preserve of the scandal press. Suddenly serious writers, reporters, and, above all, photographers were being tempted with extraordinary sums by reputable publications to invade the privacy of celebrities—people in many instances famous for nothing more than being famous. And, at just the time that popular fascination with celebrities was being pushed to this new pitch, two of the Grimaldi children were reaching dating age. The combination was explosive, with profound and lamentable effects on the family.

To quote Tracy Lord in *High Society*, Caroline was now "examined, undressed, and generally humiliated" by sharp-edged speculation and omnipresent paparazzi. The seventeen-year-old was portrayed as an habitué of the posh nightclubs and discos, who fought with her parents, and flunked her courses. She was linked with every eligible male (and more than a few ineligible) on the social horizon, most notoriously with Prince Charles of England, with whom it was said she was carrying on a secret romance. (Grace wrote "one of my 'outraged mother' letters to the American magazine that said that." Caroline hadn't ever met Charles.)

Reporters and writers could at least be answered or ignored. Worse by far than their violences was the invasion of photographers—the ubiquitous paparazzi who staked out the Grimaldi townhouse day and night, tailing Caroline with unflagging zeal and ingenuity no matter how she (or her family and friends) tried to elude them. The pictures they took were adorned with captions that turned any young male in Caroline's company into her "current beau." The stories they illustrated carried headlines like "Princess Heartbreaker" and texts that "detailed" her "affairs" and nights of dancing till dawn. The facts of the girl's life made these allegations ludicrous, but that did not even slow down the cottage industry that was Caroline-speculation. "I really would shoot these people if I had my way," Rainier said with uncharacteristic brutality as he watched his daughter's life made wretched with the strain and embarrassment of this harassment. Legal suits, which the Prince brought time and again, accomplished little more than affording Rainier a bit of relief in the illusion he was doing something. Bodyguards were of small help; they protected persons, not privacy. They could not block photo lenses, and they unintentionally proved a further encumbrance to a self-conscious teenager.

Anyone would have been overwhelmed by this kind of attention, but Caroline more so than most, for Grace was right: her daughter *was* vulnerable. Isolated from the world for sixteen years, she was suddenly attacked by it. The mob scenes that took place every time she went out on a date or even got home from school; the necessity of guards and chauffeurs; the discomfort she unwillingly wrought in the lives of her friends—all weighed on Caroline. "Why do I have to be a princess? I hate it," she would yell through tears of frustration.‡

Grace was as distraught by these circumstances as by any she had ever known. Sorely missing her husband and son, burdened with her usual load of Monaco's business (and the vexation of having to conduct it on weekends and by telephone), Grace's pain at her daughter's distress was exacerbated by her own helplessness. There was *nothing* she, or anybody, could do; no amount of self-discipline, hard work, or sacrifice on her part could be of any help to her beleaguered daughter. Speaking of these years, Caroline would later say, "I believe that for

‡ As Grace told her (and Caroline's) close friend, Fleur Cowles. Interview with Cowles. May 12, 1983.

her, as for us, there were moments where we truly couldn't take it anymore."

Gradually the mood in the Avenue Foch residence took on aspects of a bunker mentality. In her anguish, loneliness, and futile rage at "them," Grace underwent a subtle change. Always an exacting woman where her children were concerned, Grace in Monaco was not rigid, nor did she envelop them. Rainier's indulgent presence had a relaxing effect on family members as well as on rules, and Grace's busy workload kept her occupied. Now, alone with two young girls in a large townhouse that much of the time resembled a besieged fortress, missing her husband and son, without an office for escape, and with fewer obligations to occupy her time, Grace clung tenaciously—to her standards, her self-discipline, her mask, her fears, and to Caroline. Needless to say, she did *not* return to Monaco after a semester, for by then she regarded herself as her daughter's only ally in a battle royal.

In truth, the contest had just begun, and Grace was not so much an ally as an adversary.

§   §   §

Q. *If you had to summarize it in one trenchant sentence, "this is what [Mother] was to me," what would you say?*

A. *She was a point of reference in all things, from the smallest detail to the most important thing.*

—Caroline of Monaco

In the teeth of the press, the gossip, the embarrassment, her mother's hovering presence and her own emerging needs, Caroline also changed. She passed her bac in the spring of 1975 and entered the École Libre ("Sciences Po") that fall, but her heart was not in it. During the last half of 1975, she began to discover *la vie mondaine* and acquire a taste for it (perhaps thinking that if the press kept saying she was having a good time, she might as well have one). The society pages of *Le Figaro, Le Quotidien de Paris, Paris Match,* and especially the all-seeing "Oeil" of the French *Vogue* kept an unblinking eye on Caroline's movements and provided readers with a minute chronicle of her appearances at "New Jimmy's," "Régine's," and every other trendy discotheque or cabaret in Paris. The "Caroline brigade" of paparazzi was rewarded for its patience over the months of uneventfulness in the previous year with weekly, biweekly, and sometimes triweekly photographs of their prey as she made her sensational debut with the *jeunesse dorée.*

Not only Caroline's behavior but her personality underwent some changes at this time. A certain hardening set in, as she became less concerned with other people's opinion of her—notably her mother's.

Grace herself, though displeased by what she saw, struggled to hold herself back. She would confide to her friends that Caroline was "impossible," but to her eighteen-year-old daughter, she put on as tolerant a face as she could. But there was smoldering underneath, as was evident in both women's words to the press. Grace would talk of how "much more together Caroline is than I was at her age"—which Caroline heard as a euphemism that meant "I wasn't as headstrong and frivolous as my daughter." For her part, Caroline began stressing the differences between herself and Grace, though always doing so in a laudatory, admiring way: "My mother is beautiful but she is rather reserved. She is a marvelous housewife, full of self-control, always impeccable down to the smallest detail. I sometimes find it difficult to do the things Mother expects of me." On another occasion, she commented "We are so different. She was shy. I am not." Grace had "thank[ed] God Caroline doesn't want to be an actress," to which her daughter's revealing response was: "I don't want to compete in mother's field. My own ambition is to keep on being a student for a while." Caroline also stressed her resemblance to her father, emphasizing qualities that she obviously felt were underrepresented in Grace. "In private, we wear old sweaters and jeans and race around like kids. And even when my father is busy he still finds the time to sit in an armchair and listen to me. I hope I'll find a man like my father . . . a man who'll *know how to lead a private life without being bored*" (Emphasis added). Finally, Caroline let it be known that Stephanie was getting away with more than she had been permitted at her age.

It was unlikely that Grace did not "listen" to Caroline, but it was equally likely she didn't really hear her. Few were more theoretically aware of all the angles in child-rearing than Grace—including the "rebellion" that came with the late adolescent's identity crisis. She was aware that "our children are growing up in a very different world from the one we lived in [as kids]." She quoted Gibran that children were "arrows that fly forth" from "bows that are stable," and she reminded journalists of her own "breakaway": "Kids have to do it." Nevertheless when one of hers did it, Grace wasn't ready, she wasn't happy, and she didn't *really* understand why. Why, for example, couldn't Caroline see through the life she was leading and many of the people she was leading it with? Why couldn't she buckle down to her studies, which Grace knew she loved? Why was she so sullen with people one minute and nearly seductive the next? Why those overtight jeans and transparent blouses? And why, dear God, all that makeup? To put a fine point on it: why couldn't Caroline be more like she had been at her age?

Meanwhile, Caroline's "private life" continued to be far from "boring," and despite her protest, she was no longer much interested in being a student. That became clear at the end of Sciences Po's fall term. For the first time, Caroline did poorly on exams. She would stick it out at the École through the end of the year, but then she intended to withdraw. At this point, Rainier, who had been removed from the immediate situation and inclined to indulge Caroline somewhat in her newfound enjoyment of life, worried that things might now be getting out of hand. Discos and high living were tolerable but not if they interfered with his daughter's education. In long and intensive discussions among Rainier, Grace, and Caroline, the parents managed to convince their daughter that a change of place would be best for her. Princeton, it seemed to Rainier, was the ideal spot for a driving, intellectual student like Caroline, in ways that it would not have suited Albert. The competitiveness of the academic environment there would absorb his daughter's energy. Caroline reluctantly agreed. She applied to the university and was accepted, and she notified Princeton she would enter in the fall. Nevertheless, her heart was not in it; she was going to please her parents. Then, during the summer of 1976, she met Philippe Junot.

§   §   §

Nobody wants to hear about a love affair unless there's some reason that it shouldn't be one.
                                        —*George Kelly*, The Deep Mrs. Sykes

His past and profession were something of a mystery. The son of a successful French businessman who was *not* related to the famous Napoleonic marshal named Junot (though he liked having people think he was), Philippe was a sophisticated man-about-town. "He works in investments" was the most definitive statement his friends would make about his career, while Junot himself avoided the question. He claimed to have graduated from the New York Institute of Finance, though the Institute was not granting diplomas at the time Junot studied there. Caroline met him at a discotheque and was charmed by his insouciance and casual knowledgeability. There were surface qualities about Junot that recalled Oleg Cassini, but he hadn't the designer's strength of personality nor his mad romanticism. But he had savvy self-assurance and a dab hand that more than concealed his lack of emotional and spiritual depth—especially from a girl momentarily fleeing "the examined life." Philippe, for all his seventeen years of seniority to Caroline and all his apparent "control" over her, was first and last a blank slate on which she wrote her life script.

Their romance blossomed quickly and visibly, within the parochial world of swinging Paris. Philippe, though he got angry at individual journalists and photographers, didn't mind the publicity and taught

Caroline a needed lesson in relaxing with the paparazzi. They went to Maxim's and the Alcazar, to Normandy and Switzerland, and they sunned at St.-Tropez, where Caroline was photographed in the nude (much to the annoyance of her parents who had been led to believe she was in Paris that weekend). But they led far less of the high life than the press imagined. Mostly, they just spent a lot of time in Philippe's apartment, enjoying each other and their friends, and satisfying Caroline's desperate wish to create another life than the restricted one she had always known. "Philippe has given me the first freedom I've ever known in my life," Caroline said later. "His apartment helped me to have some independence and provided me with an escape from my normal routine." Late in the summer of 1976, Caroline put her foot down and absolutely refused to go to Princeton. Instead, she offered to enter the Sorbonne and work toward a *licence* (bachelor's degree) in psychology. Six months later, in the winter of 1977, she sat down with Grace and Rainier and told them that Philippe had asked her to marry him.

The Grimaldis did not like Junot. Rainier had once assured his biographer that "children who are normally brought up . . . like Caroline, would not allow themselves to be flipped over in some adventure." Now he could barely bring himself to believe she had fallen for a man who was (to Rainier's thinking) so palpably a seducer and fortune hunter. Grace appreciated the qualities in Philippe that attracted Caroline, but she did not think there was much to him and could not respect him. Both parents admitted that their viewpoints might well be skewed by protectiveness for their daughter, whose life under Junot's influence was not something they approved of. In the final analysis, however, neither their private opinions nor Philippe's age nor his indeterminate profession—"I think he has something to do with investment counseling," Rainier would say on the eve of Junot's becoming his son-in-law—were the decisive factors in their displeasure at learning of Caroline's wish to marry him. Caroline was in their eyes too young and emotionally inexperienced to marry *anyone*, and nothing she could say would dissuade Grace and Rainier from this belief.

Grace, in particular, was desperately unhappy. Much of the press attributed her distress to the thwarting of her wish for a "brilliant match" for her daughter; an English magazine had her scheming for the Prince of Wales. Other journalists blamed Grace's unhappiness on the scandal that Caroline's behavior brought down on Grace herself and her reputation for "perfection," especially as a mother. The truth in the former speculations was nil, and in the latter minor. Grace's anguish stemmed consciously from her fear that Caroline was going to make herself terribly unhappy. But what troubled Grace most was her intuition that Caroline's actions were, at bottom, motivated by rebellion against maternal authority. Her beloved daughter was caught in an emotional *itinéraire obligatoire* (roller coaster) to disaster, and it was partly Grace's doing; *that* was what finally ate away at her, for it made Grace doubt the hard-won lessons around which she had built her own life and raised her children. If you raised your children in fidelity to self-discipline, sacrifice, faith, authority, family unity, was *this* where you led them? Had she been wrong? Grace grew anxious pondering the issue, and her grief alarmed Rainier and close friends.

Doubts, disappointment, and even moments of near despair profoundly shook Grace's beliefs; they did not shake her love for her daughter nor her intention, come what may, to hold on to her. Beliefs were of little enough usefulness, anyway. As she had told a journalist in the pre-Junot era, "I don't think there is any formula for raising children. The best a parent can do is play it by ear and hope for the best." She added, beware "when you start slamming the door [on your children]. Sometimes they drive you right up the wall, you want to strangle them, but you have to leave that door open because when it's closed, it's finished." Grace now had a chance to live up to that difficult advice—to leave the door open to a daughter who appeared nude in weekly magazines, neglected her studies, got drunk in cabarets, and dated a man who thought it clever to pull down his pants on the dance floor at "New Jimmy's" and pour a bottle of Johnnie Walker over himself. It was a hard chance to take, especially when leaving the door open might mean acquiescing in an "indissoluble marriage."

Ironically, Grace was the one who pushed the matter to a sacramental conclusion. Caroline had first mentioned marriage in early 1977, before she had her degree and having known Philippe hardly nine months. At her parents' fervent pleas, she consented to postpone the question for a period while she worked at her studies, and, the Grimaldis hoped, forgot about Junot. Caroline did the first, not the second. By autumn of 1977, the question of a wedding once again hung fire. Rainier was now willing to use his authority over the princely family and forbid Caroline to marry. If he had done so, Caroline would have had to break openly with her family and marry outside of Monaco, and perhaps outside of the church.

Husband and wife discussed a ban at great length. Some measure of Grace's distress may be seen in the fact that, initially at least, she insisted her husband use it. Rainier implored her to remember what a sensitive girl Caroline was, how ineradicable an impression a formal ban would make on her. Did Grace want to lose her? In short, he begged her to leave the door open. For a time, Grace then waffled back and forth, at times in favor of a ban, other times opposed. Caroline, after all, had said she wouldn't break with the family in order to marry Philippe. She had told her father that if he withheld his permission, she would bow to his authority, but she and Junot would settle down together out of wedlock. Rainier, actually, was prepared to accept this as a preferable solution to marriage, but Grace was not. Partly, she objected for appearance's sake—the couple's "living in sin" would cause a major uproar in conservative, Catholic Monaco—and partly because her own view of romantic love was (like Caroline's) inextricably tied to the Church and its teachings. So finally, reluctantly and with many second thoughts, she cast her decisive vote for what Caroline wished: a formal church wedding. Who knew, she'd say to her husband, maybe marriage would improve Philippe. But even with the decision made, Grace remained prey to doubts and would wonder aloud to Rainier if they shouldn't alter their position and let Caroline live with Philippe. The very eve of the wedding, she said to her husband, half wryly, half seriously, "Well, perhaps it's for the better. This way she'll have a successful second marriage."*

In late 1977, the speculation that was rampant in the society pages was confirmed: Caroline Louise Marguerite de Grimaldi would become Mrs. Philippe Junot in June of the following year. They would reside in a flat in Paris and Caroline would pursue her work toward a master's degree in philosophy at the Sorbonne. Until the wedding, Caroline would continue to live with her mother and sister on the Avenue Foch. Grace had candidly admitted to a few journalists that Caroline's marriage was "her own decision" and "not something I was strongly in favor of." Rainier was formally polite to Junot, but nothing more. Caroline, meanwhile, buckled down to her work in the 1977–78 academic year and completed her *licence*. She was happier now; soon she would no longer be mainly Grace's daughter, but a wife, and then mother, in her own right.

The wedding itself was a comparatively subdued affair. Originally planned for a mere forty to fifty guests, it gradually grew to five times that number (including the usual contingent of Grace's Hollywood friends), but it never approached the extravaganza of 1956. The press assumed this decision reflected the princely couple's lack of enthusiasm for the groom, but the greater truth was that it reflected their earnest desire to avoid inflicting on Caroline the misery they had gone through at their own wedding. Local shopkeepers were warned unofficially not to commercialize the event by selling souvenirs of the wedding, while reporters and photographers were very severely limited in number and controlled in their movements. A British journalist was even detained by the police for questioning locals about the wedding. A couple of reporters had their revenge by unearthing and publishing an obscure

* Interview with Rainier, September 12, 1983.

Monégasque legend about a witch who condemned the Grimaldis to
unhappy marriages.

One curious note was the reporting of Junot's occupation. He had
always been evasive and defensive about it—in part no doubt because
the assumption was so rank that he was a fortune hunter hoping to
profit from his wife and her family's connections. "The question I hate
most," he told one reporter, "is 'what do you do?'" The result was that
many stories of the wedding described him as an "investment counselor," using quotes, which gave it an unintended ironical twist.

The couple was joined in matrimony in the courtyard of the Palace
by the same bishop who had married Grace and Rainier. Caroline experienced the same problem with getting the ring on her finger that
Grace had had; she laughed nervously, and Philippe said, "Hey, relax
your finger." At the reception afterwards, a guest walked over to the
Prince and, trying to make small talk, asked cheerfully, "And what
does your son-in-law do, Monseigneur?" "Anything," Rainier replied.

Caroline's short-lived marriage to Philippe Junot is, sadly, a classic
study in disillusionment leading to dissolution. With her immense res-
ervoirs of energy, intelligence, and good faith, Caroline was going *to
make it work,* by which she blissfully understood duplicating (or rivaling) her parents' marriage. Her ignorance of her husband's true character was a direct measure, maybe a direct result, of her fervent intention to become her own Grace. Junot actually entered the marriage
more knowledgeable about himself and his wife than Caroline was and
certainly far more aware than she that marriage was something two
people created freely, without hidden agendas and *idées fixes.*

If Caroline had any hopes that Philippe would be a Rainier, they
must have started fading at the very start, when he permitted a favored
photographer to come along on the South Pacific honeymoon and take
pictures. In fact, between the long honeymoon and several trips immediately afterward to Scotland, the United States and the West Indies,
the Junots did not settle down in their luxurious penthouse on the
Avenue Bosquet until the late fall of 1978.

Caroline immediately began talking about having babies. Rumors
and the scandal sheets had in fact had her pregnant before the wedding; then, when her unfaltering slimness confounded their allegation,
maintained that she'd suffered a miscarriage. Grace, for all that she
very much wanted grandchildren, was distressed by her daughter's
wish to get pregnant soon. "I adore children," she told a reporter, "but
I hope Caroline will not experience motherhood immediately," adding,
"I was twenty-eight when Caroline was born." In part, Grace believed
the only hope for survival the Junot marriage had was for husband and
wife to come to know each other and begin working out "the series of

concessions" that she and Rainier once called marriage. But at a deeper level, Grace was not eager to see Caroline more deeply implicated in an alliance that she still couldn't bring herself to believe would last.

The Grimaldis continued to remain in close touch with their daughter, only now the impetus was more from Caroline's side. Being married and anticipating motherhood, Caroline felt able to draw close to her mother again—but this time, she believed, in the role of equal, not of little girl feeling oppressed by external and (mostly) internalized standards and expectations she was heartily tired of. In her public words, Caroline continued to defer respectfully to her mother, as she had throughout even the most difficult period. But the twenty-one-year-old's actions betrayed her tacitly felt equality with a mother whom she now strove mightily to imitate. She instantly took on heavy obligations for Monaco, notably the presidency of the Monégasque organizing committee for the International Year of the Child. She organized and led a very successful "Youth Walkabout" in Monaco to raise money for the Year, and she and Philippe attended many public and charitable events in the Principality. Indeed, Caroline's work there occupied so much of her time that she had temporarily to suspend her graduate work.

But it was in her public statements about children, family, and the ills of society that Caroline most faithfully aped her mother. She deplored the effects of too much television on children: "Television suffocates all forms of creativity. It's too easy for parents to let their children sit in front of the TV while they get on with other things." (These words came only a year or two after Caroline had complained that Stephanie was being allowed to watch more TV than she and Albert had been able to do.) She decried permissiveness and spoke of the need for authority (albeit "enlightened"), and she criticized excessive violence, sex, and nudity in the media. The family, she opined, "is of value in itself and it has a vocation—the family is, above all, centered on the children." A child, she continued, "learns to live through his mother, because mother love is the indispensable soil in which the child's personality grows." Caroline was described by the press as "decidedly old-fashioned."

Few rebels have turned coat as swiftly as twenty-one-year-old Caroline Junot became an apostle of counterrevolution. Could it be doubted that had she fulfilled her project of becoming a mother, she would perhaps have raised a rebel or two of her own?

In the event, words and hopes and all the effort of make-believe could not long keep intact a relationship that never really existed. The one figure whom Caroline omitted from her felicitous calculus was her husband, Philippe, whose thoughts on marriage and intentions for living life had nothing in common with his "old-fashioned" wife. Only someone as fixated as Caroline was on her own hopes could have ignored the innumerable warnings from close friends of her own and her husband's that Philippe was "a cool temperament." As Junot himself said, before he met Caroline he believed that "staying single was the natural condition for a man and marriage was a social convention." Philippe's commitment to the marriage was very much "in his fashion." That fashion included extramarital affairs, and the appearance of same; a taste for parties, nightlife, and society that left little room for domestic quiet and solitude; and a demanding workload and a new preoccupation with professional success that required him to travel inordinate amounts of time. For a girl who had many times signaled the world that she wished to marry "a man like my father," Caroline had not chosen well. But perhaps a girl does not choose well when imitating her mother.

The denouement of the marriage was sad, sordid, and minutely reported by the press, whom Philippe the play-around husband did not appreciate as much as Philippe the courtier had. Junot was out of Paris on business frequently, and when he was in town, he spent a great deal of time away from home—playing soccer, seeing his friends, or going (with or without Caroline) to parties and nightclubs. Word of his amorous adventures—real and imagined—began circulating within a few months of the wedding. A paparazzo caught Philippe off guard dancing with an ex-girlfriend, Countess Agneta von Furstenberg, at Studio 54 when Caroline believed he was in Montreal on business. Distraught and humiliated, Caroline indulged her temper and produced a counter scene of her own, visiting a Parisian nightclub with an ex-beau.

From there, it was a downhill slalom of eighteen months of heartbreak as Philippe persevered in his indiscreet behavior (and tongue-lashed the press), and Caroline alternately fought him on his own terms or took tearful refuge in her home or with her family. Nobody watched these events more closely or with greater pain than Grace. That her private predictions about the marriage were coming true in no way diminished the agony she shared with her daughter or the blame she felt at having been a psychological cause of Caroline's actions. Rainier at least got some relief in fury at Junot, but Grace, now as before, had thoughts only for Caroline. Gently, but firmly, without a trace of "we-told-you-so," she reached out to her unhappy daughter. The "door" that her parents had kept open turned out to be Caroline's escape from her self-made disaster and perhaps her only alternative to a complete breakdown.

Publicly, Grace and Nadia Lacoste kept up a front with the press: "Every marriage has its ups and downs. Philippe and Caroline are human;" "I think Caroline *is* happy" (this appearing in print when Caroline had already left Junot). But behind the scenes Grace and Rainier maneuvered very delicately—at least vis-à-vis Caroline; Philippe was treated differently. When he came to Monaco, the son-in-law was treated to frozen, almost menacing silences by Rainier, even in public. "I really believe the Prince would have throttled him at the end [if Junot had showed up]," Rupert Allan said.† Caroline, however, was another matter. Without pushing her, or even discouraging her from further effort, Grace and Rainier tacitly led her to understand that, contrary to the general impression, they would *not* be scandalized by a separation and divorce. As mutual indiscretion mounted on savage altercation and finally broke out into a public contretemps at the 1980 Grand Prix, the Grimaldis finally intimated to Caroline their feeling that if she thought enough was enough, they did, too.

By then, their daughter's friendship with Robertino Rossellini, the son of Ingrid Bergman and the Italian director Roberto Rossellini, was being touted in the press as a romance, which it was not at the time. Caroline commuted to Monaco often in the early summer of 1980. Sometimes she kept to herself there; other times she would try to share her misery and dispel her confusion in talks with her parents. By now the feeling among the entire family ran against further attempts at reconciliation but they were careful not to press it on Caroline, who was still in love with Philippe and half dedicated to the idea that marriage was forever. Mostly, what people close to Caroline sensed in conversations with her was shock that this could be happening, shock at the magnitude of her misperception of her husband, and shock at the dawning, horrible realization that there may never have been anything there to begin with.

Caroline gradually arrived at a more accurate assessment of the nature of her husband, her own motivations, and the state of the marriage. Sustained by her parents whose tacit approval of her thought of divorce had by now become almost a suggestion of that course, Caroline decided to act on her intuition. She did so with a remorselessness reminiscent of Craig in her great-uncle's play *Craig's Wife*: "My mind . . . appreciates this situation so thoroughly that it has no illusions about the impossibility of my continuance here." Without returning to Paris even to speak to her husband, Caroline directed Nadia Lacoste to issue a communiqué soon after the Red Cross Gala (August 8, 1980) saying the marriage was definitively over; divorce would ensue. Without the "open door," it was unlikely Caroline could have come to so clean a decision so quickly, and without her husband's participation.

Now it was Junot's turn to be stunned. Although he had had a profounder grasp of Caroline than she had of him, he found it impossible to believe she would act this resolutely and that no further chance

† Interview with author, April 14, 1983.

of reconciliation existed. In his fashion, he had truly loved her, and he did not want a divorce. He had hoped that eventually Caroline would come round to accepting (or at least tolerating) his open-ended and casual idea of marriage. "I want a woman who can be an accomplice and a companion," he told a journalist afterwards. Now he alternately blamed the press and her parents for what had come to pass—the press for magnifying and distorting "our disagreements," Rainier and Grace for intruding and interfering. However, the burden of Junot's charges against his in-laws weighed less on their direct intervention (he offered no instances) than on the way they had raised their daughter. Caroline, he said, had been spoiled and overprotected, and the consequence was that such a woman could not "cope with the reality of life." He noted in passing that she had little genuine interest in him or his business ("Caroline never seemed the least bit aware"). His final gripe was that "She was going through so many changes—psychologically, emotionally, intellectually—that it was hard to keep up with her."

No doubt it was hard for Junot to keep up with Caroline; no doubt he needed a simpler kind of "accomplice" from the complicated, changing, talented Grimaldi girl, so absorbed in her own subliminal conflict with her mother and the "project" that it gave rise to, that she had little grasp of Philippe or genuine interest in his work. Junot was perhaps a shallow cad, but he was so transparently so that the question intrudes itself: if people far less gifted than Caroline understood Philippe, why didn't she? Love may be blind, but one wonders if she loved him in any meaningful sense of the word. Philippe Junot had a legitimate gripe, if he had cared to voice it: all along he had been a weapon which a beautiful, complex, gifted, and unhappy young girl used in her unconscious struggle with the mother whom she consciously loved and respected, but toward whom she unconsciously felt rivalry and resentment. Once that weapon proved worthless, it was flung down as quickly as it had been picked up.

Caroline's brother, Albert, later called his mother "a great woman in every sense." It cannot have been easy being her eldest child, particularly when she embodied a hovering, insistent perfectionism for herself and her offspring. A child could "hate" so impossible a model as Grace, though only unconsciously. A child could upset and destroy lives by trying to rival her mother. It had happened before.

There was no rapid recovery from the Junot episode for Caroline. As for her mother, it was one of the three great crises of her life (after 1955 and 1962). In some regards it was the worst (certainly the most drawn out) because it involved the pain of another, her own child. Grace cannot have been ignorant of the psychological components of the drama. The degree of her anxiety and distress pointed to an inchoate awareness that Caroline's actions were dictated at some level by the frustration she felt at thinking she had to follow her mother's example, by Grace's being too impossible "a point of reference in all things."

Grace was far too intelligent a mother to try to mold her children in any coarse sense; they were never expected to garner top honors or "be the best," nor still less to "marry well" or "play the part." Rather, they were saddled (unintentionally) with a heavier burden—the burden of having to be *good* like their mother, who also just *happened* to be "the best," to have married well, to have won top honors, etc. The burden of Grace's unrelenting unintentional "perfection" sat hardest on Caroline, for she was the eldest and, as a female, identified with her mother. With her own intelligence, beauty, and many gifts, Caroline early began to believe that she *could*, as well as should, rival her mother. As she reached her middle and late teens, these amorphous drives (intensified by adolescent sexuality and Caroline's hearty satedness with Catholic schooling) took shape in a "project": at one and the same time, she would escape from childhood and rules and vault into equality with her mother, by becoming a wife and mother in her own right. Simultaneously, she would take a master's in philosophy and perform important jobs for Monaco. So misconceived a project could never have worked, even if the mate whom Caroline had chosen had been a worthier mate.

Grace's single overt mistake was to mistrust her daughter, which she expressed by being overprotective—specifically, by moving to Paris with Caroline. Caroline's one hope of weathering her crisis—without externalizing it by getting married—lay in getting distance from her mother and acquiring the freedom to find herself *by* herself. Grace's hovering presence on the Avenue Foch, intensified by her own loneliness, her frustration at not being able to act, and the siegelike conditions imposed by the press, put Caroline in a double bind—at school and in her social life, she was undergoing heady new experiences and being bombarded by very powerful stimuli (internal as well as external). At home, however, she faced a regime more or less contiguous with the restricted life of convent schools—only directed by her real mother superior. The pressure grew too great and Caroline broke away. Under the circumstances, what was remarkable was how close the two remained immediately before, during, and after the break.

Once the break occurred in the form of Caroline's declaration of her love for Philippe and strong wish to marry him, Grace—surprisingly and brilliantly—down-shifted, perhaps because her heart warned her that now all could be lost. Rather than hand down orders to Caroline— as Albert I had done to his son, Louis, when he wished to marry the washerwoman's daughter—Grace quietly relaxed her authority; in her love for her daughter and determination to hang on to the relationship,

Grace forced herself (with Rainier's help) to become flexible and re-
sourceful. A woman as "reactionary" and enamored of authority, as
Grace's own statements had sometimes made her out to be, would not
have withstood the temptation to hold back from gross interference—
up to, and including, a princely ban. A narrowly "strict" Roman Catholic and an appearance-bound princess would not have readily counseled divorce, but would have clung to the indissolubility of marriage.
Indeed, if Grace and Rainier were the people they were often portrayed to be, they would have *liked* the wily "investment counselor"
named Junot, whose father was deputy-mayor of Paris and whose family had important connections in conservative French business circles.
But they were not drawn to him; from the start, they saw him for what
he was.

In sum, as important as form and appearance were to Grace, she
gave them away for content every time.

§   §   §

Everything I do is connected to my husband.

—*Princess Grace*

As they had tried on her fortieth birthday, so the reporters tried on
her fiftieth (in 1979) to get Grace to say she was bothered by losing
some of her remarkable beauty. But her vague replies weren't very
gratifying to the cosmetic-conscious. "I'm used to the lines [on my
face]," she told a writer from the *Ladies' Home Journal*, "and, quite honestly, I don't mind the gray hair. You see, I feel every age has its
beauty." She minded much more the extra ten to twenty pounds she
carried around from the days when Edith Head thought her almost too
slim. She had an excuse she'd occasionally give the press—her travel
and social schedule made adherence to a diet impossible—but the truth
was, as Grace's friends and family knew, she liked to eat. Sometimes at
Roc Agel, she'd cook herself. She'd learned a lot of French (especially
Mediterranean) dishes by now, but she would still, from time to time,
offer up a good old American barbecue.

Sometimes the price she paid for enjoying a good meal had its amusing consequences—nobody being more amused than Grace. At the
Shah of Iran's gigantic celebration of the twenty-five-hundredth anniversary of the founding of the Peacock Throne in 1971, Grace and
Rainier flew to Persepolis to join dozens of other international celebrities, dignitaries, and statesmen in the festivities. There were rounds of
wonderful meals with all manner of exotic dishes; and few guests did
themselves prouder than Grace, who, by the time the last, formal dinner rolled around, was sitting *very* snugly in her glittering Givenchy.
At dessert, the man sitting next to Grace (the premier of a Warsaw Pact

country) lit up his cigar, and the smoke from it set off in the Princess of Monaco a foursquare, lumberjack sneeze. Instantly, several buttons holding together the back of her glittering gown shot to the floor, and the back of the dress fell open. Madame Ardant, her very proper lady-in-waiting, cast a look of such horror on the spectacle of her mistress's undoing that she nearly fainted. That finished Grace, who until then, was barely managing to control her impulse to break down in helpless laughter. With Ardant practically swooning, and Rainier uselessly pulling at the dangling threads that once held buttons on his wife's dress, Grace, between paroxysms of mirth, may have vowed she'd lose a few pounds.

And she did, but then she put them back on again. The one impulse that would have made her take the weight off for keeps, she said once, was if her husband told her to. But he didn't. Rainier liked his wife pretty much as he got her. The pain for both of them in the late seventies was that they lived apart. The press aggravated this ache to the point of fury in the Prince by speculating that Grace was a "self-exile" in Paris. He ordered Monaco's New York consul, Frank Cresci, to file a complaint against the National *Star* (circulation one million) with the National News Council for reporting that he and Grace were separated. The Council found for the plaintiff, saying that the *Star* had "cloaked its sources in anonymity" and that its editors had been remiss in failing to report letters in which Grace, and her brother, had asserted the untruthfulness of the article.

The gossip that all but invariably attended such allegations was that Rainier was keeping a woman, or two, on the side—for example, at the Hotel Negresco in Nice. The ludicrousness of it amused the Prince when it didn't enrage him. He would say to close friends that he wished the prices weren't so high at the Negresco so he could keep more "chorus girls" there. Grace faced far less of this silly libel (though every so often a "history of the JFK/Grace Kelly liaison" would pop up). She, too, would occasionally joke about "getting to that age where I'll run off with a skiing instructor." Neither the Prince or Princess ever graced these charges with a public denial, and no serious publication ever trafficked in them; yet they remained a staple of the scandal press, hence of the literary diet of many millions of readers.

That Rainier cast an appreciative eye on some of the women he met was probably as likely as that some of them might have liked to have an affair with him. The same thing could be said of Grace, who, to the end of her life, remained in the opinion of many one of the most attractive women in the world. (In the first decade of their marriage, Rainier in fact tended to be rather sensitive about the almost involuntary reactions that his wife evoked from men, though he told a journalist, "I'm not jealous of other men. One could only feel jealous if given any

reason." It stood to simple reason, however, that in lives as unremit-
tingly illumined by klieg lights as theirs, it would have been impossible
to carry on an outside affair—even had one or the other wished to do
so. Some serious evidence would almost unquestionably have come to
light; yet none ever did. Barring a full-dress affair, someone in the
Grimaldis' position would be left with only the possibility of an occasional momentary dalliance. In Grace's case, this was extremely unlikely because totally out of character. In Rainier's, on the other hand,
it was entirely plausible (at least in the opinion of several of the
Grimaldis' closest friends), but no hard evidence ever confirmed it.

What was undoubtedly the case was that Grace and Rainier, like
most couples who lead independent lives, very occasionally met individuals with whom they felt a mutual emotional-physical chemistry
that, under other circumstances, might have developed into an affair,
but couldn't now, and didn't. Had it happened, had, for example, the
Prince acted like what *Le Monde* once called "le French husband" and
taken a mistress, not one among Grace or the Grimaldis' friends interviewed for this book felt that this would have, of itself, ended, or even
badly harmed, their relationship. For one thing, Grace had her mother's example of self-possession under marital strain to draw on. But
more to the point, the Grimaldis "were too mature as a couple," said
one close friend, who had once worked for them, "for some indiscretion to have destroyed anything important. They respected and depended on each other too much to let it all go over something like a
fling. I can even imagine Grace saying to [Rainier], 'Well, do what you
must, but for god's sake, be discreet.' "

The seventies brought no changes from the sixties in the rich patterns of discussion, concession, collaboration that steadily deepened
and matured Grace and Rainier's love. Without the Prince's strength
and counsel—even across the five hundred miles separating Paris and
Monaco—Grace would never have got through the Junot affair as well
as she did. His frequent appearances in Paris or her trips to Monaco
helped Grace to tolerate the helplessness and distress as she watched
the fusillades of mutual recriminations and vengeances that punctuated the Junot marriage in its disintegration. Numerous people who
saw her in this period—for example, Earle Mack, the producer of *Children of Theatre Street*, who worked intensively with Grace in 1977 (see
Chapter 11)—commented on the difference Rainier's presence wrought
in her spirits.‡

What confused even well-intentioned journalists was the independence of two extremely busy, responsible lives. Even if Grace hadn't
moved to Paris, she would have been able to spend much less time than

‡ Interview with Earle Mack, November 8, 1983.

usual in Monaco after 1976, for her schedule—now augmented by poetry readings in England and the United States, and active membership on the board of 20th Century-Fox (see Chapter 11)—was a marvel of organized activity. The years when Grace emotionally depended on the Prince and needed him as a frequent companion were long past. The "présence" that Grace lacked then, now filled her waking hours with obligations. Finally, it remained true that the Grimaldis had different tastes in pastimes and leisure. As they grew older and surer of themselves as a couple, there was perhaps less need for one to do something he or she didn't especially enjoy just to please the other. Rainier spent much of his spare time on the yacht, while Grace was never happier than walking in the mountains and along the coast—sometimes alone, sometimes with Monsieur Kroenlein or a member of the Garden Club, collecting flower cuttings for her collages and enjoying nature. But it should perhaps be noted that when the walkers reached the luncheon rendezvous, more often than not it was no servant or lady-in-waiting who drove up with the meal, but Rainier come to see what she'd found.

If the seventies brought no new sources of argument between husband and wife, they failed to remove all of the old. Even Rainier's temper would sometimes flare up, though Grace could stand up to it better now and wasn't reduced to long sulky silences to make *her* points and hurt known. Grace continued to remain close and available to her Philadelphia family—a habit that Rainier and many of her close friends both admired and felt exasperated by at the same time, for Grace's solicitousness, if not her affection, seemed such a one-way street. Some of the Kellys, notably Kell, continued to make shameless use of her, it seemed to Rainier. Into the early years of the decade, he had nursed serious political ambitions, which, like his father's, met frustration. Grace figured as an important resource to her brother, who made frequent calls on her for appearances at his fund-raisers and speeches. Two years older than she, he even took to calling himself "Princess Grace's baby brother," which annoyed his sister enough that she made a point of talking about it to a journalist. Still, she loyally turned up as often as she possibly could, even when it meant entirely rearranging her schedule or inconveniencing herself.

Ultimately, Kell's political hopes collapsed in 1975 when Ma not only refused to support him but even told the local Democratic Party potentates that she would oppose her son if he ran. The "old Prussian general," as Kell called Ma, had had enough of politics with J.B.; she knew the effect it could have on a family. Kell's marriage to Mary Freeman was in trouble, and rumors of his affairs were as common as they had been about John Sr. Ma felt she was helping her son by stepping in. (His marriage nonetheless ended in divorce, as had two of Peggy's.)

His political future rather dimmed, Kell stayed active in public affairs, among other ways, by pleading guilty to a drunk driving charge in 1977. In the late seventies he concocted a scheme to bring Philadelphia inner-city dropouts to Monaco on a sort of student program. He explained it to Grace, who dutifully pitched the idea to her husband. Kell even appeared in Monaco with some of his young wards in tow. There had been talk in the Principality of launching a small, open university. Anthony Burgess, among others, strongly favored it, and might have served as a professor of literature. Rainier was interested in the project, but only under the right circumstances—and Kell and his Phillie dropouts, some of them looking scruffy and wearing long hair, weren't his idea of a good idea. He said no.

§　　§　　§

The late seventies brought more than trials for Grace, they brought her sublimations of her actorly impulse which—by their variety, difficulty, and her prowess at them—almost compensated her for her renunciation of her art.

CHAPTER XI

TOWARD SYNTHESIS
1976-82

I'm looking forward to being a grandmother and having lots of beautiful grandchildren . . . I'm looking forward to having more time to myself now that the children are nearly all grown up. I have a passion for new things, new jobs, new ways to enjoy my life with my husband. Believe it or not, I'm actually adventurous.

—Princess Grace (1980)

On the neglected front of artistic self-expression, the years also brought Grace certain pleasures, the pleasures of well-considered, well-accomplished sublimations. These were not the triumph or fulfillment she would have had as an actress, to be sure, but they were not meager and not to be scorned. Within the limits that Grace had set herself, in these final years she achieved success—as an artist, and in other ways, too. She was able to synthesize and resolve some longstanding conflicts in her role as Princess and wife and in her past as actress and celebrity. With Grace one must always pose the question—often asked of those prematurely dead, "What would have happened had she lived?" So much was coming together just at the moment it all accidentally came apart.

Her first artistic success concerned wild flowers—little creatures that she described in words that another might have used to evoke Grace herself: "I love their delicacy, their disarming innocence, and their defiance of life itself."* Hiking in the hills around the Principality, Grace would often lose herself collecting wild flowers but then—too soon, it seemed to her—she would lose the flowers, as they eventually died in their vases. An American, from Philadelphia—Mrs. Henry King—introduced Grace to a wonderful way of keeping her "pick and gather" forever: pressed flowers. She made a convert.

Grace delighted in creating designs with pressed flowers, finding "a

* Princess Grace of Monaco, with Gwen Robyns, *My Book of Flowers* (Doubleday & Company, Inc., 1980), p. 71, and subsequent quotes from pp. 41–47.

deep satisfaction to know that without any formal training, it is possible for everyone to express themselves." Grace made eighty to one hundred pressed flower pictures and wrote about her work lyrically in *My Book of Flowers*, a volume that she co-authored with Gwen Robyns.

Pressed flowers meant Roc Agel. Grace loved this place, even on clear and sunny days—the so-called "Princess Grace weather" that had first so annoyed her with its monotony. But in the mountain retreat she now delighted that she could see up and down the Riviera Coast and out to sea—on a good day, all the way to Corsica. She found the bad weather scenic too, especially the whirling mists that suddenly enclouded the desolate site. Grace loved to laugh about the time that she heard a guest interrupting a phone call to observe, "Just a moment, I must close the window, a cloud has come in."

Roc Agel meant family. Grace did her best work with flowers at Roc Agel because it was a place where the whole family relaxed. Here Rainier tended an orchard and puttered in his toolshed; the children cluttered the insides of the house with tennis rackets, cameras, games, and half-empty boxes of chocolates. It was more like a home than the Palace, or rather, it was a farm, exactly like so many others in the mountains above the coast, with its pigs, chickens, cows, and Sicilian donkeys. In the summer Rainier even brought his beloved zoo creatures to Roc where they roamed—often into the house.

Grace added to the informality by fussing over her flowers in the garden room—an enclosure copied from a Hitchcock residence near San Francisco with three glass walls and a see-through ceiling. There she would work in a "self-made clutter," surrounded by flowers, telephone books, pressing materials, glue, and other paraphernalia. Rainier sometimes complained about the untidiness, but Grace found the casual atmosphere perfect for flower pressing. To her, it was a hobby, not a regal activity, and deserved the kind of casual den she had created.

Grace followed no set methods with her collages and used no prior designs. Indeed, she hardly used any equipment, substituting her fingers for tweezers and old phone books rather than the usual corrugated cardboard to press the flowers. After pressing them for a month, Grace would excitedly lay them out, then sit amid her elements and start to improvise, fitting petals, leaves, and stems in whatever way suited her impulse. She often compared her designs to jigsaw puzzles: "By moving the flowers around, the main shape gradually falls into place," she wrote. Often she would find an appealing design, then leave it sitting a while before re-examining it with fresh eyes. No sighing or sneezing was allowed, she jested.

This casual process produced fine results, and not just artistic. Grace compared the tranquillity she achieved through flower pressing with the effect of needlework, crocheting, or knitting. "No wonder Victorian ladies spent hours making pressed flower albums and pictures," she wrote. Her family claimed the work so absorbed her that she actually talked to herself "like a cat purrs." For her part, she was able to lose herself in the flower work despite the surrounding family helter-skelter. "I am fortunate," she wrote, "to be able to concentrate no matter how much noise is going on." It was, perhaps, a habit that she had developed early, amid the noise of another household.

Despite the fact that she achieved some remarkable designs—all of them signed "GPK"—she never entered them in a contest, though she did exhibit them in Monaco and twice in Paris, where they sold rapidly. Unlike many flower pressers, she never repeated a design, but kept developing new ones of increasing complexity and delicacy. She matched freely and imaginatively with simple, as well as with more complex, flowers, with primroses and periwinkles, lavender and jasmine, daisies and violas (Johnny-jump-ups), forget-me-nots and hydrangeas, Queen Anne's lace and the rare tropical orchid brought her by a visitor from Africa or the East. Many designs were photographed and reprinted in the chapter of *My Book of Flowers* where Grace poured out her love for this offbeat but satisfying form of self-expression. The flower collages there seem like pastels or two-dimensional watercolors: they are delicately beautiful and only apparently without depth.

They fit their maker.

§ § §

Among the scripts that passed over Grace's desk in the seventies, none produced in her the pang of *The Turning Point*. The director of the film, Herb Ross, conceived the idea of casting Grace, but he wisely approached her through her old agent and friend, Jay Kanter, now an executive with Ladd Productions. Kanter privately doubted seriously that his ex-client would accept any offer, but he knew how much it pleased Grace to receive scripts and remain in small ways part of the "business," so he told Ross he'd send it on to the Palace. The screenplay told the story of two women, one an aging ballet star who finds it hard to cope with her fading glamour, the other a former dancer who might have been a star, but who chose instead the domestic route of having a family. Riveted by both topics, Grace devoured the script, then almost wept, not for the story, but for Ross's remarkable offer: Grace could play *either* lead, but wouldn't she please consider making *The Turning Point her* turning point by making a comeback?

Moved, and terribly flattered, Grace nonetheless told Kanter what he had figured she would. She could not even consider a return to feature film acting, she said, but please convey to Ross her gratitude and very best wishes. When Grace later learned that the parts had gone to Anne Bancroft and Shirley MacLaine, she was proud. Going on forty-seven, two decades away from the soundstages, she was still regarded as having "sex appeal" at the box office. She sighed a few times over it and confided to her sympathetic husband at least *thrice* that it would have been fun.

Not long after, Grace got a cable from Jean Dalrymple, her old friend from the New York theatrical world who had tried so hard to get her the part of Roxane in the 1953 production of *Cyrano de Bergerac.* The two had stayed in loose touch over the years, and Grace trusted her. The cable spoke vaguely of a film project. Thoughtfully, Jean had prepaid a return cable in which Grace would say if she wished Jean to call her to explain things. Grace was too excited to go through this rigmarole. She got on the horn and plied Dalrymple for details. This was what her old friend had to say.†

An American real estate financier and enthusiastic breeder of racing horses named Earle Mack had developed an improbable case of balletomania. A man of means and dreams, Mack dashed off in 1975 on a ballet tour of the Soviet Union, where he had been particularly impressed with the world-famous Vaganova Institute. Standing in baroque Russian glory on St. Petersburg's old Theatre Street, this institution (formerly the School of the Russian Imperial Ballet) had given the world most of its greatest classical dancers. As he admiringly studied the committed and hardworking students and staff, it seemed to Mack that they cried out to be memorialized on film—specifically, in a documentary that he would produce. Incredibly, Mack's thought wasn't the pipe dream it ought to have been, given the previous inaccessibility of the U.S.S.R. to American filmmakers. When he approached the relevant office of the Ministry of Culture that dealt with such requests, Mack encountered several key apparatchiks who were sympathetic to Westerners. They told him that if he could assemble a strong production team, he was welcome to film a documentary about the Vaganova. But he should act with dispatch; one couldn't trust this temporary thaw, and possibly very soon the hole in the ice would freeze over.

Nothing if not quick to take advantage of an opportunity, Mack overnight assembled a lean, tough team of professionals—including the noted ballet artistic director, Oleg Briansky, a fine young Austrian film director, Robert Dornhelm, and Jean Dalrymple as his associate producer. They had dashed into the Soviet Union with a small camera team and had, in two incredible weeks of working fifteen hours a day, got most of the footage they needed. A later trip, virtually a fly-by-night thriller, took place just as the "hole" was indeed starting to freeze

† Details come from interview with author, November 15, 1983.

over. Eventually, Mack's sympathizers in the Ministry of Culture lost their battle with the hard-liners, but Mack completed his work in time. Carting their treasure back to the United States, the directors had edited the footage into a ninety-minute documentary of inestimable value: not again in many years, if ever, would the Vaganova be opened up to Americans. In short, this remarkable cake was now baked and needed only the icing before it could be offered to the public.

Would Grace like to narrate *The Children of Theatre Street*, Dalrymple asked? If she did not, they were intending to ask Dame Margot Fonteyn.

Forget Fonteyn; Grace would do it. With incredibly uncharacteristic impulsiveness, after just the briefest discussion with Rainier, the Princess shot off her provisional acceptance of an offer that would put her back in commercial films for the first time since *High Society*. Dalrymple was pleased, but a little surprised. Grace, in listening to Dalrymple, had realized quickly that here was the perfect concoction—a movie about one of Monaco's greatest traditions, ballet, where Grace would be herself. Obviously the project was reminiscent of those old TV features about the Principality which Grace had worked on, but altogether grander, longer, and artistically far more interesting.

Grace was so enthusiastic that she invited Mack to lunch on the Avenue Foch at his very earliest convenience and asked Rainier to come up to meet him. Though it was a chilly October day, Grace walked out beyond her front garden to greet Mack and say how "happy" she was to meet him.‡ She couldn't wait to hear about the film. The producer explained that this was a very low budget ($500,000) documentary with himself as sole investor. Grace couldn't be spared much of a fee, therefore—a few thousand dollars—but he offered her a small percentage of the gross. He realized that these amounted to small remuneration for a star of her caliber, but—

That was fine, Grace assured him before he could finish his formulaic regret. She wasn't concerned with money (the fee and percentage were turned over to Besobrasova for the Academy); indeed she had no conditions, not even script approval. Her only concern was fitting this project into her other obligations, especially to her family, she added. She very badly wanted to do this film.

Grace very much liked the monologue by Beth Gutcheon, which included this lovely description of the Vaganova students "reaching through the difficult to achieve the beautiful." Then she made her first tentative suggestion, based on a wish to please and placate her subjects. Since Monaco's link with Russian ballet was direct and renowned—the Ballets Russes de Monte Carlo had been filled with Imperial Ballet

‡ Details come from interview with Mack, November 8, 1983.

School products—would Mack and the others mind, Grace inquired, if a preface about the Principality were added to the film? Strictly speaking, the documentary's thematic unity was slightly compromised by the short proem that Grace worked up with Beth Gutcheon. Monaco's link with the Russian school was strong, but no more pressing than Balanchine's, yet the New York City Ballet wasn't a subject of the film (nor was American Ballet Theatre, which had its share of Vaganova alumni, including Makarova and Baryshnikov). Nevertheless, the Princess had by then so charmed the filmmakers that they accepted her small request without demur; some, indeed, thought it a good idea.

Finally, Grace had one small editorial suggestion; she objected to a line of text: "Leningrad used to be the Venice of the north and now it is the Venice of nowhere." That was gratuitous and provocative to the Soviets, she said, adding that she had understood this was not to be in any sense a political film. The producers agreed; the line was deleted. In the event, the Russians banned the film anyway—for a reference to the three Vaganova stars who defected to America: Nureyev, Baryshnikov, and Makarova.

The work began. A camera team came to Monaco to shoot Grace on the stage of the Monte Carlo Opera and in an open boat in the harbor. They had all wondered if Grace would be nervous in her first appearance before a movie camera in a generation. They got their answer: she was not, not in the least. Rather, her cooperation flowed in direct proportion to her excitement at being "back." Shooting and dubbing were accomplished in under a week. Grace developed a close affection for Robert Dornhelm, the boyish and gifted thirty-year-old director of the film, who became utterly devoted to her and, in the opinion of some of his colleagues, enamored of her. Grace and he spent some of their free time together, going around Paris to museums, talking incessantly. Grace's feelings for Dornhelm were, in Dalrymple and Mack's opinion, those of a proud older sister. She felt that he had great talent and deserved more attention than he was getting. She hoped to help him; in the meantime, she invited him to come to Monaco to do a film for her Garden Club.*

If not as close to Grace as Dornhelm, Earle Mack certainly won his narrator's confidence enough to be invited occasionally to the Avenue Foch. There, he soon sensed the great tension in his star-narrator's life caused by the problem of Caroline. Mack came to know the girl slightly and liked and admired what he saw in her. Soon Grace spoke

---

* Dornhelm stayed in occasional touch with Dalrymple after the film was finished. He excitedly reported to her his work for Grace in Monaco. When the Princess died, Dornhelm was so distraught that he dropped entirely out of touch with anyone connected with *The Children of Theatre Street*. Interview with Jean Dalrymple, November 15, 1983.

openly to him of the heartache her daughter's infatuation with Junot was causing her. Mack advised her to try to pull back from her own intense involvement with the situation, but he realized it would take Grace a long time to do that.

The other great tension Mack (and his colleagues) felt in Grace was her frustration as a film artist. Her eagerness and excitement about the project at hand were far out of proportion to the difficulty or interest of a narrator's part in a documentary, however sensitive the monologue or fascinating the subject. Not knowing Grace well, Mack wasn't sure precisely what *The Children of Theatre Street* signified to her. At times, he thought it might be Grace's "halfway point" on her journey back to features; at other moments, he believed that "benign" narrator roles constituted a sort of private "game she played with herself—pretending to keep the door open to a return, even though she understood she wouldn't actually step through it."

The documentary proved to be a hit. Grace herself drew mixed, if passing, mentions from critics concentrating on the subject of the film, not the narrator, whom they nearly always referred to as "Grace Kelly" (or, in one instance, "Kelley"). Some thought that she got the "proper hint of poetry in her voice," while others felt she was "curiously wan" or "curiously flat." Grace's presence in fact lent the project a further cubit of class as well as wider box office appeal. The opening shot of her in the Monte Carlo Opera shows a middle-aged princess against a baroque background, hands clasped matronly together, speaking in somewhat stilted English about her realm's balletic grandeur. But this inauspicious tableau fades suddenly and is replaced by a shot of Grace on the Bay of Monaco, the wind blowing her hair back, speaking with animation about the dance. Grace Kelly never looked more beautiful and rarely spoke this warmly. The contrast of the two Graces could not have been greater, for all that it was probably unintentional on the director's part.

Grace's major accomplishment in the subsequent ninety minutes of narrative (she is not on camera again) is to keep the uninitiated viewer interested in what is, finally, a balletomane's film. Off camera, Grace's accent doesn't seem so anglicized; her voice is steady, melodious, soothing, and sometimes poetical. The film won an Academy Award nomination for Best Documentary, and Grace herself won an Award of Excellence from the Film Advisory Board. (Grace used her clout to get *The Children of Theatre Street* into the Cannes Film Festival after the deadline.)

Commercially, the film took years to make back its money, despite the fact that its dissemination was very extensive, in movie houses and on television all over the world. Grace happily did promotional tours for the documentary in Los Angeles, New York, and in various Euro-

pean capitals; the trips especially pleased her by bringing her in touch
with the people now running the movie industry. But the fee scale for
documentaries is a fraction of that for features. It wouldn't be until
eighteen months after Grace's death that her beloved Académie would
get its first income from the percentage points that Grace assigned to
Besobrasova.

Grace's only sharp disappointment with *Children of Theatre Street* concerned the French version of the film. She had fretted and prepared
carefully and done a narration entirely in her adopted tongue—in
which, by now, she was entirely fluent, but still slightly accented. She
even consented to Dornhelm's suggestion that they shoot a new preface with Grace standing on the roof of the Paris Opera (a scary experience for her), speaking a line about French ballet history, with nothing
on Monaco. Despite these concessions to Gallic pride, however, *Les
Enfants de la Rue du Théâtre* was never shown in France. French distrib-
utors offered an insulting, miserly sum. It was the only offer, out of
dozens and dozens around the world, that Mack turned down (with
Grace's full accord).

In the United States, the documentary set off a spate of speculation
that "Grace Kelly would soon be back on the silver screen," as *Variety*
hyped it. Grace gave an interview to Judy Klemsrud of the New York
Times to issue an explicit denial of any such intentions (the headline of
the subsequent article: "Princess Grace Makes a Movie—But It's No
Comeback").† What emerges clearly from the interview was Grace's
slight exasperation that her former countrymen so steadfastly refused
to understand that "Grace Kelly" was long, *long* gone. The "return"
that everyone—even friends like Earle Mack—prattled and wondered
about endlessly hadn't been a remote possibility for years. "I made a
decision long ago," Grace told Klemsrud, "a decision I had to make."
Then she said, "There is too much to look forward to, and we can't
dwell on the past."

In sum Grace enjoyed doing *The Children of Theatre Street* fully as
much as she thought she would from the moment she heard about the
project. Neither a "turning" nor a "halfway" point of some mythical
return, there is no reason to construe her work on the film as an elaborate "game" with herself. Grace knew herself and her world too well to
get away with games of that sort. She leaped to do the documentary
because it was fun, worthwhile, and possible. Period.

Grace's fondness for movies was never limited to acting and film
artistry. Particularly after 1962, and the exclusion of acting as a possi-

† December 18, 1977.

bility for her, she broadened her interests to all sides of the business. In mid-1976, she got the chance to do this in earnest.

In the spring of 1976, a vacancy occurred on the ten-*man* board of Twentieth Century-Fox. Given the spirit of the times, the members figured they'd better elect a woman to join them. One of the members, Alan Ladd, Jr., mentioned this to his colleague Jay Kanter, who suggested Grace. Ladd thought that a terrific idea: in Grace's election, they could kill two birds with one stone, for she had been an actress, and the board needed artists as well as women to provide some color in their unbroken rank of corporate gray. But would she do it, he asked Kanter; the job, after all, entailed three to six annual meetings and a good bit of preparation. Kanter said he would find out.

Soon after, he called his old client and said, "Well, since you won't take a part in one of Fox's movies *[The Turning Point]*, they figure the only way to get you is with an offer to sit on the company's board. How about it?"‡ Grace was both very surprised and very flattered. Until now, only charities in need of money or organizations crusading for causes had shown any interest in her. Certainly no profit-making corporation had ever asked her to enter their elite circle of governors. But though she felt like blurting out "yes" on the spot, Grace said she'd better think about it and talk it over with Rainier. In a fortnight, she called Jay to say she'd be "delighted" to accept. It is not likely that Grace or anyone else on the Fox board savored the irony of a situation that saw this apostle of female traditionalism attain one of her most exciting and preferred activities thanks to a doctrine she was opposed to: "affirmative action."

The reality was that Grace was a token, but she did not act like one: having surprised Grace, the Fox board was now surprised *by* Grace. She might almost have been called a "model" member—as she certainly was for her indefatigability and preparation—but Grace was a tad too "interventionist" and unpredictable to really qualify for that title. She demonstrated a real skill for what was euphemistically termed "balancing artistic innovation with corporate responsibility," or, freely translated, increasing profits while decreasing the amount of schlock turned out. According to board chairman, Dennis Stanfill, Grace was "anything but a rubber stamp."* Having poured over the material sent her, she came to meetings better prepared than many members and didn't hesitate to speak out. On at least one occasion, she challenged the reputation of a highly touted director who was having terrible problems bringing in his film on budget and on deadline. As a rule, board members hesitated to criticize specific films and projects,

‡ Interview with author, December 2, 1983.
* Interview with author, November 23, 1983.

but Grace never did, and in this instance, her judgment turned out right: the company lost money on that movie. Grace made frequent use of the Fox screening room in Paris to keep up with American movies, and when she came to board meetings, she plumped for her values—less sex and violence, more intelligence and wholesomeness—and no one was in doubt about which films she liked and which she didn't. One of her favorites was, of course, *The Turning Point*, which was released at nearly the same time as Grace hosted a meeting of the Fox board in Monaco. She gave the movie all the push she could. In her four years among the Ten (Grace left the board when the studio was sold in 1980), Grace became, in Stanfill's opinion, "one of the most respected members of the board." Grace herself simply confided to Kanter that she "loved being in the business, even if it's not in front of the camera."

Grace loved poetry. Her friendship with the clothes designer Vera Maxwell arose out of a shared fondness for Shakespeare's sonnets, which they often recited to one another when they were together. Grace also read poems with Fleur Cowles and, in French, with Jacqueline Ardant, and when her children were young, she read them verse. Thus, it was surprising to no one but the man who called to ask her that Grace agreed to read publicly for the first time at the Edinburgh Festival of 1976.

John Carroll, in addition to being every bit the nephew of Margaret Rutherford, was a distinguished impresario of poetry readings. In his long years at his honorable trade, he had directed Sybil Thorndike, Flora Robson, Edith Evans, Vivien Merchant, Judy Dench, Michael Williams, and Laurence Olivier, to name only a few. An excitable, loquacious, slightly deaf, slightly addlepated, profoundly endearing little man, Carroll couldn't believe that Grace of Monaco would be free to read at the renowned Edinburgh Festival, but he was somewhat desperate. The theme of that bicentennial year was the "American Heritage," and John didn't know many Americans. He had listened to clips of Grace's voice in the BBC file and found that "she has a *very* slight American accent" (this said in earnest; Carroll did not truck with ironies of any sort).†

Grace invited Carroll to lunch in Paris where he recounted, with wonderful excitement, the challenge and joy of poetry reading. When he paused for breath, Grace said she would be *delighted*. The director then threw himself into assembling the right collage for her. It was a small voice, "a speaking voice—not one of your stentorian Shakespearean voices." The room and the audience could not be large; the

† Interview with author, September 9, 1983.

poems must suit the voice and its owner. When they arrived in Edinburgh in the fall of 1976, Carroll had a chance to rehearse Grace—"She took direction like a duck, unlike that batty old dowager, Edith Evans." The problem for actors with poetry recitation is that it isn't acting, it's reading. The poems, not the readers, are central. If the reader acts, he hams it up. "The single most important key to good poetry reading is restraint," said Carroll.

For Grace, John had selected a long selection from *Wild Peaches*, by the American poet Elinor Wylie. As Wylie was a Southerner, Carroll cautiously suggested that a slight drawl was in order, but *nothing heavy*. Grace worked at it; the poem was of lush verse, and she had a hard time to get color and emotion in her voice, as well as the right accent. She wasn't helped any by the knowledge that her co-readers were eminent: Richard Pasco of the Royal Shakespeare Company and Richard Kiley, the fine American stage actor. "Grace worked hard, but not like most actors, who would read and re-read and re-read it aloud, playing with phrasing, intonation, modulation, and so on. Grace tried principally to get an intellectual grip on the poem itself." Carroll, meanwhile, made certain the lovely St. Cecilia's Hall in Edinburgh was available, for it was a cosy eighteenth-century chamber and wouldn't permit an audience of more than two hundred.

The result was a great success. To be sure, Grace's particular celebrity played a role in the enormous draw—long box office lines for all four performances; the producer of the Festival said he could have sold tickets for two weeks. But brute fame wouldn't have garnered her the warm reception she got from poetry lovers or critics. The BBC was prompted by the praise to replay her rendition of *Wild Peaches* on New Year's Eve as one of the "poetry highlights" of the preceding year. But then if anyone had restraint down cold, it was Grace.

As in so many of her artistic activities, the one who enjoyed it most was the performer herself. But after Edinburgh, Grace really glowed. Despite John's instruction that the requirement of good poetry reading was *not* to act, this performance of *Wild Peaches* was the closest Grace had actually come to her beloved stage acting since Elitch Gardens in the summer of 1952. She awaited the reviews, praying they be good and was delighted when they were. A year or so later, when Thomas Quinn Curtis gave another poetry reading a rave in the *International Herald Tribune*, she wrote with relief to her old acting chum Natalie Core O'Hare, "I'd have just crawled into a hole and died if they hadn't liked me."‡

Grace immediately agreed when Carroll proposed a Shakespeare reading at Stratford-upon-Avon in the summer of 1977. On a balmy

‡ Interview with author, June 1, 1983.

midsummer night in Holy Trinity Church, with the Bard placated in his tomb for this disturbance (Grace had brought a red rose for "dear William"), Grace joined Richard Pasco and John Westbrook (he, too, of the Royal Shakespeare) to read from *Twelfth Night* and other selections —including one of her own favorite sonnets, "Let me not to the marriage of true minds admit impediments . . ." By now, Grace was learning, at Carroll's direction, how to take better care of her "instrument," as poetry readers (and singers) call their voices. Knowing that the night was long and the poetry *very* demanding, she husbanded her energy, planning in advance when to lean hard on her voice, and when not.

Word of these doings reached the United States. The American International Poetry Forum invited Grace to read in Pittsburgh, asking that she simply repeat her selection from Edinburgh. John Carroll, however, would be damned if he would let "you take coals to Newcastle." He set about creating a new collection that would deal with some of Grace's favorite poems on three of her favorite topics: birds, beasts, and flowers, with selections from Whitman, D. H. Lawrence, Tennyson, Robinson Jeffers, Shelley, and many others. These included a favorite of Grace's by Blake ("To see a world in a grain of sand/And a heaven in a wild flower . . ."), and one by Hopkins that Grace came to care for very much, "Glory be to God for dappled things . . ."[*]

American audiences appreciated Grace less as the refined leader of poetry that she had become than as "our own Grace Kelly" returned to "acting" in a new guise. In fairness to spectators, the American presentation of "Princess Grace" took on a starchy formality—the "picture-postcard princess"—that, curiously, had been absent in presumably more tradition-conscious Europe. As Grace had control over how she was exhibited, the blame was hers; on the other hand, she may have recognized at the start that audiences were usually there to gawk, and this would have made her nervous and sent her reaching for her mask. The 1978 tour took her around the East Coast and to Minneapolis, often to houses that the fastidious and knowledgeable Carroll felt were far too large for her voice, and before listeners who, in their large majority, hadn't been to a poetry reading in their lives and probably wouldn't go again. (Grace's brother Kell arrived late at his front row seat in a Philadelphia theater, then proceeded to chat in stage whispers with his date through the readings.) Mel Gussow wrote in the New York *Times* that Grace "clearly upstaged her own performance," but whose fault was that? His generally favorable review unintentionally

---

[*] After Grace's death, Carroll published a popular, splendidly illustrated edition of *Birds, Beasts, and Flowers* (Exeter: Webb & Bower, 1983), with a frontispiece of one of "GPK's" pressed flower collages. The book did very well in England and wants for an American edition.

epitomized the problem with the American attitude that wouldn't let Grace be other than Grace Kelly. Wrote the good newspaper critic, "The evening will probably not bring back poetry as a popular platform art, although it certainly does lend it glamour. But perhaps it will encourage Princess Grace to attempt a real performance."

English audiences were more appreciative and not because their artistic standards were lower. In the fall of 1978, Grace presented a shorter version of "Birds, Beasts, and Flowers" for the Queen Mother at St. James's Palace. This was the first unpaid reading Grace did—on behalf of one of the Queen Mum's personal charities (the Family Service Units, an organization that looked after broken families).

Grace's technical proficiency was improving steadily. From her good, but tentative early readings, she was now confident in a wider range of parts. She had also developed an excellent working relationship with her co-reader, John Westbrook. An old pro at this, Westbrook had privately wondered how "a romantic leading lady like Grace had been would do at serious poetry reading. The difference between reading and [the acting roles she was used to] was great—like shifting to lieders if you're used to grand opera."† After he saw Grace capture the character of an incipient Irish bag lady in *An Old Woman of the Roads,* Westbrook stopped wondering. "What a fine character actress she would have made. What surprised me most was how intellectual her approach was to [poetry reading]. She would study it like a student." Later, Grace did read romantic leads, often in tandem with Westbrook —e.g., Rosalind and Orlando from *As You Like It;* Perdita and Florizel from *The Winter's Tale.* She didn't engulf or eroticize these roles but "assumed them sweetly, lovingly. She tended to follow my lead. She was one of the most generous colleagues I have worked with onstage, never wrapped up in herself. Whenever I needed moral or technical support during a program, she sensed it and gave it."

In effect, Grace's disabilities as a Broadway stage actress contributed to her success at poetry reading. The small- to medium-range voice with the "slight American accent," the intellectual method of capturing character, the restraint that yet permitted the reader's heart, humor, and personality to shine through, the highbrow subject matter and refined audience, the controlled presentation and historical surroundings—were all "too, too" for Broadway, but just right in Goldsmiths' Hall, City of London or St. James's Palace.

The readings went on—in Aldeburgh, Dublin, and Vienna, where Grace read a short poem in German, followed by her first genuinely funny reading: some verse of Morris Bishop's about Rubens's painting his wife in a see-through coat—a poem that opened, "Artists' wives

† Interview with author, September 9, 1983.

lead such peculiar lives . . ." Grace made another tour to the United States in 1980, reading a new Carroll anthology called "Evocations" that included work by Ogden Nash, Stephen Vincent Benét, Robert Frost, and Edmund Burke. In March of 1981, she read in a charity gala for the Royal Opera House Appeal and afterwards attended a supper at Buckingham Palace given by the patron of the Opera, Prince Charles. The event happened to coincide with Charles's first appearance in public with his fiancée, Lady Diana Spencer, who wore the "famous" strapless evening gown that provoked murmurs from the bored or the moralistic. Sensing the young girl's timidity, Grace went out of her way to put her at ease, an act that Diana never forgot. (In July of 1981, Grace and Prince Albert attended the royal wedding and stayed as a guest of the Queen at Buckingham Palace.)

Returning by car to London from a reading in Chichester in early 1982, Carroll excitedly told Grace about their next invitation—St. George's Chapel, at Windsor Castle. The Windsor Festival was one of England's poshest cultural dos, he began, and the Chapel itself surely one of the most beautiful, with the second choir in the land after King's College Chapel in Cambridge. And, oh, John went on, he had the "perfect setting" in mind for Grace that would blend "in just the right mix": the boys' choir, music by Sir William Walton, poetry of W. H. Auden, and "the proper lighting—nothing garish"—so that when the Princess stood alone by the pulpit, she would have the presence of the Queen herself.

Grace smiled and said it sounded wonderful, but she would have to set aside the time now on her calendar for although it was early in the year, her schedule was already filling to the end of 1982. When was the Festival, she asked? Sunday, the twenty-sixth of September, he replied.

The development of Monaco's attitude to its Princess's new hobby was well expressed in the changes of heart of its Sovereign Prince. At first, Rainier took little note of Grace's reading other than to offer vague encouragement. There were so many things she did that it was impossible to keep up with them all. Then, for a time, he grew annoyed that the readings were getting out of hand, taking Grace away from Paris or Monaco much more than any other commitment. But as the Princess scored success after success with audiences that included royalty, aristocracy, the Presidents of Ireland and Austria, and many representatives from the diplomatic, political, and business elite of four countries, Rainier changed his mind. Monaco had never had an Ambassador like this. This wasn't the old Grace Kelly glamour and celebrity that the Prince, the Princess, and the Principality all knew well, and disliked; this was an entirely new kind of effulgence which Grace accomplished *as Princess* in a context entirely appropriate to her rank and position. After the formal banquet at St. James's, where Grace and Rainier sat with the Queen Mother, the former King and Queen of Greece, and Lord Mountbatten, the Prince took John Carroll aside and thanked him for his loyalty and good service.

The Monégasques, too, and more particularly, the permanent foreign residents of the Principality (who tended to be far less parochial in their outlook and awareness than the native Monégasques) were proud of the acclaim their Princess was winning in her new "role." *The Children of Theatre Street*, though not shown on French television, nevertheless evoked sufficient reactions around Europe and the United States to become talked about in Monaco. So did the exhibitions of Grace's flower collages at the prestigious Galeries Drouant in Paris. Indeed, the turn of the seventies saw the convergence and "ripening" of so many of Grace's patient efforts in Monaco. The Garden Club, the Flower Show and Arrangement Competition, the Ballet Academy and its distinguished director, the Festival of the Arts, the Princess Grace Foundation (fattening off the fees of Grace's works, as well as a widening spectrum of donors) were all emerging into international significance. Even her fondest hope—the refounding of the Ballet de Monte Carlo—might see itself realized, Grace was told by Rainier. The government, particularly the Council and the treasury, were continually impressed with her financial responsibility and success at fund-raising. Maybe a ballet wouldn't turn out to be too much of a drag on the budget.

Grace's final theater of artistic operations was just that—a theater. Monaco had not had a functioning playhouse since before the war. The old Monte Carlo Theater had fallen into such disrepair that plays had to be mounted in the Salle Garnier at the Opera—that is, when they could be fitted in between a full schedule of operas, ballets, and concerts. Realizing his realm needed a theater, and of course fully aware of Grace's interest in such things, Rainier suggested to Grace the idea that a playhouse be included in the new Convention Center that went up in the seventies (on the site of the old theater, which had been razed to the disgruntlement of many to make way for "progress").

Husband and wife pursued the project together. The theater that they created was not a restoration of the old *belle époque* edifice but a modern construction. They worked closely with the architects and decorators; indeed they chose the decor themselves—the varying shades of blue for the carpets and walls, the varieties of light woods and the yellow upholstered seats giving a gilt effect, the Venetian-style lamps. Grace saw to it that the lighting, curtains, and stage machinery were the finest quality. It was widely assumed, as the time for the theater's inauguration drew near, that it would be named for Rainier himself, or for Louis II, his grandfather. In fact, the Prince had quietly requested that the theater bear another name. On December 18, 1981, the Princess Grace Theater opened.

Grace had a personal mission in mind for her theater. This studio board member, narrator, flower presser, knitter, and ex-actress-turned-poetry-reader had thought she might eventually *produce*. If not, perhaps, in name, then by initiative. While the theater was still under construction, Grace was already telling people she hoped to see (among other things) light comedy staged there—maybe, she was thinking, some revivals . . . such as *The Torch-Bearers*, by George Kelly. The truth was, it had pained Grace over the years to watch her uncle's reputation and plays gathering dust in old anthologies. "There's a whole new generation that doesn't know him as well as I wish they did," she told Budd Schulberg in 1977. And to buttress her point, she had quoted the critic H. H. Brown's opinion of Uncle George's *The Show-Off* (1924) "the best comedy yet written by an American." In March of 1982, George Kelly was inducted posthumously into the Theater Hall of Fame, and Grace went to New York to "accept" for her uncle, who was presented by the playwright Robert Anderson. A fine tribute, it was nonetheless a sign of the times that it had taken the American Theater Critics Association a decade to get round to electing George Kelly, whom they had not included in the original ninety-five "theatrical greats" admitted into the Hall of Fame at its inception in 1971. In a small way, the Princess Grace Theater would try to fill this lacuna in the "new generation's" culture.

§   §   §

The early eighties brought Grace American tributes that pleased, embarrassed, and annoyed, for they all focused on Grace Kelly. But Grace of Monaco put on a gracious smile. She accepted stage producer Alex Cohen's invitation to appear at his *Night of 100 Stars* at Radio City Music Hall to raise money for the Actors' Equity fund for a home for retired actors. Along with Elizabeth Taylor, Bette Davis, Lee Strasberg, Tony Randall, Van Johnson, James Cagney, Helen Hayes, and many others, Grace re-became a "star" for an evening, reading some poetry at the opening of the long program.

Six weeks later, it was Philadelphia's turn to appeal to Grace of Monaco for an appearance of Grace Kelly. On the occasion of the City's tricentennial, its "Century IV Commission" wished to honor Grace. Would she please come "home" for "A Tribute to Grace Kelly, Actress"? This genuinely moved and embarrassed Grace all at once, for she truly didn't think her three-and-a-half-year career in films deserved something like this. On the other hand, it *was* a great honor, and from Philadelphia, to boot, so she accepted the invitation, saying she considered it a "lovely tribute to the Kelly family as a whole, not just to myself."

Rainier did not accompany her to this star- and luminary-studded affair that situated his wife in the municipal pantheon somewhere between Benjamin Franklin and Eugene Ormandy. He was pleased for Grace and told her she had no reason not to be proud of the tribute, but personally, he felt once was enough for Rainier III to have to stand, unfranchised and disespoused, in the Philadelphia limelight beside "Grace Kelly, Actress." Grace should definitely have this evening to herself. And she did. But she did not forget Monaco or its Prince. Among the many actors on hand to honor her was Celeste Holm, who asked Grace if she might recount for the audience the story of the famous lunch at M.G.M. where Dore Schary put his foot in his mouth by telling Rainier that Metro's back lot was bigger than his Principality. "Yes, dear," Grace replied, "but will you also say that today Dore is dead and the Metro back lot sold, but the Prince and Monaco are doing just fine?"

The final honor that the United States paid "Grace Kelly, Actress" was presented by ABC. The network announced it was putting in production a movie of the week called "Once Upon a Time Is Now—Grace Kelly's Early Years." One of its producers described the script as "a fairy-tale story." Here Grace drew the line. "I think no one has the right to exploit what I have done—my name and my life and my career —without permission," she told *People* magazine in April of 1982, adding that she had written letters of protest to the network—futile as usual.

In several interviews, Grace tried hard that spring to stop Americans from "pigeonhol[ing] me." She demurred at being spoken of as a "great actress" when she clearly hadn't had the time to develop as a screen artist beyond, in her words, "promising." She called it "very unlikely" she would return to films, protested the suppositions that her life hadn't been fulfilling, and spoke at length about the ways in which it *was*. She noted the things she was doing—her poetry readings ("I would rather do it for people who enjoy poetry"), her work in Monaco, and her life as "a producer in the artistic and cultural fields." Yet she was aware, she told *People*, that the press "doesn't seem to be interested in that side of my life." As for the ABC movie, Grace made three judgments in the course of discussing it that were revealing of the difference between her self-perception and the world's view of her. Her childhood, she said, was "uninteresting" ("except to myself"); the view of her life as a fairy tale was "revolting"; and as a girl, she was "never pretty or cute," she said, when asked about the choice of Cheryl Ladd to portray her in the ABC film. Shortly after, in answer to the question, "And your future, Princess?," she told the writer, R. T. Kahn, "My future, like the past twenty-six years, is entirely devoted to the Principality of Monaco, and to my husband."

At their tenth anniversary, Grace had told her husband the present she wanted most was a "year off for good behavior." At their twentieth, she said she still wanted a year off, but with him and nobody else around.

For their twenty-fifth anniversary, the Grimaldis went to a party at Frank Sinatra's home in Palm Springs, where the singer-host chided the actress-guest about having won a Gold Record before he did (Grace won it for "True Love" from *High Society*). It was a warm, intimate gathering of old friends. Natty O'Hare was charmed by the rapport between Grace and Rainier, except when she was amused at Grace's "mothering of him." Overhearing her scold him, "Now you take off those wet clothes this minute and get into a hot tub," O'Hare thought it might be Albert she was talking to.

And for their final anniversary, Grace and Rainier went to Taiwan, where, among other activities, Grace rebaptized the refurbished steamship *Constitution* which had brought her to Rainier twenty-six years before.

But they were rarely alone and too infrequently together. The demands on their lives were staggering, and Grace continued to spend much of her time on the Avenue Foch while Stephanie went to private school nearby. So Grace created her own circle of friends in Paris, as she had in New York—and again, many of them were older women. Jacqueline Ardant, her retired lady-in-waiting lived in the neighborhood and visited often, as did Aniela (Madame Arthur) Rubinstein. Vera Maxwell flew in occasionally from New York, as did Fleur Cowles from London. Virginia Gallico, the widow of Grace's closest writer-friend, Paul Gallico, was her lady-in-waiting and often accompanied her on trips or spent time on the Avenue Foch. Nadia Lacoste, closer to Grace's age, had a home in Paris as well as Monaco. Over the years she had become a confidante as well as employee. With these people, Grace felt a special rapport that she shared with no one outside her husband and children. "Two kisses aren't enough," she'd say when she greeted Fleur, "let's have a third, and a fourth."‡ "She was emotive without being coy." The approval, security, and affection offered so freely by these older friends may have touched a little girl deep within Grace who had often "clung" to a mother that hadn't always appreciated, or had time for, clingers.

Although the topics they talked about were usually serious in these

‡ Interview with author, May 12, 1983.

years—Caroline, Stephanie, the paparazzi, or this or that outrageous lie in a German or American scandal sheet—the memories of Grace etched the sharpest in their minds were the times of laughter. "I was mischievous. I'd try to get her going," Cowles said. "She would tell funny stories, usually in accents—her Brooklyn Jewish-mama accent was one of her best. We'd all get quite wild with laughter. She had absolute control of her audience and no inhibitions at all. She was the opposite of the glacial princess. In fact she reminded me then of a little girl."

In Monaco, the Prince and Grace counted among their newer friends the fine English writer and musical composer, Anthony Burgess, who had moved to the Principality from Italy in the late seventies, after learning of a kidnapping plot on his young son. This was a somewhat improbable friendship between the decrier of excessive violence and the author of *A Clockwork Orange*, yet it grew because Burgess's violent energy and expansive genius awed and captivated Grace. They also had things in common—from monarchism and Catholicism, through a taste for the writings of Alberto Moravia and for potent cocktails, to a shared ability to move rapidly back and forth from hominess to elegance. On one of her early visits to the Burgess's apartment in the Condamine, the author told Grace that he and his wife slept on the floor. "Excellent idea," she replied, "but don't forget to pick up the mattresses occasionally and air them." When Burgess and his Italian wife went to the Palace, Grace concocted drinks for them "that knocked your head off." Then, while Mrs. Burgess and Rainier spoke Italian (Genovese dialect—though the Prince could also "talk Piedmontese"), Grace and the writer talked about music or literature. She was delighted to find out from him that the last, never-mounted comic opera of Gilbert and Sullivan was a pungently satirical story of a "Prince of Monte Carlo" who tried to wed his "beautiful daughter" to an English prince. The last book Grace read was Burgess's novel *Earthly Powers*, a powerful, but also erudite philosophical novel. Grace worked at it assiduously until she got it. Grace, the author said, was one of the few who "had the wit to recognize that it is a Catholic book about what the French call *'libre arbitre'* [free will]."

§　§　§

An individual's religious convictions (i.e., his actual beliefs, not those he professes to believe) will strongly influence his ability to cope with suffering . . . The individual's actual beliefs are stressed since it is quite one matter to be philosophical about suffering, when one is not

suffering, and quite another to accept and find meaning in this experience when one is feeling its full impact.
                                    —*Joyce Travelbee, Professor of Nursing**

Of course religion does yield high dividends, but only to the man whose resources are within him.
                                                        —Timothy 6:6

Nothing that Grace had was more important to her, nor more definitive of her, than her faith, yet nothing is harder to capture, for in this realm, more than in any other, she kept herself to herself. One can observe her religiousness and take note of her works of charity, but these are, at best, undependable indices of an interior process.

A practicing, even fervent Catholic, Grace was never "churchy"—a fact which the press *never* fathomed about her. Yet, in this, she was simply being the daughter of two independent-minded, not to say freethinking, parents. To say the least, Jack and Margaret Kelly never stood in awe of the Roman Catholic Church's rules or its hierarchy. Meat was generally avoided on Fridays; mass was pretty regularly attended on Sundays, but these and all the other pronouncedly Catholic "outer signs of inner grace" were worn with an affable looseness reminiscent of Pascal's description of his belief in dogma—"in general and from a distance."

When she was "holding forth" and inveighing, Grace could certainly sound *very* Catholic. "I think religious education for children is of the utmost importance," she told a Philadelphia meeting of the International Eucharistic Congress. "It helps them develop and gives a strength that those without it seem to lack. As family traditions break down, children with no religious background or spiritual enrichment are left drifting and confused. Only religion, whatever the faith, can help with the disintegration and uncertainty around us."

On the other hand, Grace eventually came to believe it had been a mistake to send Caroline to the stern nuns at St. Mary's College in Ascot, and she did not force Stephanie into overstrict parochial schools. Although she was strongly opposed to abortion (as are many non-Catholics as well), she disagreed with the Church on birth control. Nor was her attitude on divorce dogmatic, as evidenced by her thinking about Caroline's wedding and her tacit advice to her daughter when the marriage was disintegrating. Grace was capable of going to services at an Anglican church because a Catholic one wasn't available, or of skipping mass altogether if she were exhausted from work and travel and needed to conserve her strength. She mildly scandalized

* *Interpersonal Aspects of Nursing* (Philadelphia: F. A. Davis, 1971).

several "proper" Monégasque women when she casually noted one day, "I do isometrics in church so while I'm doing my soul some good, I'm doing my body some good, too." Grace and Rainier drew close to Father James Boston, the American priest who replaced Francis Tucker as their personal chaplain. In the early sixties, Boston left the cloth to marry *before* being laicized by the Vatican, but the Grimaldis never wavered in their friendship or support. Grace occasionally lunched with Boston and his wife when she was in Washington, D.C., where they lived.

Peter Jacobs was another example where Grace and Rainier planted themselves squarely against what they considered to be an unfair, cruel, and ultimately self-defeating decision of the Roman Catholic hierarchy. The priest, who had become a friend of the Grimaldis at the end of the seventies, opened a restaurant in Manhattan's theater district as a means of raising money for scholarships for students at the Catholic high school at which he taught and counseled. He named it Palatine after the chapel in the Grimaldi Palace. The Archbishop of Washington, D.C., Jacobs's nominal superior, disapproved of the Palatine and ultimately suspended Jacobs from his priestly functions until he gave it up. Clerical involvement in profit-making enterprises, as Grace and Rainier were well aware, was an old and honorable tradition of the Catholic Church. An order of nuns owns and operates a superb restaurant, L'Eau Vive, in the shadow of St. Peter's in Rome. Grace and Rainier wrote letters and made interventions on Jacobs's behalf, to no avail. Typically, Grace then began to worry that in frustration or anger, Jacobs might lose his vocation. She talked to him about it many times and told him she prayed often that he would stay a priest.†

Grace's public charitable activity and the work of her Foundation occupied a large portion of her life. She did biblical narratives on television to raise money for religious causes—notably her friend, Father Patrick Peyton and his Rosary Crusade (whose motto was "The family that prays together stays together"). At one of the busiest times in her life, she got a call from her friend Bill (William F.) Buckley begging her to help him out of a jam by doing a television narrative of a New Testament parable in the Sistine Chapel. Grace agreed to do two (the Prodigal Son and the Good Samaritan). What was far less well-known —because she kept it strictly under wraps—was her private charitable work with individuals and families. In Monaco, these were extensive, as her secretaries, Paul Choisit and Louisette Lévy-Soussan testified, though they felt obliged not to reveal details.‡ Anthony Burgess, who

† Interview with Jacobs, November 18, 1983.
‡ Interviews with author, September 13, 1983.

often went for walks with Grace through the Principality, noted "I observed her concern for the older and poorer Monégasques, all of whom she knew personally."

But her private charitable reach extended beyond Monaco. In the United States, she worked quietly, almost secretly, through people like Father Jacobs. He brought to her attention individual cases—often of young people—who needed varieties of help which Grace provided. From time to time, she brought Jacobs to Monaco to discuss their collaboration. On one of these trips, he became friendly with Caroline who later (1981) worked with Jacobs to set up a telephone hot line for desperate or depressed young people in Monaco—the burnouts of Régine's and the other nightclubs. Caroline herself manned one of the phones for a time.

Turning from practice and "works" to faith, it seemed that Grace, for all her independence of judgment vis-à-vis the clergy, had mystical and spiritual sides which expanded as she grew older. Her first Easter in Monaco, she and the Prince went out into the medieval town before the Palace to watch the Good Friday torchlight procession. Rainier frankly wondered how she would respond to this very Mediterranean-Catholic ceremony, with townspeople fervently impersonating Christ and His followers and persecutors. The procession could become lurid and passionate, and many Americans, even Catholics, would have found it superstitious, almost pagan, and certainly jarring to their religious sensibilities. Not Grace. She surprised her husband with how evidently moved she was—and not as a spectator with "anthropological" interest, but as a believer watching fellow Christians express their faith.

In her own piety, Grace leaned heavily on private prayer, especially as she grew older. She often made novenas and lit candles for various wishes (frequently for Caroline or Stephanie) and was a fervent sayer of the rosary, which she could be found praying by herself in the tiny chapel at Roc Agel or the Palatine Chapel (the Prince's personal chapel) in the Palace. Indeed Grace was a profound devotee of the Virgin, to the point that her intensity "surprised" Father Jacobs who wasn't used to encountering "so traditional and strong a marian faith among people of Grace's position and intellectual ability." As early as the first few years after her marriage, Grace and Rainier (at her request) made a two-day pilgrimage to Lourdes, where Grace attended mass in the Grotto with a crippled Monégasque girl whose fare and expenses she had paid. Later she visited the Shrine of Fatima in Portugal and made other pilgrimages. Grace later became avidly interested in two other saints—the Theresas, of Lisieux and of Avila. She liked to quote lines of the latter's mystical writings, one of her favorites being

"I live and yet I do not live, and yet so high a life I hope that I die and yet I do not die."

In the course of his work with Grace in the years after 1979, Peter Jacobs became not only a close friend but something of a spiritual adviser to the Princess, though he said he felt more like observer or admirer. His feeling was that Grace had a profound and intense, but very "inner" faith. Rainier said the same thing but spoke of it as a development over time: "I think [her faith] became a deeper part of her life than it was in the younger days when she may have turned to it [mainly] as a consolation in time of need."

The effect of Grace's faith was strongest, not surprisingly, on her family. Even more than his wife, Rainier was unenamored of "official" Catholicism and aware of the foibles and prejudices of its hierarchy. But the seriousness of his wife's commitment to the Christian faith eventually moved him, too, and was very possibly what kept the Prince from lapsing into the kind of formal Catholicism so pervasive in Europe among the upper classes who, for social or political reasons, choose not to abandon "religion" altogether. In Anthony Burgess's view, the intellectual side of Rainier, more pronounced as he grew older, might very easily have made him (factually if not nominally) into what in Europe is called a "freethinker"—i.e., an agnostic. The presence of Grace's piety and faith moved Rainier, however. In an interview, after a long pause, he said that "yes," faith was one of the most important factors in helping him to adjust to Grace's death.

In raising her children, Grace stressed religious content over form. They could (and did) miss mass occasionally, but they were not to forget their prayers—which their mother said with them until they got older. It would appear that Grace's emphasis on faith over religion has saved her children for both faith *and* Catholicism—at least through 1983. Albert attended mass regularly while at Amherst and did so by free choice. Caroline, according to the friends of her mother who were particularly close to her, has deep-running Christian faith and remains a practicing Catholic. The fate of her application for an annulment of her marriage to Junot is rooted mainly in her wish to be able one day to marry in the Church and remain a practicing Roman Catholic in good standing.

Finally, faith may perhaps best be measured by the way a person defines, and leads, her life. There is "cheap grace" and "costly grace," wrote the German theologian and martyr, Dietrich Bonhoeffer, and the difference between them is the degree of obedience, of commitment, exacted and offered. Cheap grace is often the grace of sacraments taken routinely, garnished with ceremony, piety, music, and vestments. Sometimes, however, cheap grace can become costly. Few reli-

gious ceremonies were more solemn or beautiful than the mass cele-
brating the marriage of Grace and Rainier in the Cathedral of St.
Nicholas. In the seven years following their wedding, Grace discovered how costly the nuptial grace that Bishop Barthe invoked on them
would be. To her surprise, she found that the price she was paying in
artistic self-suppression to be Rainier's wife was very high and painful;
simultaneously she discovered that the job of Princess was exceptionally difficult and elusive.

So the question arose, as it would for anyone, "Must I, shall I, go on
paying the price of my vows?" Grace answered yes and kept repeating
the answer for the rest of her life. Her life as princess then became an
ongoing "act of submission," to use the apt phrase of her friend William F. Buckley. He continued, "If she had decided to become a nun
rather than a princess, there would not have been a distinctive difference in her approach to her vocation."* In short, after she came to
Monaco—and more especially after the *Marnie* affair gave her her first
real test of faith—Grace came to *define* her life in Christian terms and
then proceed systematically to try to follow the "will of God" as best
she could perceive it.

Submission to one's vows, hence to one's faith, need not, should not
be, blind. One does not agree to be run over; one accepts to run *with*.
Grace certainly looked at it thus. In her life as Rainier's consort, she
submitted—accepting, against her own judgment and taste, his modernization policy for Monaco—yet all the while she worked indefatiga-
bly and creatively to save the Principality's beauty and history. As a
mother, Grace had the hardest time submitting. Through clenched
teeth and fists, she supported Caroline in her trials even though pun-
ishing or rejecting or preaching to her would have been justifiable, and
far more satisfying. But if the daughter was never in doubt of her
mother's love and presence, neither was she in doubt as to her views
and beliefs. Grace was her ally, definitely not her accomplice.

Enduring the hardships of costly grace, Grace eventually found its
joys. Service and submission have their pleasures, too, and their sweet
triumphs. In the last years of her life, Grace began to reap some of the
harvest of her submission. The financial reserves provided by Rainier's
development of Monaco permitted works of charity and culture that
brought great happiness—to no one more than to the woman who
initiated most of them—while the alliance between man and wife
brought its partners a strength and meaning that only years of mutual
respect and concession-making could bring. It wasn't a fairy-tale romance; it was a married life in which love blossomed at its own pace

* Interview with author, November 30, 1983. See also Buckley's obituary, "Princess
Grace, RIP, *National Review*, October 15, 1982.

and toward its own ends. As a parent, moreover, Grace lived to reap one very real joy: Caroline's testing eventually made her a deeper, wiser, and more compassionate person than she might have been if she hadn't married Junot. In the Christian vision, "truth comes wrapped in darkness, wisdom comes *through* the mystery of sin."† *Felix culpa*, the prodigal daughter.

§   §   §

At Amherst College, the blond, handsome student prince of Monaco was still the dream son who gave no one any heartache and many much pleasure. Like his Sigmund Romberg counterpart, Albert was beloved of his schoolmates and known to throw one or two back now and again, but as to complicated or troublesome romantic involvements, he left that to his sisters.

Rainier actively wished that his son's college years be a happy, comparatively relaxed time of sports, fun, friend-making, and "being himself." His father knew what work, worry, and mask-wearing lay in store for the Prince Hereditary, and he was determined that Albert have happier years of youth to look back on than he had had. Thus the boy grazed on a broad range of subjects, including many cultural and "impractical" ones in literature and the fine arts (though he majored in political science), was expected to attain only passing marks, not to perform brilliantly, which in any case would have been out of the question for he hadn't Caroline's scholastic flair.

Rather, the Prince's *spécialité* was his human qualities. He had needed only two months, if that, to make the whole college stop nudging one another when he walked by and saying "Do you know who *that* is?" Now, when they saw him, guys waved and said "Hey Al, how's it going?" Noted an acquaintance Dennis Markell, "It was absolutely uncanny how completely at ease he put people without *seeming* to try, for any effort would have looked phony. He's a genius at making you think he cares about you, and putting you at ease, without a trace of insincerity."‡

He appeared regularly at Father Quigley's Sunday mass, and he held down a baritone's spot in the Amherst Glee Club, where his voice, like his mother's, was pleasant but on the small side. But the sleeper quality that permanently preserved Albert from all taint of goody-goodiness was, as his family could have readily predicted, his wicked sense of humor. Grimaldi's Steve Martin imitations were, going away, the best on campus. And if the muffler on a friend's Fiat broke loose late on a Saturday night when everyone was tired and lethargic, it was Al who

† Martin E. Marty, *A Cry of Absence, Reflections for the Winter of the Heart*, (New York: Harper & Row, 1983), p. 123.
‡ Interview with author, December 4, 1983.

crept under the car and did what he could. He joined a fraternity, Chi Psi (at that time all male; later co-ed), he played varsity soccer, and he lived in a reassuringly messy room. (His mother, despite her taste for her own "self-made clutter" was appalled at Albert's untidiness.) Beyond having a private telephone whose number was not given out by the college switchboard, he endured no special security measures and, at isolated Amherst, didn't seem to require any, not even for protection from the "Smithies," one of whom he was rather keen on.

In the summer of 1979, the Glee Club made a tour of Europe and was invited to give an evening concert in the Cathedral of St. Nicholas in Monaco. Then, Al's confreres got a lucid glimpse of the "other" side of their buddy's life. None was surprised, yet all remarked, at how easily Albert assumed the demeanor and accepted the protocol of his rank. Markell again: "he was as popular there as he was at school."

Before his beaming parents, Albert graduated from Amherst in the spring of 1981, then served in the French Navy, after which he spent a year learning finance as an intern at Morgan Guaranty Trust in New York. The decision that he rather than his father would accompany Grace to the marriage of Prince Charles and Lady Diana was largely Rainier's. His son was twenty-three; it was time he began to assume some of the obligations and taste some of the perquisites of rule. The wedding, moreover, was a good place to start because Albert would be meeting people nearer his own age among the friends of the bride and groom.

Grace strongly supported her husband's intention to abdicate one day in the not-distant future. Neither wanted to see their son put through the dual trauma of simultaneously losing a father and ascending the throne. Rainier wanted to be on hand to advise Albert in his early years as Prince Sovereign. But the time of rule was not yet at hand. "Al" still had a while yet to live.

His slight stutter continued—the only sign that maybe *some* repression or inner tension were buried here and might lead to consequences further down the road.

Although the scandal press had Caroline involved romantically with every conceivable (and a few inconceivable) partners, and although Caroline was certainly not living a nun's life in the post-Junot years, she was no longer a headache or a heartache to her parents. Quite the contrary, Caroline was a changed person for the better. It could be said that divorce, not marriage, made her not only a woman, but a valued helpmeet to her parents in the work of Monaco. Meanwhile she waited for the Vatican to process her annulment request. What small margin of sympathy, if not honor, that accrued to Junot's account by the sincerity of his pain on getting word of the separation was lost when he challenged the annulment with the vindictive absurdity that "according to my religious beliefs, one cannot look upon marriage as something you undertake very lightly."

The press did not leave Caroline (or her siblings) alone, though they wrote about her selectively, ignoring her good work, such as the establishment of the hot line for Monégasque youth, and focusing on her dates. The German scandal sheets got so gross in their distortions about all three children that Grace let fly with an indictment of the entire nation ("a horrible country"). This outburst was reported with sanctimonious hypocrisy by the London press, which regularly dealt in more than its fair share of Grimaldi speculation.

Having a [teenage] daughter is like riding a young horse over an unknown steeplechase course. You don't know when to pull up the reins, when to let the horse have its head—or what.

—*Princess Grace*

With Albert and Caroline off to the races, so to speak, there nevertheless remained a "steeplechase" for Grace to run: Stephanie. Thankfully, the psychodynamics between Grace and her youngest were far simpler and less fraught than those between Grace and Caroline. Perhaps because the two were so dissimilar, Grace's example didn't saddle this daughter like an incubus, nor did Stephanie create a phantasm out of her mother. Where Caroline had gone through a tortured and tortuous rivalry with her mother, Stephanie proved merely obstreperous, a royal pain-in-the-ass.

But, dear God, a lovable one. In some ways, the youngest child was her mother's pet and shadow, or as Stephanie herself put it in a gracefully balanced flourish, "As I was always very close to my mother, so was I also very near to her." On the one hand, Grace adored this constancy and devotion, but on the other—wiser from her experience with Caroline—she took greater pains not to fuss over Stephanie as she had her sister. This was made easy by the fact that Grace was physically absent from the Avenue Foch residence a great deal more often than she had been in the early years of living there. In short, the younger daughter had it a lot easier—as her siblings kept reminding her. More TV, later curfews, louder stereo, and less nagging—even in her "punk" period of dressing. When she hated the ultrastrict Catholic school in the suburbs, Grace put her in a more liberal Catholic one in town, and when she refused to go back even to that, Grace enrolled her in a secular private school (Charles-de-Foucauld) in nearby Neuilly.

Sometimes Grace didn't give way, but then neither did Stephanie. She was not, she informed everyone loftily, going to wear a dress at the ball before her sister's wedding because she was "wearing slacks these days." Grace forbade her to attend the ball unless she did, so she didn't come at all but watched the event from various cubbyholes and aeries that only a thirteen-year-old in a large palace would know about.

Grace's worry about Stephanie was nevertheless *not* her daughter's willfulness or occasional temper. It was her emotional immaturity. This rendered her endearingly affectionate, to be sure, but it also made her terribly vulnerable on the romantic front—no less than Caroline had been, if for different reasons. And indeed, the "problem of Stephanie" came into existence in October of 1981 at a posh private club called the Elysées-Matignon. Sixteen going on seventeen, Stephanie met Paul Belmondo, seventeen going on eighteen, the handsome, athletic son of France's most famous movie star. And within a few months she was in love as only Stephanie could be: compulsively, hopelessly, inseparably.

It was no replay of the Junot affair, though not from Stephanie's lack of aspiration or effort. Rather, Paul was too firmly planted with his feet on the ground (or in a racing car) to give any consideration to marriage at an early age. A well-brought up, polite, and charming young man, the Grimaldis liked him from the start and never stopped liking him. It was Stephanie, and her mad obsession with Paul, that they worried about. She couldn't just be a girl with a boyfriend and go about her life; she devoted herself to it with something approaching the single-mindedness of an *Adèle H.* Stephanie eked her way through high school and graduated in the spring of 1982, but it took a ton of moral support and imposed discipline from her mother for her to concentrate on studying for the state-administered examinations for her baccalaureate.

Stephanie pulled out her bac, but she had no interest in college. Paul failed his, but in his dedication to racing, he was disciplined and hardworking, and this argued for his seriousness in Grace and Rainier's eyes. The Grimaldis now hewed steadfastly to their determination that Stephanie had to do *something* besides date Paul. God only knew, she might wear down her boyfriend's reserves of common sense and elope with him. She had early shown a flair for clothes design; she created her own gown for the 1980 Red Cross Gala, and it had so impressed Marc Bohan, the head designer at Dior, that he invited her to apprentice at Dior. This, Stephanie *thought* she *might* do. After all, it would mean she lived in Paris—near Paul.

Through the summer of 1982, Grace worried about her lovesick daughter. She insisted that Stephanie live in Monaco (or Roc Agel) with the family, which the girl reluctantly did, but the two of them argued often and violently. As Grace had to have asked herself, was a daughter of hers once again headed, in a boat with another, for an emotional Niagara Falls, all because Grace had overprotected her as a child? To be sure, the "extra" psychological scaffolding of the Caroline-Grace rivalry was missing, but that fearsome vulnerability abided . . .

§   §   §

That summer was knocked out of sync (or catawampus, as Rainier might have said) by the load of work that pushed vacation into August, usually a Roc Agel month. Grace and Rainier had taken a wonderful cruise by themselves to Norway. It wasn't the year alone with her husband that Grace wanted, but it beat commuting from Paris on the weekends, and it was a promise of things to come, she hoped. Now, in September, there was the upcoming Windsor Festival to plan for ("The program arrived safely, and I *love* it," she wrote John Carroll), and then a trip to the States. There was the board meeting of the Red Cross and a charity gala in Paris; Peter Jacobs had written that he needed to talk to her about several difficult cases; and the Garden Club needed—

But her mind was on Stephanie. The two of them were leaving for Paris on the night of the thirteenth, on the *train bleu*. This would be a crucial test of an autumn. The girl must buckle down to other things than just Paul, whether it be the apprenticeship at Dior or admission to the Paris School of Design. She must not push herself and that nice young man into emotional disaster.

Grace was no driver and didn't care if she wasn't. Before she was married, she had told a reporter that if she ever had money, she would get a chauffeur before any other luxury. Now she had one, but sometimes she still found herself behind the wheel. As, for example, this Monday morning, the thirteenth of September. Grace had laid out some of her dresses on the back seat of her Rover 3500, so there was no room for three people. The chauffeur remained at Roc Agel with Albert and Rainier. Grace would drive. The kids joked that when "Mom" drove down from Roc Agel, they could run ahead on foot and be there before her. To which she would smile and admit she drove slowly, but she got there.

There was one safety convention Grace flouted, however: seat belts. She felt uneasy, claustrophobic in them, she told Phyllis Blum Earl every time her ex-secretary would nag her to wear them.

Grace and Stephanie left Roc Agel around 9:30 A.M., waving at the guard at the little station on the edge of their property, then driving the winding County Highway 53 they knew so well. Around a quarter to ten, the car passed the intersection of 53 and the main route from Menton; the French policeman usually on duty there recognized the car, with Grace at the wheel. The Rover now pulled onto the Moyenne Corniche, with its sharp hairpin curves, all of which had barriers as a precaution to keep careless drivers from careening over the mountain side. The one turn that did not have a barrier was the last. Grace would not have been driving faster than twenty-five or thirty miles per hour at the maximum as she traveled the last five miles toward home. The Palace indeed was already visible in the distance.

In his truck, the French teamster Yves Raimondo was following the Rover. He saw it take the first two of the final three turns normally, slowing down to a crawl for the curve, then picking up speed on the straightaway. Suddenly, however, about two hundred yards before the final curve—the one without the barrier—Raimondo saw the Rover begin to zigzag, to the point of sideswiping the mountain itself on the left. Later he would say it looked as if the driver had lapsed in her attention to the road. He sounded his horn and the car ahead straightened in its course, but then Raimondo saw that it wasn't turning to make the curve. It wasn't even braking. With surprise and horror, he watched it drive straight off the road, onto the bank, and off the side.

The Rover fell approximately 110 feet down a steep slope covered with small trees and shrubbery, through which the car plowed a path, coming to rest, more or less right side up, at the edge of a garden. The garden belonged to a man who worked in the Principality for the S.B.M. This man, who wishes to remain unnamed, was the second to arrive on the scene; his wife had preceded him by a half-minute or so. We shall call them Mr. and Mrs. P. Another man, Monsieur Pierre, who was nearby supervising construction on a home he was having built, arrived third. Sesto Lequio, the owner of the home rented by the P's arrived fourth. When Mr. P arrived, Stephanie had already been helped out of the car by Mrs. P and was sobbing hysterically in her arms, yelling "Get my mother out of there!"

Lequio would later tell some reporters—notably from the scandal press—that he arrived first and that the Rover's engine was in flames, which he doused with the aid of a hand extinguisher from his truck just in time to spare Stephanie a hideous fate. The P's and Pierre saw no flames, merely steam from the radiator, which Lequio, when he arrived, indeed doused.

Stephanie soon identified herself to the P's just as they realized for themselves who she was. Several other people had by now arrived. Mr. P telephoned the Palace, which in turn notified the French authorities, called for an ambulance and galvanized the staff at the Princess Grace Hospital. In fact two ambulances arrived from the Principality, and their attendants were able, with some effort, to extract Grace from the rear seat of the Rover, where she had been thrown in the accident. She was completely unconscious, with bruises, a wound on her scalp, and an obviously broken right leg.

Slightly less than half an hour after the accident, Grace arrived at the hospital named for her. Her husband and son arrived there from Roc Agel before the ambulance. Caroline was in London and returned that evening. Unable to see Grace immediately, they visited Stephanie who, though in great pain in her back, wept uncontrollably, repeating to her father, "Oh, Mommy panicked. She didn't know what to do. She lost control." In a broken, incomplete narrative, Stephanie also indicated she herself had tried to grab hold of the emergency brake, but couldn't.

It was clear to any medically informed personnel who had access to Grace that she was severely injured. Her deep unconsciousness, pallor, her difficulty in breathing, and unresponsiveness to all external stimuli indicated major internal trauma. In his examination of the Princess, Dr. C. L. Chatelin, the chief of surgery at the hospital, concluded on the basis of one of her eyes' nonreaction to light that she had sustained a severe brain injury in addition to the severe fractures of her right leg (femur), collarbone, and ribs. He sent for Dr. Jean Duplay, a renowned neurosurgeon in Nice, but in the meantime before he could arrive (around 1 P.M.), Chatelin treated Grace for her fractures and other external injuries. Because she was having trouble breathing, he hooked her up to a mechanical respirator, a procedure which called for her to be injected with a rapidly acting narcotic called Gamma O. H. At no time did Grace come close to regaining consciousness. Stephanie, for her part, sustained a fracture of a vertebra which narrowly missed paralyzing her from the neck down for life.

Nadia Lacoste and her chief press officer were both gone on vacation. In their absence, no one from the press office had enough rank or courage to appear at the hospital and "take charge" of public relations. Rainier, in any case, was in no condition to draft a communiqué, though he was consulted. The task of telling the press *something* eventually devolved to someone attached to his personal household, who was inexperienced with the press, but aware of the Prince's attitude toward it, hence eager to protect his own flanks lest Rainier later accuse him of saying too much. The doctors, for their part, were strongly against divulging much information. The release that appeared early Monday afternoon wasn't even what in Watergate vocabulary would have been termed a "limited hang-out"; it was closer to "disinformation." Grace, it said, had suffered various breaks and contusions and was in "satisfactory condition but strict observation is necessary to diagnose any secondary complications." Two sentences were virtually lies. One said that the Princess had "ascertained a brake failure." Nothing of the kind had been proven nor would be. Another said that Stephanie was "suffering from superficial bruising." Yet even a casual look at the girl indicated she had suffered more serious injury to her back than that.

By midafternoon, Dr. Duplay, too, shared the opinion that Grace had sustained very serious, perhaps fatal, brain injuries, but he couldn't know what exactly was wrong with her until they did a CAT scan. That procedure would entail moving her, however, for the Princess Grace Hospital hadn't yet acquired that apparatus. Not until close to 11 P.M. was Grace moved to a nearby private doctor's office and a CAT scan administered. It revealed two areas of bleeding in her left brain, one deep, near the thalamus, one, more superficial, in the temporal lobe. In layman's terms, it corroborated everyone's suspicions from the start: Grace was dying, and if by some miracle, she did not die, she would never recover the use of her intellectual faculties. She would be a "vegetable," as they say.

Rainier, who had been pacing the hallway in front of the Intensive Care Unit, had known since late afternoon that things were quite serious. Now this news removed any hope. He communicated it to his children, who frequently embraced their father. The entire family was in tears (as were many of the staff at watching them); it was the first time anyone had seen Prince Rainier cry. Father Penzo, the Prince and Princess's chaplain, was on hand, but he could not administer the sacrament of the sick because Grace was totally unconscious. He simply prayed over her. Around 6 A.M., the family assembled around Grace's bed in the Intensive Care Unit. The oscilloscope indicated life existed in only a technical sense. Albert and Caroline kissed Grace tenderly, then left their father alone with her for a time. He emerged presently and took his two older children home to the Palace. Around noon, at the Prince's request, the doctors ceased all life support. Grace lingered through the day of Tuesday and died that night, at 10:30 P.M.

§   §   §

An example [of media exaggeration] is that you have a bump with your car. Five minutes later it has become a bad accident. Next it is really dramatic; the car is wrecked and you are injured. It ends up with you being thrown out into the road and are killed.
                                                            —Prince Rainier III (1966)

These lines were sadly prophetic in one way, but not at all in another. The *scandale* that began smoldering in the wake of the first press communiqué and exploded after the second—issued on the night of Tuesday, the fourteenth, to announce Grace's death—was mainly provoked by misinformation or lack of information from the Principality, not hype from the press, at least the serious press. The first release, influenced strongly by the two physicians' reluctance to provide anything approaching the real facts, was the major mistake, for it laid a groundwork of suspicion on which the speculation built. Given the dearth of official information in the wake of both communiqués, reporters—particularly from the scandal tabloids—conducted hasty investigations and drew false conclusions. They invaded the site of the crash, taking what turned out to be false and self-flattering testimony from Lequio, and drawing a wrong inference from his claim to have seen Stephanie get out of the driver's side of the car, while Grace was lying in the backseat. In fact, Stephanie was already out of the car when Lequio arrived on the scene, while Grace had been thrown into the back seat during the crash. Lequio, moreover, did not put out a raging fire under the hood of the Rover. Indeed, he was the only witness to speak of a fire at all. The rest saw only some steam from the radiator and engine. Whatever else he was, Rainier III was the sort of man and Prince who, if he had any reason to believe that Sesto Lequio had saved his wife and daughter from burning or indeed rendered them any service whatever, would have acknowledged it publicly and rewarded the man. But he has said nothing, while Lequio has retreated from his earlier pronouncements and now tells reporters: "Ask Stephanie what happened, not me."

The conclusion that many rushed to at the time was that Stephanie had been driving, and her father was trying to cover up this fact because the girl was under age. Such appears not to have been the case. First, Grace was not the sort of mother to indulge a child in as dangerous and malfeasant an act as letting a seventeen-year-old negotiate the Moyenne Corniche on a busy Monday morning. Second, witnesses (the guard, the policeman at La Turbie) saw Grace driving. Third, Dr. Chatelin told Lacoste, who had immediately returned from her vacation, that some of the head injuries on Grace had been caused when she bumped violently against the steering wheel during the crash.

The next large issue is harder to resolve: what *did* happen in the car in the moments before the accident? The problem was not the brakes. British Leyland, the manufacturer of the Rover, sent a team to investigate. They found the car's brakes, and indeed all its systems, to be in perfect condition. In the press and among the Grimaldis' close friends, there was a good deal of speculation that Stephanie and her mother were having a violent argument which either precipitated a stroke or in some other way badly compromised Grace's concentration (e.g., so that she put her foot on the accelerator instead of the brake).

It is entirely plausible that mother and daughter could have been having one of their "usuals." On the other hand, it is equally likely that they were telling jokes or laughing at Stephanie's favorite "stupidity" from her mother's dialogue in *Mogambo* ("I didn't know monkeys climbed trees"). Only Stephanie knows what went on in the car, and thus far she has said nothing more to anyone than what she excitedly told her father at the hospital immediately after the accident. No one close to her has seen fit to interrogate Stephanie about what remains an excruciating set of memories.

Did Grace have a stroke at the wheel? The little that Stephanie did tell her father—"Oh, Mommy panicked. She didn't know what to do.

She lost control."—could support argument pro. On the other hand, Grace did not have high blood pressure, was not on any medication and had none of the other high-risk factors known to cause strokes (though she was still passing through menopause). Strokes, moreover, rarely hit with such devastating swiftness and totality as to render a victim helpless in a few seconds. Finally, Stephanie's report could be adduced to prove, not that Grace had a stroke, but that she accidentally put her foot on the wrong pedal.

Nevertheless, undeniable evidence of the CAT scan shows that she had two "cerebral-vascular hemorrhages"—one, deep in the brain; one in the frontal lobe. Nadia Lacoste, under pressure from all sides to "prove" that Stephanie was not driving, got Drs. Duplay and Chatelin to sign an overconfident statement certifying "that the verifications and medical examinations carried out, one of which was by scanner, prove that Her Serene Highness, the Princess Grace was driving the car at the time of the accident." The doctors later amplified this with an explication that the deeper stroke occurred before the accident and precipitated it, while the more superficial, massive one in the frontal lobe was caused by the external trauma of the crash.

The CAT scan, however, does not *prove* that Grace was driving, only that she had a stroke. By itself, the scan cannot even *prove* that the one (deeper) stroke precipitated her loss of control, or that it occurred in the car, for the scan is not dependable for pinpoint chronology. A report in the New York *Times* (September 21, 1982) by its medical editor, Dr. Lawrence K. Altman, challenges Chatelin and Duplay's certitude on this matter. That is the single value of the article. The other "questions" it raises—Should Gamma O. H. have been given? Shouldn't the CAT scan have been given sooner? Were there slight "inconsistencies" in the French doctors' description of Grace's symptoms? Were life-support systems terminated too quickly?—are based on *a priori* reasoning, or reasoning from statistics and probabilities, in the absence of Grace's X rays, scanner results and other tests, or of having seen the victim herself. Altman's doctors and "inquisitive laymen" were not present in the crush of those events, and to question by hindsight the wisdom of a physician like Duplay, whom the *Times* article acknowledged to be an "internationally respected brain surgeon," is jejune and feckless. No wonder Altman's sources preferred to remain nameless.

The fact remains that Chatelin and Duplay were wrong to let themselves be pushed into permitting their "medical certainty" to be utilized for argumentation that was not medical but political and circumstantial. Chatelin did tell Lacoste that some of the exterior lacerations on Grace's head corresponded to the shape of the steering wheel, but this was not specified in any release.

The question of what caused the accident—stroke, argument, panic, mistake, or a combination of them—thus remains open. What no one seriously contests is that Grace died of a massive cerebral hemorrhage, and that, if she had been "saved," it would have been for a circumscribed "life" she would not have wanted, and her family did not want for her.

§ § §

And so she died, very likely without knowing that the end was at hand. No one would have begrudged death his claim more stubbornly than this wisher for grandchildren, yet probably few people are readier to die than she was. Only once did Grace make a public statement about anything connected to death:

Q: I know it's much too early in your life to ask you this question, but . . . how are you going to want to be remembered?

GRACE: Well, I suppose mostly in terms of my children and their children, how they will remember me. I would like to be remembered as trying to do my job well, as being understanding and kind.

Q: Are there any things about your [screen] career that you would want remembered?

GRACE: Well, I don't know. I don't feel as though I achieved enough in my career to stand out more than many other people. I was very lucky in my career and I loved it, and— but I don't think I was accomplished enough as an actor to be remembered for that, particularly. I'd like to be remembered as a decent human being and a caring one who tried to help others.

Everything about this answer, even the reasons for the discussion of which it was part, said "Grace." Overburdened with business and prior commitments, she was approached by Cable TV for a taped interview.* This, she told the Monégasque Consul in New York, she needed "like another hole in the head," but because the assistant producer of the show was an old friend, Grace wedged it into the end of her prevacation schedule—in July 1982, two months before her death. After Grace agreed to do the show, Pierre Salinger was found to ask the questions. He posed (among others) the ones cited above toward the end of the show. A transcript does not indicate how long Grace paused before she began her answer, nor the pauses at the end of each

---

* The interview was eventually sold to ABC News which ran it on "20/20."

sentence. But they are as much a part of her answer as the words themselves. So is the "from-the-ground-up" construction of her carefully pondered answer. Grace thought first of her children and of the grandchildren she so badly wanted to know, and then of her life as Princess. Salinger had to bring up her movie career, to which Grace offered her frank and (in the opinion of many) underappreciative judgment. Then finally—after thinking about the question and getting into the "flow" of it—she got to the heart of the matter: "a decent human being . . . who tried to help others."

What is impressive about the postdeath period is how predictably "in character" people and events were and remained. The funeral was the second biggest event the Principality had seen since the 1956 wedding. It was televised, and it brought to Monaco a large contingent of luminaries from the political and entertainment worlds, the great majority of whom, from the Princess of Wales to Nancy Reagan, seemed genuinely stunned and grieving.

The tributes and obituaries each took Grace from the perspective familiar to the writer or his audience, beginning with the scandal sheets who, in their democratic search for more readers, careened wildly back and forth between libelous tales (Grace's "cruelty" to her children; her "affair" with JFK) and hagiography (Grace the "saint"), saying anything to sell a tabloid. The Hollywood press was syrupy— Roderick Mann telling his readers "When a beautiful Hollywood star marries a European prince they're supposed to live happily ever after. I always thought they would." A French television commentator got himself taken off the air for a brisk obituary that would have irritated Grace less than Mann's and come closer to her self-estimate: "Curious destiny," said Bernard Langlois of Channel 2 in the French Midi, "that of Grace Kelly, a talented actress chosen by a Prince who one day offered her his hand, his crown, and a throne planted on a wealthy rock in an operetta land. [Her death] changes nothing in the destiny of humanity . . . just the ordinary grief of a well-known family."

To the end, Americans hung on to their movie star. Even *The New Yorker* regretted that Grace hadn't "been allowed to grow older, [for then] it might have become easier to separate the screen queen from the real princess." But since it was not, the writer (Natacha Stewart) rued that "once again, the distinction between truth and fiction remains blurred forever." One wonders whether, if Grace pursued her work as Princess of Monaco until she was 106, the "distinction" would have got any clearer for the writer. *Le Monde* split the difference with the United States, calling the deceased, "Grace Kelly, Princess of Monaco."

John Vinocur, barely three months after Grace's demise, was already trying to show that "the death of Grace means the loss of an important element for stability in a time of change for Monaco's economy, which is based on tourism, real estate and light industry."† However, the author conceded that real estate and industry probably wouldn't register much change, so he concentrated on tourism. His argument and implications were bereft of meaningful figures and proved nothing. Certainly they demonstrated no connection whatever between Grace's death and a decline in tourism, which, in any case, would have been hard to show since tourism was up 11 percent in the Principality that year (and nearly 16 percent the next).

The Kellys, too, stayed in character, coming to Monaco for the funeral and scandalizing close friends of the Grimaldis with the insensitivity of their behavior, then returning home where Peggy and Kell gave interviews to the *National Enquirer* saying they suspected "foul play" in Grace's death.‡

The measure of the Grimaldis' grief is perhaps best seen in the photo of them leaving the Cathedral of St. Nicholas after the memorial mass, *one year later*. Time has done little to ease their pain, but they carry on, perhaps inspired by Grace's sense of duty. Stephanie was perhaps sufficiently sobered by her mother's death to check her own pace and defuse somewhat the obsessiveness of her relationship with Paul, whom she has not yet married. Albert, on the other hand, finally began to let go of himself, to feel his oats and sow some seeds. And Caroline continues her steady progress on all fronts. On December 29, 1983, she married a wealthy young Italian businessman from Milan, Stefano Casiraghi. She did so in a civil ceremony for the Vatican was still taking its celestial time about granting an annulment of her marriage to Junot.

Grace's death advanced her work for Monaco by providing the fillip that finally broke the Ballet de Monte Carlo out of the thicket of political infighting among Besobrasova, the National Council, and others. Under the artistic direction of Ghislaine Thesmar and Pierre Lacotte (formerly of the French National Opera Ballet in Paris), the company seemed a good bet to make its debut sometime in 1984. Grace's passing also gave an impetus to the launching of the American branch of the Princess Grace Foundation, whose February 1984 fund-raising Benefit was hosted by Ronald and Nancy Reagan and proved a great success.

---

† "Monaco: Bereft of a Princess and Down on Its Luck", the New York *Times,* November 25, 1982.

‡ Peggy and Kell both denied speaking to the *Enquirer,* but the publication's General Editor, Raymond Villwock, insists they did. The *Enquirer* preceded its quotations with the words "Peggy [or Brother Jack Kelly] told the *ENQUIRER,"* which it uses only in cases where a subject knowingly spoke to a reporter from the publication. Villwock added that both siblings are considered good sources. No one around the Grimaldis in Monaco doubts that they probably did speak to the scandal sheet that Grace so loathed.

Perhaps with these works, Grace's story comes to its most natural close. Or should the last word be those of a French television commentator at Grace's funeral apostrophizing the Princess in the name of "the people of Monaco":

"Au revoir, madame, you have perfectly fulfilled your contract."

INDEX